How to Use This Book 1
Suggested Itineraries 2
Planning Map 9
Why Visit New England? 13
Practical Tips 19
1 Boston 25
2 Cambridge 53
3 Lexington and Concord 61
4 Salem 69
5 Cape Ann 79
6 Coastal New Hampshire 89
7 Southern Maine 97
8 Mid-Coast Maine 107
9 Acadia 119
☆ Scenic Route: Schoodic Peninsula 131
☆ Scenic Route: Sargent Drive 132
10 Inland Maine 133
11 The White Mountains 143
☆ Scenic Route: Kancamagus Highway 156
12 New Hampshire Lakes 157
13 Northern Vermont 167
14 Central Vermont 175
15 Southern Vermont 183
16 The Berkshires 193
17 Western Connecticut 207
18 Heart of Connecticut 215
19 Coastal Connecticut 227
20 Newport 237
21 Martha's Vineyard 251

22 Nantucket 261
23 Cape Cod 273
☆ Scenic Route: Route 6A Cape Cod 285
24 Plymouth and the South Shore 287
New England Festivals 297
Appendix 305
Index 308
Map Index 312

Parade, Hartford, Connecticut

NEW ENGLAND

TRAVEL SMART®

Anne E. Wright

John Muir Publications
Santa Fe, New Mexico

Acknowledgments
For Randy and Jennifer, whose patience and understanding allowed me to complete this book. Special thanks go to my sister, Martha, and to my parents for their research assistance.

John Muir Publications, P.O. Box 613, Santa Fe, New Mexico 87504

Printed in the United States of America.
Second edition. First printing May 1998.

ISSN 1097-5004
ISBN 156261-403-7

Editors: Peg Goldstein, Chris Hayhurst
Graphics Editor: Steve Dietz
Production: Marie J. T. Vigil, Nikki Rooker
Design: Janine Lehmann and Linda Braun
Typesetting: Marcie Pottern
Map Style Development: American Custom Maps—Albuquerque, NM USA
Map Illustration: Kathleen Sparkes—White Hart Design
Printing: Publishers Press
Cover photo: *large*—© Fridmar Damm/Leo de Wys, Inc.
small—© Jeff Greenberg/Unicorn Stock Photos
Back cover photo:© Jeff Greenberg/Unicorn Stock Photos

Distributed to the book trade by
Publishers Group West
Berkeley, California

HOW TO USE THIS BOOK

This *New England Travel•Smart* guidebook is organized in 24 destination chapters, each covering the best sights and activities, restaurants, and lodging available in that specific destination. Thanks to thorough research and experience, the author is able to bring you only the best options, saving you time and money in your travels. The chapters are presented in geographic sequence so you can follow an easy route from one to the next. If you were to visit each destination in chapter order, you'd enjoy a complete tour of the best of New England.

Each chapter contains:

- User-friendly maps of the area, showing all recommended sights, restaurants, and accommodations.
- "A Perfect Day" description—how the author might spend her time if she had just one day in that destination.
- Sightseeing highlights, each rated by degree of importance: ★★★ Don't miss; ★★ Try hard to see; ★ See if you have time; and No stars—Worth knowing about.
- Selected restaurant, lodging, and camping recommendations to suit a variety of budgets.
- Helpful hints, fitness and recreation ideas, insights, and random tidbits of information to enhance your trip.

The Importance of Planning. Developing an itinerary is the best way to get the most satisfaction from your travels, and this guidebook makes it easy. First, read through the book and choose the places you'd most like to visit. Then, study the color map on the inside cover flap and the mileage chart (page 12) to determine which you can realistically see in the time you have available and at the travel pace you prefer. Using the Planning Map (pages 10–11), map out your route. Finally, use the lodging recommendations to determine your accommodations.

Some Suggested Itineraries. To get you started, six itineraries of varying lengths and based on specific interests follow. Mix and match according to your interests and time constraints, or follow a given itinerary from start to finish. The possibilities are endless. *Happy travels!*

SUGGESTED ITINERARIES

With the *New England Travel•Smart* guidebook you can plan a trip of any length—a one-day excursion, a getaway weekend, or a three-week vacation—around any special interest. To get you started, the following pages contain six suggested itineraries geared toward a variety of interests. For more information, refer to the chapters listed—chapter names are bolded and chapter numbers appear inside black bullets. You can follow a suggested itinerary in its entirety, or shorten, lengthen, or combine parts of each, depending on your starting and ending points.

Discuss alternative routes and schedules with your travel companions—it's a great way to have fun, even before you leave home. And remember: don't hesitate to change your itinerary once you're on the road. Careful study and planning ahead of time will help you make informed decisions as you go, but spontaneity is the extra ingredient that will make your trip memorable.

J. David Bohl/Society for the Preservation of New England Antiquities

Beauport House, Gloucester, Massachusetts

New England in One to Three Weeks

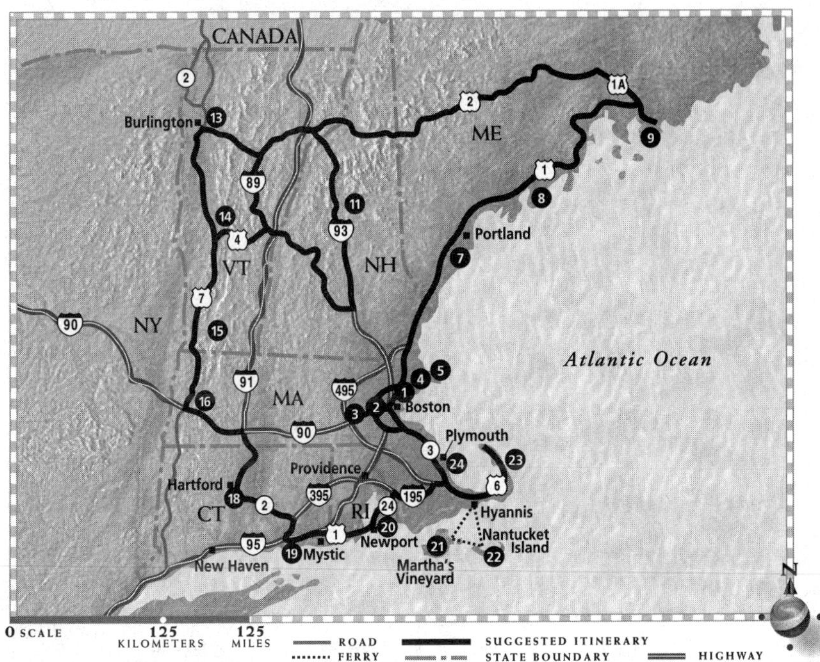

If you have one week to visit New England, see:

1. **Boston**
2. **Cambridge**
3. **Lexington and Concord**
4. **Salem**
5. **Cape Ann**
7. **Southern Maine**
8. **Mid-Coast Maine**

If you have two weeks to visit, add:

9. **Acadia**
11. **The White Mountains**
13. **Northern Vermont**
14. **Central Vermont**
15. **Southern Vermont**
16. **The Berkshires**

If you have three weeks to visit, add:

18. **Heart of Connecticut**
19. **Coastal Connecticut**
20. **Newport**
21. **Martha's Vineyard**
22. **Nantucket**
23. **Cape Cod**
24. **Plymouth and the South Shore**

Nature Lovers' Tour

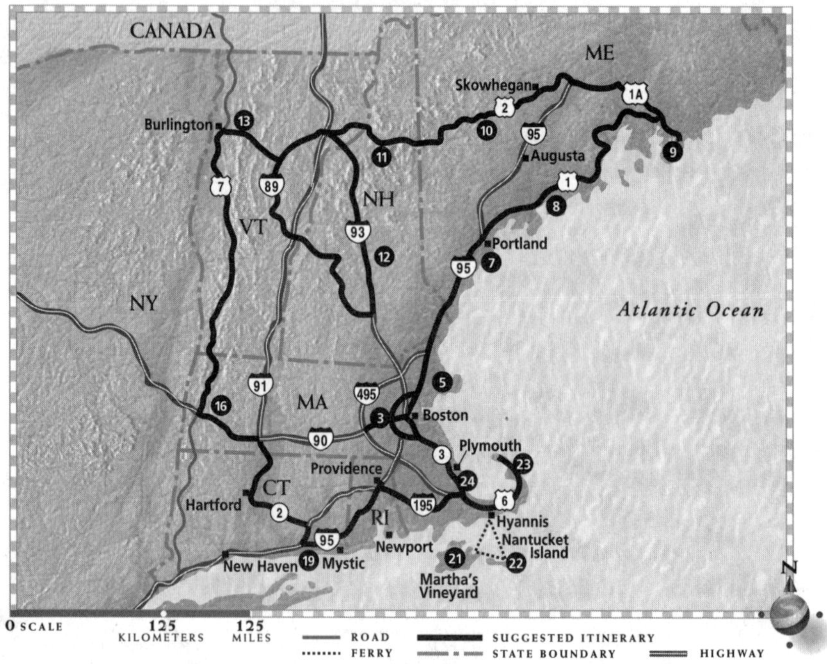

- ❸ **Lexington and Concord** (Great Meadows, Walden Pond)
- ❺ **Cape Ann** (Parker River Wildlife Refuge, Plum Island)
- ❼ **Southern Maine** (nature preserves)
- ❽ **Mid-Coast Maine** (Monhegan Island)
- ❾ **Acadia** (Acadia National Park)
- ❿ **Inland Maine** (Baxter State Park, lakes, rock-hounding)
- ⓫ **The White Mountains** (state parks, Mt. Washington, Kancamagus Highway)
- ⓬ **New Hampshire Lakes** (Lake Winnipesaukee, Squam Lake)
- ⓭ **Northern Vermont** (Mt. Mansfield, hiking)
- ⓰ **The Berkshires** (Mt. Greylock, Berkshire Botanical Garden)
- ⓳ **Coastal Connecticut** (Denison Pequotsepos Nature Center, beaches)
- ㉑ **Martha's Vineyard** (beaches and wildlife sanctuary)
- ㉒ **Nantucket** (beaches)
- ㉓ **Cape Cod** (national seashore)
- ㉔ **Plymouth and the South Shore** (wildlife refuges, World's End)

Time needed: 3 weeks

Arts and Culture Tour

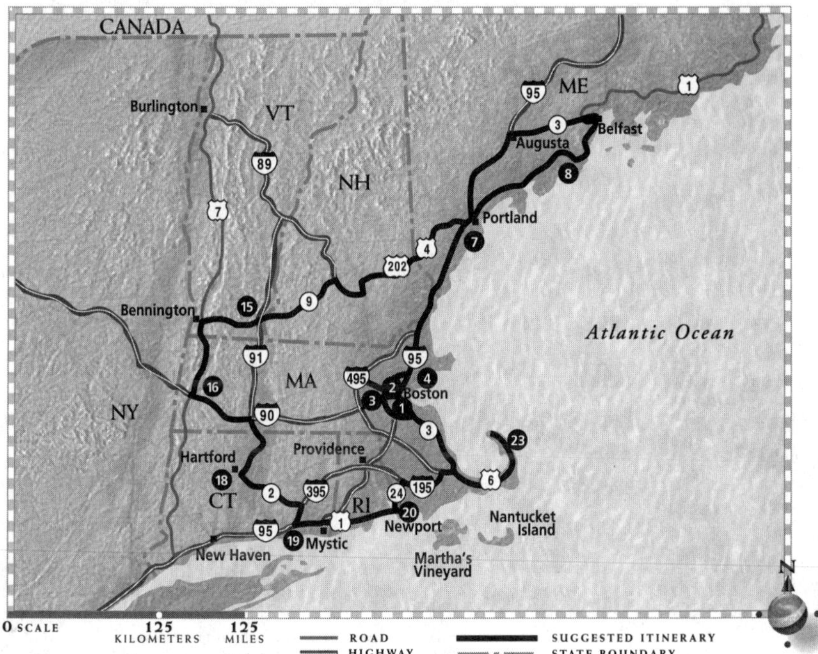

❶ **Boston** (museums, music, theater)
❷ **Cambridge** (museums, Henry Wadsworth Longfellow's home)
❸ **Lexington and Concord** (Alcott and Emerson homes, Thoreau Lyceum)
❹ **Salem** (Peabody Essex Museum, House of Seven Gables)
❼ **Southern Maine** (Portland Museum of Art)
❽ **Mid-Coast Maine** (Farnsworth Art Museum)
⓯ **Southern Vermont** (museums)
⓰ **The Berkshires** (Norman Rockwell Museum, Chesterwood, Tanglewood, Jacob's Pillow, Arrowhead, The Mount)
⓲ **Heart of Connecticut** (Wadsworth Athenaeum, Stowe and Twain homes, Hill-Stead Museum, Goodspeed Opera House)
⓳ **Coastal Connecticut** (Yale museums)
⓴ **Newport** (mansions)
㉓ **Cape Cod** (galleries and museums)

Time needed: 2 weeks

Family Fun Tour

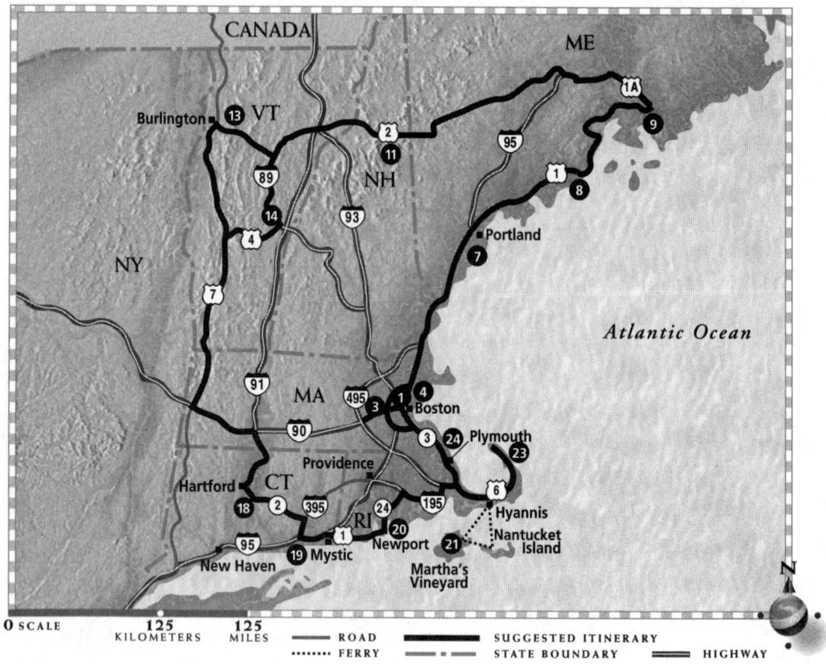

❶ **Boston** (museums, Boston Tea Party Ship)
❸ **Lexington and Concord** (Walden Pond)
❹ **Salem** (wax museum, Pioneer Village)
❼ **Southern Maine** (Children's Museum, Seashore Trolley Museum)
❽ **Mid-Coast Maine** (Boothbay Railway Village)
❾ **Acadia** (outdoor activities)
⓫ **White Mountains** (outdoor activities, Storyland)
⓭ **Northern Vermont** (Ben & Jerry's Ice Cream Factory)
⓮ **Central Vermont** (Sugarbush Farm, Quechee Gorge, Simon Pearce Glass)
⓲ **Heart of Connecticut** (train and riverboat ride)
⓳ **Coastal Connecticut** (Mystic Seaport, Mystic Marinelife Aquarium, beaches)
⓴ **Newport** (Green Animals topiary gardens)
㉑ **Martha's Vineyard** (Flying Horses Carousel)
㉓ **Cape Cod** (museums, seashore, Cape Cod chip factory)
㉔ **Plymouth and the South Shore** (history)

Time needed: 2 weeks

History Lovers' Tour

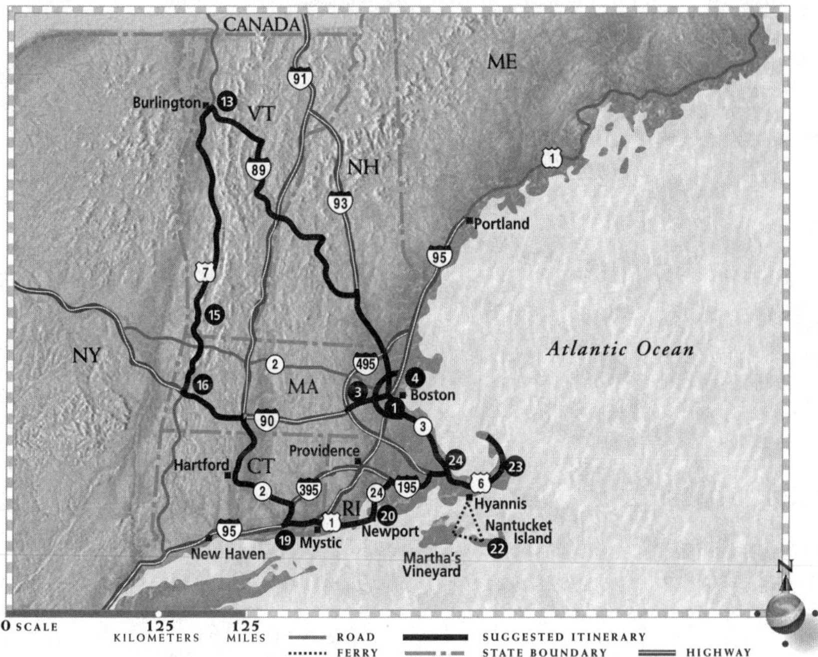

- ❶ **Boston** (Freedom Trail, Kennedy Library, Boston Tea Party Ship)
- ❸ **Lexington and Concord** (North Bridge, Sleepy Hollow Cemetery, Concord Museum)
- ❹ **Salem** (Peabody Essex Museum, Salem Witch Museum)
- ⓭ **Northern Vermont** (Shelburne Museum)
- ⓯ **Southern Vermont** (Bennington Museum, Bennington Monument)
- ⓰ **The Berkshires** (Deerfield, Hancock Shaker Village)
- ⓳ **Coastal Connecticut** (Mystic Seaport)
- ⓴ **Newport** (mansions)
- ㉒ **Nantucket** (restored buildings)
- ㉓ **Cape Cod** (Heritage Plantation, museums)
- ㉔ **Plymouth and the South Shore** (museums, historic buildings, Plimoth Plantation and the *Mayflower II*, Plymouth Rock)

Time needed 2–3 weeks

The Literary Tour

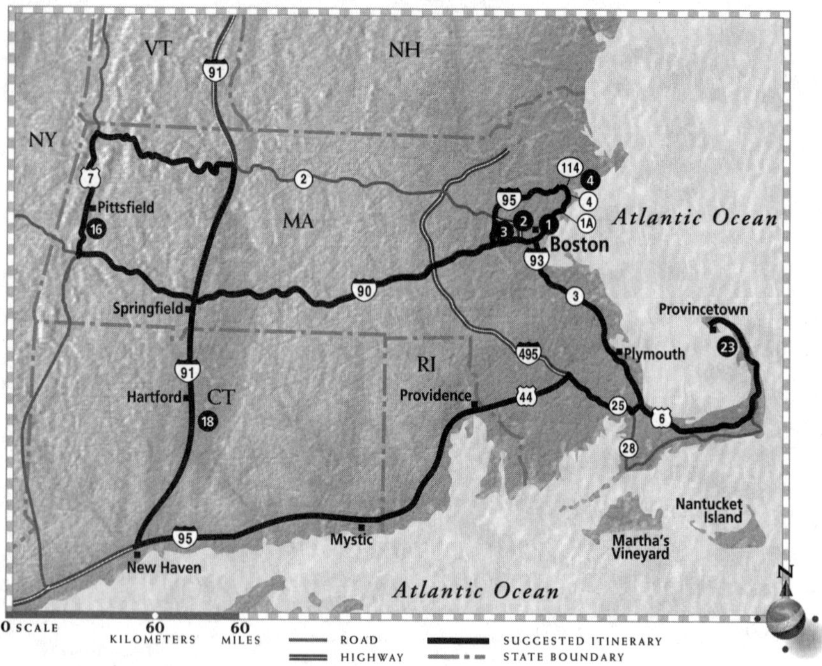

❶ **Boston** (Old Corner Bookstore)
❷ **Cambridge** (Longfellow National Historic Site)
❸ **Lexington and Concord** (Concord Museum, Thoreau Lyceum, Wayside, Old Manse, Emerson's House, Sleepy Hollow Cemetery, Walden Pond)
❹ **Salem** (House of Seven Gables)
⓰ **The Berkshires** (The Mount, Arrowhead)
⓲ **Heart of Connecticut** (Twain and Stowe homes)
㉓ **Cape Cod** (Thornton Burgess Museum, Green Briar Nature Center)

Time needed: 1–1½ weeks

USING THE PLANNING MAP

A major aspect of itinerary planning is determining your mode of transportation and the route you will follow as you travel from destination to destination. The Planning Map on the following pages will allow you to do just that.

First, read through the destination chapters carefully and note the sights that intrigue you. Then, photocopy the Planning Map so you can try out several different routes that will take you to these destinations. (The mileage chart that follows will allow you to calculate your travel times and distances.) Decide where you will be starting your tour of New England. Will you fly into Boston, Hartford, or Providence, or will you start from somewhere in between? Will you be driving from place to place or flying into major transportation hubs and renting a car for day trips? The answers to these questions will form the basis for your travel route design.

Once you have a firm idea of where your travels will take you, copy your route onto the Planning Map in the Appendix. You won't have to worry about where your map is, and the information you need on each destination will always be close at hand.

The Conway Scenic Railroad, North Conway, New Hampshire

Planning Map: New England

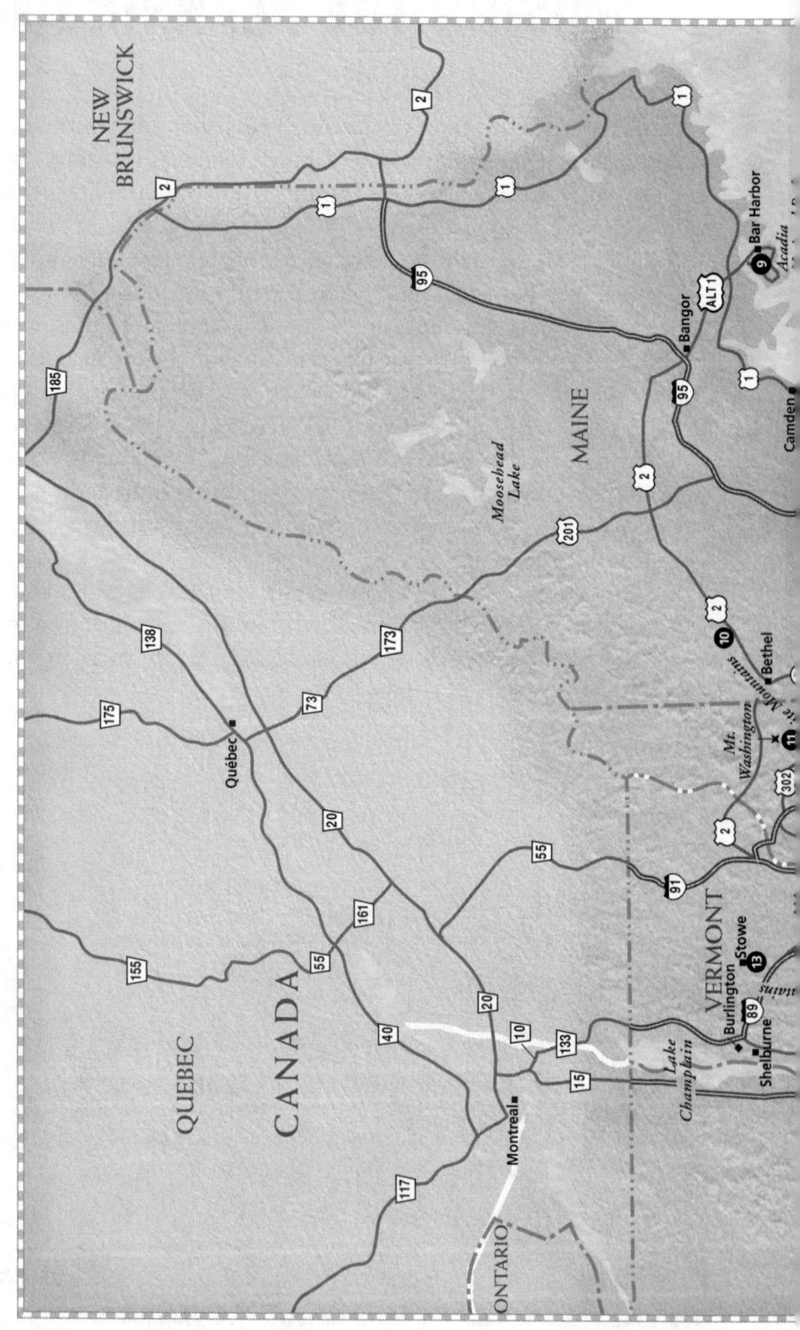

You have permission to photocopy this map.

NEW YORK
NEW HAMPSHIRE
MASSACHUSETTS
CONNECTICUT
RHODE ISLAND
Atlantic Ocean

Conway
12
Boothbay Harbor
8
Freeport
Portland
Lake Winnipesaukee
Rutland
Woodstock
Gre
14
Connecticut River
Kennebunkport
7
Portsmouth
6
Bennington
15
Berkshire Hills
16
Cape Ann
5
Gloucester
Salem
4
Lexington
3
Cambridge
2
Boston
1
Stockbridge
Hudson River
Provincetown
Cape Cod
24
Plymouth
Providence
Litchfield
17
18
Hartford
23
Danbury
New Haven
19
Mystic
20
Newport
21
Martha's Vineyard
Nantucket Island
22
New York

87 · 7 · 4 · 91 · 93 · 302 · 89 · 4 · 95 · 90 · 91 · 90 · 495 · 7 · 24 · 3 · 138 · 6 · 28 · 91 · 95 · 95

N

0 SCALE
100 KILOMETERS
100 MILES

ROAD
HIGHWAY
INTERNATIONAL BOUNDARY
STATE BOUNDARY

NEW ENGLAND MILEAGE CHART

	Boston, MA	Concord, MA	Salem, MA	Cape Ann, MA	Portland, ME	Augusta, ME	Acadia, ME	North Conway, NH	Weirs Beach, NH	Burlington, VT	Woodstock, VT	Bennington, VT	Stockbridge, MA	Litchfield, CT	Hartford, CT	Newport, RI	Martha's Vineyard, MA	Nantucket, MA	Cape Cod, MA
Concord, MA	20																		
Salem, MA	15	30																	
Cape Ann, MA	38	55	25																
Portland, ME	116	125	96	68															
Augusta, ME	159	162	142	145	54														
Acadia, ME	290	305	270	250	180	103													
North Conway, NH	147	164	132	109	70	93	247												
Weirs Beach, NH	91	96	89	105	83	123	240	4											
Burlington, VT	218	218	230	238	221	218	401	146	150										
Woodstock, VT	175	175	190	139	155	223	335	141	75	100									
Bennington, VT	152	132	168	169	198	282	378	235	133	123	96								
Stockbridge, MA	141	131	156	179	249	275	429	288	194	169	142	46							
Litchfield, CT	131	127	146	165	224	282	400	258	201	254	157	89	42						
Hartford, CT	100	98	115	142	201	251	381	251	170	220	140	111	65	32					
Newport, RI	74	94	89	112	190	212	370	221	153	326	238	225	179	120	116				
Martha's Vineyard, MA	108	128	123	146	224	234	404	255	159	326	284	260	250	188	217	116			
Nantucket, MA	113	133	128	151	229	232	409	260	157	331	289	265	255	192	222	121	15		
Cape Cod, MA	121	141	136	159	237	257	417	268	182	339	297	273	263	218	230	129	65	70	
Plymouth, MA	40	60	55	78	156	196	336	187	121	258	216	192	182	163	149	90	68	73	81

WHY VISIT NEW ENGLAND?

New England is the birthplace of our nation in many respects. The Pilgrims landed here in 1620, the first battle of the Revolutionary War was fought on Massachusetts soil, Harvard University in Cambridge is the cornerstone of American education, and founding fathers such as John Adams spent their lives here. You'll feel history all around as you pause on centuries-old town greens, drive past crusty stone walls that define property lines, ramble over covered bridges, and visit time-weathered historic homes and monuments. Along the way you'll see where Shakers worshipped, poets penned, colonists rebelled, whalers toiled, and presidents were born.

Nature has endowed New England with a beautiful landscape. Atlantic currents and Ice Age glaciers have sculpted this part of the country to near-perfection. During your holiday you'll have the opportunity to stretch out on sparkling white-sand beaches, picnic in rocky coves, watch playful seals in their natural habitat, hike pine-covered trails, stand atop the highest peak in the Northeast, swim in bubbling mountain streams, and dine on fish recently snatched from the ocean, all while you breathe in the salty sea air. If you visit in the fall, you'll also see the hills ablaze with vibrant colors.

This guide opens the door to your New England adventure.

HISTORY

New England unquestionably played a major role in our country's development, and is therefore one of the most historically rich regions of the United States. The arrival and settlement of the Pilgrims at Plymouth in 1620 established New England's place in our nation's history, while events a century and a half later solidified the region as a guiding force in the creation of our democracy.

In the 1760s, Britain imposed a series of taxes on the colonists. New Englanders—Bostonians in particular—were the most vocally opposed to the increasing tariffs. In 1770 a skirmish between British soldiers and angry colonists resulted in the deaths of five colonists. The incident is now known as the Boston Massacre. Three years later another act of defiance, the Boston Tea Party, further escalated the hostility between the British and the colonists. Eventually the conflicts culminated in the Revolutionary War.

In April 1775, Paul Revere made his fabled ride from Boston to Lexington and Concord to warn the revolutionary minutemen of the advancing British troops. The next day the first shots of the Revolutionary War were fired. During the course of the war, a number of key battles took place in New England, such as the battle of Bunker Hill and a confrontation in 1777 at Bennington, where the colonists soundly defeated the British.

New England contributed to the country's growth in other areas as well. In the early days, the region's whaling operations and foreign trade helped produce a thriving economy for the infant nation. With the advent of the Industrial Revolution, area factories began to churn out yards upon yards of fabric from southern-grown cotton. In more recent years, high-tech New England firms have helped bring about a revolution of a completely different nature.

Finally, New England has been the site of at least one regrettable but highly memorable incident in our nation's history—the Salem Witch Trials. In 1692, some 200 residents of the town of Salem, Massachusetts, were accused of being witches. Nineteen of the accused met their fate at the gallows before the governor stepped in to stop the paranoia. The infamous event no doubt helped to shape our constitution when it came to a U.S. citizen's right to a fair trial.

CULTURES

As New England was often the first American gateway that immigrant groups entered, the region is naturally culturally diverse. Long before the Pilgrims arrived, New England was home to Native American groups. They included the Penobscots in what is now Maine, the Pequots in what is now Connecticut, and the Wampanaogs in what is now Massachusetts.

Until the mid-1800s, the cultural heritage of most New Englanders was primarily British. Many Irish came to New England after the potato famine of 1846, and African Americans began moving to the north to escape the oppressive slavery of the south. Several decades later the Boston area became a popular destination for large numbers of Italian immigrants, and Portuguese, often drawn by a thriving fishing industry, settled in places such as New Bedford and Rhode Island. Closer to home, clusters of French-Canadians relocated from Canada to Vermont and New Hampshire.

Representatives from all of these cultures still reside in New

England, and each group, in its own way, has affected the societal tenor of the region as a whole.

THE ARTS

While the arts are celebrated throughout New England—there are outdoor concerts on the town green during the summer in Bar Harbor and regular theatrical performances in season in places such as the Dorset Playhouse in southern Vermont and the Goodspeed Opera House in East Haddam, Connecticut—Massachusetts boasts the region's highest concentration of prestigious art organizations. Those organizations are based primarily in two regions: the Berkshires and metropolitan Boston.

Boston is a regular stop for traveling productions of Broadway musicals and top-notch dance companies such as Alvin Ailey. The Boston Ballet has made *The Nutcracker* a requisite part of many area residents' annual holiday celebrations, while the Boston Pops Orchestra, led in the past by legendary conductors Arthur Fiedler and John Williams, has been a longtime favorite. The Boston Symphony Orchestra, considered one of the best in the country, spends its winter season in the city then moves to Tanglewood in the Berkshires for the summer months.

While the BSO at Tanglewood is one of the best-known attractions in the Berkshires, it's not the only one. Lovers of the arts will have no trouble filling up their calendars with other performances during a summer visit to the area. For dance, there's Jacob's Pillow; for theatrical performances, the Williamstown Theatre Festival, the Berkshire Theatre Festival, and the Mount.

CUISINE

Boston baked beans, Parker House rolls (named for Boston's famed Parker House Hotel), Boston cream pie, and New England clam chowder—each of these celebrated foods is deeply rooted in New England. The traditional fare of the region developed for the most part from food sources and ingredients that were readily available, and therefore tends to have fewer spices than cuisine native to other regions of the United States.

Clams are plentiful in New England. Fried or steamed, the clams on Cape Ann are often considered the best in the world. Of course, no trip to New England would be complete without succulent Maine lobster, either broiled or steamed then dipped in melted butter. Clams and lobster are the two main ingredients in a typical New England clambake—along with juicy corn-on-the-cob. Another seafood dish, broiled scrod, is a New England staple.

Native fruits have also left their mark on the regional cuisine. Bountiful fields of Maine blueberries are transformed into baked blueberry muffins, pancakes, and pies. Southern Massachusetts has always been a prime cranberry-growing region. In fact, cranberries—along with native turkey—were an important part of the Pilgrims' first Thanksgiving. Both still appear on Thanksgiving tables everywhere.

New England cuisine also reflects the area's English and Irish cultural heritage. You're probably more likely to find properly British roast beef and Yorkshire pudding on a New England menu than elsewhere in the United States, and the so-called New England boiled dinner, consisting of corned beef, cabbage, and potatoes, was really brought over by Irish immigrants and is traditionally eaten on Saint Patrick's Day.

FLORA AND FAUNA

With temperatures that can dip well below freezing during winter, particularly in the northernmost part of the region, you're not going to find palm or citrus trees in New England. Nor will you see cacti or other plants that favor arid climates, or blooming beauties such as orchids that require a tropical environment. New England flora depends on ample rainfall and must be hardy enough to withstand occasionally harsh winters. Variations in climate and elevation within the region dictate what you'll ultimately see on your trip.

In coastal areas such as Cape Cod, and islands like Nantucket and Martha's Vineyard, beach roses and spiky beach grass cover sandy dunes. Inland, forest floors are blanketed with lush, leafy ferns; and maple trees, interspersed with white birches, offer a colorful show during autumn months. In Maine, where the climate is more severe, the evergreen is the dominant tree. Blueberries are also abundant in Maine, while the marshy terrain of southern Massachusetts provides the perfect environment for cranberry bogs. Corn grows successfully in every New England state, and wildflowers thrive in all rural areas during summer.

Deer are common throughout the region, as are small animals

such as woodchucks, raccoons, rabbits, squirrels, and skunks. If you travel deep into the Maine wilderness, you may spot moose and bear. Atlantic whales are the largest mammals to inhabit New England, while clams, lobster, and bluefish are among the abundant sea life that shares the coastal waters with the gentle giants.

Seagulls make their homes all along the coast, while robins and blue jays are common farther inland. The New Hampshire lakes, such as Squam and Winnipesaukee, are especially hospitable to loons, and hawks can sometimes be seen soaring over New England's more mountainous areas.

THE LAY OF THE LAND

A tour of New England will reveal a landscape that is as interesting and as beautiful as it is varied. In eastern Connecticut, eastern Massachusetts, and Rhode Island, the land is relatively flat, leading out to a shore lined with white-sand beaches. Traveling north along the Maine coast, the shoreline becomes increasingly more rugged and rocky, reaching a crescendo at Acadia National Park, which contains both Cadillac Mountain, the highest point on the Atlantic coast, and Somme Sound, the only natural fjord on the coast.

Farther inland, Maine becomes more mountainous, and the almost completely landlocked states of Vermont and New Hampshire (a tiny section of southeastern New Hampshire does touch the sea) are all but dominated by the majestic Green and White Mountain ranges. New Hampshire lays claim to Mt. Washington—the tallest mountain in the northeast at over 6,000 feet. While the Berkshires of western Massachusetts do not reach such lofty heights, they are respectable nonetheless. Traveling south from the Berkshires, the mountains give way to the more subtle rolling hills of western Connecticut, and the Connecticut River cuts a swath across the center of the state as it makes its way to the Atlantic.

OUTDOOR ACTIVITIES

Naturally, in terrain as varied as New England's, outdoor activities are plentiful and diverse enough to suit all tastes. Hundreds of miles of shoreline ensure that surfers, swimmers, windsurfers, and sailors have ample opportunities to pursue their hobbies. Inland lakes, rivers, and streams provide outlets for fishing, kayaking, rafting, and canoeing enthusiasts, while thousands of acres of mountainous forest offer the perfect setting in which to hike the Appalachian Trail, rock climb, backcountry camp, hunt, or mountain bike. (Since campfire and fishing regulations vary from state to state, it is wise to check with each state prior to engaging in either activity.)

Hot-air balloon trips are offered in certain parts of New England, and the region's coastal waters are popular for whale-watching. Bird-watchers will find numerous wildlife sanctuaries throughout the region. In winter, the Berkshires and the White and Green Mountains come to life with snowmobilers and downhill and cross-country skiers.

PRACTICAL TIPS

HOW MUCH WILL IT COST?

The cost of your trip to New England will be determined by a number of factors, such as how long you will be visiting the region, how many people are in your party, whether you fly to your destination or drive from a neighboring state, whether you rent a vehicle or travel in your own car, whether you eat primarily in restaurants or prepare your own meals, and whether you camp or stay in expensive hotels. What you spend depends on the style in which you travel. I have listed average costs for car rentals, lodging, and meals in the Transportation, Camping and Lodging, and Food sections of this chapter. More specific price information is provided throughout the book for lodgings, restaurants, and sights.

WHEN TO GO

The best time to visit New England is between mid-May and mid-October. Many historical sites, restaurants, and hotels listed here are open only during those warmer months. Of course, New England is known worldwide for its spectacular fall foliage, which generally reaches its peak in Vermont and New Hampshire in early October. Winter skiing is also a popular attraction there. Do keep in mind that if you visit New England for the foliage or for skiing, many of the suggested sightseeing highlights will already be closed for the season.

July and August are the busiest months in terms of tourists, and, particularly in the coastal regions, the most expensive. Vermont and New Hampshire are naturally very crowded during peak leaf-peeping season, when places like North Conway in the Mount Washington valley of New Hampshire turn into veritable parking lots on Columbus Day weekend. If you plan to travel during peak periods, advance lodging reservations are a necessity. I've been told that churches have had to open their doors to stranded tourists, or worse, weary travelers have spent frosty New England nights upright in their cars. Call ahead for reservations to ensure that your trip runs as smoothly as possible.

In my experience, the best time to see New England is in September. The weather is usually sunny and pleasant without the heat and humidity of July and August, ocean temperatures are at their

NEW ENGLAND'S CLIMATE

Average monthly high and low temperatures in degrees Fahrenheit, plus monthly precipitation in inches.

	Boston	Portland	Hartford	Burlington
Jan.	37/23 3.6	32/12 3.5	36/18 3.4	27/10 1.8
Mar.	46/31 3.7	41/25 3.7	45/27 3.6	38/20 2.2
May	67/50 3.3	64/42 3.6	71/47 4.1	66/44 3.1
July	82/65 2.8	79/57 3.1	85/62 3.2	81/59 3.7
Sept.	73/57 3.1	69/4 3.1	75/52 3.8	69/49 3.3
Nov.	52/36 4.2	48/30 5.2	52/32 4.0	44/30 3.1

warmest, and many sights are still operating on their extended summer schedules. You may miss the foliage at its peak (although I'll bet you'll see a few leaves turning in the northern regions), but you'll also miss many of the summer tourists. Off-season rates begin just after Labor Day in some coastal towns.

June is another good time to travel and avoid the crowds, but the weather is less predictable than in September, and high-season rates generally go into effect on Memorial Day weekend.

TRANSPORTATION

Just about all major airlines have several daily nonstop flights to Boston from most major U.S. airports. Prices vary depending upon your departure city, but fares from airline to airline are generally comparable. Your travel agent can help you find the cheapest flight available for your desired departure date. It is usually best to purchase your ticket at least 30 days in advance to secure the lowest fare.

Feb. 1, 2006

Dear Chuck and Jani-

Hope this finds you both well. [illegible]veryday here is good as John improves.

Here are the books John told you about, he also says keep them no need to send them back.

The photos of Chuck and the business and Chuck and "Rocky" are really nice. Hope all is well with both. Rocky is a cute little guy - guess you've decided to keep him, lucky boy. Have to get ready now to take John to P.T. By the way did you have any luck with those numbers I gave you for Sharon? [illegible] not let me know if there is an[illegible] else I can do, I know its [illegible] you are so far. Take care [illegible] the kids.

Love,
Fay

While metropolitan Boston is readily accessible by public transportation and a network of commuter trains and buses, the rest of New England is not. Greyhound, Bonanza, Peter Pan, and Vermont Transit bus companies serve rural areas of New England to some extent, but you will find it hard to travel to all the sights once you reach each destination by bus.

This book is designed for those traveling by car, RV, or motorcycle. With the exception of Sargent Drive along Somme Sound in Maine, all suggested routes are open to those types of vehicles. However, the auto roads to the summits of Cadillac Mountain in Acadia National Park and Mount Washington in New Hampshire may be too precarious for large motor homes and too demanding for older cars.

You'll find that states such as Maine, New Hampshire, and Vermont are very good about providing directional and mileage signs for historical sites, lodging, and eating establishments that are off secondary roads.

If this is your first trip to New England, it may also be your first experience with rotary traffic circles. A word of caution: These circular intersections—found most often in Massachusetts when three or more roads come together—can be dangerous, so approach them carefully. A Massachusetts driver's approach to rotaries is, "Close your eyes and go." While this is not recommended, neither is timidity. Many unaccustomed drivers get hit because they wait too long. Try to blend into rotary traffic as easily as possible, moving at a slow but steady speed. Do not stop in the middle of a rotary! If you miss your exit, just continue around and exit on your next circuit.

All major car rental agencies have offices in Boston. Compact cars generally run about $225 per week with unlimited mileage, and mid-size cars rent for $250 per week or more. Subcompacts are somewhat cheaper and get better gas mileage, but can feel cramped when you spend a lot of time inside them.

CAMPING AND LODGING

Country inns are one of the best ways to truly immerse yourself in New England tradition. Inns, some of which have been operating for 100 years or more, serve regional specialties, are often furnished with priceless antiques, and generally offer comfortable to exceptional lodging, sometimes at little more than the cost of a motel room. A night in a country inn will generally cost at least $100 for two during summer and can cost as little as $60 in the off-season (of course, rates vary greatly depending upon location and type of accommodation offered). In many cases, the room rate includes a full breakfast, making the cost more appealing.

Motels in the area average about $55 for two but often provide only half as much in the way of amenities and atmosphere. However, if you're traveling with a family, motels may be the only affordable lodging other than camping. For those who want to travel lavishly, I have also listed luxury accommodations.

Camping is a much cheaper alternative to staying in either bed and breakfasts or motels, although many campgrounds are not as convenient to sights. Campgrounds operated by state, national, and municipal park services usually charge less than private campgrounds—about $12 per night. Park-run campgrounds tend to be more wooded and less crowded than private ones, but often don't have facilities such as hot showers, grocery stores, playgrounds, or swimming pools. Of course, there is a price to pay for convenience: Nightly rates at private campgrounds run at least $15. To get the most satisfaction from your trip, choose the type of lodging that best suits your lifestyle and budget.

FOOD

Preparing your own meals is the most economical way to eat on your trip, and you shouldn't have any trouble finding adequate provisions at any point along the way. If you're not equipped for food preparation or prefer to leave that task to others while on vacation, be prepared to spend an average of $5 for breakfast, $7 for lunch, and at least $10 for dinner, per person, when eating out. The restaurants I suggest are ones that I've personally enjoyed, or that have local reputations for their quality, uniqueness, convenience, or price. Fresh seafood is what first comes to mind when one thinks of New England cuisine, but places like Boston and Cambridge offer the visitor a wide variety in ethnic dining as well.

A cooler stocked with soda, juice, yogurt, cheese, and other snacks can save both money and time. If your bed and breakfast sends you off with a hearty morning meal, you can often get by until dinner with just a snack in the early afternoon. If your lodging establishment doesn't provide breakfast, a chilled fruit cup from the cooler may be just the thing to start the day. By cutting out one restaurant meal a day, you can reduce your total trip cost significantly. A cooler will also save you time, since you won't have to pull off the highway every time you feel a pang of hunger or thirst. Besides, the less time you spend looking for a place to eat, the more time you'll have to explore the New England you came to see.

WHAT TO BRING

Mark Twain once said, "One of the brightest gems in the New England weather is the dazzling uncertainty of it." The best way to deal with New England weather is to come prepared. Even in the hottest summer months, it is possible to run into cool evenings in parts of Maine, Vermont, and New Hampshire. Bring at least one heavy sweater no matter when you visit the area. The sweater will also come in handy any time you are out on the Atlantic, whether it's on a whale-watching vessel, the ferry to Nantucket, or a small pleasure craft, for the ocean breezes can be quite chilling.

Although I hope you won't have occasion to use it, rain gear is a must when traveling through New England. It is unlikely that you'll be able to spend a week or two in the area without encountering some form of precipitation, even if it's only a soft island mist on Martha's Vineyard. I recommend packing a lightweight hooded poncho to use while cycling or hiking and a fold-up umbrella for city sightseeing.

Make room in your suitcase for a pair of binoculars. They'll help bring the scenic vistas and wildlife of Acadia and the White Mountains National Forest into closer view, and ensure that you won't miss seeing the seals basking on the rocks just off the Maine coast.

Also pack a small empty knapsack or day-pack. It should be large enough to hold your sweater, poncho, guidebook, map, camera, and binoculars, but light enough for you to carry easily on your back. You'll find it invaluable when hiking, traveling to the islands, or simply transporting a picnic lunch.

RECOMMENDED READING

Reading (or rereading) *The House of Seven Gables* by Nathaniel Hawthorne, *Little Women* by Louisa May Alcott, *Ethan Frome* by Edith Wharton, and *Walden* by Henry David Thoreau will complement your New England sojourn as you visit the haunts and homes that inspired these American literary classics. The many layers of Newport, Rhode Island, society were the basis for Thornton Wilder's enjoyable *Theophilus North*, while Henry Beston spent a Thoreau-like year in a tiny house on Nauset Beach in Cape Cod recording the passage of nature in *The Outermost House*. Either book will add an extra dimension to your trip. Robert McCloskey's *Make Way for Ducklings*, a delightful tale of a duck family living in the Boston Public Gardens, brings the city to life for young children.

RESOURCES

Connecticut Tourism Office: (800) CT-BOUND
Maine Publicity Bureau: (207) 623-0363
Massachusetts Office of Travel and Tourism: (617) 727-3201, fax: (617) 727-6525, Web: www.mass-vacation.com, e-mail: vacationinfo@state.ma.us
New Hampshire Office of Travel and Tourism: (603) 271-2666
Rhode Island Tourism Division: (800) 556-2484 or (401) 277-2601, Web: www.visitrhodeisland.com
Vermont Chamber of Commerce: (802) VERMONT, Web: www.travel-vermont.com

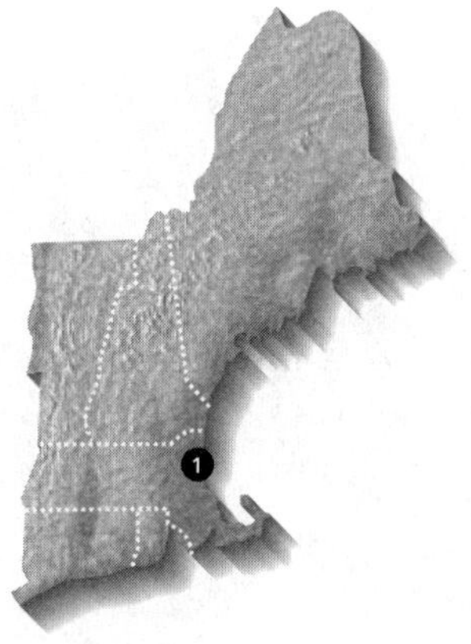

1 BOSTON

Boston's long history—the city was established in 1630—becomes apparent the moment you arrive. It's hard to walk more than a block in downtown Boston without seeing some kind of historic marker. If it weren't for the parked cars, a walk at dusk along Beacon Hill's gaslit brick sidewalks and cobblestone streets might convince you that you'd traveled back in time to the nineteenth century. With the exception of Back Bay, a former tidal marsh area that was filled in and laid out in the mid-nineteenth century, Boston's complex network of narrow streets, distinct neighborhoods, and old brick buildings give it more the feel of a European city than a modern American metropolis.

However, you need only look at the numerous glass skyscrapers in the city's financial district to realize that progress has by no means passed Boston by. In addition to the thriving financial community, countless high-tech firms have their headquarters in the Boston area. Boston Harbor, once the city's mainstay, is still a busy port. Long a center of learning, Boston boasts one of the greatest concentrations of colleges and universities in the nation and is on the cutting edge of medical research. Consequently, it is an interesting, culturally diverse, and attractive city, steeped in its past yet vibrantly alive in its present. ◪

DOWNTOWN BOSTON

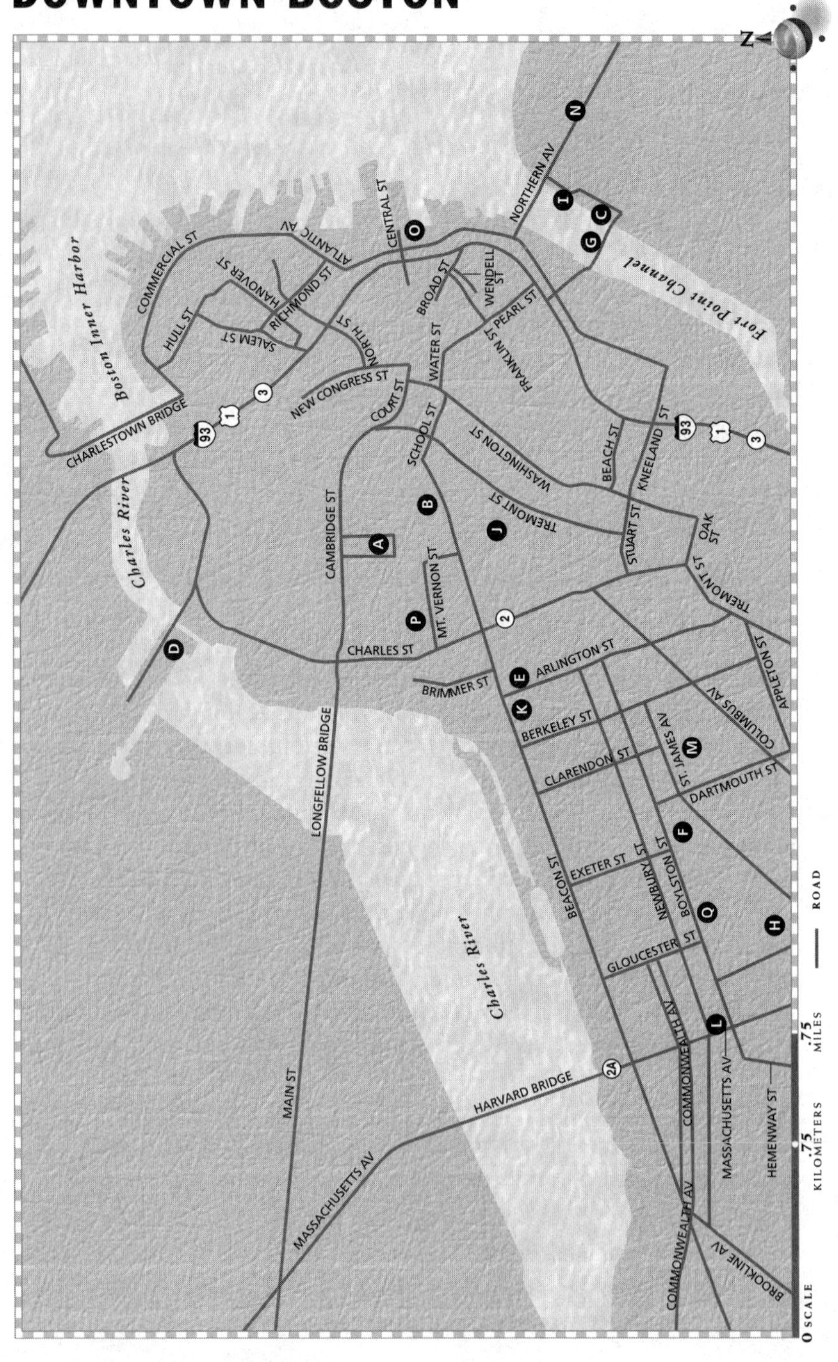

N
Boston Inner Harbor
Fort Point Channel
Charles River
Charles River
COMMERCIAL ST
ATLANTIC AV
CENTRAL ST
NORTHERN AV
HANOVER ST
RICHMOND ST
HULL ST
SALEM ST
NORTH ST
BROAD ST
WENDELL ST
PEARL ST
WATER ST
FRANKLIN ST
NEW CONGRESS ST
COURT ST
CHARLESTOWN BRIDGE
SCHOOL ST
WASHINGTON ST
BEACH ST
KNEELAND ST
TREMONT ST
CAMBRIDGE ST
STUART ST
OAK ST
MT. VERNON ST
CHARLES ST
ARLINGTON ST
BRIMMER ST
BERKELEY ST
APPLETON ST
COLUMBUS AV
ST. JAMES AV
CLARENDON ST
DARTMOUTH ST
LONGFELLOW BRIDGE
EXETER ST
NEWBURY ST
BOYLSTON ST
BEACON ST
GLOUCESTER ST
COMMONWEALTH AV
MASSACHUSETTS AV
HEMENWAY ST
HARVARD BRIDGE
MAIN ST
MASSACHUSETTS AV
COMMONWEALTH AV
BROOKLINE AV
93
1
3
2
2A
A
B
C
D
E
F
G
H
I
J
K
L
M
N
O
P
Q
ROAD
0 SCALE
.75 KILOMETERS
.75 MILES

Downtown Boston Sights

- Ⓐ Black Heritage Trail
- Ⓑ Boston Athenaeum
- Ⓒ Boston Children's Museum
- Ⓓ Boston Museum of Science
- Ⓔ Boston Public Gardens
- Ⓕ Boston Public Library
- Ⓖ Boston Tea Party Ship and Museum
- Ⓗ Christian Science Center
- Ⓘ Computer Museum
- Ⓙ Freedom Trail (starting point)
- Ⓚ Gibson House Museum
- Ⓛ Institute of Contemporary Art
- Ⓜ John Hancock Observatory
- Ⓝ Massachusetts Bay Brewing Company
- Ⓞ New England Aquarium
- Ⓟ Nichols House Museum
- Ⓠ Skywalk at the Prudential Tower

A PERFECT DAY IN BOSTON

Begin with a breakfast picnic in the Boston Public Gardens where you'll enjoy the beauty of the flowers and birds in the quiet calm of the early morning. Then hop on the T (subway) and travel to the Museum of Fine Arts to be one of the first ones through the door when the museum opens at 10 a.m. After a few hours wandering through the galleries and visiting the gift shop, break for lunch in the museum's fine restaurant.

After lunch walk over to the Gardner Museum and leisurely linger in its divine courtyard. Later, head to Newbury Street and browse through its shops and galleries—perhaps finding a treasured used book at the Victor Hugo Bookshop (at number 339) or the latest bestseller at Waterstones' (on the corner of Newbury and Exeter). Just before dusk go up to the observation deck of either the Prudential or John Hancock Building and watch the lights come on all over the city. From there, travel across town to the North End for a marvelous Italian meal. If you have any energy left after dinner, stroll through Quincy Market to see whatever street acts might still be performing, or unwind to music in a piano bar.

ARRIVING IN BOSTON

Although Logan Airport is only 2½ miles from downtown Boston, getting to the downtown area can often be an exhausting experience. (If you're renting a car for your trip through New England, I recommend waiting to pick it up until after you've visited Boston and Cambridge. Driving in the city can be confusing at best, and parking is both limited and expensive.) From the airport, cab fare into the city will run at least $10, and can be much more expensive in the likely event you get stuck in traffic. Share a cab if possible. Some downtown hotels pick up guests from the airport, so before you jump into a taxi you may want to call and check with your lodging to see if they offer such a service.

If you are traveling light, the **MBTA** (Massachusetts Bay Transportation Authority) is the fastest and least expensive means to reach the downtown area. A free shuttle bus that stops regularly at all airline terminals will take you to the Blue Line subway stop. A subway token is 85 cents, and in ten minutes you'll be in the heart of Boston. Board the train on the "Inbound" side of the tracks. A map of the entire subway system is clearly posted in every subway station.

Another option when traveling to downtown is to take the **Water Taxi** from Logan Airport (617-330-8680 or 800-23-LOGAN). This is a quick and scenic method, but unless your hotel is located on the waterfront, you'll still have to transfer to some other mode of transportation once across the harbor.

Amtrak (800-USA-RAIL) trains arrive at South Station several times a day from New York and points south. South Station is on the main subway line, and no doubt your hotel will only be a short subway or cab ride away.

Greyhound (800-231-2222) operates a terminal in the city, providing access to Boston from many smaller towns. The depot is near the Arlington Street subway stop of the Green Line in Back Bay.

By car, Boston can be reached from the west by the Massachusetts Turnpike, from the north by I-95 to Route 1, and from the northwest and south by I-93, known locally as the Southeast Expressway.

GETTING AROUND BOSTON

Walking is the preferred form of transportation in this compact city. Be sure to wear comfortable shoes, since many of the old brick and cobblestone streets were in place long before high heels came into vogue.

The subway system is the oldest in the country and sometimes operates like an antique. Subway stations are marked by a "T" symbol. The network of lines (Red, Green, Blue, and Orange) is quite extensive in the heart of the city, but check your street map before hopping on a train. Often three stops on the subway are only three physical blocks apart, and it takes more time to wait for the train than to walk the distance yourself. The farther you're going from the city center, the more sense it makes to travel by subway, but it is best to avoid subway travel at rush hour. Although tokens cost 85 cents, in some areas additional fare is required. If you plan to use the subway often, you can buy short-term visitor passes at the Logan Airport MBTA station and at the Visitor's Information Center on Boston Common. Or you can call the MBTA (617-222-3200) or inquire at any of their offices for additional sales locations. A one-day pass costs $5, a three-day pass is $9, and a seven-day pass is $18.

If you have a car, leave it at your hotel. Boston has been settled for more than 350 years, and a great number of roads were laid down over centuries-old cow paths that follow no logical design. The haphazard pattern of streets can be a nightmare for out-of-town drivers, and parking spaces are hard to come by. Don't try to demystify Boston driving, or to tame Boston drivers, in a few short days. You'll have fewer headaches and enjoy the city much more if you travel on foot.

SIGHTSEEING HIGHLIGHTS

★★★ **Boston Museum of Fine Arts**—This is one of the most highly respected art museums in the country. The collection consists of ancient Greek, Roman, Egyptian, and Asian art, with classic European and American artists represented as well. There are also American period rooms, early American furniture, silver, and fine musical instruments. The West Wing addition, designed by I. M. Pei, houses changing exhibits, an attractive restaurant, and a superlative gift shop. Courtyard dining adjoins the lower-level cafeteria. Details: 465 Huntington Avenue, across from Northeastern University. The Huntington Avenue branch of the Green Line stops right in front of the museum; (617) 267-9300; open 10 a.m. to 5 p.m. Tuesday through Sunday, until 10 p.m. Wednesday. The West Wing is open until 10 p.m. Thursday and Friday. Admission is $8 adults, $6 seniors and students, $3.50 ages 6 to 17. Everyone is admitted free on Wednesday from 4 to 9:45 p.m. (2 hours–half day)

★★★ **Freedom Trail**—This 3-mile walking tour of many of Boston's most important historical sites may be the best way for a first-time visitor to become acquainted with the city's roots. The trail begins at the information booth in Boston Common on Tremont Street between the Park Street and Tremont Street subway stations. You can get tour information from the visitor information kiosk (617-242-5642). Should you decide to tackle the trail on your own, it is well-marked by a red line on the pavement, but it's a good idea to get a map at the information booth in case you decide to stray from the main route. The map also contains background information on each site.

The first stop on the Freedom Trail is the "new" **State House**, designed by respected architect Charles Bullfinch and built in 1795. The capitol was built on land belonging to John Hancock's family, and Samuel Adams laid the cornerstone. With its gleaming golden dome, it has long been a cherished Boston landmark. Details: (617) 727-3676; open 10 a.m. to 4 p.m. Monday through Friday.

The next stop is the **Park Street Church** (617-523-3383) and **Granary Burying Ground**, where John Hancock and Samuel Adams lie buried near victims of the Boston Massacre. A little farther down Tremont Street is **King's Chapel** (617-227-2155), built in 1754. Behind the chapel on School Street is the **Old City Hall**, now home to a marvelous French restaurant, Maison Robert, and a commemorative statue of Benjamin Franklin. Several doors down, on the corner of School and Washington Streets, is the **Old Corner Bookstore** (now called the Globe Corner Bookstore, 617-523-6658) in a lovely brick building that dates to 1712. Now known for its fine selection of regional and travel titles, the store is steeped in literary history: Such notable figures as Henry David Thoreau, Henry Wadsworth Longfellow, Ralph Waldo Emerson, and Judge Oliver Wendell Holmes met here in the 1800s to discuss topics of the day.

Diagonally across from the Old Corner Bookstore at the **Old South Meeting House** you can view a multimedia presentation on the building's role in history: Boston Tea Party rallies were held here. The meeting house was built in 1729. Details: (617) 482-6439; open 9:30 a.m. to 5 p.m. daily April through October; 10 a.m. to 4 p.m. weekdays, and 10 a.m. to 5 p.m. weekends during the rest of the year. Admission is $2.50 adults, $2 seniors and students, $1 ages 6 to 18.

The **Old State House**, the next stop on the trail, was built in 1712 and currently houses exhibits on Boston history. Just outside the State House is the site of the Boston Massacre, where five colonists were slain by British soldiers in 1770, foreshadowing the Revolutionary War. Details: Washington and State Streets; (617) 720-3290; open 9:30 a.m. to 5 p.m. daily. Admission to the state house is $3 adults, $2 seniors and students, $1.50 ages 6 to 18.

From the State House you'll pass through **Faneuil Hall** (617-242-5642) and **Quincy Market**, old buildings that have been refurbished to serve as a major focal point for entertainment, dining, and shopping in the city. Because of the number of dining options, this is a good place to stop, have lunch, and recharge your batteries for the rest of the trail. If you find the shops tempting, you can always return in the evening for a more leisurely visit; many of the stores stay open late.

From the marketplace, cross under Interstate 93 to Boston's thriving North End district where a large Italian population keeps its customs alive through restaurants, groceries, and bakeries. If you didn't dine at Quincy Market, you may want to treat yourself to a memorable lunch in one of the North End's fabulous bistros while you're here. Paul Revere is perhaps the North End's most famous former resident, and his home at 19 North Square is the next stop along the Freedom Trail. The **Paul Revere House**, built in 1676, is the oldest building still standing in the city of Boston. On exhibit in the home are Revere documents, memorabilia, and, of course, silver. Details: (617) 523-2338; open 9:30 a.m. to 5:15 p.m. daily mid-April through October, 9:30 a.m. to 4:15 p.m. during winter, closed Mondays January through March. Admission is $2.50 adults, $2 seniors and students, $1 ages 5 to 17. The **Pierce/Hicborn House** next door, circa 1711, can be toured with the Revere House for a combined admission charge of $3.25 for adults, $2.25 for students and seniors, and $1 for children.

From the Revere House, follow the trail to the **Old North Church** (617-523-6676), where the famed lanterns ("one if by land, two if by sea") warned of the British arrival the night of Paul Revere's ride. Farther up Hull Street you'll pass the old **Cop's Hill Burial Ground**, where Edward Hartt, the builder of the USS *Constitution*, is buried. Cross the Charlestown Bridge to the Charlestown Navy Yard to view his creation, also known as Old Ironsides. The ship was built in 1797, saw active duty in the War of 1812, and is the oldest commissioned warship afloat today. Guided tours of the ship are given from 9:30 a.m. to 3:50 p.m., but if you get there after 3:50 p.m. you can tour the top deck of the ship on your own until sunset. There is also a **USS Constitution Museum**, open year-round. Details: (617) 242-5670;

open 9 a.m. to 6 p.m. in summer, 9 a.m. to 4 p.m. in winter, 9 a.m. to 5 p.m. in spring and fall; closed Thanksgiving, Christmas, and New Year's Day. Admission to the museum is $4 adults, $3 seniors and students, free for children under 6. The ship itself is free.

Just outside the entrance to the Navy Yard you can see a multimedia re-creation of the battle of Bunker Hill at the **Bunker Hill Pavilion**. Details: (617) 241-7575; open 9:30 a.m. to 4 p.m. daily, until 5 p.m. during summer; reenactments every half hour. Admission is $3 adults, $2 seniors, $1.50 ages 5 and up, $8 families.

After visiting the pavilion, walk up the hill to the 220-foot-tall **Bunker Hill Monument**, which commemorates the major Revolutionary War battle. Details: (617) 242-5641; open 9:30 a.m. to 6 p.m. June through August, 9:30 a.m. to 4 p.m. September through May. Admission is free.

Once you've reached the end of the trail there is no need to retrace your steps back into town. MBTA buses run frequently from Charlestown to downtown Boston. (full day)

★★ **Boston Museum of Science**—First test your strength, then discover the power of electricity. Learn about the earth's gravitational force, then explore faraway planets in the planetarium. You can spend hours in this fascinating museum unearthing the secrets of nature's unseen energy sources, as well as those that are visible to the naked eye, and seeing how people try to tame and control them. Many of the exhibits are participatory. Details: Science Park (the museum has its own subway stop on the Lechmere branch of the Green Line); (617) 723-2500; open 9 a.m. to 5 p.m. daily, until 9 p.m. Friday. Admission to museum is $8 adults, $6 seniors and ages 4 to 14. Admission to planetarium shows is $7.50 adults, $5.50 seniors and children; combination tickets are available. (2 hours–half day)

★★ **Boston Public Gardens**—Founded in 1897 and designed by Frederick Law Olmstead, who also created New York's Central Park, these are the oldest public gardens in the United States. The gardens are in full bloom from April through October, but the stately trees and beautiful landscaping make them a pleasure to visit in any season. Children will love the *Make Way for Ducklings* sculpture—depicting a scene from the book of the same name—and will enjoy a ride on the swan boats. A swan boat ride (about $2 per person) is a relaxing way for adults to get a perspective on the city as well. Details: (617) 635-4505;

swan boats operate from 10 a.m. to 4 p.m. mid-April through mid-June and 10 a.m. to 5 p.m. mid-June through Labor Day. (¼–1 hour)

★★ **Computer Museum**—With high-tech industry centered in Boston and with nearby Massachusetts Institute of Technology turning out the computer geniuses of the future, it is no wonder that Boston had the first museum devoted to the computer. Get a close-up look at the first computers, then test your skills in the PC gallery, explore the internet, try virtual reality, or check out the remarkable robots. Details: On Museum Wharf next to the Children's Museum; (617) 423-6758; open 10 a.m. to 6 p.m. daily in summer, until 9 p.m. Friday; 10 a.m. to 5 p.m. Tuesday through Sunday September through May. Admission is $7 adults, $5 students and seniors, free for children under 3. Admission is half-price on Sundays from 3 p.m. to 5 p.m. (2 hours)

★★ **Isabella Stewart Gardner Museum**—My favorite museum in Boston, this Venetian-style palazzo on the Fenway just two blocks from the Museum of Fine Arts houses Gardner's extraordinary private collection. Imagine having a chapel in your home with a thirteenth-century stained-glass window and living with not one but three Rembrandts. Gardner, an avid patron of the arts, made it her life's work to amass this collection, ranging from early Italian religious paintings to American and French impressionists of the last century to beautifully intricate European laces. The courtyard, complete with Roman statues and mosaics, is abloom with flowers in every season and makes a splendid haven from the outside world. Concerts are given frequently in the halls, usually on Sunday afternoon at 3 p.m. There is also a café on the premises. Despite the much-publicized theft of some of the museum's most famous works in 1990, it remains a treasure well worth unearthing. Details: (617) 566-1401; open 11 a.m. to 5 p.m. Tuesday through Sunday. Admission is $7 adults, $5 students and senior citizens, $3 ages 12 to 17, free for children under 12. (2 hours)

★★ **John F. Kennedy Library and Museum**—Your visit begins with a film on Kennedy in an imposing building designed by noted architect I. M. Pei. Then it's on to the exhibits, which include Kennedy's presidential desk, video presentations of the former president on the campaign trail, and important speeches from his term in office. More than just a tribute to one man, the library gives you a fascinating look into the United States' recent past. Details: Columbia Point, Boston; (617)

929-4523; open 9 a.m. to 5 p.m. daily; closed Thanksgiving, Christmas, and New Year's Day. The last film of the day starts at 3:50 p.m. Admission is $6 adults, $4 seniors and students, $2 children. (2 hours)

★★ **John Hancock Observatory** and **Skywalk at the Prudential Tower**—From the top of either the John Hancock Tower in Copley Square or the Prudential Tower nearby, you'll see magnificent views of the city and beyond on clear days and the city's sparkling lights as night falls. The Skywalk is not as tall as the John Hancock but has views in all directions (the Hancock is closed off on one side). Details: John Hancock Observatory, 200 Clarendon, (617) 572-6429; Skywalk at the Prudential, 800 Boylston, (617) 236-3318. The observatory is open 9 a.m. to 10 p.m. Monday through Saturday, noon to 10 p.m. Sunday. Admission is $3.75 adults, $2.75 seniors and ages 5 to 15. Skywalk open 10 a.m. to 10 p.m. Monday through Saturday, noon to 10 p.m. Sunday. Admission is $2.75 adults, $1.75 seniors and ages 5 to 15. (1 hour)

★★ **New England Aquarium**—What trip to the coast would be complete without a look at the inhabitants of the sea? The aquarium has a magnificent cylindrical glass tank several stories high. You can view hundreds of species of sea life, including sharks, barracudas, and giant sea turtles, as you wind your way down the spiral ramp. Dolphin shows are included in your admission. If you don't have time to go inside, at least take a few minutes as you stroll along the waterfront to watch the seals play at the outside entrance to the aquarium. Details: On Central Wharf, 3 blocks from Faneuil Hall Marketplace next to the Aquarium T stop on the Blue Line; (617) 973-5200; open 9 a.m. to 5 p.m. daily, later in summer. Admission is $8.75 adults, $7.75 seniors, $4.75 ages 3 to 11. (1½ hours)

★ **Boston Children's Museum** (★★★ if you are traveling with children)—The museum is known for its "hands-on" exhibits, Native American collection, and Japanese home painstakingly moved here piece by piece from Kyoto. Children magically become hushed when they enter the Japanese house, but in the rest of the museum laughter prevails as they try on clothes in Grandmother's Attic, scramble up and down over several levels in the climbing structure, and blow bubbles as big as they are. Teens will enjoy "faultless jamming" in the clubhouse designed especially for them. Details: Congress Street at Museum

Wharf; (617) 426-5466; open 10 a.m. to 5 p.m. daily, until 9 p.m. Friday; closed Monday Labor Day through June and on New Year's, Thanksgiving, and Christmas. Admission is $7 adults, $6 seniors and ages 2 to 15, $2 for 1-year-olds. Admission Friday from 5 p.m. to 9 p.m. is $1. (2 hours–half day)

★ **Boston Tea Party Ship and Museum**—You get to throw a tea chest overboard in protest of the British tax on this replica of the eighteenth-century ship where the famous revolt took place. (The chests aren't actually filled with tea and are connected to the ship by rope, but at least you get to feel like a rebel.) Details: 300 Congress Street on Museum Wharf; (617) 338-1773; open 9 a.m. to 6 p.m. daily during summer, until 5 p.m. the rest of the year; closed December through March. Admission is $6.50 adults, $3.50 children over age 5. (1 hour)

Arnold Arboretum—For an outdoor excursion, a visit to the arboretum at the Arborway in Jamaica Plain is well worthwhile—especially during lilac season. The 265-acre landscaped arboretum has more than 7,000 varieties of trees and boasts the second-largest collection of lilacs in North America, with over 400 varieties. Details: 125 The Arborway, (617) 524-1718; visitors center open 10 a.m. to 4 p.m., grounds open sunrise to sunset. Admission is free. (1–2 hours)

Black Heritage Trail—This walking tour highlights significant places in Boston's black history. The **African Meeting House**, the oldest standing black church in the United States, is one of the stops on the trail. Details: The African Meeting House is at 8 Smith Court; other sites on the trail can be visited only with an organized tour; (617) 742-5415; open 10 a.m. to 4 p.m. daily. (½ hour–half day)

Boston Athenaeum—The Athenaeum is a long-standing Boston institution. The library's collection includes early American publications and a gallery of American art. Details: 10½ Beacon Street near the State House, (617) 227-0270. (½ hour)

Boston Beer Company—The brewery is known for local favorite Samuel Adams Lager. Details: (617) 522-9080, call for directions by car or subway; tours are held Thursday and Friday at 2 p.m., and run continuously from noon to 2:30 p.m. on Saturday. A $1 donation is requested. (1½ hours)

GREATER BOSTON

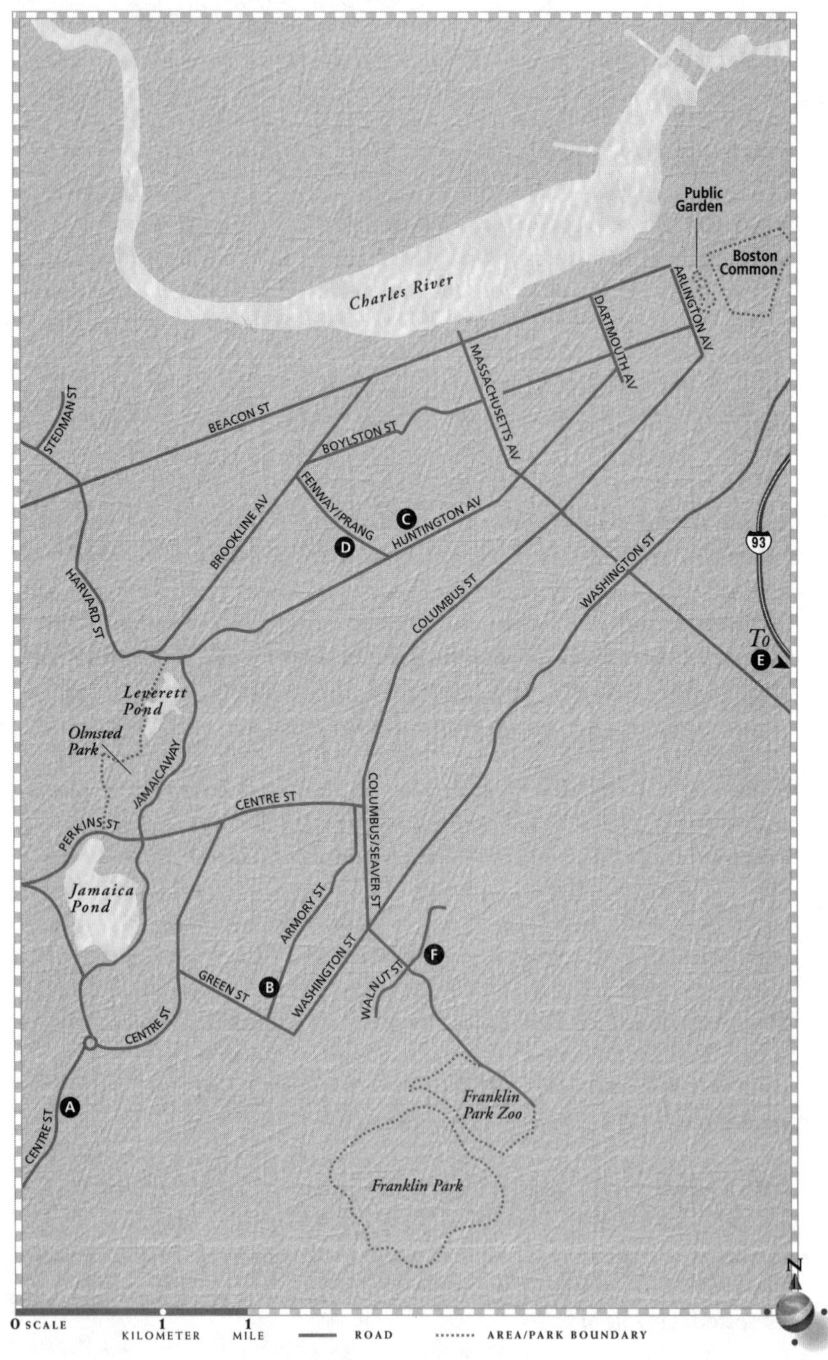

Charles River
Public Garden
Boston Common
ARLINGTON AV
DARTMOUTH AV
MASSACHUSETTS AV
BEACON ST
STEDMAN ST
BOYLSTON ST
FENWAY/PRANG
HUNTINGTON AV
BROOKLINE AV
HARVARD ST
COLUMBUS ST
WASHINGTON ST
93
To E
Leverett Pond
Olmsted Park
JAMAICAWAY
CENTRE ST
PERKINS ST
Jamaica Pond
COLUMBUS/SEAVER ST
ARMORY ST
WASHINGTON ST
GREEN ST
WALNUT ST
CENTRE ST
CENTRE ST
Franklin Park Zoo
Franklin Park
N
0 SCALE
1 KILOMETER
1 MILE
ROAD
AREA/PARK BOUNDARY

Greater Boston Sights

- **A Arnold Arboretum**
- **B Boston Beer Company**
- **C Boston Museum of Fine Arts**
- **D Isabella Stewart Gardner Museum**
- **E John F. Kennedy Library and Museum**
- **F Museum of the National Center of Afro-American Artists**

Boston Public Library—Located in Copley Square, the Italian Renaissance–style library is of interest because it was designed by the highly regarded architectural firm of McKim, Mead, & White. Details: 666 Boylston, (617) 536-5400. (½–1 hour)

Christian Science Center—This headquarters of the First Church of Christ Scientist is architecturally impressive. The *Christian Science Monitor* is published here, and the 30-foot stained-glass globe called the Mapparium, inside one of the center's buildings, is frequented by tourists. Details: 175 Huntington Avenue behind the Prudential Building; (617) 450-3790. Admission is free. (1 hour)

Gibson House Museum—The museum is an 1859 Victorian home. Details: 137 Beacon Street in Back Bay; (617) 267-6338; tours at 2, 3, and 4 p.m. Wednesday through Sunday May through October; same hours Saturday and Sunday November through April. No tours are offered on major holidays. Admission is $3. (1 hour)

Institute of Contemporary Art—This museum features changing exhibits of contemporary art. Details: 955 Boylston Street; (617) 266-5153; open noon to 5 p.m. Wednesday through Sunday, until 9 p.m. Thursday. Admission is $5 adults, $3 students, $2 seniors and children under 16. Free Thursday evenings. (1 hour)

Massachusetts Bay Brewing Company—Brewery tours are offered on Friday and Saturday at 1 p.m. Details: 306 Northern Avenue, Boston, (617) 574-9551. (1 hour)

Museum of the National Center of Afro-American Artists—This museum focuses on visual arts by African Americans. Details: 300

Walnut Avenue in the Roxbury section of Boston; (617) 442-8614; open 1 to 5 p.m. Tuesday through Saturday, until 6 p.m. during summer. Admission is $4 adults. (1 hour)

Nichols House Museum—This 1809 period home once belonged to Rose Standish Nichols. Details: 55 Mt. Vernon Street atop Beacon Hill; (617) 227-6993; open noon to 4:15 p.m. Tuesday through Saturday; hours more limited during the rest of the year. Admission is $5. (1 hour)

FITNESS AND RECREATION

Since Boston is a compact and walkable city, and most sights are best reached on foot, you'll probably get plenty of exercise just walking around sightseeing. However, if you desire a more active vacation, a bike trail begins at the Museum of Science and ends at Watertown Square. If you're adventurous or a frequent bicyclist, the 17-mile distance should not be challenging, but most visitors stick to the section that runs along the banks of the Charles River from the Esplanade to the far end of Back Bay. This portion of the path is also favored by runners and in-line skaters. Bicycles can be rented from **Earth Bikes** at 35 Huntington Avenue near Copley Square, (617) 267-4733.

For those who wish to try their hand at sailing or windsurfing on the Charles, **Community Boating** (617-523-1038) offers programs for short-term visitors (a two-day membership runs about $50, a seven-day membership is around $70). The boat dock is located on the river near the Charles Street MBTA station, and is open April through October.

The city operates a number of ice-skating rinks in the metropolitan area, and public skating hours are built into the schedule. The most convenient rink to downtown Boston is located on the far side of the North End.

FOOD

While Boston has no shortage of good restaurants, four eateries have remained popular for more than 100 years. The **Locke Ober Cafe** (617-542-1340), down an alley off Winter Street, was established in 1875. It is an old-money institution with dark wood paneling, hard-backed leather chairs, and a men's-club atmosphere. Menu items are expensive and include lobster Savannah and Wiener schnitzel. **Jacob**

Wirth's (617-338-8586), across from the New England Medical Center on Stuart Street near Chinatown, has changed little over the last century. The wooden floors are well worn, the home-brewed beer (both light and dark) is full-bodied, the hearty meals have a German flavor, and prices are moderate. **Durgin Park** (617-227-2038) in Faneuil Hall Marketplace is yet another Boston landmark noted for New England–style meals, large portions, and surly waitresses. The restaurant originally served the men who worked the docks (big meals at low prices), and has tried to retain the same atmosphere—although prices, which range from $8 to $18, are no longer dirt cheap. Just around the corner, the **Union Oyster House** (617-227-2750), established in 1826, has a raw oyster bar and specializes in seafood. Entrées range in price from $15 to $25. The quality of the food has slipped somewhat in recent years at Locke Ober, Durgin Park, and the Union Oyster House, and the restaurants seem to be riding on their reputation a bit. However, they are still worth visiting for tradition's sake.

Although **Maison Robert** (45 School Street, 617-227-3370) and **Cafe Budapest** (90 Exeter Street, 617-266-1979) aren't a century old, they've still been around long enough to become venerated Boston eateries. Maison Robert is located in lovely Old City Hall, and fine French fare is the restaurant's specialty. Continental cuisine, with an emphasis on Hungarian dishes, is the focus of Cafe Budapest's menu. A violinist adds a touch of romance to the evening atmosphere. You should expect to pay a price for dining at either restaurant, but Maison Robert does operate a more moderately priced café downstairs from its main restaurant.

On the trendy side, Boston has a **Hard Rock Café** (131 Clarendon, 617-424-7625). While not as much a novelty as these cafés were when there were only a few, a meal at the Hard Rock can still be a fun experience if you're a rock 'n' roll fan—and of course the memorabilia is different in each restaurant.

Anthony's Pier 4 (140 Northern Avenue, 617-423-6363), overlooking the harbor and the city, serves seafood on a grand scale. In size, Anthony's is more like a factory than a restaurant, and while its standards are not what they used to be, it manages to maintain a pleasant atmosphere. Tasty dishes from the sea come with freshly baked popovers, and if you have room for dessert, the baked Alaska is sure to please. Try to get a seat outdoors in the summer. Call for reservations, and expect to pay at least $20 per person at dinner.

The **Boston Sail Loft** at 80 Atlantic Avenue also specializes in seafood and overlooks the water, but in a crowded yet relaxed milieu. The menu includes sandwiches, chowder, salads, and pub fare at moderate prices. About a five-minute walk from Faneuil Hall, it is a popular nightspot with local young professionals. Even more casual and crowded is **No Name** (617-338-7539) on the Boston fish pier off of Northern Avenue. What it lacks in ambiance, No Name makes up for in low prices ($8 to $10 for dinners, $15.95 for lobster) and the freshness of its seafood. The restaurant is hard to find, so call ahead for directions. Be prepared to wait in line—they do not take reservations. **Skipjack's** (199 Clarendon Street, 617-536-3500), a relative newcomer, is quickly gaining acceptance for its innovative seafood dishes. The fresh-baked rolls that accompany meals are a nice touch, and on Sundays the restaurant offers a jazz brunch.

While you can get fresh fish almost anywhere in New England, Boston is the only place to offer a variety of excellent ethnic restaurants. Try several of them while you're here. The **King & I** restaurant at 145 Charles Street on Beacon Hill (617-227-3320) has delicious Thai cuisine with prices ranging from $6.95 to $10.95. **Lala Rokh**, on Mount Vernon Street about a block up from Charles Street, specializes in Persian dishes (dinner entrées $13 to $16). The spicy aroma of **Kebab 'n' Kurry** (Massachusetts Avenue and Beacon Street, 617-536-9835) can easily entice you into ordering more than you can possibly eat. Everything you sample at this restaurant will be delectable. The basement Indian restaurant is casual and affordably priced. Try the samosas and chicken saga. A bit pricier, **Casa Romero** (617-536-4341) specializes in gourmet Mexican and southwestern dishes. Located in the alley just off Gloucester and Newbury Streets, the restaurant is open Monday through Saturday. The chef's talents are renowned in the area and, therefore, reservations are recommended. **Jae's Cafe** (617-421-9405) on revitalized Columbus Avenue in the South End serves delicious Korean noodle and rice dishes, and prices are reasonable (entrées start at $7.95). At **Nara** (617-338-5935), on Wendell Street deep in the heart of the financial district, a wide variety of sushi selections are rolled to order. The teriyaki dishes are also terrific. Busy during weekday lunch hours, this cozy restaurant is refreshingly quiet in the evenings.

The North End—where the smell of garlic and anise waft through the streets—is the place to go for Italian cuisine. You can pick up the makings of a picnic meal at one of the neighborhood's many Italian groceries and bakeries, or follow your nose to pick out a restaurant. **Villa Francesca** (617-367-2948) on Richmond Street is somewhat expensive, but the food is worth its price. Lively murals are painted on Francesca's walls, and in good weather the streetside windows recede to give the bistro the flavor of an open-air café. **La Piccola Venezia** (263 Hanover Street, 617-523-3888) serves traditional Italian specialties such as manicotti, veal parmigiana, and lasagna in an informal setting. The menu is written on chalkboards throughout the tiny restaurant. Bring a hearty appetite because the portions are huge! Prices range from $10.95 to $14.95. Prices are also moderate at **L'Osteria** (109 Salem, 617-723-7847). The restaurant serves melt-in-your-mouth eggplant parmigiana and, for shrimp-lovers, savory shrimp Francese. The **Daily Catch** on Hanover Street is a casual spot where seafood—calamari in particular—is the specialty. It is not unusual to see lines of people waiting outside North End restaurants on weekend nights since most do not take reservations. If you're too full for dessert at the end of your restaurant meal, stop by **Mike's Pastry** at 300 Hanover Street (617-742-3050) for some canolis to go. If you visit Boston during the summer, you may be lucky enough to come upon one of the neighborhood's Italian festivals. You can literally eat your way through the streets! Call (617) 536-4100 for festival information.

Chinatown, with the third-largest Chinese population in the country, has a wide selection of Asian restaurants. Walk down the street and eat at whichever one appeals to you the most.

As cold as the region gets in winter, oddly enough New England has the highest per-capita consumption of ice cream in the country. New Englanders are passionate about their ice cream! Bostonians are connoisseurs; hence a number of locally famous rival parlors vie for business. Wherever you decide to sample the sweet frozen dessert, you're bound to be pleased.

Steve's, possibly the best known of the lot, has locations throughout the area, including one at Quincy Market and another on Massachusetts Avenue in Back Bay. Try their mix-ins: crushed Oreos, Heath Bars, chocolate chips, and the like are hand-blended into fresh ice cream made the old-fashioned way. Their hot-fudge sundaes are amazing. Steve Herrell, who originally founded Steve's and later sold the company, is back with his own parlor, Herrell's, on Dunster Street in Cambridge. **Emack & Bolio's** on upper Newbury Street also turns out a good product. For basic family-style ice cream, **Brigham's** operates several restaurants in the city. Caffe Bella Vista on Beacon Hill's Charles Street serves Italian gelato.

LODGING

Cosmopolitan city that it is, Boston has plenty of high-class hotels to bathe you in luxury. Lodging in downtown Boston can be quite pricey but many of the hotels listed here have special weekend packages, making them a little more affordable than during the week. **Hotel Meridien** (617-451-1900 or 800-543-4300), at 250 Franklin Street in the financial district, has one of the better restaurants in the city—Julien's. Doubles midweek are in the $300 range and can run less than $200 on weekends. The hotel also has an indoor swimming pool. The **Regal Bostonian Hotel** (617-523-3600 or 800-222-8888), adjacent to Faneuil Hall Marketplace and Haymarket, and a short walk from the North End, has one of the best locations in the city for sightseeing, as well as one of the better restaurants—Seasons—with a rooftop view. Doubles average about $245. The hotel also offers a "Boston Kids" package that includes milk, cookies, popcorn, videos, and board games for children, and a complimentary continental breakfast for up to four people. The **Ritz-Carlton** (617-536-5700 or 800-241-3333), at 15 Arlington Street overlooking the Public Gardens, has been accommodating guests since 1927. Its high tea is a classy affair, and this is where visiting heads of state stay when they come to town. Double rooms average $215 to $385. The **Four Seasons** (617-338-4400 or 800-332-3442), at 200 Boylston Street, is also adjacent to the Public Gardens. It offers elegant Old World style in a new building (the hotel opened in the mid-1980s). Doubles start at $285 on weekends, $345 during the week. Special amenities for children with the hotel's "weekend with the kids" package include child-size robes and Nintendo games. The hotel also has a lap pool and sauna. The **Copley Plaza** (617-267-5300 or 800-WYNDHAM) has one of the most sumptuous lobbies in Boston and is conveniently located right on Copley Square. Every President since William Howard Taft has stayed at the hotel. Doubles range in price from $210 to $260 per night. For families, the hotel has a suite with two bedrooms and a connecting bath, and kids can borrow books and games from the hotel's lending library. **Boston Harbor Hotel** (617-439-7000 or 800-752-7077), at 70 Rowes Wharf on the waterfront, is an elegant addition to the Boston lodging scene. Water taxis from the airport stop right at its doorstep. Double rooms with a city view start at $305, and those with a harbor view start at $365. The hotel has a health club: Use of the swimming pool and spa is included in the room rate, there's a $10 charge if you'd like to use the fitness facilities. If you're traveling with a family, ask about the hotel's family-vacation packages where kids under 18 stay free in the room with parents. The hotel is super convenient to the kid-friendly Children's Museum, Tea Party Ship, Computer Museum, and Aquarium.

What the **Marriott Hotel Long Wharf** (617-227-0800 or 800-228-9290) lacks in personality it makes up for in an outstanding location and friendly staff. At 296 State Street, it's on the water, directly adjacent to the Aquarium and Faneuil Hall Marketplace. The Italian North End is nearby. Doubles range in price from $189 to $269.

The **Lenox Hotel** (617-536-5300 or 800-225-7676), at 710 Boylston Street at Copley Square, and the **Omni Parker House** (617-227-8600 or 800-843-6664), at 60 School Street on the Freedom Trail just a few blocks from Quincy Market, are more reasonably priced than the hotels listed above and are still convenient to sights. So too is the **Eliot Hotel** (617-267-1607 or 800-44-ELIOT) at 370 Commonwealth Avenue next door to the Harvard Club in Back Bay. Suites at the Eliot are comfortable and elegant with chintz fabrics, antiques, botanical prints, and Italian marble baths. Guest rooms at the Eliot range in price from $185 to $265 for double occupancy. Doubles at the historic Parker House—Parker House rolls were made famous here—tend to be on the small side and start around $200 during the week, but can go for as little as $109 on the weekends. Double-occupancy rooms at the Lenox start at $190. The Lenox also has a family rate which includes breakfast for two adults and two children, and four one-day passes to the subway. Even more of a bargain are two hotels in the Kenmore Square area—**The Buckminster** (645 Beacon, 617-236-7050 or 800-727-2825) and **Howard Johnson's** (575 Commonwealth Avenue, 617-267-3100 or 800-654-2000). Rates at the Buckminster, including breakfast, start at $69. The hotel is wheelchair accessible, and several rooms have been especially designed to accommodate travelers with disabilities. Rates at the Howard Johnson's range in price from $95 to $165, and kids under 16 stay free in the same room with their parents. Parking at the Howard Johnson's is also free, which can be a significant savings, as downtown parking garages can be quite expensive.

Boston International Hostel (12 Hemenway Street, 617-536-9455) offers basic dormitory accommodations for only $15 per night for AYH members and $18 per night for nonmembers, but the hostel is

DOWNTOWN BOSTON

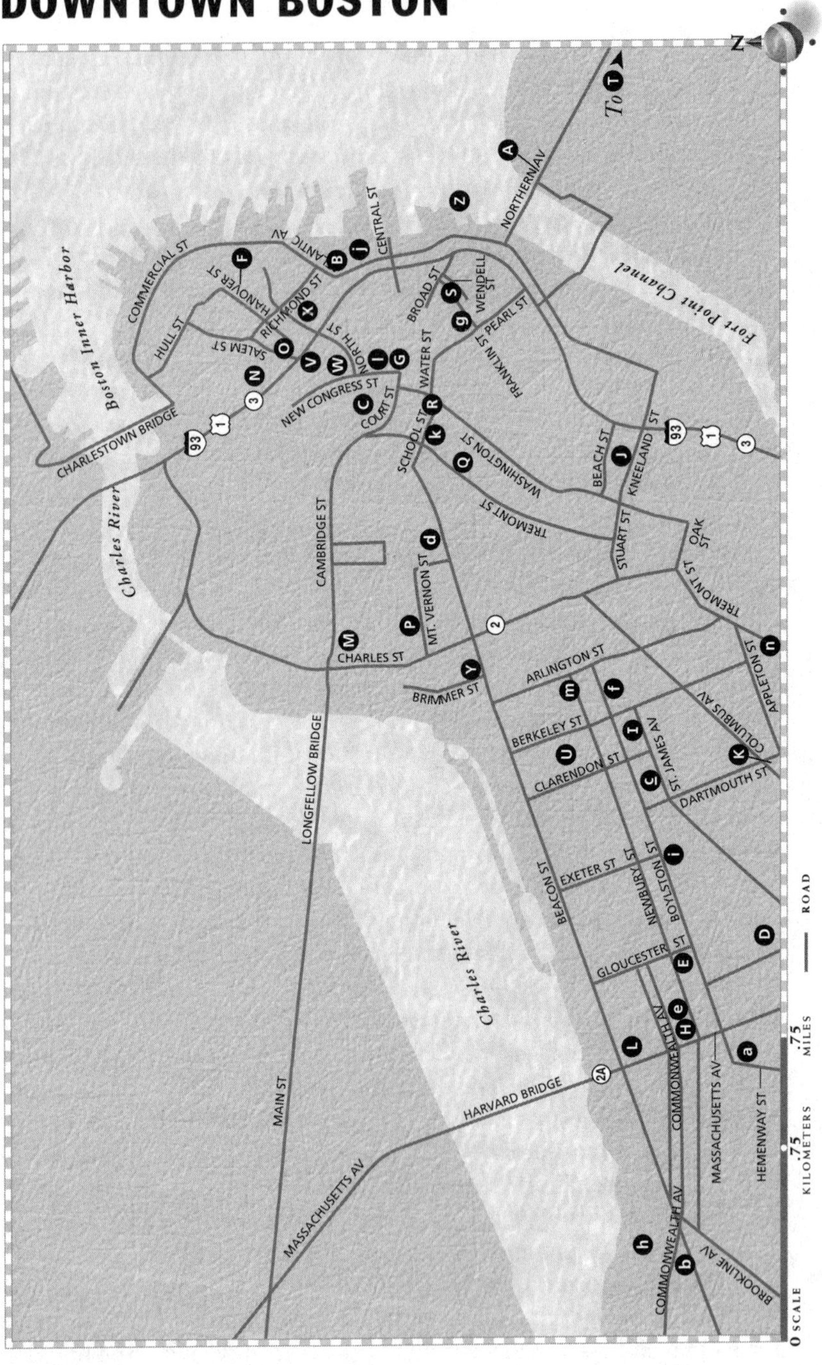

To T

NORTHERN AV

Fort Point Channel

CENTRAL ST

ATLANTIC AV

COMMERCIAL ST

Boston Inner Harbor

HANOVER ST

RICHMOND ST

BROAD ST

WENDELL ST

HULL ST

SALEM ST

NORTH ST

PEARL ST

FRANKLIN ST

WATER ST

NEW CONGRESS ST

COURT ST

CHARLESTOWN BRIDGE

SCHOOL ST

WASHINGTON ST

BEACH ST

KNEELAND ST

Charles River

TREMONT ST

CAMBRIDGE ST

STUART ST

OAK ST

MT. VERNON ST

CHARLES ST

ARLINGTON ST

BRIMMER ST

APPLETON ST

COLUMBUS AV

BERKELEY ST

LONGFELLOW BRIDGE

CLARENDON ST

ST. JAMES AV

DARTMOUTH ST

EXETER ST

NEWBURY ST

BOYLSTON ST

BEACON ST

GLOUCESTER ST

COMMONWEALTH AV

MASSACHUSETTS AV

HEMENWAY ST

HARVARD BRIDGE

MAIN ST

BROOKLINE AV

ROAD

0 SCALE

.75 KILOMETERS

.75 MILES

Food

- Ⓐ Anthony's Pier 4
- Ⓑ Boston Sail Loft
- Ⓒ Brigham's
- Ⓓ Cafe Budapest
- Ⓔ Casa Romero
- Ⓕ Daily Catch
- Ⓖ Durgin Park
- Ⓗ Emack & Bolio's
- Ⓘ Hard Rock Café
- Ⓙ Jacob Wirth's
- Ⓚ Jae's Cafe
- Ⓛ Kebab 'n' Kurry
- Ⓜ King & I
- Ⓝ L'Osteria
- Ⓞ La Piccola Venezia
- Ⓟ Lala Rokh
- Ⓠ Locke Ober Cafe
- Ⓡ Maison Robert
- Ⓕ Mike's Pastry
- Ⓢ Nara
- Ⓣ No Name
- Ⓤ Skipjack's
- Ⓥ Steve's
- Ⓦ Union Oyster House
- Ⓧ Villa Francesca

Lodging

- Ⓨ Beacon Hill Bed & Breakfast
- Ⓩ Boston Harbor Hotel
- ⓐ Boston International Hostel
- ⓑ The Buckminster
- ⓒ Copley Plaza
- ⓓ Eliot and Pickett Houses
- ⓔ Eliot Hotel
- ⓕ Four Seasons
- ⓖ Hotel Meridien
- ⓗ Howard Johnson's
- ⓘ Lenox Hotel
- ⓙ Marriott Hotel Long Wharf
- ⓚ Omni Parker House
- ⓛ Regal Bostonian Hotel
- ⓜ Ritz-Carlton
- ⓝ YWCA

Note: Items with the same letter are located in the same area.

only open to members during the summer. The hostel is close to the Boylston subway stop on the Green Line, to Newbury Street, and to the Prudential Center, and only a five-minute walk from the Museum of Fine Arts. It has a fully equipped kitchen and showers and is wheelchair accessible. The **YWCA** (40 Berkeley Street, 617-482-8850) in the South End has budget accommodations for women only. Rooms with shared baths run about $30 per night for one person, $45 per night for two, and long-term rates are available.

If you'd like to be situated on residential Beacon Hill try the **Eliot and Pickett Houses** (617-248-8707). The nineteenth-century brick townhouses are located on quiet Mt. Vernon Place, and although you'll feel removed from the hustle and bustle of downtown, you'll actually be conveniently situated for city sightseeing. In fact, the lodging is directly adjacent to the state capitol building. The 20 guest rooms are attractively decorated with antiques, and most have private baths. Rooms with private baths range in price from $105 to $120 for two, while the rooms with shared baths are $85 for a couple, and a self-serve continental breakfast is included. On the "flats" of Beacon Hill near the Charles River, the **Beacon Hill Bed & Breakfast** (27 Brimmer Street, 617-523-7376) has rooms with private baths and fireplaces. Rates including breakfast start at $150 per night in low-season and top out at $200 per night in high-season. The B&B has only three guest rooms, so reservations should be made well in advance.

For a more complete listing of hotels in the area, write the Massachusetts Lodging Association at 148 State Street, Suite 400, Boston, MA 02109. They produce a free lodging directory. Bed & Breakfast Agency of Boston (617-720-3540 or 800-CITY-BNB) can help you find a bed and breakfast in the area that's right for your needs. In general, if you are willing to stay outside the city, you'll probably find a wider range of inexpensive hotels. You will not, of course, have the convenience of the city at your doorstep.

ARTS AND ENTERTAINMENT

Music lovers should not miss the world-famous **Boston Pops** or the **Boston Symphony Orchestra's** more traditional classical performances. Both make their home in Symphony Hall, except during summer when the BSO travels to Tanglewood and the Pops gives its annual Fourth of July concert at the Esplanade on the Charles River. Call (617) 266-1492 for ticket information. Boston also has its own ballet company, the **Boston Ballet**. Call (617) 695-6950 for their schedule. Annual performances of *The Nutcracker* are a holiday favorite.

If you prefer comedy to dance, the **Comedy Connection** in Quincy Market's upper rotunda features comics nightly. Call (617) 248-9700 for a schedule and cover charge information. **Shear Madness**, a "whodunit" that's more comedic than mysterious, has been running in Boston since the 1970s. For show times, call the box office at (617) 426-5225. Tickets are in the $25 to $30 range.

The **BOSTIX** booth in Faneuil Hall Marketplace and at Copley Square sell tickets for all major theatrical productions. Check with them to see what's in town during your visit. It is sometimes possible to get reduced ticket prices there the day of performance. Call (617) 482-BTIX for up-to-date schedule and ticket information.

NIGHTLIFE

If you're in a bar-hopping mood, the Quincy Market area is a good place to start because of its high concentration of drinking establishments. **Houlihan's** is primarily a restaurant but has a dance floor that packs them in after dinner. **Cricket's** attracts the business-suit set, while **Lily's** has a piano bar and outdoor seating, and is a great place to people-watch on hot summer nights. The **Black Rose** is a lively Irish pub near Faneuil Hall, and the place to go on Saint Patrick's Day, if you can get in.

Back Bay has a number of popular night spots including **Friday's**, on Newbury Street, which has a fun menu, tasty appetizers, and a crowded bar area in which to mix and mingle. **Daisy Buchanan's**, also on Newbury Street, used to be a Red Sox hangout but is now dominated by swinging singles.

The **Eliot Lounge**, on Massachusetts and Commonwealth Avenues, sports a relaxed and casual atmosphere. This is where the runners flock after completing the Boston Marathon. The **Top of the Hub**, atop the Prudential Building, has a terrific view of the city. The drinks aren't cheap, but the view is worth it. If your tastes run to Broadway show tunes, try **Diamond Jim's** piano bar at the Lenox Hotel. Patrons are welcome to stand up and try their hand at a song or two.

On Beacon Hill, one of my favorites is **Seven's Pub** at 77 Charles Street. They serve great sandwiches with homemade potato salad at rock-bottom prices, and have a good selection of imported beer. The milieu is smoky and very casual. The clientele is mixed but always friendly. Hidden away on lower Chestnut Street (#75) is the **Charles**

Restaurant, a classy establishment with an intimate bar. Several blocks away on Beacon Street is the **Bull 'n' Finch Pub,** which inspired the TV sitcom *Cheers*. Although it has lost some of its neighborhood appeal to fame, it is still a fun place to go, especially if you were a fan of the show. For more elegant sipping, try upstairs in the lounge at the **Hampshire House**.

Landsdowne Street, across from Fenway Park, is lined with nightclubs catering to a young crowd. One of the most popular clubs is **Venus de Milo** (11 Landsdowne Street, 617-421-9595). If Venus de Milo is packed, you may want to try **Avalon** at 15 Landsdowne (617-262-2424). **Zanzibar** (1 Boylston Place, 617-451-1955) is a Caribbean-themed nightspot complete with palm trees and exotic drinks.

SPORTS

If you enjoy a good game of baseball, you'll especially appreciate watching one in **Fenway Park**, home of the **Boston Red Sox**. The ballpark's relatively small size makes attending a game more a participatory than a spectator sport. Call (617) 267-1700 for schedule and ticket information.

Wintertime visitors can catch either the **Boston Celtics** or the **Boston Bruins** at the **Fleet Center**, which replaced the aging Boston Garden in 1995. You can call the Fleet Center for event information (617-624-1000), but tickets can be purchased only in person at the center's box office or by calling Ticketmaster at (617) 931-2000.

Racing buffs will be drawn to **Suffolk Downs** (617-568-3225) for horse racing and **Wonderland** for dog racing. Both tracks have their own stops on the Blue Line subway. Hard-core sports enthusiasts can now visit the **Sports Museum of New England**, located in the Cambridge Side Galleria near the Lechmere stop on the Green Line. Call (617) 57-SPORT for hours and information.

You'll have to travel outside of Boston if you wish to attend an NFL game. The **New England Patriots** play in Foxboro Stadium, about an hour from the city. Call (617) 931-200 or (800) 543-1776 for schedule and ticket information.

SHOPPING

Boston shopping affords enough variety so that any visitor should be able to find what he or she is looking for. The best shopping is clustered in four different sections of the city.

Back Bay: The best shopping in Back Bay can be found on Newbury Street, a handsome street that runs from the edge of the Public Gardens to Massachusetts Avenue; the lower end of Boylston Street paralleling Newbury; and at Copley Place adjacent to Copley Square. Newbury Street is home to the city's chic boutiques and art galleries. The Vose Galleries (238 Newbury, 617-536-6176) is well respected by art collectors. Sumptuous shops range from the trendy to antiques to traditional favorites such as Burberry's, Brooks Brothers, Cartier, Pierre Deux, and Laura Ashley. Designers Armani (617-262-7300) and Versace have stores here, and you can find several interesting secondhand clothing stores toward the Massachusetts Avenue end of the street. Along the way are plenty of sidewalk cafés catering to weary shoppers. Louis of Boston, the exclusive clothing store, is located on Berkeley Street between Newbury and Boylston; while Boylston street is home to venerable Shreve, Crump & Low (Boston's answer to Tiffany & Co.), the Women's Educational & Industrial Union (a crafts and gift shop that benefits women's causes, 617-536-5651), Hermes, Escada (617-437-1200), Sonia Rykiel, and chain stores FAO Schwartz, Eddie Bauer, and Talbots (617-262-2981). Nearby Copley Place is a high-class shopping mall anchored by the Westin and Marriott Hotels. Neiman Marcus (617-536-3660) and Gucci are located here, as is an excellent newsstand carrying a wide variety of American and continental magazines, a six-cinema movie complex that features the fine *Where's Boston* documentary film in one of its theaters, and a Rizzoli's bookstore. Saks Fifth Avenue (617-262-8500) and Lord & Taylor are at the adjacent Prudential Center.

Downtown Crossing: This Washington Street area is one block east of Park Street station. Though not a visually appealing place to shop, the "World-Famous Filene's Basement" (617-348-7974) is worth a stop, especially for bargain hunters. (It's important to note that there is no tax on clothing in Massachusetts, making the bargains at Filene's even more affordable to many out-of-state visitors.) Across the street from Filene's is the Jordan Marsh flagship store (617-357-3000). Barnes and Noble also operates a large bookstore at Downtown Crossing, and fast-food addicts can have their fill at either The Corner or the fast-food hall upstairs at Lafayette Place.

Faneuil Hall Marketplace: The market is a good place to browse after sightseeing, since many of the stores are open until 9 p.m. The pushcarts adjacent to the food hall sell everything from Celtics souvenir shirts to batik sarongs. Stores include mall standards such as

Brookstone, Banana Republic, Crate & Barrel (617-742-6025), and Warner Brothers (617-227-1101), as well as specialty shops such as April Cornell (617-248-0280) and Celtic Weavers (617-720-0750), which sells imported goods.

Haymarket: This open-air fruit and vegetable market is held every Friday and Saturday alongside Interstate 93 between Quincy Market and the North End. Many of the vendors are true characters, and the market is a ritual that has remained generally unchanged through the years. Haymarket can be a good place to stock up on fresh fruit and nuts for your trip, but beware: Some vendors display gorgeous merchandise at rock-bottom prices but fill your bag with overripe fruit from the back of the pile. Make sure you pick what you want before you hand over the money. The best selection is in the morning, while the best prices are at the end of the day when the vendors try to unload their wares rather than carry them home.

HELPFUL HINT

If a foreigner walks up to you on the streets of Boston and asks you, "Where is this place that you have war?" they are probably not referring to the Bunker Hill area but to an unsavory area known locally as the Combat Zone. The zone lies between the theater district and Chinatown and is comparable to New York City's Times Square district. Although the zone is shrinking due to new development, a strip of X-rated movie houses still remains. The area is best avoided.

SIDE TRIPS FROM BOSTON

A quick and refreshing way to get out of the city is by taking a cruise in Boston Harbor. There are dinner cruises, brunch cruises, jazz cruises, cruises to the harbor islands, and sightseeing cruises. The cost depends upon the length and type of cruise you select, but the view of the city from the harbor is almost always impressive. If you plan to venture out to the harbor islands you may want to bring along a picnic lunch and make a day of it. A number of companies operate harbor cruises, and each has its own schedule and list of specialty cruises. **Bay State Cruises** (617-723-7800) and **Boston Harbor Cruises** (617-227-4321) are located on Long Wharf. **Massachusetts Bay Lines** (617-542-8000) and **Odyssey Cruises** (617-654-9700) are located at Rowes Wharf. The **Charles Riverboat Company** (617-621-3001) at the

Cambridge Side Galleria adjacent to the Museum of Science offers narrated cruises of the Charles River as well as tours of Boston's inner harbor via working locks. The tour of the Charles lasts about an hour and is $8 for adults, $6 for seniors, and $5 for children.

If you wish to travel further afield, one of New England's foremost attractions is **Old Sturbridge Village** (508-347-3362), about an hour west of Boston. A living museum that re-creates everyday life in an 1830s New England village, Sturbridge has more than 40 restored buildings on 200 acres. A "Friends Meetinghouse," a print shop, gristmill, and a nineteenth-century school are among the structures in the village; and crafts demonstrated by costumed guides include candlemaking, blacksmithing, and woodworking. Although children especially enjoy the village, adults will certainly be impressed as well. The village is open year-round (10 a.m. to 4 p.m. during the winter, 9 a.m. to 5 p.m. the rest of the year), except for major holidays and Mondays during winter months. Admission is high—$15 for adults, $13.50 for seniors, $7.50 for children ages 6 to 15—but the visit is an all-day event. From Boston, take the Massachusetts Turnpike (I-90) west to exit 9 and follow signs to the village.

The Sturbridge area is also one of the largest apple-growing regions in the state. Many of the orchards have "pick your own" programs, making a Sturbridge outing fun for the whole family, especially on a crisp autumn day. The trip from Boston is about 60 miles each way. If you want to spend the night in Sturbridge, the **Publick House & Country Motor Lodge** (508-347-3313 or 800-782-5425) is a popular spot. It's located on Sturbridge's common about five minutes from the museum village. Rates range from $89 to $155 July through October and from $59 to $135 during the rest of the year. The less expensive rooms are located in the motor lodge.

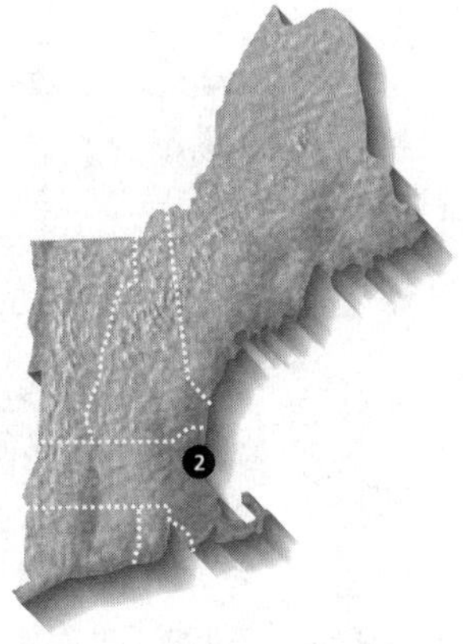

2 CAMBRIDGE

Cambridge, like Boston just across the Charles River, has been around for more than 360 years. Originally called New Towne in 1630, it was renamed Cambridge—after Cambridge, England—in 1638. With just under 100,000 people, Cambridge has about a fifth the population of Boston, yet within its boundaries are two of the nation's top schools—Harvard University and Massachusetts Institute of Technology (MIT).

Harvard, founded in 1636, was America's first college. It began as a school for ministers and gradually expanded to a full-scale university that now includes respected medical, law, business, and dental schools. Presidents John and John Quincy Adams, Teddy and Franklin D. Roosevelt, and John F. Kennedy were all Harvard graduates. Harvard's classic red brick buildings and houses dominate the landscape around Cambridge's Harvard Square. Farther down Massachusetts Avenue (the city's main thoroughfare), MIT's more subdued buildings line both sides of the street. MIT, perhaps the country's best school for technology and science, was founded in 1865.

Bustling Harvard Square tends to be the focal point for most visitors to the city. Visitors will find a good selection of museums, shops, and restaurants in "the Square." From there, it is only a short walk to the river to watch crew teams in racing sculls, or to Brattle Street, where handsome residences belie the urban locale. History buffs might want to explore bucolic Mount Auburn Cemetery, where notables such as Winslow Homer and Henry Wadsworth Longfellow are buried.

CAMBRIDGE

N
WASHINGTON ST
BOW ST
SUMMER ST
BEACON ST
KIRKLAND ST
CAMBRIDGE ST
BROADWAY ST
MASSACHUSETTS AV
DIVINITY AV
QUINCY ST
OXFORD ST
WENDELL ST
Harvard University
DUNSTER ST
HOLYOKE ST
2A
MASSACHUSETTS AV
Cambridge Common
GARDEN ST
WINTHROP ST
JOHN F. KENNEDY ST
ELIOT ST
BENNETT ST
Anderson Bridge
Western Av Bridge
WESTERN AV
NORTH HARVARD ST
BRATTLE ST
CONCORD AV
MT. AUBURN ST
BRATTLE ST
Charles River
ALEWIFE BROOK PKWY
FRESH POND PKWY
Mt. Auburn Cemetery
A B C D E F G H I

0 SCALE .75 KILOMETERS .75 MILES
ROAD
AREA BOUNDARY

Sights

Harvard University:

- **A Busch Reisinger Museum**
- **B Fogg Art Museum**
- **C Museums of Cultural and Natural History**
- **D Sackler**
- **E Semitic Museum**
- **F Widener Library**

G Longfellow National Historic Sight

H MIT Museum

I Mount Auburn Cemetery

A PERFECT DAY IN CAMBRIDGE

Begin your day with a pastry from Au Bon Pain in Harvard Square. Sit and watch commuters on their way to work and students on their way to class, and enjoy the fact that with your day of leisure ahead, you are doing neither. Divide your morning between the Fogg Art Museum and the Busch Reisinger at Harvard. After lunch at one of the restaurants in the square, stroll down Brattle Street, past some of Cambridge's loveliest homes, to Longfellow's house. After touring the home, head back to the square and spend what is left of the afternoon browsing in the many shops there—especially the bookstores. Dinner could be casual—either a salad from Grendel's salad bar or a Chinese meal at Yenching—or in high style at Upstairs at the Pudding. End the day with an art film at the Brattle Theater or a play at the American Repertory Theatre, and an ice cream from Herrell's.

SIGHTSEEING HIGHLIGHTS

★★★ **Harvard University**—This is the oldest university in the United States. Its ivy-covered buildings and quiet courtyards make it one of the prettiest as well. Stop in at **Widener Library** as you walk through "The Yard." It has one of the most extensive collections of any library in the country. The library has a small exhibit depicting Cambridge history which may help put the city in perspective.

Harvard's huge endowment has given the school outstanding museums and innumerable buildings of interest. See if you can guess which one was funded by a major camera company (hint: it's near the Yard). The **Fogg Art Museum** (32 Quincy Street), with its fine collection of Impressionist works, including a Degas ballerina, and Romanesque and medieval works, is my favorite Harvard museum. At the **Busch Reisinger Museum** (29 Kirkland Street), the specialty is German expressionism. The **Sackler** (Quincy Street and Broadway), the newest of the Harvard museums, concentrates on Far Eastern and Islamic art. Details: (617) 495-9400; open 10 a.m. to 4:45 p.m. Monday through Saturday, 1 to 5 p.m. Sunday. Admission to all three museums is $5 adults, $4 seniors, $3 students; free Saturday mornings and for children under 18.

Also operated by Harvard are the **Museums of Cultural and Natural History** and the **Semitic Museum**. The natural history museums are located on Oxford Street and have exhibits on comparative zoology and geology as well as a unique glass flowers exhibit. Details: (617) 495-3045; Museums of Cultural and Natural History are open 9 a.m. to 5 p.m. Monday through Saturday, 1 to 5 p.m. Sunday, closed on major holidays. Admission is $5 adults, $4 seniors and students with valid ID, $3 ages 3 to 13. Like the art museums, they are free to all on Saturday morning. The Semitic Museum is open 11 a.m. to 5 p.m. Monday through Friday, 1 to 4 p.m. Sunday. (1 hour per museum)

★★ **Longfellow National Historic Site**—This was the home of poet Henry Wadsworth Longfellow for 45 years until his death in 1882. His major works were written here, among them *Hiawatha* and *Evangeline*. The house, one of many beautiful homes along Brattle Street, was built in 1759, and has additional historic significance as George Washington's headquarters during the siege of Boston in 1776. Details: 105 Brattle Street, (617) 876-4491; open 10 a.m. to 4:30 p.m. Wednesday through Sunday, closed Thanksgiving, Christmas, and New Year's Day. Admission is $2, free for seniors and children under 17. (1 hour)

★ **MIT Museum**—In addition to exhibits on holography, engineering, science, and architecture—exhibits you'd expect from a university that has produced some of the world's greatest scientific minds—this museum also has an art collection and a model ship gallery. Details: Main museum, 265 Massachusetts Avenue near Central Square, (617)

253-4444; open 9 a.m. to 5 p.m. Tuesday through Friday, noon to 5 p.m. weekends, closed major holidays. Admission is $3 adults. The Compton Gallery is in building 10 of the school's main campus (open 9 a.m. to 5 p.m. Monday through Friday), Hart Nautical Galleries is in building 5 (open 8 a.m. to 8 p.m. daily). (1 hour)

✯ **Mount Auburn Cemetery**—This is one of the most beautifully landscaped urban cemeteries anywhere. There's even a small lookout tower where you can view the surrounding cities of Cambridge and Boston. Charles Bullfinch (the architect who designed the Massachusetts State House), American artist Winslow Homer, Henry Wadsworth Longfellow, and Oliver Wendell Holmes are all buried here. The cemetery is a bit of a walk from Harvard Square but may be worthwhile if you appreciate historic tombstones. Details: 580 Mt. Auburn Street. (½ hour)

FOOD

Harvard Square's restaurants run the gamut from fast-food establishments to upscale bistros. Try **Yenching** (617-547-1130) on Massachusetts Avenue near the T station for good Chinese food at moderate prices ($7–$13). **Au Bon Pain**, next to Yenching, is the place to people-watch at outdoor tables. Study chess players intent on their game as you sample croissants in every flavor imaginable, gourmet sandwiches such as tarragon chicken or chicken with bernaise, and creamy soups. **Grendel's Restaurant** (617-491-1050), at JFK and Winthrop Streets, has a terrific salad bar, good Greek combination plates, and a pleasant atmosphere. Prices are reasonable. Popular with the young set, the **Border Café** packs them in for tasty fajitas and other Mexican dishes. Expect long lines, scruffy wooden tables, and a spirited crowd if you choose to dine here.

The Garage on the corner of Mt. Auburn, JFK, and Dunster Streets is filled with out-of-the-ordinary fast-food restaurants. **Formaggio's** (617-547-4795) creates unique sandwiches with fillings such as ratatouille and boursin cheese on fresh homemade bread. Upstairs, **Café Aventura** serves great pizza for a song. In the basement on the Dunster side of the complex is **John Harvard's Brew House** (617-868-3585). The restaurant serves home-brewed beer and pub grub. Smoked meats are the house specialty. Prices range from $5.95 to $15.95.

CAMBRIDGE

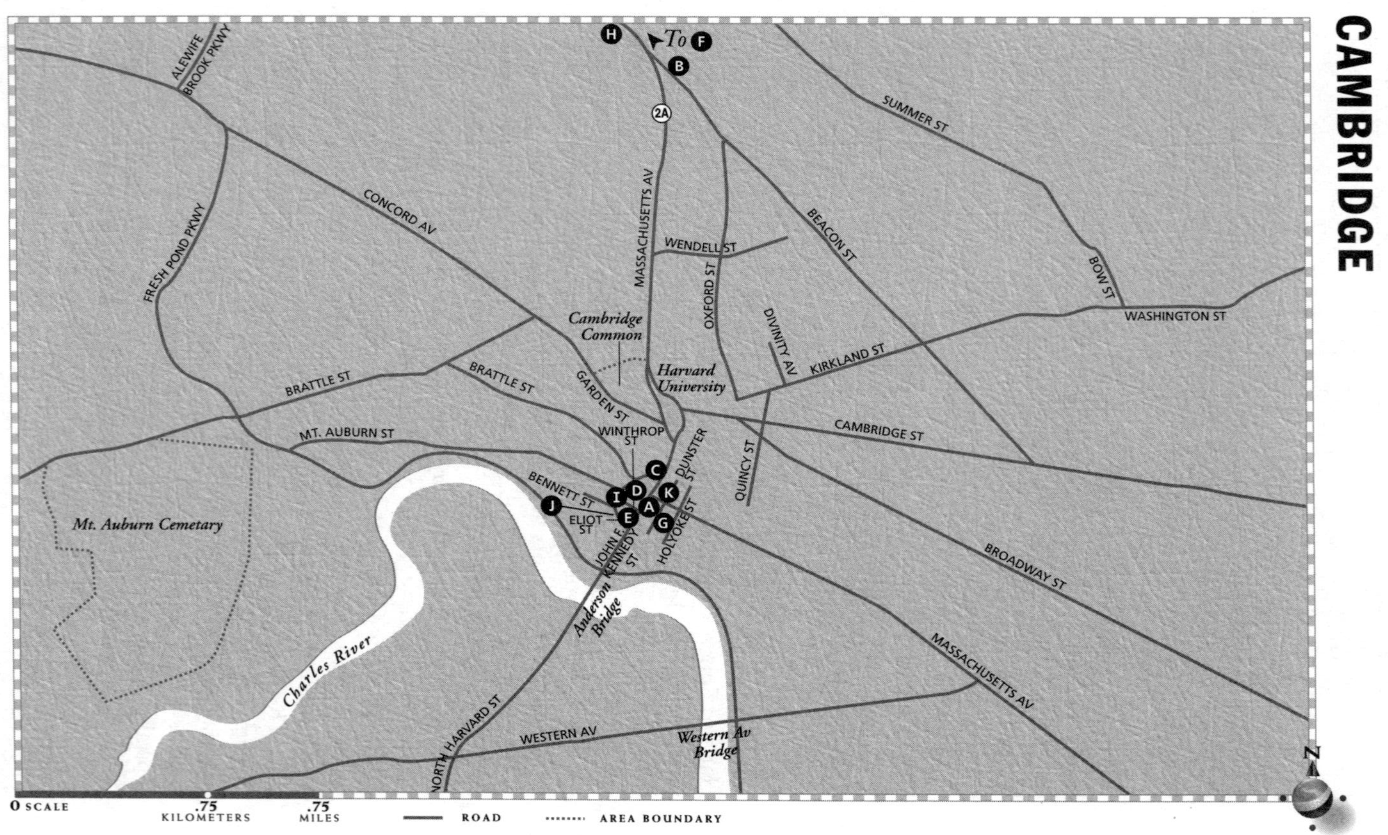

H
To F
B
2A
ALEWIFE BROOK PKWY
SUMMER ST
CONCORD AV
MASSACHUSETTS AV
BEACON ST
WENDELL ST
BOW ST
FRESH POND PKWY
OXFORD ST
DIVINITY AV
WASHINGTON ST
Cambridge Common
Harvard University
KIRKLAND ST
BRATTLE ST
BRATTLE ST
GARDEN ST
WINTHROP ST
MT. AUBURN ST
CAMBRIDGE ST
DUNSTER ST
QUINCY ST
BENNETT ST
C
I
D
K
A
J
E
G
ELIOT ST
HOLYOKE ST
JOHN F. KENNEDY ST
Mt. Auburn Cemetary
BROADWAY ST
Anderson Bridge
MASSACHUSETTS AV
Charles River
NORTH HARVARD ST
WESTERN AV
Western Av Bridge
N
0 SCALE
.75 KILOMETERS
.75 MILES
ROAD
AREA BOUNDARY

Food

- A Au Bon Pain
- B Averof
- C Border Café
- D Café Aventura
- D Formaggio's
- D The Garage
- E Grendel's Restaurant
- D John Harvard's Brew House
- F Redbones
- G Upstairs at the Pudding
- A Yenching

Lodging

- H A Cambridge House Bed & Breakfast
- I Charles Hotel
- J Harvard Square Hotel
- K Inn at Harvard

Note: Items with the same letter are located in the same area.

At the other end of the spectrum is **Upstairs at the Pudding** (617-864-1933). The "Pudding"—as in Harvard's notorious Hasty Pudding Club—is at 10 Holyoke Street. The restaurant has an herb garden terrace, and reservations are recommended. Meals at this fine-dining establishment are expensive.

If southern barbecue is your thing, and you don't mind hopping on the subway for two stops to Davis Square in Somerville, try **Redbones** (55 Chester Street, 617-628-2200). The open kitchen turns out everything from pork pulled sandwiches and fried Louisiana catfish to ribs done Memphis, Texas, or Arkansas style. Prices are reasonable ($5.95–$13.95). At the **Averof** (617-354-4500), in Porter Square (the subway stop between Harvard and Davis Square), belly dancers perform while patrons dine on Greek specialties.

LODGING

If you want to be in the heart of things, stay in Harvard Square. The **Charles Hotel** (1 Bennett Street, 617-864-1200 or 800-882-1818) is the upscale lodging choice with a health club and spa. Doubles range from $179 to $329. The **Harvard Square Hotel** (617-864-5200 or 800-458-5886) across the street offers simpler accommodations for about $175 per night. One of the newest lodgings to grace Harvard Square is the **Inn at Harvard** (1201 Massachusetts Avenue, 617-491-2222 or 800-222-8733). With its elegant atrium lounge and attractive guest rooms, the inn is both comfortable and convenient (doubles range from $155 to $249). At 2218 Massachusetts Avenue beyond Harvard Square in North Cambridge, **A Cambridge House Bed & Breakfast Inn** (617-491-6300 or 800-232-9989) offers romantic lodging in a nineteenth-century home. Rooms have large, inviting canopy beds, and a gourmet breakfast is included in the room rate ($119 to $225 for two people).

ARTS AND ENTERTAINMENT

Ryles Jazz Club (617-876-9330) in Inman Square has long been recognized as one of the Boston area's best jazz bars. The **Regattabar** at the Charles Hotel in Harvard Square also has live jazz most evenings. Blues musicians perform nightly at actor Dan Ackroyd's **House of Blues** (96 Winthrop Street, 617-491-BLUE). The cover charge varies, and there's a gospel brunch on Sundays. The **Brattle Theatre** (617-876-6837) on Brattle Street in Harvard Square shows current art films, revives old film classics, and occasionally runs film festivals. The **American Repertory Theatre** (64 Brattle Street, 617-547-8300) has live theatrical productions. Call the theater for schedule and ticket information.

SHOPPING

Because of its proximity to Harvard University, Harvard Square has more than its share of bookstores. **The Coop** (Harvard Cooperative Society, 617-499-2000), Harvard University's main bookstore, also has a considerable music and art-print department. **Wordsworth** and the **Harvard Square Bookstore** are two bookshops where you can browse to your heart's content. Both stores are open late. When you run out of bookstores, there are plenty of clothing stores and specialty shops—particularly in the **Galleria** and **Charles Hotel** shopping complexes—to keep even the most determined shopper busy for hours. Don't miss the newsstand in the center of Harvard Square: Its selection of magazines and newspapers is varied and extensive.

3 LEXINGTON AND CONCORD

The "Shot Heard 'round the World" was fired in Concord on April 19, 1775. On that infamous spring day (still celebrated as Patriot's Day in Massachusetts), some 700 red-coated British troops stormed into Concord hoping to plunder the ammunition and provisions that colonists had stored there. Although the British called for reinforcements, they were outnumbered by American minutemen and ultimately retreated back to Boston.

During the hundred years that followed the war, Concord was home to some of America's foremost literary figures—Ralph Waldo Emerson, Nathaniel Hawthorne, Louisa May Alcott, and Henry David Thoreau. Because of Thoreau's strong naturalist influence, parts of Concord have been set aside as nature preserves. Today, with many of Concord's lovely colonial homes still intact, it is easy to see what inspired writers to live in this charming village.

Neighboring Lexington also has its share of charm and history. The first battle of the Revolutionary War took place in Lexington on that same April day in 1775. Some buildings that played an important role in that initial skirmish (such as the Munroe Tavern, which served as a field hospital for the retreating British) are still standing. Lexington today is a quiet, well-to-do residential community, popular because it is within easy commuting distance of Boston and outlying high-tech employers.

LEXINGTON AND CONCORD

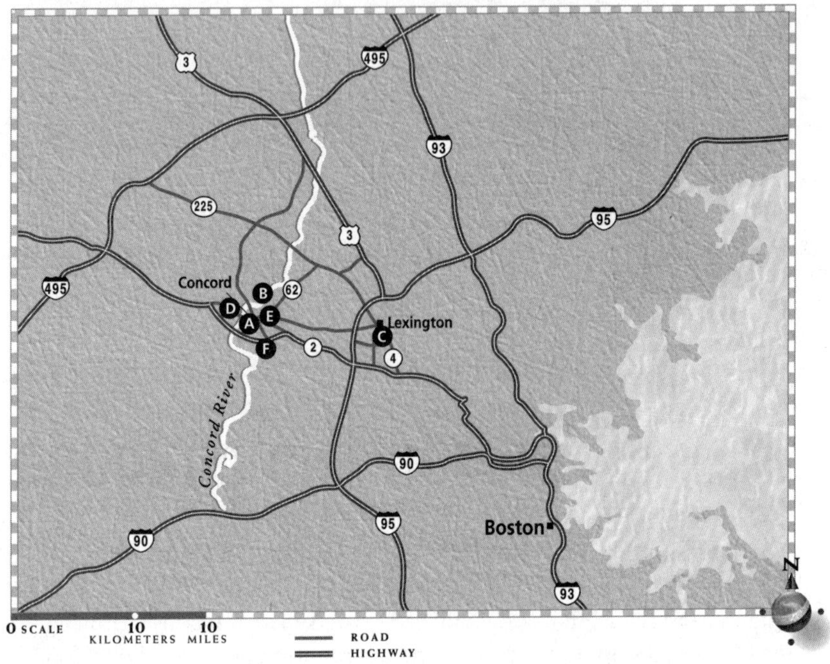

Sights

- **A** Concord Museum
- **A** Emerson's House
- **B** Great Meadows Wildlife Refuge
- **C** Museum of Our National Heritage
- **D** North Bridge
- **D** Old Manse
- **E** Orchard House
- **B** Sleepy Hollow Cemetery
- **A** Thoreau Lyceum
- **F** Walden Pond
- **E** The Wayside

Note: Items with the same letter are located in the same town or area.

A PERFECT DAY IN LEXINGTON AND CONCORD

To set the stage for the day to come, begin at North Bridge in Concord. Then tour the Concord Museum. Spend the better part of midday picnicking, swimming, and hiking at Walden Pond. After enjoying the outdoors for a few hours, head back inside, catching the last tour of the Alcott family home—Orchard House. For a relaxing end to the day, dine in the historic Colonial Inn in the center of Concord.

SIGHTSEEING HIGHLIGHTS

★★ **Concord Museum**—The museum brings together Concord's military and literary histories. Items of interest on the museum tour include Paul Revere's lantern, which hung in the Old North Church in Boston the night of his famous ride, and personal articles of Henry David Thoreau and Ralph Waldo Emerson, who were friends as well as fellow writers. Details: 200 Lexington Road, just east of the intersection of Routes 2 and 2A; (978) 369-9609; open 9 a.m. to 5 p.m. Monday through Saturday, noon to 5 p.m. Sunday, closed on major holidays. Hours are shortened January through March. Admission is $6 adults, $4 seniors and students, $2 children. (1½ hours)

★★ **North Bridge**—This is the site of the first clash between British and Revolutionary troops. Visit the bridge more for its historical significance than for what you'll see here today. *The Minute Man* statue now stands at the site in memory of that fateful battle. The statue was made by noted sculptor Daniel Chester French, whose grave is in nearby Sleepy Hollow Cemetery. The visitor center on the hill above the bridge houses a gift shop and replicas of military attire that the minutemen used. Details: On Monument Street about a mile from the center of Concord; (978) 369-6993. Admission is free. (¼–1 hour)

★ **Emerson's House**—Ralph Waldo Emerson lived here for almost 50 years until his death in 1882. Many of the writer's personal artifacts are on display, including a desk he used and part of his personal library. Details: 28 Cambridge Turnpike just across from the Concord Museum; (978) 369-2236; open mid-April through October 10 a.m. to 4:30 p.m. Thursday through Saturday, 2 to 4:30 p.m. Sunday. Admission is $4.50 adults, $3 ages 6 to 17. (1 hour)

★ **Great Meadows Wildlife Refuge**—This marshy area was frequented by Thoreau in his study of nature. Today you can follow the 1¾-mile Dike Trail loop and perhaps see a fox, muskrat, or weasel in addition to the various species of waterfowl that nest in the wetlands. Details: From Sleepy Hollow Cemetery, continue on Bedford Road for about ¾ mile, then turn left onto Monsen Road. Stay on Monsen Road to the refuge entrance. Admission is free. (2 hours)

★ **Museum of Our National Heritage**—The museum is devoted to preserving and showing virtually all facets of America's heritage through changing exhibits that range from antique quilts to decorative arts to early military paraphernalia. Details: 33 Marrett Road on Route 2A in Lexington; (781) 861-6559; open year-round 10 a.m. to 5 p.m. Monday through Saturday, noon to 5 p.m. Sunday, closed Thanksgiving, Christmas, and New Year's Day. Admission is free. (1 hour)

★ **Old Manse**—Old Manse was built in 1770 and was, at different times, home to both Emerson and Hawthorne. Details: On Monument Street just below the North Bridge; (978) 369-3909; open 10 a.m. to 4:30 p.m. Monday and Wednesday through Saturday, 1 to 4:30 p.m. Sunday June through October. Admission is $4.50 adults, $2.50 senior citizens, $1.50 ages 6 to 16. (1 hour)

★ **Orchard House**—This was the home of Louisa May Alcott from 1858 to 1877 and the setting for her famous novel *Little Women*. Many actual furnishings are on display, including sketches done by an Alcott sister which still remain on one of the bedroom walls. The chapel in back of the house was built in 1884 to house meetings of the Concord School of Philosophy. The school was founded by A. Bronson Alcott, Louisa's father. Details: 399 Lexington Road (Route 2A traveling toward Lexington); (978) 369-4118; open April through October 10 a.m. to 4:30 p.m. Monday through Saturday, 1 to 4:30 p.m. Sunday and holidays; November through March open 11 a.m. to 3 p.m. weekdays, 10 a.m. to 4:30 p.m. Saturday, 1 to 4 p.m. Sunday. Admission is $5.50 adults, $4.50 senior citizens and ages 13 to 18, $3.50 ages 6 to 17. (1 hour)

★ **Sleepy Hollow Cemetery**—As you travel back toward Concord center from the North Bridge, turn left onto Bedford Street. The entrance to the cemetery will be on your left. Follow signs to Author's Ridge. Ralph Waldo Emerson, Henry David Thoreau, Nathaniel

Hawthorne, Louisa May Alcott, and sculptor Daniel Chester French are all buried here. (½ hour)

★ **Thoreau Lyceum**—The lyceum is filled with Thoreau memorabilia and includes a replica of his house at Walden Pond and a bookshop and library specializing in his works. Details: 156 Belknap Street; (978) 369-5912; open 10 a.m. to 5 p.m. Monday through Saturday, 2 to 5 p.m. Sunday, closed major holidays and in January. Admission is $2 adults, $1.50 students, free for children under age 8. (1 hour)

★ **Walden Pond**—Henry David Thoreau's famous retreat from civilization is now a popular escape for Boston city dwellers and their suburban counterparts. Being relatively mud-free compared to most ponds, and much warmer than the Atlantic, Walden Pond is a popular place to swim in the area. The pond can get crowded on a hot summer day, but the farther you walk from the main beach, the better chance you have of finding a secluded pond-side picnic spot. In recent years there has been a major crusade—spearheaded by celebrity musician Don Henley—to save the woods surrounding Walden Pond from developers. There is a model of Thoreau's house next to the parking lot, but the actual house is about a ten-minute walk from Route 126. Details: Follow Walden Street from Concord center south for about a mile, then cross Route 2. The pond will be on your right, the parking lot on your left. (978) 369-3254. There is a charge for parking. (½ hour–half day)

★ **The Wayside**—Louisa May Alcott and Nathaniel Hawthorne both lived in this nineteenth-century home. Details: 455 Lexington Road, Concord, (978) 369-6975; open seasonally, call ahead for hours. Admission is charged. (1 hour)

FOOD

Picnic at Walden Pond or Great Meadows Wildlife Refuge if the weather is nice. There are a number of roadside farm stands in the area to augment the goods in your picnic basket. Otherwise, for fine indoor dining in Concord, **Merchants Row** (978-369-9200) at the Colonial Inn is the place to go. In addition to breakfast, lunch, and dinner, the restaurant also serves a buffet Sunday brunch and afternoon tea. Reservations are recommended.

LEXINGTON AND CONCORD

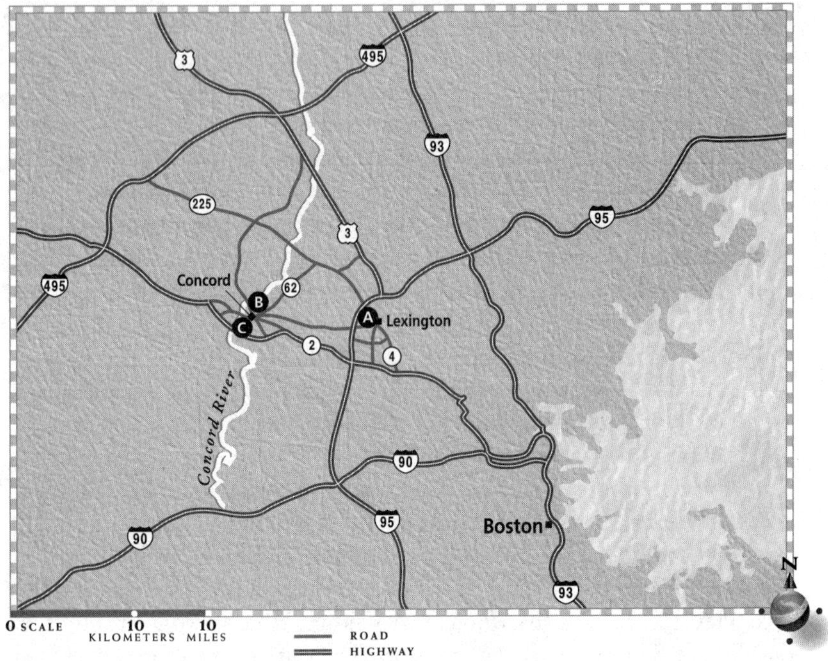

Food

- Ⓐ Lemon Grass
- Ⓐ Mario's
- Ⓑ Merchants Row
- Ⓐ Yangtze's

Lodging

- Ⓒ Colonel Roger Brown House
- Ⓑ Colonial Inn
- Ⓐ Holiday Inn Express
- Ⓐ Sheraton Tara Lexington Inn

Note: Items with the same letter are located in the same town or area.

Lexington has a handful of restaurants that offer ethnic variety at reasonable prices. For Thai food try the **Lemon Grass** (1710 Massachusetts Avenue, 781-862-3530). **Mario's** (Massachusetts Avenue in the center of town, 781-861-1182) is popular with families because it offers large portions of Italian dishes at low prices. The restaurant is casual, and often crowded and lively. Entrées are generally under $7. For delicious Chinese food, try the evening buffet at **Yangtze's** (781-861-6030). The restaurant is also in the center of town and the buffet costs $10.95 per person.

LODGING

The **Colonial Inn** (978-369-9200 or 800-370-9200) on Monument Square in the center of Concord is one of the best-known inns in the area. The oldest part of the inn dates back to 1716, and at various times has been everything from a general store to a storehouse during the Revolutionary War. It's been run as a hotel for the last century. Guest rooms are attractively appointed with colonial style and country furnishings. Room prices range from $90 to $285; price depends on the season, type, and room location (rooms in the oldest section are the most expensive). Connecting rooms are available for families in the Prescott wing; and the Cottage has two two-bedroom suites, each with a full kitchen. About 3 miles from Concord center, the **Colonel Roger Brown House** (1694 Main Street, 978-369-9119 or 800-292-1369) offers bed-and-breakfast accommodations in a relaxed atmosphere. The home was built in 1775 by minuteman Colonel Roger Brown. Today each guest room has a private bath and color television. A continental buffet breakfast is included in the room rate ($75–$100). As a bonus for active travelers, guests get a complimentary membership to the health club next door during their stay.

If you prefer to stay in chain hotels, try the **Sheraton Tara Lexington Inn** (727 Marrett Road, 781-862-8700 or 800-325-3535) or the **Holiday Inn Express** (440 Bedford Street, 781-861-0850 or 800-HOLIDAY). Doubles at the Sheraton range between $170 and $235 per night; rooms at the Holiday Inn are about $100.

SIDE TRIPS FROM LEXINGTON AND CONCORD

Lincoln, another attractive town in the area, is adjacent to both Concord and Lexington. In Lincoln, the **DeCordova Museum and**

Sculpture Park is worth a visit if you have time. Exhibits change regularly but focus on twentieth-century American art, and the grounds are always lovely. The museum is open from noon to 5 p.m. Tuesday through Sunday. Admission is $4 adults, $3 children and seniors. Call (781) 259-8371 for current exhibit information.

Lowell, northwest of Lexington and Concord, was once a major center for textile manufacturing. Today the city's better days may be over. There are, however, almost 40 restored buildings related to Lowell's manufacturing past that survive as part of the **Lowell National Historical Park** (call 978-970-5000 for information). The park's visitor's center is located at 246 Market Street, adjacent to the Merrimack Canal. (Tours of the canal are also available.)

Also in Lowell, The **New England Quilt Museum** offers changing exhibits of handcrafted quilts. Details: 18 Shattuck Street; (978) 452-4207; open 10 a.m. to 4 p.m. Monday through Saturday year-round, noon to 4 p.m. Sunday May through November. Admission is $4 adults, $3 seniors and students. The **Whistler House Museum of Art**, the early-nineteenth-century house where James McNeill Whistler was born, displays his paintings as well as those by his contemporaries such as John Singer Sargent. Details: 243 Worthen; (978) 452-7641; open 11 a.m. to 4 p.m. Wednesday through Saturday, 1 to 4 p.m. Sunday. Admission is $3 adults, $2 students and seniors.

Cobblestones Restaurant (91 Dutton Street, 978-970-2282), in a brick building adjacent to the canal, has a varied menu and is convenient to many of Lowell's sights. Lunch entrées range between $6 and $8; dinner prices are $10 to $17.

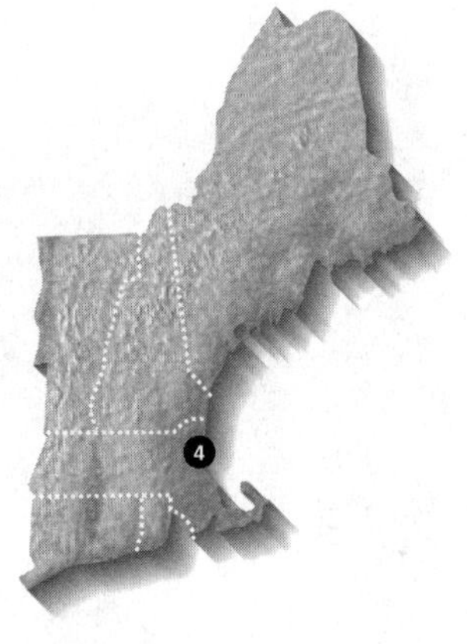

4 SALEM

First settled in 1626, Salem is both beguiling and bewitching. It is a small city struggling to preserve its past glory while striving to keep pace with the twentieth century. In the late 1700s Salem was one of the largest communities in the United States—due to an active maritime trade network with Europe, the West Indies, and Asia. The staging ground for the infamous witch trials of 1692, Salem is also home to the House of Seven Gables, immortalized by Nathaniel Hawthorne who was born in the city in 1804. All these facets of Salem's past are worth exploring.

In 1692, mass hysteria gripped the city when several girls claimed to have been bewitched by a West Indian servant named Tituba. The claims started a rash of accusations, and just about anyone exhibiting strange behavior was said to be a witch. More than two hundred townsfolk in all were arrested for allegedly practicing witchcraft. Nineteen of the accused were hanged, and one was stoned to death before Massachusetts governor William Phipps put a stop to the executions in 1693.

Today Salem is called "the Witch City"— a reputation the city has turned to its advantage. The witch trial legacy attracts many curious tourists to Salem, particularly on Halloween. ◘

SALEM

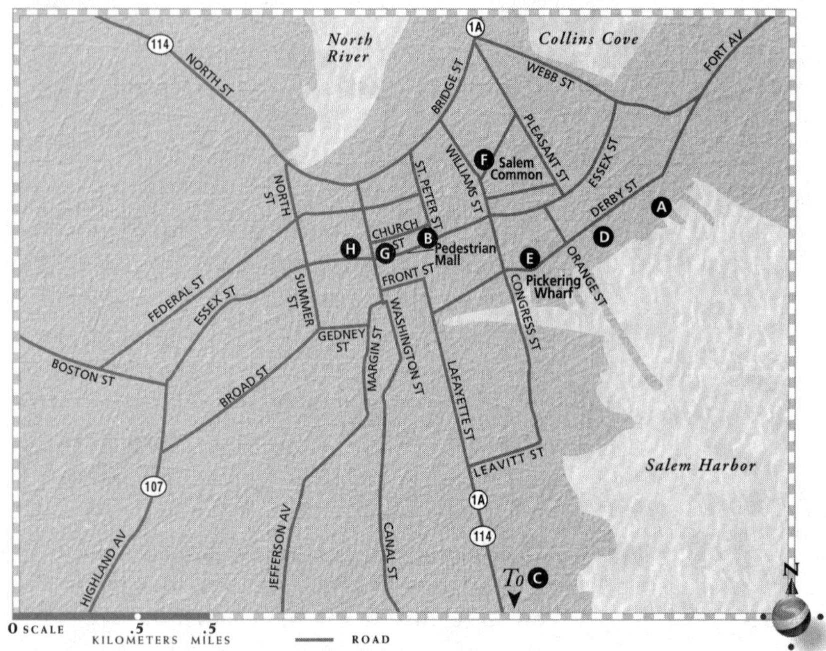

Sights

- **A** House of Seven Gables
- **B** Peabody Essex Museum
- **C** Pioneer Village
- **D** Salem Maritime National Historic Site
- **E** Salem Wax Museum of Witches and Seafarers
- **F** Salem Witch Museum
- **G** Witch House
- **H** Witches Dungeon

A PERFECT DAY IN SALEM

Start your day at the wonderful Peabody Essex Museum. Enjoy lunch on the waterside at Victoria Station. In the afternoon visit the House of Seven Gables and then tour the Witch House or watch the Witch Museum's media show. If you have time to spare, window-shop at Pickering Wharf before heading to nearby Marblehead for dinner and overnight accommodations.

SIGHTSEEING HIGHLIGHTS

★★★ **Peabody Essex Museum**—The Peabody is a gem, with extraordinary depth for a small-city museum. There are exhibits of nautical paintings and instruments and ships' figureheads, as one might expect in a city whose livelihood came from the sea. However, the most fascinating exhibits are those devoted to goods brought back to this country through foreign trade. The collection includes fine china from the Orient, tribal artifacts from the Pacific islands, exotic furniture, silver, and even a miniature Taj Mahal carved in ivory. For children, there are several rooms devoted to natural history. At 132 Essex Street, Plummer Hall houses a collection of art, silver, dolls, toys, and military artifacts from Essex County, as well as special exhibits. Details: East India Square at Liberty and Essex Streets, (978) 745-9500; open 10 a.m. to 5 p.m. Monday through Thursday and Saturday, 10 a.m. to 8 p.m. Friday, noon to 5 p.m. Sunday; closed Monday November through Memorial Day. Admission is $7.50 adults, $6.50 senior citizens and students, $4 ages 6 to 16, $18 for a family of four. The museum also offers tours of historic homes dating from 1690 to 1819. Combination tickets to the galleries and homes are available. (2 hours–half day)

★★ **House of Seven Gables**—This is the house that inspired Nathaniel Hawthorne to write the well-known novel by the same name. The house was built in 1668 and harbors a secret staircase. The house in which Hawthorne was born has been moved to the grounds in recent years, and the complex includes two other buildings dating back to the 1600s. Details: 54 Turner Street on the water, (978) 744-0991; open 9:30 a.m. to 6 p.m. July 1 through Labor Day, 10 a.m. to 4:30 p.m. the rest of the year; closed Thanksgiving, Christmas, New Year's Day, and the first two weeks in January. Admission is $7 adults,

$4 students, $3 ages 6 to 12. The tour includes a short introductory film. (1½–2 hours)

★★ **Pioneer Village**—Grazing sheep, thatched cottages, blacksmithing, hand-churned butter, and hand-spun wool are a few of the things you'll see in this re-created 1630s village. Costumed guides reenact the Puritan way of life here, and 12 structures are spread throughout the village's 4 acres. Details: Forest River Park, (978) 744-0991; open late May through October 10 a.m. to 5 p.m. Monday through Saturday, noon to 5 p.m. Sunday. Admission is $4.50 adults, $3.50 seniors and ages 13 to 17, $2.50 ages 6 to 12. Family rates are available, as are combination tickets to the village and the House of Seven Gables. (2 hours)

★★ **Salem Witch Museum**—In a Romanesque-style building that's hard to miss on Salem Common, the museum features an audiovisual presentation of the events of 1692. It is an engaging introduction to the history of the witch trials. Details: Washington Square, Salem, (978) 744-1692; open 10 a.m. to 5 p.m. daily, until 7 p.m. in July and August. The presentation is shown on the hour and half hour. Admission is $4 adults, $3.50 seniors, $2.50 students and ages 6 to 14. (½ hour)

★ **Salem Maritime National Historic Site**—Run by the National Park Service, the site includes the Custom and Derby Houses along with several wharves and warehouses illustrating Salem's former dominance as a port. Details: 174 Derby Street, (978) 745-1470; open 9 a.m. to 5 p.m. daily. Admission is free. (2 hours)

★ **Salem Wax Museum of Witches and Seafarers**—Wax figures represent Salem's past in a variety of historical scenes that include the founding of Salem, the witch trials, and the city's prosperous seafaring days. A 23-minute multimedia show on the witch trials is included in the admission price. Details: 288 Derby Street, Salem; (978) 740-2929 or (800) 298-2929; hours vary (the museum has extended hours during summer), so call ahead. Admission is $4 adults, $3.50 seniors, $2.50 children under 14. (1 hour)

★ **Witches Dungeon**—The trial of Sarah Goode, one of the accused witches, is reenacted in a re-creation of the dungeon where alleged witches awaited hanging. Details: 16 Lynde Street, (978) 741-3570;

open 10 a.m. to 5 p.m. daily May through November. Admission is $4 adults, $3.50 seniors, $2.50 ages 6 to 14. (1 hour)

★ **Witch House**—Those accused of being witches were interrogated here by Judge Jonathan Corwin before going to trial. Built around 1642, it is one of the oldest houses still standing in the United States. Tour guides explain uses of eighteenth-century everyday household items and how expressions such as "sleep tight" and "turning the tables" originally came into our language. Details: Corner of Essex and Washington Streets, (978) 744-0180; open 10 a.m. to 4:30 p.m. mid-March through November, until 6 p.m. in July and August. Admission is $5 adults, $1.50 ages 5 to 16. (1 hour)

FITNESS AND RECREATION

Devereux Beach runs along the narrow strip of land that connects the town of Marblehead to Marblehead Neck about 6 miles from Salem. There are facilities at Devereux, but as the beach tends to be a little rocky, some residents prefer a tiny slip of sand set back in a cove within walking distance from downtown Marblehead. If Devereux does not appeal to you, perhaps you can persuade one of the locals to give you directions to their "secret" beach.

FOOD

Pickering Wharf has the highest concentration of restaurants in Salem. Generally they're fast-food and take-out operations ranging from Chinese to pizza. **Victoria Station** (Pickering Wharf, 978-745-3400) has outdoor seating in summer and good steak and seafood dinner entrées ranging from $14 to $20. Lunch prices are moderate. Seafood gets top billing at the **Chase House** (Pickering Wharf, 978-744-0000), with dinner entrées ranging from $9 to $14. The **Lyceum Bar and Grill** (43 Church Street, 978-745-7665) offers fine fare in an attractive building. Baked scrod, grilled pork tenderloin, and fish chowder are specialties at this popular restaurant. Dinner entrées range from $16 to $21.

In Marblehead, **The Barnacle** (781-631-4236) and **The Landing** (81 Front Street, 781-631-1878) both overlook the harbor and serve fresh seafood. Prices are moderate at the Barnacle; they range from $12 to $21 at the Landing. The **King's Rook** (12 State Street,

SALEM

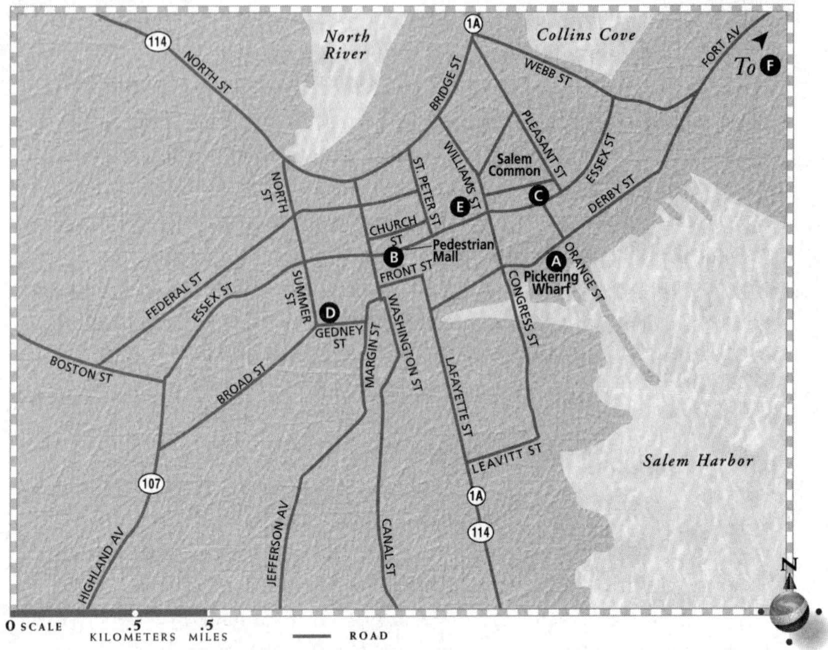

Food

- A Chase House
- B Lyceum Bar and Grill
- A Pickering Wharf
- A Victoria Station

Lodging

- C Hawthorne Hotel
- D Salem Inn
- E Stepping Stone Inn

Camping

- F Winter Island Maritime Park

Note: Items with the same letter are located in the same area.

781-631-9838) is a cozy coffeehouse that serves copious salads and tasty desserts. Chocolate lovers must find their way to **Stowaway Sweets** (154 Atlantic Avenue, 781-631-0303) candy shop. The "chocolate meltaways" are positively out of this world.

LODGING

In Salem, the following inn establishments are all close to the main tourist attractions. The **Salem Inn** (7 Summer Street, 978-741-0680 or 800-446-2995) is in an attractive brick Federal-style building constructed in 1834 by a local sea captain. Rooms are furnished with antiques, and suites with fully equipped kitchens are available. The inn is diagonally across from the Witch House. Double rooms start at $119, and suites run from $129 to $189. The **Hawthorne Hotel** (978-744-4080 or 800-SAY-STAY), an elegant small hotel on the town common, keeps company with Salem's stateliest homes. Doubles start at $99 per night. The **Stepping Stone Inn** (adjacent to the Witch Museum at 19 Washington Square, 978-741-8900 or 800-338-3022) is a cozy bed and breakfast with a cheery breakfast room. Prices range from $75 to $95 and include a continental breakfast.

While staying right in Salem is certainly convenient for sightseeing, you may wish to travel 6 miles to the charming seaside town of Marblehead for lodging. A stroll down its winding streets, a seafood dinner overlooking the water, and a drive out to affluent Marblehead Neck are all excellent ways to relax after a busy day of sightseeing. Two bed and breakfasts that overlook the ocean are **Spray Cliff** (25 Spray Avenue, 781-631-6789 or 800-626-1530) and **Harborside House** (23 Gregory Street, 781-631-1032). The Harborside is within easy walking distance of Marblehead's restaurants, and the helpful innkeeper can steer you in the direction of the right one for you. The Spray Cliff has a Tudor exterior, and a crisp, airy feel inside. Innkeepers Sally and Roger Plauche welcome their guests with wine and cheese, and guests are always free to help themselves to soft drinks or refreshments from the bar. In the morning, guests are served a continental breakfast with home-baked goods. Room prices range from $175 to $205. A continental breakfast is also included in Harborside's rates ($70 to $85). For a $15 booking fee, Bed & Breakfast Reservations North Shore, Greater Boston & Cape Cod (617-964-1606 or 800-832-2632) can help you locate a bed and breakfast suited to your tastes in Marblehead, Salem, or anywhere you visit on the North Shore.

MARBLEHEAD

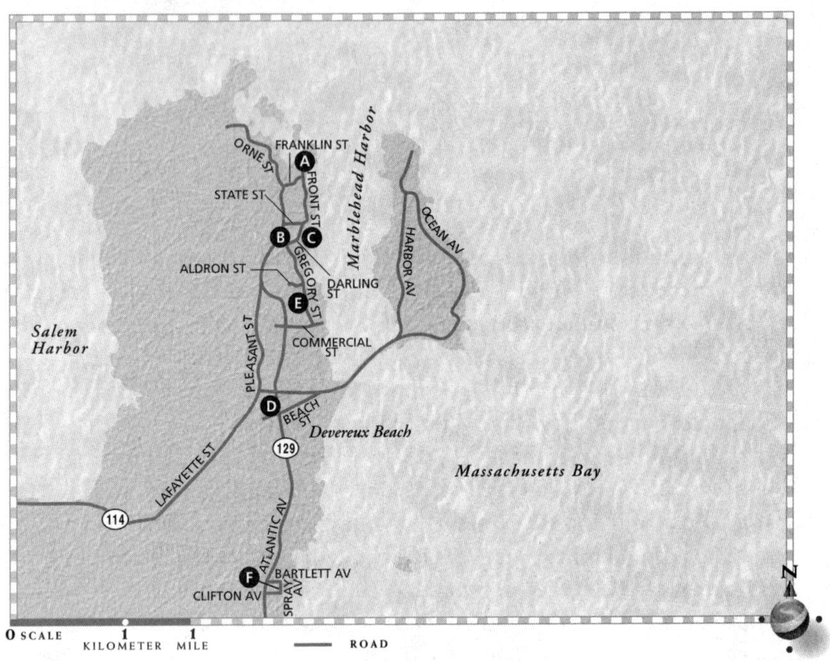

Food

- **A** The Barnacle
- **B** King's Rook
- **C** The Landing
- **D** Stowaway Sweets

Lodging

- **E** Harborside House
- **F** Spray Cliff

CAMPING

There are campsites at **Winter Island Maritime Park** (50 Winter Island Road) in Salem. Sites rage between $15 and $18, and the campground is open May through October. The Salem Trolley stops at the campground, and can take you to Salem's historic sights. Call (978) 745-9430 for information.

HISTORIC HOMES

Salem has many notable homes, dating from the 1600s through the 1800s, that are open to the public. The **Ropes Mansion** (318 Essex Street), several doors down from the Witch House, was built in 1727 and remodeled in 1894. It's open June through October from 10 a.m. to 4 p.m. Monday through Saturday, and from 12:30 to 4 p.m. on Sunday. Admission is charged for adults, seniors, and children over age 6.

You will come across other historic homes as you walk around the town; pick up a map at the Chamber of Commerce in the Town Hall at 32 Derby Square. There is a National Parks Tourist Information Office on Derby Street adjacent to Pickering Wharf, open until 6 p.m. in summer. There is free parking behind the building. (I have had no trouble parking in the lot for several hours, but you may want to check with the park office to see if there is a time limit on the day of your visit.)

If you prefer not to spend the entire day on your feet, the **Salem Trolley** (depot at 9 Pickering Way, 978-744-5469) offers one-hour narrated tours, and stops at most of the major sights every hour. Tickets, which are good for one day, cost $8 for adults, $7 for seniors and students, and $4 for children ages 5 to 12. A family rate of $20 is available, and the trolley tickets entitle you to discounts at a number of local businesses. The trolley runs Monday through Friday from 10 a.m. to 5:30 p.m. (the last tour of the day leaves the Salem Visitor's Center at 4:30 p.m.) April through October, and on weekends in November and March.

SIDE TRIPS FROM SALEM

Marblehead, founded in 1629, is such a delightful town that you may wish to spend a few hours exploring its narrow streets lined with handsomely restored homes and quaint shops. One historic home of note, the **Lee Mansion**, is open to the public from mid-May through mid-October. Built in 1768 by Colonel Jeremiah Lee, the Georgian residence is now home to the Marblehead Historical Society. The house boasts famous guests such as George Washington and John Adams, and the decor includes exquisite hand-painted wallpaper, antique pewter tableware, and an engaging primitive oil painting of Marblehead Harbor. The house is open from 10 a.m. to 4 p.m. Monday through Saturday, and from 1 to 4 p.m. on Sunday. Admission is $4 for adults, $3.50 for students and seniors, and free for children under age 10.

If you'd like to get out on the water, East India Cruise Company of Salem operates whale-watch, harbor, and "attitude adjustment" cruises from May through October. The ticket booth and dock is located at Pickering Wharf across from Victoria Station restaurant. Call (978) 741-0434 or (800) 745-9594 for current departure times and ticket price information.

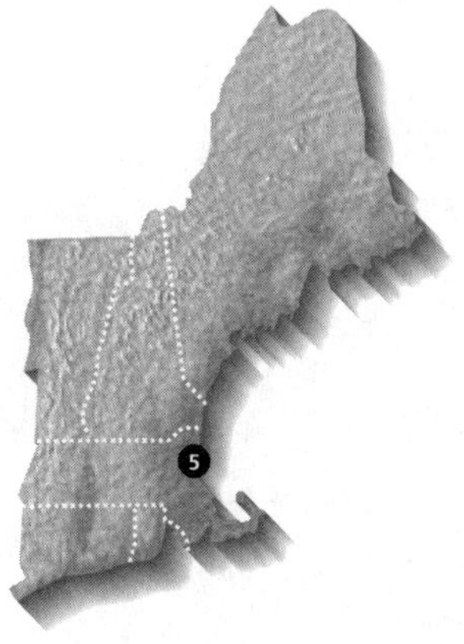

5 CAPE ANN

Cape Ann is not as famous as Cape Cod, yet it's closer to Boston and its rugged coastline typifies traditional New England scenery. The area boasts enchanting villages (many originally settled in the 1600s) and first-rate beaches, yet tourism is much subtler here than in other New England communities.

On Cape Ann's south end, the most scenic drive to the ocean is Route 127 through lovely towns such as Manchester-by-the-Sea, where New England aristocrats hide stately homes behind stone walls and vast lawns. Pride's Crossing railroad station has two waiting benches, one marked "Democrats" and one "Republicans." Often the most interesting sights are just off Route 127, so try a few side streets.

In Manchester, you can take an invigorating dip at Singing Beach, named for the sound of the wind on moving sand. (Warning to visitors: The ocean north of Boston may be a trifle colder than you expect—enter the water cautiously.) To the north is Gloucester, long a fishing port and now home to Hammond Castle. Rockport, at Cape Ann's outer tip, was an art colony for many years. Although now somewhat commercial, the town retains much of its original charm. Nearby, sleepy Annisquam has beautiful oceanside homes. Antiques lovers should not miss the shops on Route 133 between Gloucester and Rowley. Ipswich, where colonists first exclaimed, "No taxation without representation," claims more seventeenth-century homes still standing than any other town in America. Newburyport, at Cape Ann's north end, boasts fine Federalist homes and the beautiful Parker Wildlife Refuge. ◪

CAPE ANN

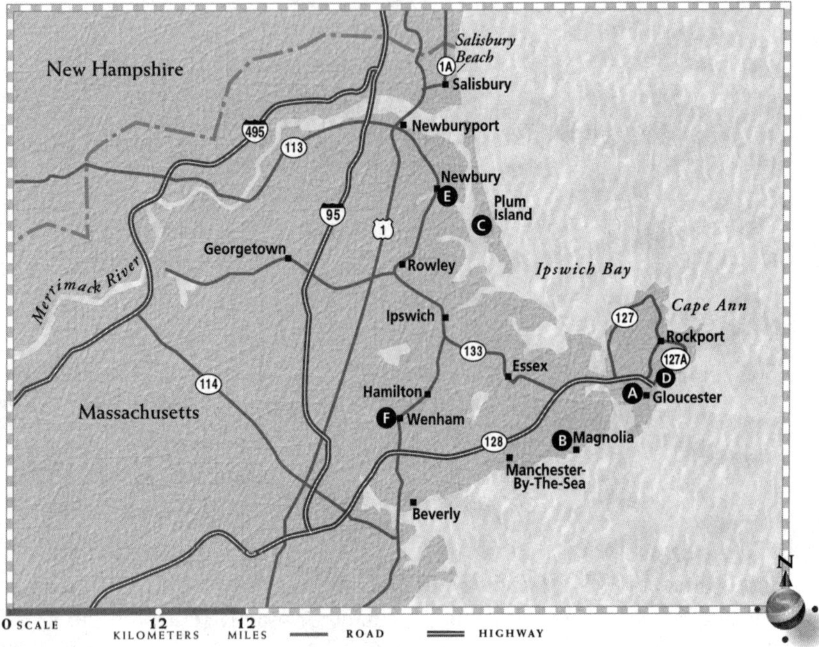

Sights

- **A** **Cape Ann Historical Museum**
- **B** **Hammond Castle Museum**
- **C** **Plum Island and Parker River National Wildlife Refuge**

Society of the Preservation of New England Antiquities Sites:

- **D** **Beauport**
- **E** **The Coffin House**
- **E** **Dole-Little House**
- **E** **Spencer-Pierce-Little Farm**
- **E** **Swett-Ilsley House**

- **F** **Wenham Museum**

Note: Items with the same letter are located in the same town or area.

A PERFECT DAY ON CAPE ANN

Start the day walking the nature trails at Plum Island, and then rest on the lovely beach there for a spell. If you're brave, take a bone-chilling plunge in the frigid ocean waters. For lunch, travel south to Essex for a heaping fried-clam plate at Woodman's. Afterward, visit Hammond Castle in Gloucester. End the day strolling the shop-laden lanes of Rockport.

SIGHTSEEING HIGHLIGHTS

★★★ **Hammond Castle Museum**—Although it was constructed during the late 1920s, much of this building and its contents actually date to medieval and Renaissance Europe. The castle was built for John Hays Hammond Jr. Though his is not a household name, Hammond holds more than 400 patents and is credited with many inventions that have shaped modern life, from radio control systems to shaving cream. The castle interior includes an organ with more than 8,000 pipes and, in the center of a medieval courtyard, a reflecting pool that Hammond used to dive into from his second-floor bedroom window. Another unique fixture in the castle is a rain-making system, which Hammond installed in the roof over the courtyard to water his plants. On Route 127, the turnoff to Hesperus Avenue is about 4½ miles from Manchester Center on your right. The street sign is not well-marked from this direction, so keep your eyes peeled. Details: 80 Hesperus Avenue; (978) 283-7673; open 9 a.m. to 5 p.m. daily (last tour at 4 p.m.), but you may want to call ahead to verify hours; the castle sometimes closes early for special events. The castle is closed Thanksgiving, Christmas, and New Year's Day. Guided tours cost $6 adults, $5 students and seniors, $4 ages 4 to 12. (1½ hours)

★★ **Plum Island and Parker River National Wildlife Refuge**—This superb wildlife refuge is home to numerous species of birds and offers miles of golden sand beaches to walk on. One word of caution: In early July, the beaches in this area are visited by "greenheads," a type of horsefly with a nasty bite. The greenhead season lasts only about two weeks and I've been told bug spray will repel them. Come prepared and you can still appreciate this beautiful park. Details: Turn right onto Rolfe's Lane from Route 1A in Newbury and follow the signs, (978) 465-5753. Entrance fee: $5 per car, but entrance is sometimes restricted for environmental reasons. (1 hour–half day)

Cape Ann Historical Museum—Devoted to Cape Ann's history, decorative arts, home furnishings, and maritime heritage, the museum is run by the Cape Ann Historical Association. Exhibits include an 1804 period home and a collection of paintings by nineteenth-century artist Fitz Hugh Lane. Details: 27 Pleasant Street in downtown Gloucester; (978) 283-0455; open 10 a.m. to 5 p.m. Tuesday through Saturday. Admission is $3.50 adults, $3 seniors, $2 students, free for children under age 6. (1 hour)

Society for the Preservation of New England Antiquities (SPNEA)—This society operates more than 40 historic sites in New England, and a number of them are on Cape Ann. **Beauport** is a gabled, turreted home designed by Henry Davis Sleeper, who is probably best known for his design of Winterthur in Delaware. The 40-room mansion is filled with Sleeper's unique architectural features as well as fine Chinese porcelain and Chippendale furnishings that belonged to Charles and Helena McCann, who bought the home after Sleeper's death in 1934. Details: 75 Eastern Point Boulevard in Gloucester; (978) 283-0800; open mid-May through mid-October 10 a.m. to 4 p.m. Monday through Friday, 1 to 4 p.m. weekends; open weekdays only the rest of the year. Tours leave on the hour (with additional tours on the half-hour during July and August) and the last tour of the day is at 4 p.m. Admission is $5 adults, $4.50 seniors, $2.50 ages 6 to 12. (1 hour)

The Coffin House and the **Spencer-Pierce-Little Farm** are also run by SPNEA. The Coffin House dates back to 1654 and has seventeenth-, eighteenth-, and nineteenth-century period rooms. Crops from Spencer-Pierce-Little Farm are still harvested as they have been for more than 350 years. Visitors can see exhibits on early farm life in the late-seventeenth-century home that still stands on the property. Details: The Coffin House is on Route 1A in Newbury; the Spencer-Pierce-Little Farm is at 5 Little's Lane; both are open for tours on the hour from noon to 4 p.m. Thursday through Sunday June through mid-October. Tours are $4 adults, $3.50 seniors, $2 ages 6 to 12.

Two other SPNEA homes in Newbury, the **Dole-Little House** and the **Swett-Ilsley House**, are open by appointment. Contact SPNEA headquarters in Boston at (617) 227-3956 for additional information.

Wenham Museum—This small museum includes period rooms and a doll collection. Details: 132 Main Street, in the center of Wenham; (978) 468-2377; open year-round 11 a.m. to 4 p.m. Monday through

Friday, 1 to 4 p.m. Saturday, 2 to 5 p.m. Sunday; closed on holidays. Admission is $3 adults, $2.50 seniors, $1 ages 3 to 14. (½ hour)

FITNESS AND RECREATION

Essex River Basin Adventures (978-768-3722 or 800-529-2504) runs guided kayak tours on the Essex River and sea-kayaking trips to offshore islands. Less strenuous tours are offered for inexperienced kayakers and instruction is provided.

FOOD

Cape Ann is fried-clam country. As Lawrence "Chubby" Woodman invented the fried clam back in 1914, **Woodman's** (978-768-6451), on the causeway in Essex, is quite naturally the best-known place to get this regional specialty. Although their prices are no longer dirt-cheap, portions are so large that two people should have no problem splitting a dinner. Parents need not worry about bringing their children to Woodman's as the atmosphere is extremely casual—patrons dine on picnic tables and are frequently seen diving into fried-clam platters hands first. The restaurant's slogan is "eat in the rough," and they mean it. Another popular place for clams is the **Clam Box** (978-356-9707) on High Street in Ipswich. Fittingly, the restaurant is shaped like a clam box. The owners take pride in their preparation—they use only the best fresh clams and change the frying oil frequently.

If fried clams are not for you, **Chipper's River Cafe** (978-356-7956) on Market Street in Ipswich has delicious, out-of-the-ordinary sandwiches at prices starting at $5. The **Wenham Tea House** (978-468-1398) serves simple home-cooked meals and corn muffins that will carry you back to your childhood. Rockport has plenty of eateries to choose from on Bearskin Neck and along Beach Street in the center of town. In Newburyport, **The Grog** (15 Middle Street, 978-465-8008, entrées $7–$12) is a fun place to go for pub grub. Nearby, **Jacob Marley's** offers a varied menu in a pleasant environment (23 Pleasant Street, 978-465-5598, entrées $7–$14).

LODGING

Bed and breakfasts are the most popular form of lodging on Cape Ann. Rockport has the highest concentration of bed and breakfasts in the

CAPE ANN

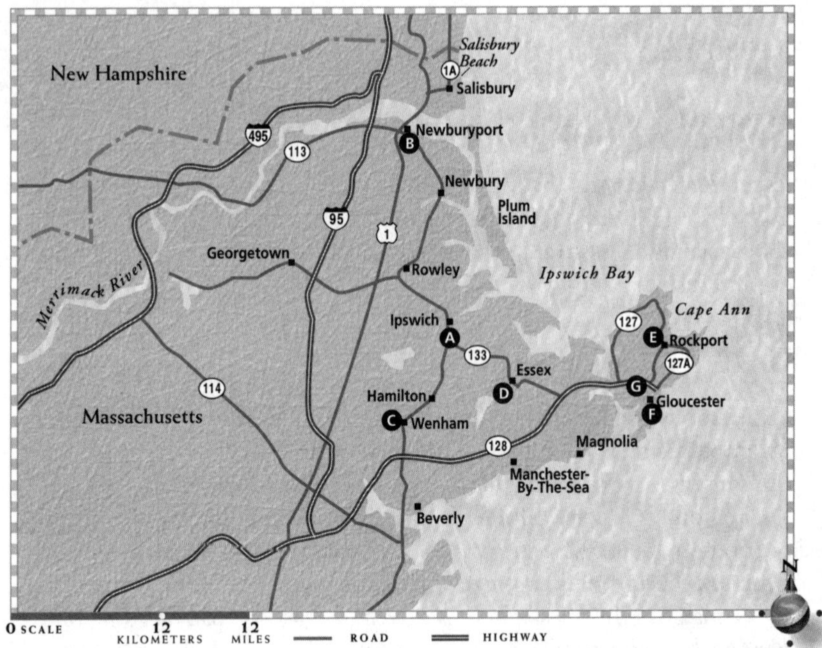

Food

- **A** Chipper's River Cafe
- **A** Clam Box
- **B** The Grog
- **B** Jacob Marley's
- **C** Wenham Tea House
- **D** Woodman's

Lodging

- **E** Addison Choate Inn
- **D** George Fuller House Bed & Breakfast Inn

Lodging *(continued)*

- **E** Linden Tree Inn
- **E** Rocky Shores
- **E** Seacrest Manor
- **E** Tuck Inn

Camping

- **F** Annisquam Campgound
- **G** Camp Ann Camp Site

Note: Items with the same letter are located in the same town or area.

area. The lovely, shingled **Seacrest Manor** (131 Marmion Way, 978-546-2211) is about a mile from Bearskin Neck and the center of Rockport. The manor's friendly hosts pride themselves on the inn's beautiful lawns and gardens. Rooms are comfortably furnished and range from $96 to $136 (ocean-view rooms in high-season are the most expensive); the price includes a full breakfast, nightly turndown service, and a morning newspaper. Across from the inn is a 9-acre nature preserve.

Rocky Shores (978-546-2823 or 800-348-4003) on Eden Road is a turn-of-the-century inn overlooking the sea and offering bed and breakfast–style accommodations. Eleven housekeeping cottages on the grounds have kitchens, making Rocky Shores a good option for traveling families. Double rooms at the inn range from $76 to $117; rates for the cottages start at $98 per day or $640 weekly for two bedrooms, $120 per day or $785 for three bedrooms.

The **Tuck Inn** (978-546-7260 or 800-789-7260), in a 1790 Colonial on High Street, is within walking distance of Bearskin Neck. A plentiful, home-baked breakfast buffet is included in your stay, as is use of the inn's swimming pool. Rates run from $55 to $95 in the off-season, and from $75 to $115 in high-season. The **Addison Choate Inn** (49 Broadway, 978-546-7543 or 800-245-7543) also has a swimming pool and breakfast buffet. Many people appreciate the inn for its colorful gardens alone. All guest rooms in the Greek Revival home have private baths and air conditioning. Doubles, including breakfast and afternoon tea, range from $101 to $130 for a suite in the summer; prices drop in the winter. Discounts for long-term stays are available. The **Linden Tree Inn** (26 King Street, 978-546-2492 or 800-865-2122) gets its name from the majestic linden tree that shades the inn's lawn. Home-baked goodies such as sour-cream chocolate cake, pineapple walnut bread, and pumpkin chocolate-chip bread often appear as part of the inn's continental breakfast. Doubles cost about $100.

In nearby Essex, the **George Fuller House Bed & Breakfast Inn** (978-768-7766 or 800-477-0148) overlooks a salt marsh. Rooms in the 1830 Federal-style home are furnished with a mix of antiques and period reproductions. Several guest rooms have their own working fireplaces. Doubles range from $90 to $150, and full country breakfasts—with dishes such as French toast topped with brandied lemon butter, or piña colada pancakes—are included in the room rate. The inn also has a sailboat for guests to enjoy.

CAMPING

Camp Ann Camp Site (978-283-8683) in West Gloucester has 250 campsites, many with hookups. The campground is about a mile from Wingersheek Beach, and the camping season runs from May through October. **Annisquam Campground** (978-283-2992) in Gloucester has 35 sites. Sites start at around $15 at both campgrounds.

BEACHES

Cape Ann, with its excellent beaches, is an enjoyable place to unwind for a few days. **Crane's Beach**, off Route 133 in Ipswich, and **Good Harbor Beach**, off Route 127 in Gloucester, are two of my favorites. The parking lot at Good Harbor is for residents only, but sometimes you can find parking within walking distance. Anyone can park at Crane's for a fee. On hot summer days, especially weekends, the lot fills up quickly. The Crane Mansion at nearby Castle Hill (978-356-4070) was built with money made in bathroom fixtures and is now rented out for elegant parties; concerts at the mansion are open to the public. **Singing Beach**, while not the largest of Cape Ann beaches, is also lovely. Parking at the beach is for residents only, but the ten-minute walk from town is pleasant. Just be certain to park legally, for the law has no qualms about ticketing or towing your vehicle.

While Crane's, Good Harbor, and Singing Beach are good for a restful day at the ocean, **Salisbury Beach**, north of Newburyport, is where people go on Cape Ann for amusement-park rides and honky-tonk. A roller coaster, carousel, miniature golf courses, and video arcades are among Salisbury's attractions.

NIGHTLIFE

A variety of musicals, celebrity concerts, and kid-oriented shows are performed at the **North Shore Music Theatre** in Beverly from April through December. Call (978) 922-8500 for ticket and show information.

SIDE TRIPS FROM CAPE ANN

Sporting types may enjoy watching a polo match. Picnics and polo go hand-in-hand at the **Myopia Hunt Club**. The action usually starts around 3 p.m. on Sunday afternoons throughout the summer and early fall. The polo grounds are off Route 1A in Hamilton. Call (978) 468-7956 for information.

Summer whale-watching expeditions are a very popular Cape Ann pastime. The **Yankee Fleet** in Gloucester operates both whale-watching cruises and deep-sea fishing trips. Call (800) WHALING or (978) 283-0313 for prices and schedules. **Capt. Bill's Whale Watch** (978-283-6995 or 800-339-4253), also based in Gloucester, offers similar excursions. **Cape Ann Whale Watch** (978-283-5110 or 800-877-5110) in Gloucester operates its cruises in conjunction with the Whale Conservation Institute. Humpback, finback, and right whales are among the species you could see on your ocean cruise. (Most cruise operations guarantee that you will see whales; if you don't you get a free trip on another day.) **Essex River Cruises** (978-768-6981 or 800-748-3706) runs nature and bird-watching cruises on the Essex River. **Moby Duck Tours** (978-281-3825) offers a unique way to tour Gloucester—by both land and sea in an amphibious vehicle. All cruise operators recommend advance reservations.

If you're in the area in early October, a side trip to the **Topsfield Fair** might be in order. The annual event claims to be the oldest county fair in the country, and it certainly offers enjoyable entertainment for the entire family. Call (508) 887-5000 for fair information.

6
COASTAL NEW HAMPSHIRE

It may not be well known outside New England, but New Hampshire has a coast, albeit a small one. Yet although the state's shoreline stretches only 18 miles, it makes the most of those miles. The coast includes the town of Hampton, the site of New Hampshire's first public school in 1649, now known more for its white sand beaches and lively boardwalk.

Located about halfway between Boston and Portland, Maine, Portsmouth is New Hampshire's second oldest city. Named for Portsmouth, England, the city was first settled in the 1620s but did not incorporate until 1849. In colonial days, Portsmouth was the capital of New Hampshire. The Treaty of Portsmouth, which ended the Russo/Japanese War, was signed at Portsmouth's Naval Shipyard in 1905.

Today, in addition to an extensive selection of fine shops and restaurants, Portsmouth boasts an interesting and historic waterfront district. An entire seventeenth-century neighborhood, Strawbery Banke, has been preserved and is well worth a visit. Once a major shipbuilding center, Portsmouth now counts seafood processing among its modern-day industries. ◪

PORTSMOUTH

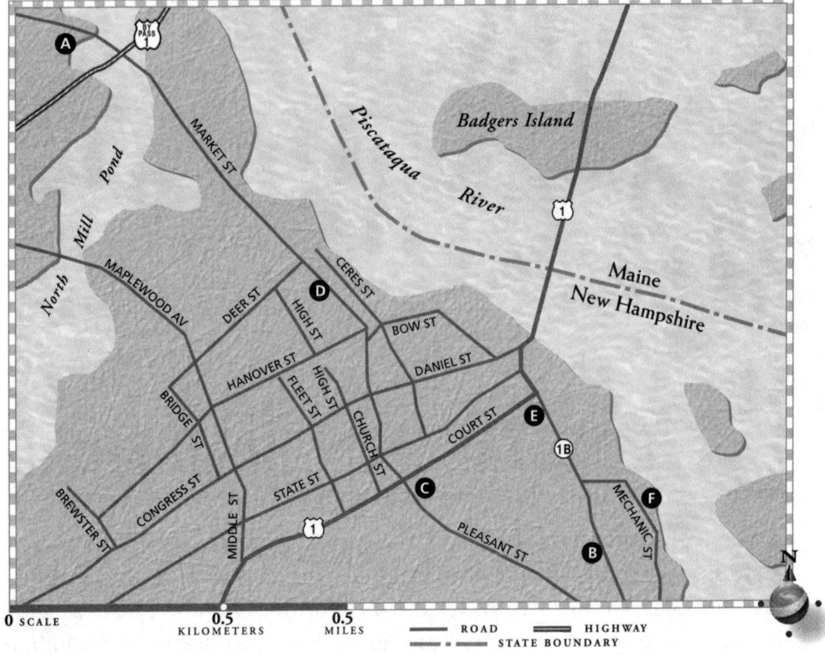

Sights

- A Albacore Park
- B Children's Museum
- C Governor John Langdon House
- D Moffat-Ladd House and Gardens
- E Strawbery Banke Museum
- F Wentworth-Gardner House

A PERFECT DAY IN COASTAL NEW HAMPSHIRE

Start at Hampton Beach first thing in the morning to beat the heat and the crowds. Have a picnic lunch on the beach, then head into Portsmouth and spend the afternoon touring the Strawbery Banke Museum. Feast on a six-course meal at the Blue Strawbery, and then spend a peaceful night in a cozy bed and breakfast.

SIGHTSEEING HIGHLIGHTS

★★★ **Strawbery Banke Museum**—Located in the heart of Portsmouth's waterfront district, the museum is really a preserved neighborhood originally settled in the 1630s. It was named for the profusion of strawberries that once grew there along the banks of the Piscataqua River. After thriving for several centuries, the area gradually deteriorated and faced demolition in the 1950s. A group of concerned citizens stepped in and began creating the 40-plus buildings and 10-acre museum there today. Some have been decorated with period furnishings, some have costumed role players, some exhibit early American tools or building methods of the day; a few can be viewed only from the exterior, as they are still awaiting restoration. The most interesting buildings at Strawbery Banke include the childhood home of Victorian writer Thomas Bailey Aldrich, the beautiful Goodwin Mansion, the Dinsmore Shop (where coopers make the wooden barrels once used extensively for transporting and storing goods), and the Drisco House. The latter, a two-family house built in 1795, is furnished on one side in the style of the 1790s and on the other as it would have appeared in the 1950s. Details: Marcy Street on the waterfront, (603) 433-1100. Open 10 a.m. to 5 p.m. daily April through October. Two-day admission is $12 adults, $8 ages 7 to 17. Admission for families with two or more children is $28. (2 hours–half day)

★ **Albacore Park**—Visitors to the park can tour a 1952 electric and diesel submarine whose cramped quarters once housed over 50 Navy men. Details: 600 Market Street, (603) 436-3680; open 9:30 a.m. to 4:30 p.m. daily May through Columbus Day; call for winter hours. Admission is $4 adults, $3 seniors, $2 children ages 7 to 17, $10 for families. (1 hour)

★ **Children's Museum**—The museum's South Meeting House, built in 1865, offers hands-on exhibits including computers, a lobster boat, and a space shuttle cockpit. Details: 280 Marcy Street, just a few blocks from Strawbery Banke, (603) 436-3853; open 10 a.m. to 5 p.m. Tuesday through Saturday, 1 to 5 p.m. Sunday; also open on school holidays and on Monday during summer. Admission is $4, free for children under 1. (1 hour)

★ **Governor John Langdon House**—Legend has it that George Washington slept in this handsome home in 1789. The home was built in 1784 for John Langdon, who served three terms as New Hampshire's governor. The restored home includes period gardens and a wing that was designed by the respected architectural firm of McKim, Mead, and White. Details: 143 Pleasant Street; (603) 436-3205; tours start on the hour from 11 a.m. to 4 p.m. Wednesday through Sunday June through mid-October. Admission is $4 adults. (1 hour)

★ **Moffat-Ladd House and Gardens**—This historic home was built in 1763 and has a secret underground passage. Details: 154 Market Street, (603) 436-1118; open 10 a.m. to 4 p.m. Monday through

J. David Bohl/Society for the Preservation of New England Antiquities

Governor John Langdon House

Saturday, 2 to 5 p.m. Sunday mid-June through mid-October. Admission is $4 adults, $1 ages 7 to 12. (1 hour)

✯ **Wentworth-Gardner House**—This 1760 Georgian-style home comes complete with period furnishings. Details: 50 Mechanic Street, (603) 436-4406. Open 1 to 4 p.m. Tuesday through Sunday late May through mid-October. Admission is $4 adults, $2 children. (1 hour)

FOOD

The **Blue Strawbery** (29 Ceres Street, 603-431-6420) overlooks the water and is Portsmouth's best-known restaurant. Its six-course meals are very much in demand (and expensive!) so reservations are a must. If you can't get into the Blue Strawbery, there's no need to panic as Portsmouth has over 80 restaurants to choose from. The **Dolphin Striker** (15 Bow Street, 603-431-5222) is the place to go for seafood (dinner averages about $18 per person), and **The Metro** (20 High Street, 603-436-0521) is popular with locals for its good food and New Orleans atmosphere. Entrée prices range from $10 to $22. **Cafe Brioche** (14 Market Square, 603-430-9225) has a good selection of breakfast pastries as well as other baked goods and soups and sandwiches at lunch. There are numerous dining choices for ethnic cuisine. Try **Szechuan Taste & Thai Cafe** (54 Daniel Street, 603-431-2226) for Thai food, **Shalimar** (80 Hanover Street, 603-427-2959) for Indian, and **Porto Bello** (67 Bow Street, 603-431-2989) for Italian. For down-home American barbecue ribs stop in at **A.D.'s Barbecue House** (107 State Street, 603-433-6330). Dinner entrées average about $12.

LODGING

There are several bed and breakfast inns in the heart of Portsmouth. All rooms at the **Sise Inn** (40 Court Street, 603-433-1200) have private baths, and several have whirlpool tubs. Breakfast is included in room rates ranging from $90 to $180. The **Oracle House Inn** (38 Marcy Street, 603-433-8827), in a Colonial home dating back to 1702, is next to the Strawbery Banke Museum. Two of the inn's four guest rooms share a bath, the other two have four-poster beds and private baths. A continental breakfast is included in the room rate. The ten rooms at the **Bow Street Inn** (121 Bow Street on the Piscataqua River, 603-431-7760) have fresh flowers and brass beds. Continental breakfast is included with overnight rates. If you prefer full-service hotels, suites at the **Sheraton Portsmouth** (250 Market Street adjacent to Portsmouth Harbor, 603-431-2300 or 800-325-3535) have living rooms and full kitchens. The hotel also has a swimming pool, sauna, and exercise room. Rates for double rooms range from $125 to $150. Call for reservations.

At Hampton Beach try **Ashworth by the Sea** (603-926-6762 or 800-345-6736). The ocean is just across the street, guest rooms have balconies, and there's a heated swimming pool. There's also a coffee shop, a fine-dining restaurant, and a lounge with live entertainment. Rates range from $65 to $225.

CAMPING

Hampton Beach State RV Park (603-926-8990), off Route 1A in Hampton Beach, has full hook-ups. However, there are only 28 sites so reservations are strongly recommended.

ARTS AND ENTERTAINMENT

Portsmouth boasts the fourth oldest operating theater in the United States. The **Portsmouth Music Hall** (603-433-3100), built in 1878, currently is home to theatrical, dance, and musical productions. The **Seacoast Repertory Theatre** (603-433-4472) performs in a former brewery, and the **Pontine Movement Theater** presents original productions in a building that was once a shoe factory.

During the summer, Hampton Beach plays host to weekly fireworks displays as well as nightly concerts at the **Sea Shell Stage**.

SIDE TRIPS FROM THE NEW HAMPSHIRE COAST

As in many New England cities, harbor and whale-watching cruises leave from Portsmouth's port. Try **Portsmouth Harbor Cruises** (603-436-8084 or 800-776-0915) for a tour of the harbor, or try the **Isles of Shoals Steamship Company** (603-431-5500 or 800-441-4620) for excursions to the Isles, tours of Portsmouth Harbor, or whale-watching expeditions. The company's whale-watching cruises are educationally oriented, and onboard activities for children are provided to keep them occupied during the journey. Fares are $25 for adults and $16 for children.

PORTSMOUTH

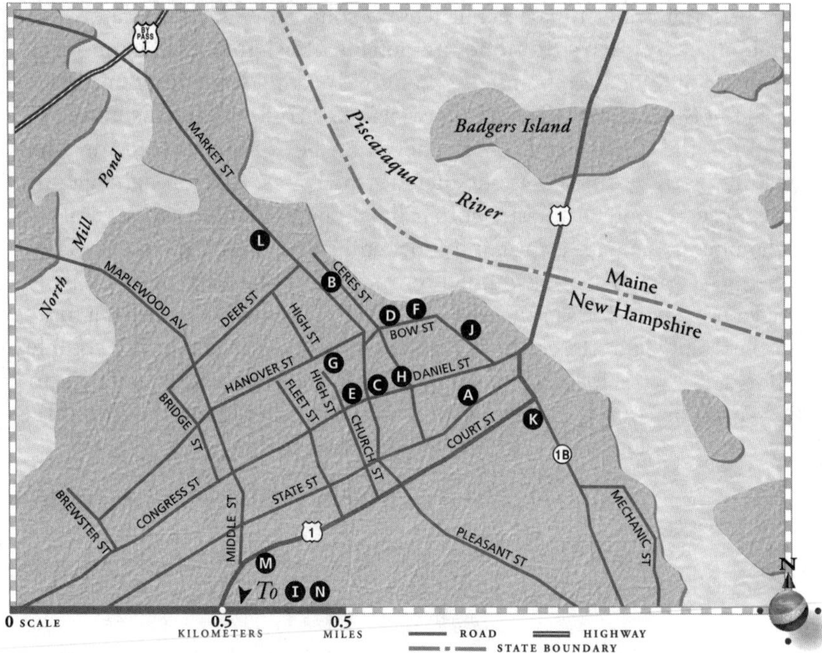

Food

- **A** A.D.'s Barbecue House
- **B** Blue Strawbery
- **C** Cafe Brioche
- **D** Dolphin Striker
- **E** The Metro
- **F** Porto Bello
- **G** Shalimar
- **H** Szechuan Taste & Thai Cafe

Lodging

- **I** Ashworth by the Sea
- **J** Bow Street Inn
- **K** Oracle House Inn
- **L** Sheraton Portsmouth
- **M** Sise Inn

Camping

- **N** Hampton Beach State RV Park

If you prefer to keep your feet on solid ground, take a detour inland to **America's Stonehenge** outside of Salem, New Hampshire. While you'll be disappointed if you go expecting something on the scale of Stonehenge (the site's local name, "Mystery Hill," is more fitting), the site—which some believe may be 4,000 years old—is interesting if you're curious about ancient ritual sites. Like Stonehenge, the Mystery Hill site is an astronomically aligned calendar, and several chambers, one with a speaking tube, still stand among the ruins. The creepiest part of the self-guided tour are the stone slabs believed to have been used for sacrifices. Details: (603) 893-8300; open 10 a.m. to 5 p.m. daily late March through November (in November the complex closes at 4 p.m.; in July and August hours are extended from 9 a.m. to 7 p.m.); the complex is also open from 10 a.m. to 4 p.m. the first three weekends in December. Admission is charged.

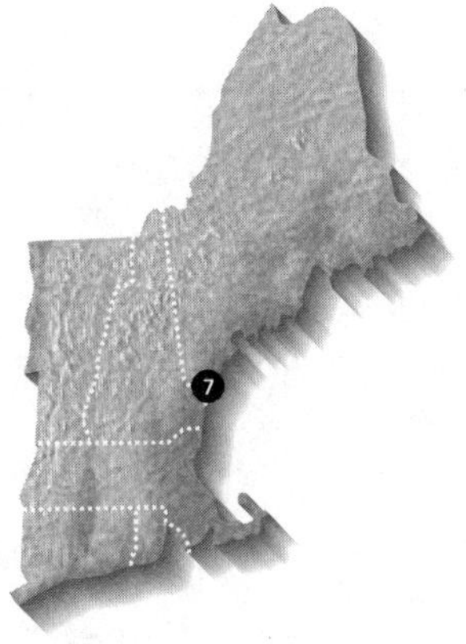

7 SOUTHERN MAINE

Maine bills itself as "Vacationland U.S.A." and often the heavily touristed areas in the state seem to be dedicated to the fine art of parting visitors from their cash. Indeed tourism is one of the state's biggest industries (tourists spend about a billion and a half dollars in Maine each year), and many of Maine's 1.2 million natives make most of their income during the three summer months.

The coast is the state's biggest tourist draw, and the southern coast is no exception. The sandy beaches of southern Maine are inviting, and they lure many vacationers year after year. With their factory outlet shops, the towns of Kittery and Freeport have become meccas for bargain hunters. In coastal Kennebunkport, scenic coves, alluring shops, and art galleries await visitors.

Southern Maine is also home to Portland, Maine's largest city, as well as a one-time state capital (from 1820 to 1832). Like many cities in the Northeast, Portland counts textile production among its most important industries. Bordering Casco Bay, the Old Port Exchange District is the heart and soul of Portland. Residents and visitors alike take pleasure in strolling down Old Port's brick sidewalks, browsing in its smart shops, and dining in one of the district's many restaurants. ◪

SOUTHERN MAINE

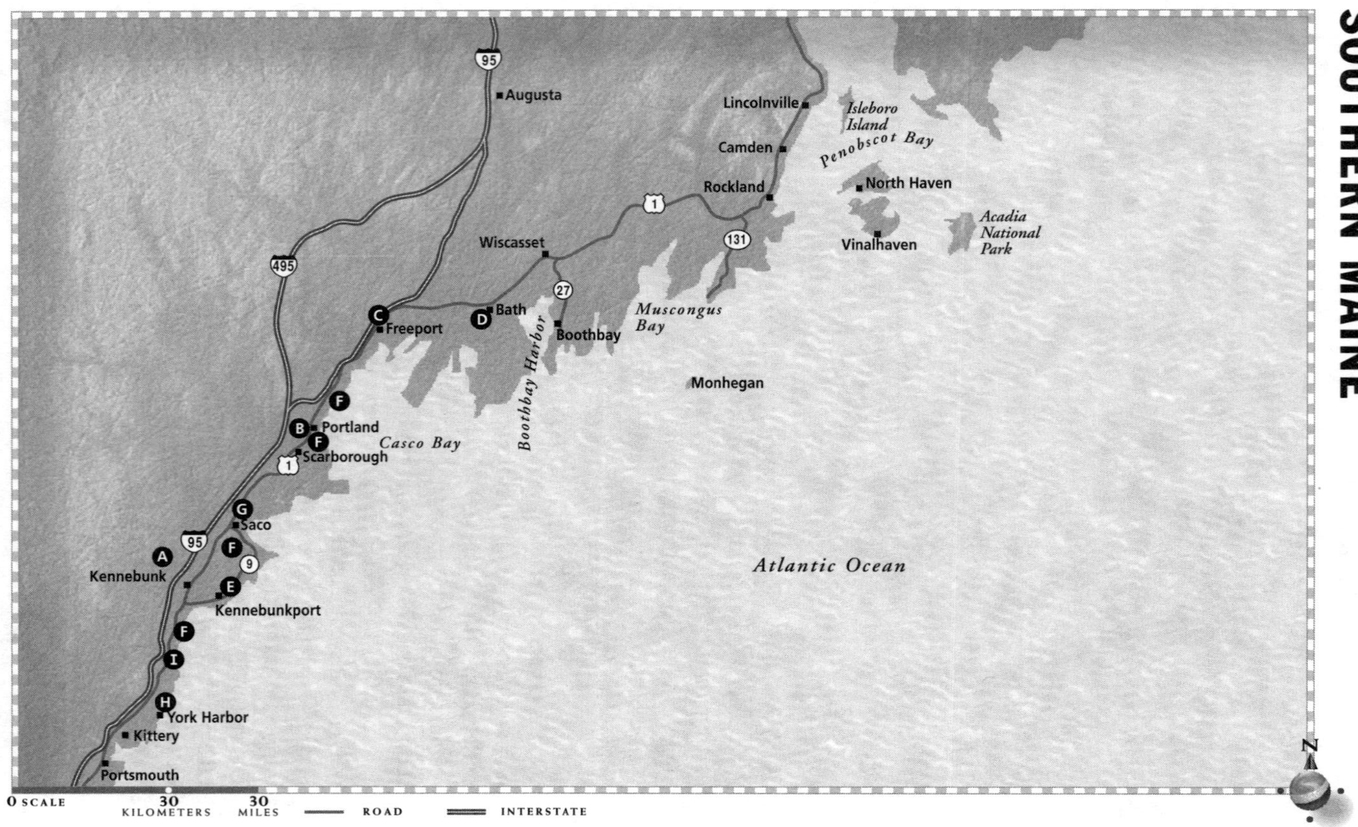

Sights

- A Brick Store Museum
- B Children's Museum of Maine
- C L.L. Bean
- D Maine Maritime Museum
- B Old Port Exchange District
- B Portland Museum of Art
- E Seashore Trolley Museum
- B Victoria Mansion
- B Wadsworth-Longfellow House
- F Wildlife Sanctuaries
- G York Institute

Food

- E Alisson's
- B Becky's
- B Fore Street
- B Fresh Market Pasta
- B Grill 36
- B J's
- B Java Joe's
- B JavaNet Cafe
- A Kennebunk Inn
- E White Barn Inn

Lodging

- E Captain Lord Mansion
- C Harraseeket Inn
- A Kennebunk Inn
- E Kennebunkport Inn
- B Regency Hotel
- H York Harbor Inn

Camping

- I Wells Beach Resort
- A Yankeeland Campground

Note: Items with the same letter are located in the same town or area.

A PERFECT DAY IN SOUTHERN MAINE

Start your day with a hearty breakfast at Becky's in Portland. Spend the morning in the Portland Museum of Art and browsing through the shops and galleries of the Old Port Exchange District. After reinforcing yourself with some fresh steamers and oysters at J's on the waterfront, head down the coast and spend your afternoon at one of southern Maine's many beaches or nature preserves. End your day with a gourmet meal at the White Barn Inn in Kennebunkport, or, if you prefer, go casual at Alisson's in Dock Square. Spend the night in the Kennebunkport area.

SIGHTSEEING HIGHLIGHTS

★★ **Portland Museum of Art**— This museum—located in an I. M. Pei–designed building—has a wonderful collection of Winslow Homer paintings and is well respected in art circles. Other American artists—including Andrew Wyeth, who often painted in Maine—are also represented here, as are European masters Degas, Monet, Renoir, and Picasso. Details: Congress and High Streets in Portland; (207) 775-6148; open 10 a.m. to 5 p.m. Tuesday, Wednesday, and Saturday, 10 a.m. to 9 p.m. Thursday and Friday, noon to 5 p.m. Sunday. The museum is also open on Monday July through Columbus Day. Admission is $6 adults, $5 seniors and students, $1 ages 6 to 12; free on Friday night. (2 hours)

★ **Children's Museum of Maine**—This might be a mandatory stop if you're traveling with small children. Located in a Victorian home, the museum's hands-on and interactive exhibits include a newsroom, science lab, and camera obscura. Details: 142 Free Street, Portland, (207) 828-1234; open 10 a.m. to 5 p.m. Monday, Wednesday, Thursday, and Saturday; noon to 5 p.m. Tuesday and Sunday; 10 a.m. to 8 p.m. Friday. Admission is $4 per person over age 1. (1 hour)

★ **L.L. Bean**—It may seem odd to list a store as a sightseeing highlight, but L.L. Bean is a Maine institution, and a midnight shopping spree at the store is a rite of passage for any New England college student. Once a rather modest store, L.L. Bean's building has grown over the years, as has the town around it. The main street in Freeport is now lined with outlet stores to take advantage of the thousands of crusading shoppers that flock to town. Details: 95 Main Street, Freeport; (800) 341-4341; open 24 hours. (1 hour)

★ **Maine Maritime Museum**—Maine's maritime past is explored through photographs, ship models, art, and a historic shipyard. Details: Washington Street, Bath; (207) 443-1316. (1 hour)

★ **Old Port Exchange District**—Portland's waterfront district has been revitalized in recent years. Many visitors enjoy spending time in the Old Port's enticing shops and restaurants between Commercial and Congress Streets. (2 hours)

★ **Seashore Trolley Museum**—The trolley, as an early form of public transportation, holds a certain romantic appeal to some. If you're one of those individuals, then this museum—with its collection of over 200 trolleys—is for you. Details: On Log Cabin Road in Kennebunkport; (207) 967-2800; open daily May through mid-October. Call for current hours and admission prices. (1 hour)

Brick Store Museum—Located in the heart of Kennebunk's Historic District, this museum focuses on the history of the Kennebunk area and includes a number of artifacts donated by former President George Bush. It also sponsors architectural walking tours at 10 a.m. on Wednesdays and at 1 p.m. on Fridays June through October. Details: 117 Main Street at the junction of Routes 1 and 35; (207) 985-4802; open 10 a.m. to 4:30 p.m. Tuesday through Saturday year-round. Admission is $3 adults; $5 with a tour of the 1803 Taylor-Barry House. (1 hour)

Victoria Mansion—This Italianate mansion, built sometime around 1860, has ornate construction including stained glass, seven marble fireplaces, hand-carved woodwork, and gilt embellishments. Details: 109 Danforth Street, Portland; (207) 772-4841; open 10 a.m. to 4 p.m. Tuesday through Saturday, 1 to 5 p.m. Sunday May through October. Tours leave 15 minutes and 45 minutes after the hour. Admission is $5 adults, $2 students and ages 6 to 17. Senior discounts available. (1 hour)

Wadsworth-Longfellow House—This is the 1786 childhood home of poet Henry Wadsworth Longfellow. Details: 489 Congress Street,

Portland; (207) 879-0427; open 10 a.m. to 4 p.m. Tuesday through Sunday June through October. (1 hour)

Wildlife Sanctuaries—There are a number of designated wildlife areas in southern Maine. Among them are the 3,100-acre Scarborough Marsh off Route 1 in Scarborough, the 30-acre East Point Sanctuary at Biddeford Pool, Prout's Neck Wildlife Preserve, and Gilsland Farm in Falmouth, operated by the Maine Audubon Society (207-781-2330). Other wildlife areas include the 800-acre Saco Heath Preserve (207-490-4012); the Rachel Carson National Wildlife Refuge (207-646-9226) in Wells, which includes a 1-mile handicapped-accessible trail; and the 572-foot Mount Agamenticus west of York where you can picnic accompanied by native birds and a view of Maine's southern coast. (1–3 hours per sanctuary)

York Institute—This museum is devoted to preserving southern Maine's history with period rooms, antique furnishings, paintings, and decorative arts. Details: 371 Main Street, Saco; (207) 283-0684 or 283-0958; open noon to 4 p.m. Tuesday, Wednesday, Friday, and Sunday; noon to 8 p.m. Thursday. Admission is $4 adults, $3 seniors, $1 students over 6, $10 per family. (1 hour)

FITNESS AND RECREATION

If your idea of enjoying the ocean involves more than simply lying on one of southern Maine's many beaches, you can learn to scuba dive or kayak with **Adventures Inc.** (207-967-5243) in Kennebunkport.

Bike rentals are available from **Cape-Able Bike Shop** (83 Arundel Road in Kennebunkport, 207-967-4382 or 800-220-0907). They can provide you with maps and will suggest good cycling routes in the area.

FOOD

The **White Barn Inn** (Beach Street, 207-967-2321) is reputedly where former President Bush dines when he wants a meal out while in Kennebunkport. (The inn also has 24 guest rooms with rates ranging from $100 to $375.) For good pub food in a casual milieu, **Alisson's** (207-967-4841) at Dock Square is a popular spot, especially on weekends when there's live entertainment. On Main Street in Kennebunk, the **Kennebunk Inn** has fine dining. The menu changes fairly regularly, but New England specialties are standard fare. Dinner entrées average between $15 and $20.

The Old Port Exchange District has the best selection of restaurants in Portland. You'll find coffeehouses such as **Java Joe's** (13 Exchange, 207-761-JOES) and **JavaNet Cafe** (where you can access the internet, 37 Exchange, 207-JAVA-NET), and bistros such as **Grill 36** (36 Market Street, 207-772-6099) and the hip **Fore Street** (288 Fore Street, 207-773-6172). If you like freshly made pasta, try **Fresh Market Pasta** (43 Exchange Street, 207-773-7146). Families will be happy to know that the restaurant also has a children's menu. On the waterfront, the casual **J's** (5 Portland Pier, 207-772-4828) is the place to go for oysters and steamers. **Becky's** (390 Commercial Street at the base of High Street, 207-773-7070) is a popular spot for hearty breakfasts despite its modest surroundings.

LODGING

There are many places to stay along the coast. Towns such as Kennebunkport have a high concentration of bed and breakfast establishments. The Kennebunk area is a good place to put up for the night at the southern end of the coast. When deciding between Kennebunk and Kennebunkport, you should know that Kennebunkport has more tourist traffic and higher prices. Kennebunk is quieter and closer to the interstate. The **Kennebunk Inn** (Main Street in Kennebunk center, 207-985-3351 or 800-743-1799), built in 1799, is as comfortable and charming as anything you'll find in neighboring Kennebunkport, and is less costly. Double rooms range from $85 to $139 during summer and start as low as $55 in winter. With the exception of Christmas Day, the inn is open year-round. There is also a good restaurant on the premises.

Should you decide to join the "Bush Watchers" in Kennebunkport (former President George Bush's summer home is here), the Federal-style **Captain Lord Mansion** (207-967-3141), listed on the National Register of Historic Places, is a good choice for accommodations. Doubles are $149 to $349 per night in summer, and include a full breakfast; rates are lower in the off-season. The **Kennebunkport Inn** (207-967-2621 or 800-248-2621) is conveniently located in Dock Square. The inn has a swimming pool, restaurant, and attractive guest rooms with antiques, private baths, and color television. Double rooms range from $70 to $230.

In the Old Port Exchange District of downtown Portland, the **Regency Hotel** (207-774-4200 or 800-727-3436) offers tasteful hotel accommodations in what was originally a nineteenth-century armory. Guest amenities include evening turndown service, a morning newspaper, and a fitness center. Doubles range from about $100 to $190, and suites are $210 to $230. Weekend packages are also available during the winter months. Call for reservations and information.

If you wish to be near Freeport's outlets, the **Harraseeket Inn** (162 Main Street, 207-865-9377 or 800-342-6423) is only a couple of blocks from L.L. Bean. Lodging is in buildings that date back to 1798 and 1850, although modern amenities such as private baths, air conditioning, and cable television have been added to all of the rooms. Suites have fireplaces, wet bars, refrigerators, and Jacuzzi tubs. Doubles range from $95 to $220 and suites start at $215 in the off-season. Rates include a buffet breakfast and afternoon tea.

Ocean views and award-winning cuisine await at the century-old **York Harbor Inn** (207-363-5119 or 800-343-3869) on Route 1A in York Harbor. The inn's 35 guest rooms are furnished with antiques and reproductions, and some have ocean-view decks as well as luxuries such as fireplaces and Jacuzzis. The dining room is well known for its fine food, and there's also a pub on the premises. Rates range from $99 to $219.

CAMPING

In Kennebunk, **Yankeeland Campground** is less than 3 miles from Interstate 95. Get off I-95 north at Exit 3; a right turn at the end of the exit ramp will take you in the opposite direction from Kennebunk. Drive straight for 2.7 miles. The campground entrance will be on your left. Hookups, hot showers, and complete recreational facilities (including swimming) are all available. Sites start at $16 per night. The campground is open from May through Columbus Day. For reservations, call (207) 985-7576.

If you want to camp near the beaches of southern Maine, try **Wells Beach Resort**. It's only about a mile from the beach and has all kinds of family-friendly amenities such as miniature golf, a swimming pool, a laundry room, a store, a recreation room with pool tables and video games, and a playground. Call (207) 646-7570 or (800) 640-CAMP for reservations.

ARTS AND ENTERTAINMENT

Portland is the hub of cultural activities in southern Maine. For classical music lovers there's the **Portland Symphony Orchestra** (tickets are available through PortTix, 207-842-0800), while the **Portland Ballet** (207-772-9671) performs classical dance. The **Portland Stage Company** (207-774-1043) and the **Portland Players** (207-799-7337) in South Portland both stage good theatrical productions. The **Ogunquit Playhouse** (207-646-5511) on Route 1 in Ogunquit has been mounting summer stock productions for over 65 years.

Sports fans should see Portland's minor league baseball team, the **Sea Dogs** (207-879-9500 or 800-936-DOGS), play a game during the summer.

BEACHES

The sandy beaches of southern Maine are quite popular, although the chilly water may be just a little too refreshing for some tastes. Seaweed-strewn **Crescent Beach** is the most easily accessible to Portland. South of the city on Cape Elizabeth off Route 77, the state parks system operates a bathhouse and snack bar there. Nearby is **Two Lights State Park** (named for the lighthouses that keep boats from running into the Cape's point) with picnic tables near the ocean and a children's playground. The lighthouses are on an adjacent road. Traveling south, there's **Old Orchard Beach**. At 7 miles long, it's one of the area's largest beaches; and with amusement park rides and arcade games it's also one of the most commercial. In the Saco and Biddeford areas there are smaller beaches such as **Fortunes Rocks**, **Biddeford Pool** (a favorite with bird-watchers; a parking permit is required), **Ferry Beach** (parking is limited), and **Bay View** (free parking). **Kennebunk Beach** is wide and sandy (a parking permit is required—check with your lodging to find out how to obtain one). South of Kennebunk, beaches such as **York**, **Wells**, and **Ogunquit** have long been drawing visitors looking for a seaside vacation. Most beaches charge for parking during the summer months.

SHOPPING

To say southern Maine is a shoppers' haven is an understatement. For years out-of-staters have been traveling to the 120-plus outlet stores just over the border in Kittery. Outlets there include Calvin Klein (207-439-8900), Napier (207-439-2276), Royal Doulton (207-434-4770), Brooks Brothers (207-439-5533), and Anne Klein (207-439-3688). In recent years, Freeport has gained stature as an outlet center thanks to L.L. Bean. The company's flagship store has grown in leaps and bounds over the last decade and now extends to a separate store just for kids. Other outlets in Freeport include Levi's (207-865-3323), The Gap (207-865-4441), Coach (207-865-1772), Donna Karan (207-865-1715), and J. Crew (207-865-3180).

If outlet shopping doesn't appeal to you, you may find the specialty shops and galleries of Portland's Old Port Exchange District more to your liking. Galleries such as Abacus (44 Exchange Street, 800-206-2166; Abacus also has stores in Boothbay, Freeport, and Kennebunkport) and the Maine Potters Market (376 Fore Street, 207-774-1633)—which sells the work of 15 Maine potters—have quality crafts. Serendipity (34 Exchange, 207-772-0219), Amaryllis (41 Exchange, 207-772-4439), Tavecchia (52 Exchange, 207-772-1699), and Wild Ginger (55 Exchange, 207-774-1435) all have women's clothes; Bears, Boats and Billygoats (50 Exchange, 207-780-0842) has delightful clothing for children; and Emerson's Booksellers (18 Exchange, 207-874-2665) has antiquarian maps and books.

Kennebunkport has a varied selection of galleries, boutiques, and souvenir shops. Kennebunk has less to offer. It does, however, have one store worth noting if you like natural products—Tom's of Maine of toothpaste fame (Lafayette Center, 207-985-3874).

SIDE TRIPS FROM SOUTHERN MAINE

If shopping is not your bag, the **Freeport Balloon Company** (207-865-1712) operates hot-air balloon rides that will take you far from the shopping frenzy in Freeport. A number of other balloon companies operate in Southern Maine including **Balloons Over New England** (207-499-7575 or 800-788-5562) in Kennebunk and **Balloon Rides** (207-761-8373 or 800-952-2076) in Portland.

HELPFUL HINT

Maine operates an excellent tourist information center in Kittery just a few miles over the state line. Accessible from I-95, the center is a good place to pick up a map and additional tourist information.

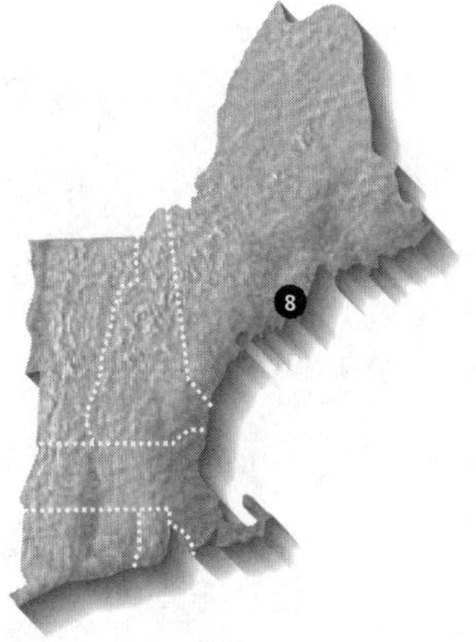

8
MID-COAST MAINE

In the mid-coast region, the sandy beaches of southern Maine begin to give way to the rocky shoreline that more often typifies the Maine coast. The region is rich in history—many towns were settled after Captain John Smith arrived here on an exploratory voyage from Jamestown in 1614. In keeping with their seaside settings, the mid-coast towns became centers for fishing and shipping.

Today the area has much to offer visitors, who can enjoy the works of fine American artists such as Andrew Wyeth at the Farnsworth Museum in Rockland, explore nature preserves on Boothbay Peninsula, and feast on a New England clambake complete with Maine lobster. Quaint seacoast towns include Camden—"where the mountains meet the sea"—a summer resort destination for almost 170 years. Wiscasset, called "the prettiest town in Maine," was once the state's chief port. It is now graced by sea captain's homes and antique shops. Flea market buffs will find Route 1 in Searsport absolute heaven.

Recreational opportunities abound here. The coast is a jumping off point for windjammer cruises and for excursions to unspoiled islands such as Monhegan—a small beauty settled in 1625 and believed to have been visited by Vikings hundreds of years before.

MID-COAST MAINE

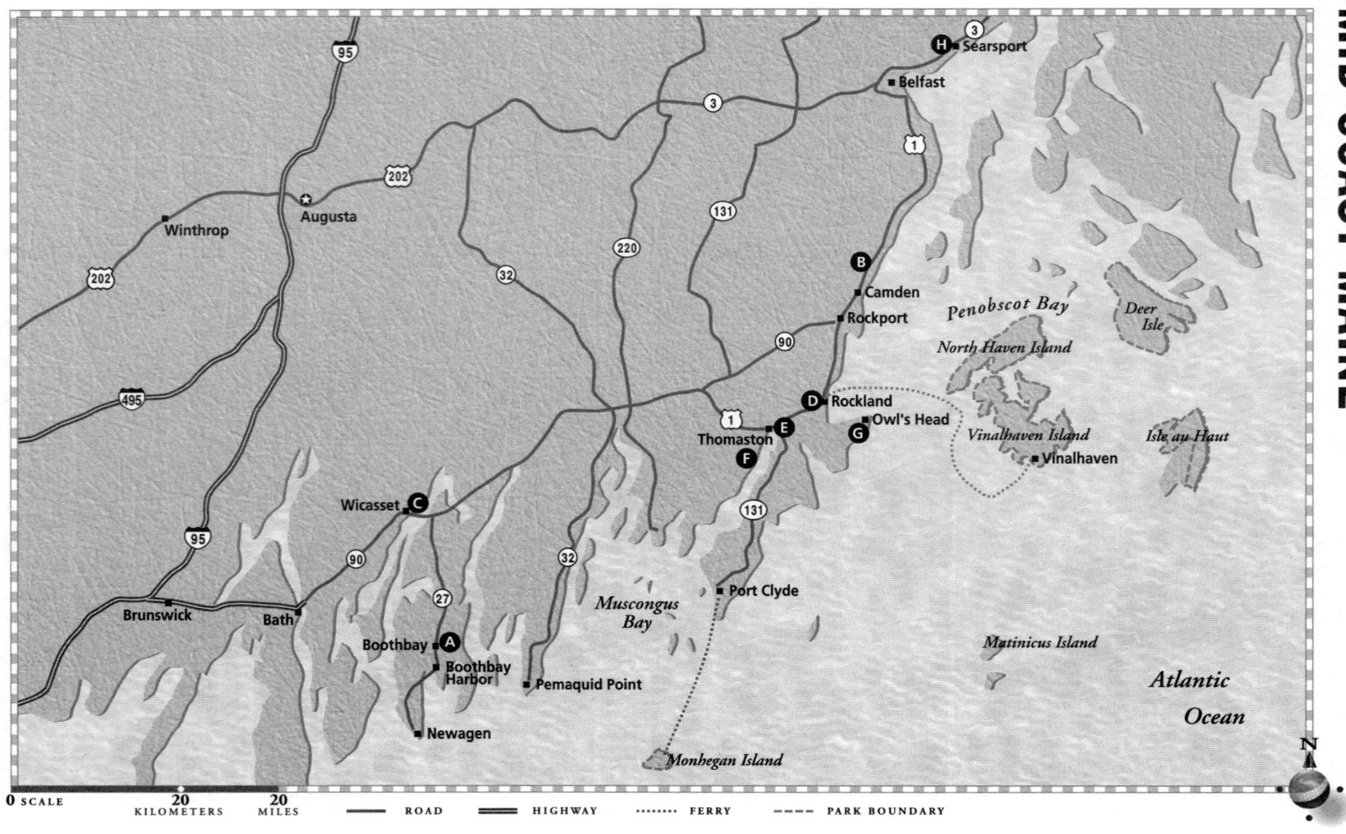

Sights

- Ⓐ **Boothbay Land Trust Preserves**
- Ⓐ **Boothbay Railway Village**
- Ⓑ **Camden Hills State Park**
- Ⓒ **Castle Tucker**
- Ⓓ **Farnsworth Art Museum**
- Ⓒ **Maine Coast Railroad**
- Ⓐ **Marine Resources Aquarium**
- Ⓔ **Montpelier**
- Ⓒ **Musical Wonder House**
- Ⓒ **Nickels-Sortwell House**
- Ⓕ **Olson House**
- Ⓖ **Owl's Head Transportation Museum**
- Ⓗ **Penobscot Marine Museum**
- Ⓓ **Shore Village Museum**

Note: Items with the same letter are located in the same town or area.

A PERFECT DAY IN MID-COAST MAINE

Start your day at the Boothbay Railway Village. Afterwards, travel to Wiscasset and visit one of the historic homes or the Musical Wonder House. From there head north to the Farnsworth Museum in Rockland. Aim for Camden late in the day so you can drive to the top of Mount Battie for picturesque views of Penobscot Bay, and stay in Camden for dinner and lodging. As an alternative, reverse the day by starting in Camden and ending up in Boothbay Harbor where you can take a cruise out to Cabbage Island for a traditional New England clambake dinner.

SIGHTSEEING HIGHLIGHTS

★★ **Boothbay Railway Village**—A one-room schoolhouse, a blacksmith shop, a Victorian parlor, an old-fashioned general store, and a barn displaying over 50 vintage autos are among the 27 exhibit buildings you can visit at this village encircled by a narrow-gauge railroad. Some of the buildings, including Boothbay's 1847 Town Hall and Freeport's 1911 train station, have been moved to the site from other locations. One building is devoted to a collection of salt and pepper shakers. Your visit begins with a 20-minute ride around the exhibits on the narrow-gauge train. Details: Route 27 in Boothbay; (207) 633-4727; open 9:30 a.m. to 5 p.m. daily mid-June through mid-October; open weekends only Memorial Day through mid-June. Admission is $6 adults, $3 children. (1½ hours)

★★ **Farnsworth Art Museum**—Fans of artists N. C., James, and Andrew Wyeth will approve of this Rockland museum. Collections include Wyeth paintings as well as works by other American artists such as Edward Hopper, Winslow Homer, Fitz Hugh Lane, and sculptor Louise Nevelson. The Farnsworth also operates the 1850 Greek Revival Farnsworth homestead behind the museum, and the Olson House, which appeared in many of Wyeth's paintings (see separate listing). Details: 352 Main Street in downtown Rockland; (207) 596-6457; open 10 a.m. to 5 p.m. Monday through Saturday, noon to 5 p.m. Sunday in summer; closed Monday and opens at 1 p.m. on Sunday in the off-season; the Olson House and the Rockland homestead close for the season in mid-October. Admission, which includes entrance to the Farnsworth homestead, is $5 adults, $4 seniors, $3 ages 8 to 18. Combination tickets, which include admission to the Olson House, are also available. (1–2 hours)

★★ **Penobscot Marine Museum**—A museum village devoted to depicting maritime life—particularly that of the Penobscot Bay area in the nineteenth century. Exhibits housed in historic buildings include model ships, nautical art, ships' figureheads, and the seafaring history of the Penobscot region. A nineteenth-century period home and an 1815 Congregational church are also part of the complex. Details: Church Street off Route 1 in Searsport; (207) 548-2529; open 10 a.m. to 5 p.m. Monday through Saturday, noon to 5 p.m. Sunday Memorial Day weekend through mid-October. Admission is $5 adults, $4 seniors, $2 ages 7 to 15. (1½ hours)

★ **Camden Hills State Park**—This park—on the north side of Camden off Route 1—offers fine views of Penobscot Bay from the top of Mount Battie. Details: (207) 236-3109. (½ hour)

★ **Castle Tucker**—In this striking Federal mansion overlooking Wiscasset Harbor, visitors can see how well-to-do sea captains lived in the 1800s. The house dates to 1807 and is furnished with Victorian decor. Details: Corner of Lee and High Streets in Wiscasset; (207)

882-7364; open noon to 4 p.m. Thursday through Saturday in July and August; tours leave on the hour. Admission is $4 adults. (1 hour)

★ **Montpelier**—Maine's Montpelier is an early twentieth-century reconstruction of the elegant eighteenth-century home General Henry Knox lived in with his family beginning in 1795. Knox served as a military advisor to George Washington and was the nation's first Secretary of War. His Thomaston home was torn down in 1871, but the reconstructed home recreated the first in many details including wallpaper, an unusual double staircase, and a lovely oval room. Costumed guides now lead visitors through the home, which is furnished with Knox-family artifacts and furniture. Details: Route 131, Thomaston, (207) 354-8062; open 10 a.m. to 4 p.m. Tuesday through Saturday, 1 to 4 p.m. Sunday late May through mid-October. Admission is $4 adults, $3 seniors, $2 children ages 5 to 11, $12 for families. (1 hour)

★ **Nickels-Sortwell House**—This handsome home in the heart of Wiscasset was built by Captain William Nickels in 1807. One of its most notable architectural features is its elliptical staircase. Although it was converted to a hotel in the 1830s, it was later reverted back to a private home and renovated in a Colonial Revival style. Details: Route 1 on the corner of Main and Federal Streets in Wiscasset; (207) 882-6218; tours on the hour from 11 a.m. to 4 p.m. Wednesday through Sunday June 1 through October 15. Admission is $4 adults, $3.50 seniors, $2 ages 2 and under. (1 hour)

★ **Owl's Head Transportation Museum**—Antique automobiles and aircraft (including a full-scale replica of the Wright Brothers' 1903 plane) are on display at this museum near the Owl's Head Lighthouse. Details: Route 73 in Owl's Head; (207) 594-4418; open 10 a.m. to 5 p.m. daily April through October; 10 a.m. to 4 p.m. weekdays, 10 a.m. to 3 p.m. weekends the rest of the year. (1 hour)

★ **Shore Village Museum**—In a state with more than 60 lighthouses, it is only natural that Maine has a museum devoted to them. This museum contains the largest collection of lighthouse paraphernalia in the United States. If you have a fascination with the inner workings of these often-mysterious coastal sentries, then a visit to the Shore Village Museum may be in order. Details: 104 Limerock Street in Rockland; (207) 594-0311; open 10 a.m. to 4 p.m. daily June through mid-October. (1 hour)

Boothbay Land Trust Preserves—The Boothbay Land Trust oversees a number of nature preserves on the Boothbay peninsula offering a total of 10 miles of marked hiking trails through tidal marshes, peaceful meadows, and other natural habitats. As the preserves are not easy to find, you should contact the Land Trust at 2 McKown Street (P.O. Box 183, 207-633-4818) in Boothbay for their brochure. It describes the various preserves and provides directions to each one. If you haven't requested a brochure prior to your trip, you might check for one at the Chamber of Commerce once you're in Boothbay. (½ day)

Maine Coast Railroad—Take this 14-mile scenic rail trip through coastal salt marshes from Wiscasset to Bath or Newcastle (on alternate days) and back. Details: The train departs from Wiscasset's waterfront, (800) 795-5404, weekends Memorial Day through late June and Labor Day through Columbus Day, daily late June through Labor Day, departing at 11 a.m. and 1 p.m. Tickets: $10 adults, $8 seniors, $5 ages 5 to 12, $25 for families. (1½ hours)

Marine Resources Aquarium—You can observe (and even touch) native marine life at this state-run aquarium. Details: McKown Point Road in West Boothbay; (207) 633-9542; open 10 a.m. to 5 p.m. daily Memorial Day through Columbus Day. Admission is $2.50 adults, $2 seniors and ages 5 to 18. (1 hour)

Musical Wonder House—This intriguing assemblage of rare music boxes and antique player pianos is part of music lover Danilo Konvalinka's private collection. It's on display in an 1852 ship captain's home complete with a flying staircase. Details: 18 High Street in Wiscasset; (207) 882-7163 or (207) 882-6373; the gift shop is open 10 a.m. to 6 p.m. daily late May through October (tours of the museum offered until 5 p.m.); hours are limited after Labor Day. (½ hour)

Olson House—This weathered 1820 farmhouse owned by the Olson family was the subject of many Andrew Wyeth paintings, including the famous *Christina's World*. Wyeth used one of the upstairs rooms as a studio. The house is run by the Farnsworth Museum in Rockland. Details: Hathorn Point Road in Cushing (get directions from the Farnsworth Museum); (207) 596-6457; open 11 a.m. to 4 p.m. daily Memorial Day weekend through October. Admission is $3 adults, $1 ages 8 to 18. (½ hour)

FITNESS AND RECREATION

Snow Bowl (207-236-3438) in Camden is a small mountain offering pleasant skiing for the whole family during the winter months.

While bicycling along traffic-laden Route 1 may prove risky, bicyclists might enjoy riding around the less congested Boothbay peninsula. **Harborside Bike Rentals** (207-633-4303) and **Tidal Transit Company** (207-633-7140) both rent out bicycles for about $20 per day with discounts for multiday or weekly rentals. Both also offer tandem bikes, and Harborside has child trailers for rental as well. In addition to bike rentals, Tidal Transit offers kayak rentals and tours.

FOOD

In Camden, meals at the **Whitehall Inn**'s dining room are definitely "Down East" with lots of seafood dishes and goodies made with Maine blueberries. At **The Belmont** (6 Belmont Avenue, 207-236-8053), local seafood such as mussels are seasoned with spices more commonly found in Asia than New England, giving meals a slightly exotic flavor. Prices range from $16 to $30. (The Belmont also has overnight accommodations; call 800-238-8053 for rates and reservations.) **Cappy's** (207-236-2254), on Main Street in the heart of town, has a varied menu at reasonable prices ($5–$14). Diners may choose from a number of seafood dishes including seafood pie and stew; and sandwiches, such as the pretzel deliwich (deli meats layered onto a soft pretzel), come with Maine potato salad. If you're looking for a fun environment try the **Sea Dog Brewing Company** (43 Mechanic Street, 207-236-6863) or the **Frogwater Cafe** (31 Elm Street, 207-236-8998). The Sea Dog serves microbrewed beer and hearty pub fare ($4–$12). Dinner entrées at the Frogwater—such as shrimp with brie, orzo, leek, tomatoes, olives, and spinach; and veal stuffed with ricotta and sun-dried tomatoes—are imaginative ($10–$16).

Boothbay also has a variety of eateries—many of them seafood restaurants right on the harbor. The **Tugboat Inn** makes a tasty seafood fettucini as well as a juicy filet mignon topped in a cognac sauce ($13–$19). The **Ebb Tide** on Commercial Street is a casual spot with a children's menu, homemade pies and chowder, and breakfast omelettes and pancakes. **No Anchovies** is the place to go for Italian cuisine, while the tiny **Blue Moon Cafe** (84 Commercial Street, 207-633-2349) is an inexpensive breakfast option ($2.50–$5.95) as well as a good place to

MID-COAST MAINE

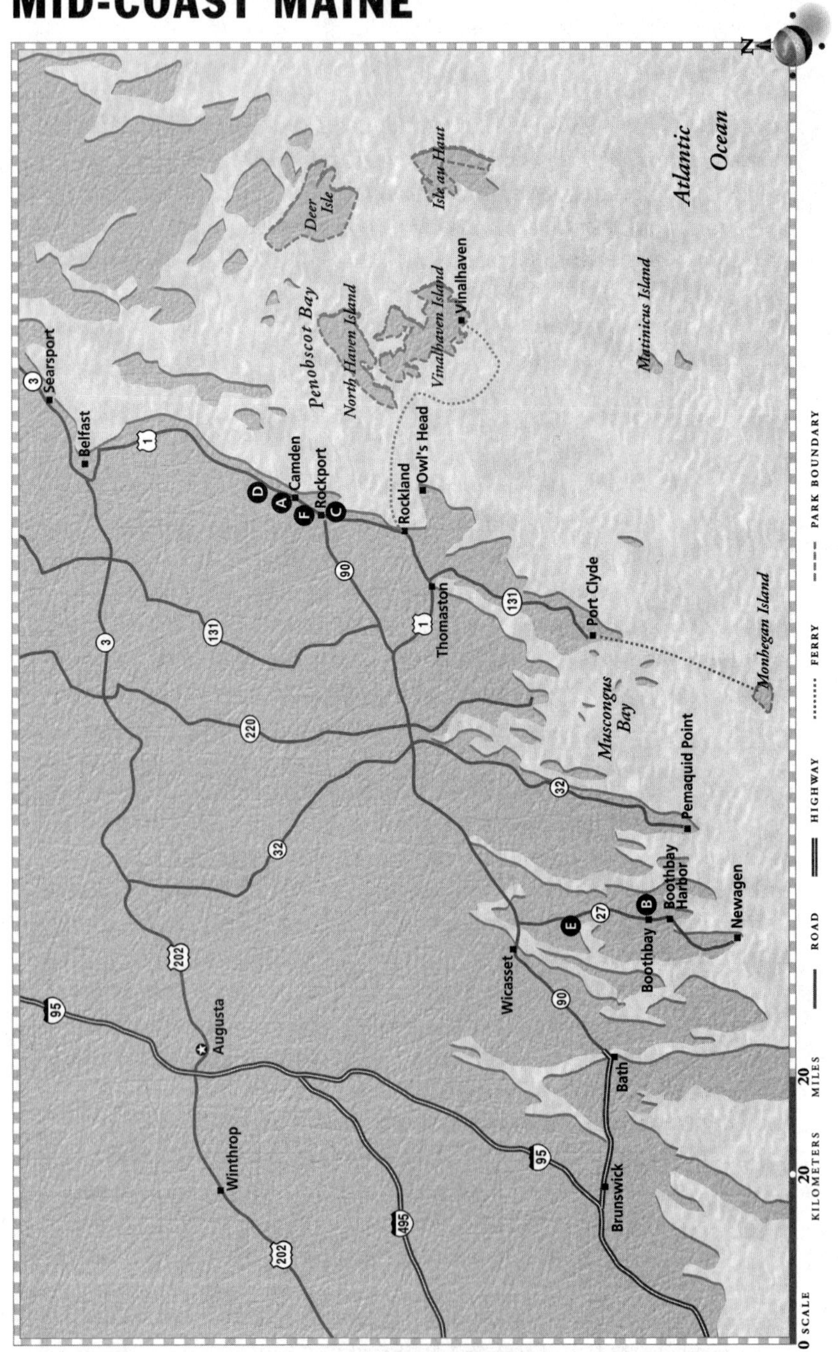

Food

- Ⓐ The Belmont
- Ⓑ Blue Moon Cafe
- Ⓐ Cappy's
- Ⓑ Ebb Tide
- Ⓐ Frogwater Cafe
- Ⓑ No Anchovies
- Ⓐ Sea Dog Brewing Company
- Ⓑ Tugboat Inn
- Ⓐ Whitehall Inn

Lodging

- Ⓐ Abigail's
- Ⓑ Admiral's Quarters Inn
- Ⓐ Blue Harbor House

Lodging *(continued)*

- Ⓐ Maine Stay Inn
- Ⓐ Norumbega
- Ⓒ Samoset Resort
- Ⓑ Tugboast Inn
- Ⓐ Whitehall Inn

Camping

- Ⓓ Camden Hills State Park
- Ⓔ Little Ponderosa Campground
- Ⓕ Megunticook Campground

Note: Items with the same letter are located in the same town or area.

pick up a flavorful sandwich or burger for lunch ($4.50–$6.95). For a uniquely New England dining experience try an island clambake. From Pier 6 at Fisherman's Wharf the Argo will ferry you to Cabbage Island for a traditional "Down East" clambake where the clams and lobsters are steamed in seaweed. The cost is about $40 per person including the boat cruise. Call (207) 633-7200 for reservations and departure times.

LODGING

Camden is centrally located for mid-coast attractions and has an appealing selection of inns and restaurants. On Route 1 north of the Camden's village center, the **Whitehall Inn** (207-236-3391 or 800-789-6565), a classic 50-room country inn, and **Abigail's** (8 High Street, 207-236-2501 or 800-292-2501), a smaller bed and breakfast, both are on the National Register of Historic Places. The Whitehall was built in 1834 as a sea-captain's home. Antique furnishings are still sprinkled about the inn. Edna St. Vincent Millay is said to have recited her poem "Renascence" for the first time to inn guests back in 1912. Doubles including breakfast are about $100 per night for a room with a shared bath, and start at $120 per night for a room with a private bath in high-season. The Whitehall is open for guests only from Memorial Day weekend through mid-October. Abigail's, just down the street in a Greek Revival home built in 1847, is run by welcoming hosts Donna and Ed Misner. Jefferson Davis was a frequent guest of the first owner, E. K. Smart, who was a member of the United States Congress. Today, guests sleep in four-poster beds (one suite has its own Jacuzzi) and dine on soufflés, quiche, and waffles for breakfast. Camden center is only a short walk away. Rates range from $75 to $145 including breakfast.

Two other inns on this stretch of Route 1 are worth noting: the **Maine Stay Inn** (22 High Street, 207-236-9636), for its hospitable innkeepers; and **Norumbega** (61 High Street, 207-236-4646), for its architecture. (The 1886 stone mansion with its turrets and multiple chimneys is quite striking.) Rooms at the Maine Stay start around $75 in the height of summer, while rates at Norumbega, which include a full breakfast and afternoon hors d'oeuvres, range from $125 to $450. On the other side of the village, the **Blue Harbor House** (67 Elm Street, 207-236-3196 or 800-248-3196) is also convenient to the center of Camden. Rooms in the restored 1810 New England Cape home have antiques, canopy beds, and hand-sewn quilts. Suites in the carriage house have their own sitting rooms, private entrances, and whirlpool tubs. Breakfasts are a real treat at the inn with dishes such as lobster quiche, blueberry pancakes with blueberry butter, or the inn's special apples, baked with raisins and granola and topped with vanilla ice cream. If you don't want to leave for dinner, the inn offers candlelit dinners by reservation only. Rates for two include breakfast and range from $85 to $135.

The mid-coast region's premier full-service resort is **Samoset Resort** in Rockport. It has both an outdoor and an indoor swimming pool, a fitness center, playground, a restaurant, lounge, outdoor tennis courts, a racquetball court, and a golf course that hugs the ocean. Cross-country skiing is allowed on the golf course during the winter, and skis are available for rent. The resort buildings, constructed with lumber from a Portland granary, are somewhat bland and industrial looking. But once you're in your room and step onto your balcony with its view of the ocean, you won't care what the building's exterior looks like. Rates at the hotel range from $95 to $305; golf packages are available. Families can enroll their children in the resort's Sam-O-Camp activities program for an additional fee. Call (207) 594-2511 or (800) 341-1650.

If you'd like to stay within walking distance of downtown shops and restaurants in Boothbay, try the **Tugboat Inn** (100 Commercial Street, 207-633-4434 or 800-248-2628)—an upscale motel overlooking the harbor. Room prices start around $95 in-season. The **Admiral's Quarters Inn** (71 Commercial Street, 207-633-2474) is also convenient. Rooms at this bed and breakfast come with private baths, decks, and entrances and range from $75 in low-season to $135 in high-season.

CAMPING

There is camping at **Camden Hills State Park** (207-236-3109) just north of Camden off Route 1. The **Megunticook Campground** (207-594-2428 or 800-884-2428), on Route 1 about 3 miles south of Camden, fronts the ocean. The campground has both tent sites and hookups for RVs. A heated swimming pool and cabins are also available. Sites range from $18 to $28 per night. About ten minutes from Boothbay Harbor on Route 27 is **Little Ponderosa Campground** (207-633-2700), an attractive camping area with spacious, wooded sites, and amenities such as miniature golf, swimming, boating, a recreation room, snack bar, store, playground, cable television, laundry facilities, full hookups, and a shuttle bus into the harbor. Both campgrounds are open from mid-May through mid-October. If you're unable to make advance reservations, you might want to try the Belfast area as numerous campgrounds are located there along Route 1.

SIDE TRIPS IN MID-COAST MAINE

There are several islands off the Maine coast that make for enjoyable summer day excursions. Because of its unspoiled beauty, **Monhegan** has long been an artists' retreat (Rockwell Kent and Jamie Wyeth painted here). You can visit this small rocky island by boat. During the summer the ***Balmy Days II*** (207-633-2284 or 800-298-2284) leaves Boothbay Harbor from Pier 8 daily at 9:30 a.m. and arrives at Monhegan at 11 a.m. Round-trip fares are about $30 for adults and

$20 for children. The return trip to Boothbay leaves the island at 2:45 p.m. so you'll have a few hours to look around, maybe hike along the island's cliffs, see how many of the 600 species of native wildflowers you can spot, or visit the artists' colony museum. If you haven't brought along a picnic, try the **Island Inn** (207-596-0371) right on the harbor, or the 1870s **Monhegan House** (207-594-7983 or 800-599-7973) in the center of the village for fresh seafood and pies. Should you decide to spend the night on the island, both the Monhegan House and the Island Inn can accommodate you. Double rooms with shared baths go for about $80 per night at the Monhegan House on peak summer weekends and are significantly less off-peak. Rates at the Island Inn range from $65 to $155 depending upon what time of the summer you stay there, whether your room has a shared or private bath, and whether you have an ocean view. (Both hotels are only open seasonally.) Bring a good pair of walking shoes, as cars are not allowed on the island.

Ferries travel to **Vinalhaven** and **North Haven** from Rockland several times a day year-round; trips take about 1¼ hours. Call (207) 596-2202 for departure and ticket information.

The exclusive **Islesboro** is only a 20-minute ferry ride from Lincolnville Beach north of Camden and may be the best island destination if your time is limited. The **Blue Heron** (207-734-6611) restaurant is the island's most popular dining establishment if you decide against a beach picnic. Call (207) 789-5611 for ferry ticket information.

Many find the Maine coast most captivating from the sea. It should come as no surprise then that windjammer cruises are a favorite pastime. Captains Ken and Ellen Barnes operate six-day cruises out of Rockland aboard their beautiful and historic schooner, *Stephen Tabor*, which was originally launched back in 1871. The *Tabor* is the oldest documented sailing vessel in continuous service in the country, and is listed on the National Historic Register. Ellen doubles as the ship's chef, and her meals are so popular that she's written a cookbook. The cost of the cruise ranges from about $650 to $720 per person. Call (207) 236-3520 or (800) 999-7352 for reservation information; cruises book up quickly so be sure to call well in advance of your visit. **North End Shipyard** (800-648-4544) in Rockland has three schooners on which they run three- and six-day cruises for $395 to $745. **Maine Windjammer Cruises** (207-236-2938 or 800-736-7981) in Camden offers three- and six-day cruises with rates ranging from $300 to $755 per person. Bring lots of warm clothing if you opt for one of these scenic cruises. It can get very chilly on the water, even in midsummer.

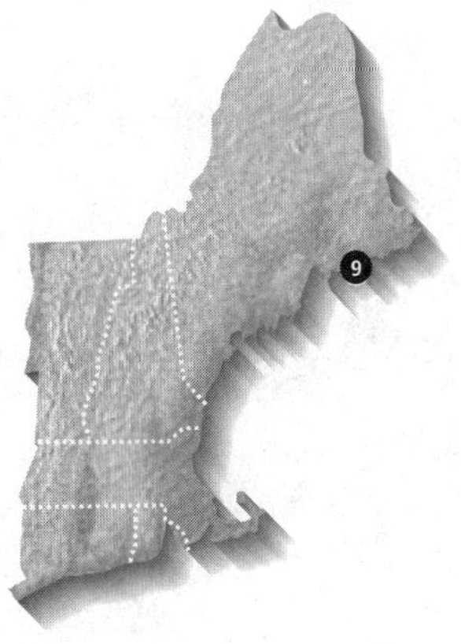

9

ACADIA

Established in 1919, Acadia National Park is the easternmost national park in the United States. If you stand atop the park's Cadillac Mountain at dawn, they say, you can be the first person in the country to see the sunrise.

The land, which encompasses rocky coastline, sheltered coves, wooded mountain trails, freshwater lakes, and ocean vistas, was originally donated by conservation-minded individuals. It is still easy to see why they felt the land should be preserved.

When visiting Acadia, most travelers establish their base at Bar Harbor—originally called Eden. Although it has a year-round population of only 5,000, Bar Harbor has been a thriving resort town for over 150 years. Famously wealthy families such as the Rockefellers, Vanderbilts, and Astors built fine summer homes in Bar Harbor in the late nineteenth century.

Today, with a multitude of souvenir shops, galleries (many of which stay open late during summer), and restaurants to suit every taste and budget, Bar Harbor has plenty to keep tourists engaged after exploring the national park. Those who prefer a quieter milieu will enjoy the less-hurried charm of Northeast Harbor on the eastern side of Mt. Desert Island. ◙

ACADIA

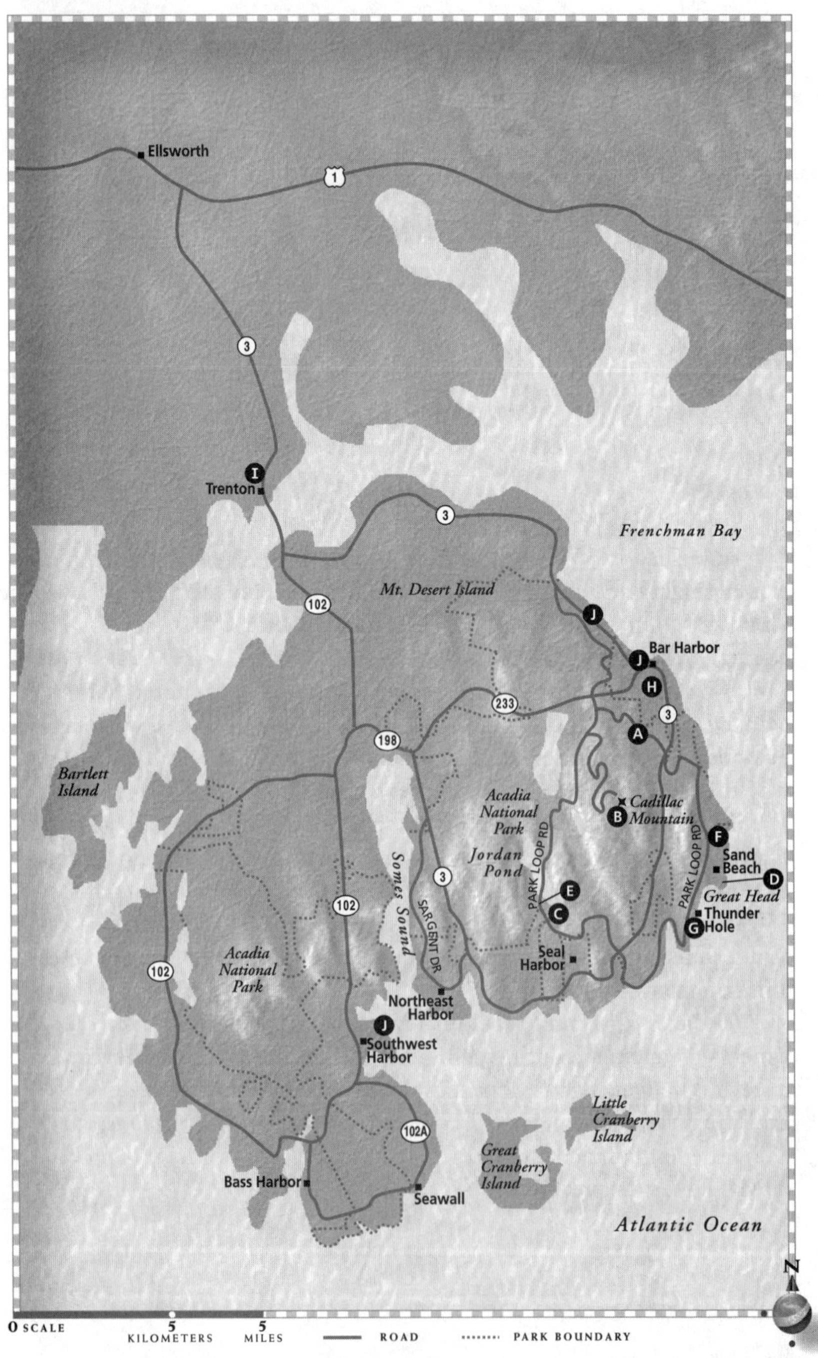

Ellsworth
1
3
I
Trenton
3
Frenchman Bay
Mt. Desert Island
102
J
Bar Harbor
J
H
233
3
198
A
Bartlett Island
Acadia National Park
Cadillac Mountain
B
F
Sand Beach
D
Great Head
Jordan Pond
PARK LOOP RD
E
C
PARK LOOP RD
Thunder Hole
G
Somes Sound
3
102
SARGENT DR
Seal Harbor
102
Acadia National Park
Northeast Harbor
J
Southwest Harbor
Little Cranberry Island
102A
Great Cranberry Island
Bass Harbor
Seawall
Atlantic Ocean
N
0 SCALE
5 KILOMETERS
5 MILES
ROAD
PARK BOUNDARY

Sights

Acadia National Park:

- **Ⓐ Abbe Museum**
- **Ⓑ Cadillac Mountain**
- **Ⓒ Gate House**
- **Ⓓ Great Head**
- **Ⓔ Jordan Pond**
- **Ⓕ Sand Beach**
- **Ⓖ Thunder Hole**
- **Ⓗ Wild Garden**

Ⓘ Acadia Zoo

Ⓙ Mountain Desert Oceanarium

A PERFECT DAY IN ACADIA

First, sit down to a hearty breakfast of blueberry pancakes at Jordan's Restaurant. Then enter Acadia National Park and visit sights along the park loop road, such as the Wild Garden, Sand Beach, and Thunder Hole. Try to time your arrival at Jordan Pond for afternoon tea. Then drive to the top of Cadillac Mountain. Once you've had your fill of the grand views, head back down to Bar Harbor for shopping and dining.

SIGHTSEEING HIGHLIGHTS

★★★ **Acadia National Park**—This park covers more than 35,000 acres. The largest portion of the park—and the most heavily touristed—is on Mount Desert Island, so named for its treeless top by French explorer Samuel de Champlain in the early 1600s. Frenchman Bay, whose name also derives from the French Colonial era, lies between Mount Desert Island and the Schoodic Peninsula (where there is an extension of Acadia). Entrance to the park is $5 per car. Be sure to bring your binoculars, as seals and otters can often be seen playing on rocks just offshore.

The visitor's information center near the Bar Harbor entrance is a good place to become familiar with the park (207-288-3338). A 15-minute film about Acadia is shown every half hour. Pick up a free map and a list of hiking trails if you wish to stray from the main road.

The **Wild Garden** is one of the first detours along the park loop. Plants in this wildflower garden are labeled, making them easier to identify when you spot them in their natural habitat elsewhere in the park. The **Abbe Museum**, at the same turnoff, is a small museum of tools and artifacts used by the island's first Indian settlers. Details: Open 10 a.m. to 4 p.m. mid-May through mid-October; open 9 a.m. to 5 p.m. July and August. Admission is charged.

Back on the loop, you come to **Sand Beach**, unusual because most beaches on Mount Desert Island are rugged and rocky. Even on the hottest of summer days, this beach is kept cool by ocean breezes. The trail to **Great Head** starts at the far end of the beach. Farther along the park road is **Thunder Hole**, where wave erosion has created a hole in the rocks which resounds with a booming noise as the waves crash to the shore.

In the summer the restaurant at **Jordan Pond** (207-276-3316) serves an afternoon tea with popovers and jam on the lawn with a splendid view of the pond and the "Bubbles"—two matching rounded mountains shaped by glaciers. If solitude is more your cup of tea, take a leisurely walk on the nature trail or on one of the flat paths alongside the pond. Find your own secluded rock and just soak up the scenery. The **Gate House** across the road from the restaurant is also worth a close look because of its unique stone architecture.

The drive to the summit of **Cadillac Mountain** is a high point of any visit to Acadia both figuratively and literally, as at 1,530 feet the mountain is the highest point on the Atlantic coast. Though an uninterrupted climb by automobile takes only about ten minutes, scores of breathtaking vistas will no doubt slow your progress. (The climb and descent will put a strain on your vehicle, so be sure to check your car's fluids and brakes before starting the ascent.) An arresting panorama awaits you atop Cadillac Mountain. (Both the mountain and the luxury automobile were named after the same Frenchman.) From the summit you can see the harbors below, the Porcupine and Cranberry Islands dotting the foreground, and Winter Harbor, Ironbound, and Schoodic across Frenchman Bay. The view is spectacular at sunrise or sunset, and the summit is also a popular star-gazing post. The road is closed from midnight until 1 hour before sunrise. (Full day)

✯ **Mount Desert Oceanarium**—The Oceanarium has three separate locations on the island with different things to see at each locale.

At the Oceanarium Bar Harbor on Route 3, about 4 miles north of the Bar Harbor Acadia entrance, you can tour a salt marsh, visit the Maine Lobster Museum, and watch harbor seals at play. The downtown Bar Harbor location is a lobster hatchery, and at the Southwest Harbor location a variety of aquatic creatures are on display in tanks. There's even a "touch tank" where you can put your hands on some of the more unusual ocean creatures—always a hit with children. Details: (207) 244-7330; Oceanariums open 9 a.m. to 5 p.m. Monday through Saturday mid-May through October; combination tickets are available. (1–4 hours)

Acadia Zoo —There are almost 50 animal species represented at this 15-acre zoo between Bar Harbor and Ellsworth. Animals range from the exotic—including leopards, tamarin, and colobus monkeys—to the indigenous, such as the moose. Details: Route 3 in Trenton; (207) 667-3244; open at 9:30 a.m. daily May through October. (1 hour)

FITNESS AND RECREATION

Many people choose to see Acadia from a bicycle rather than through a windshield. Until you're ready to climb the road to Cadillac Summit, which is demanding enough for a four-cylinder engine, two-wheeled transportation is a refreshing way to explore the park. Bicycles and mountain bikes can be rented in Bar Harbor from **Acadia Bike & Canoe** (48 Cottage Street, 207-288-9605 or 800-526-8615). The company also operates sea-kayaking tours of the park as well as guided bicycle trips *down* Cadillac Mountain. **Bar Harbor Bicycle Shop** (141 Cottage Street, 207-288-3886) rents bikes for about $14 per day ($25 per day for tandem bikes), and multiday rates are available. There are also more than 120 miles of trails within Acadia to tempt the hiker. Be sure to inquire about hiking trails while at the park's main visitor's center if you wish to explore Acadia's backcountry on foot. For the more adventurous the **Acadia Mountain Guides Climbing School** (137 Cottage Street, 207-288-8186) provides instruction and equipment rental for rock climbers of all levels.

For those who are on a rigid exercise program and can't afford to take a day off from the gym, the **Mount Desert Island YMCA** on Mt. Desert Street in Bar Harbor rents daily passes to visitors. In addition to a gymnasium, weight room, and Nautilus equipment, the Y also has a climbing wall. Call (207) 288-3511 for hours, fees, and information.

FOOD

No trip to the Maine seacoast is complete without a lobster dinner. **Abel's Lobster Pound** (207-276-5827) on Route 198 in Mount Desert won't disappoint you. A fairly casual spot—you needn't worry about bringing the kids—Abel's has a water view and picnic tables under pine trees. Prices however, which range from $15 to $35, are not cheap. Reservations are recommended. If Abel's is out of your way, there are numerous lobster pounds along Route 3 in Trenton between Bar Harbor and Ellsworth.

The **Reading Room** at the Bar Harbor Inn (base of Main Street, 207-288-3351), and the **Rinehart Dining Pavilion** (Eden Street, 207-288-5663) in Bar Harbor both offer quality dining with arresting ocean views. While seafood dominates their menus, landlubbers will enjoy the Rinehart's prime rib. **George's** (7 Stephen's Lane, 207-288-4505), behind the First National Bank on Main Street, is not situated on the water, but its elegant ambiance and unique presentation of traditional dishes warrant a visit. Dinner entrées start at about $15 in all three restaurants.

Testa's (Main Street, 207-288-3327) has been a Bar Harbor institution for over 50 years, specializing in family-style Italian cuisine and seafood dishes. Dinner entrées are reasonably priced. **Gaylon's Galley** (207-288-9706), down the street at 17 Main, is a little more upscale and offers good seafood and service. If you're willing to dine before 6 p.m., Gaylon's early-bird specials are priced right.

Had enough of seafood? **Thai Paradise** (191 Main, 207-288-5513) has Thai cuisine at prices ranging from $6.95 to $14.95. **Rupununi American Grill**, in an interesting building at 119 Main Street, has everything from salads to prime rib ($6.95–$14.95) and a lively nightclub upstairs called **Carmen Veranda** (207-288-2886). For pizza, calzones, and Italian specialties, and prices ranging from $6 to $16, there's **Carlo Ristorante** (15 Cottage Street, 207-288-4889). Try their delicious pesto pizza with veggies. Across the street, **Epi** uses natural ingredients in their sub sandwiches. Down the block at number 80, **Jordan's Restaurant** (207-288-3586) is *the* spot to go for breakfast. Jordan's is known for the best "blues" on the island, meaning blueberry muffins and pancakes. They do a brisk business, so service is fast and sometimes curt. Prices are in the $3 to $5 range.

LODGING

Many of the lodgings in Bar Harbor are open during the summer months only, so be sure to call ahead if you are traveling during the off-season. **McKay Cottage** (243 Main Street, 207-288-3531) in Bar Harbor has unpretentious lodgings at reasonable prices ($35–$95). Guests can borrow bikes, take a kayak trip at sunrise on a nearby lake, and sit down for a full breakfast for no extra charge. For those on strict budgets, the **Mount Desert Island Hostel** (207-288-5587) on Kennebec Street has dormitory beds for about $12 per night. The hostel is open only during summer, and reservations are recommended.

The 153-room **Bar Harbor Inn** (207-288-3351 or 800-248-3351), on the harbor in the heart of downtown, has much fancier accommodations. Doubles range from a low of $60 for a standard room in winter up to $265 for the most deluxe room at the height of summer. The inn also has a fine dining restaurant as well as an outdoor pool and hot tub. Two other lodgings offering fine accommodations on the water are the **Balance Rock Inn** (21 Albert Meadow, 207-288-2610 or 800-753-0494), in a handsome gray-shingled mansion, and the **Inn at Canoe Point**, a five-room inn on its own secluded rocky cove between downtown Bar Harbor and the entrance to Acadia. The Balance Rock Inn has a workout room, bar, and an outdoor swimming pool, and guest rooms have either a sauna or a Jacuzzi. Standard rooms range from $100 to $200, rooms with ocean views are $140 to $400, and deluxe suites run from $300 to $440. Rates at the Inn at Canoe Point, which include breakfast and afternoon refreshments, are $80 to $190.

Mount Desert Street, also convenient to downtown, has a whole string of inns. **Holbrook House** (number 74, 207-288-4970 or 800-695-1120) has wonderful porches, a helpful innkeeper, and rooms with private baths. Rates including a full breakfast range from $95 to $135. The attractive Victorian **Primrose Inn** (number 73, 207-288-4031 or 800-543-7842), built in 1878, is a pleasant establishment where rooms are priced from $90 to $200 in high-season. Some of the rooms at the **Mira Monte** (number 69, 207-288-4263 or 800-553-5109) have fireplaces. The home was built in 1864 but is now handicapped accessible. A continental buffet breakfast is included in the room rate (doubles are $120 to $150, suites with Jacuzzis are $180). The inn, which is on more than an acre of land, has a lovely side garden, while guest rooms come with antiques and private baths.

High Street, which intersects Mount Desert Street not far from

ACADIA

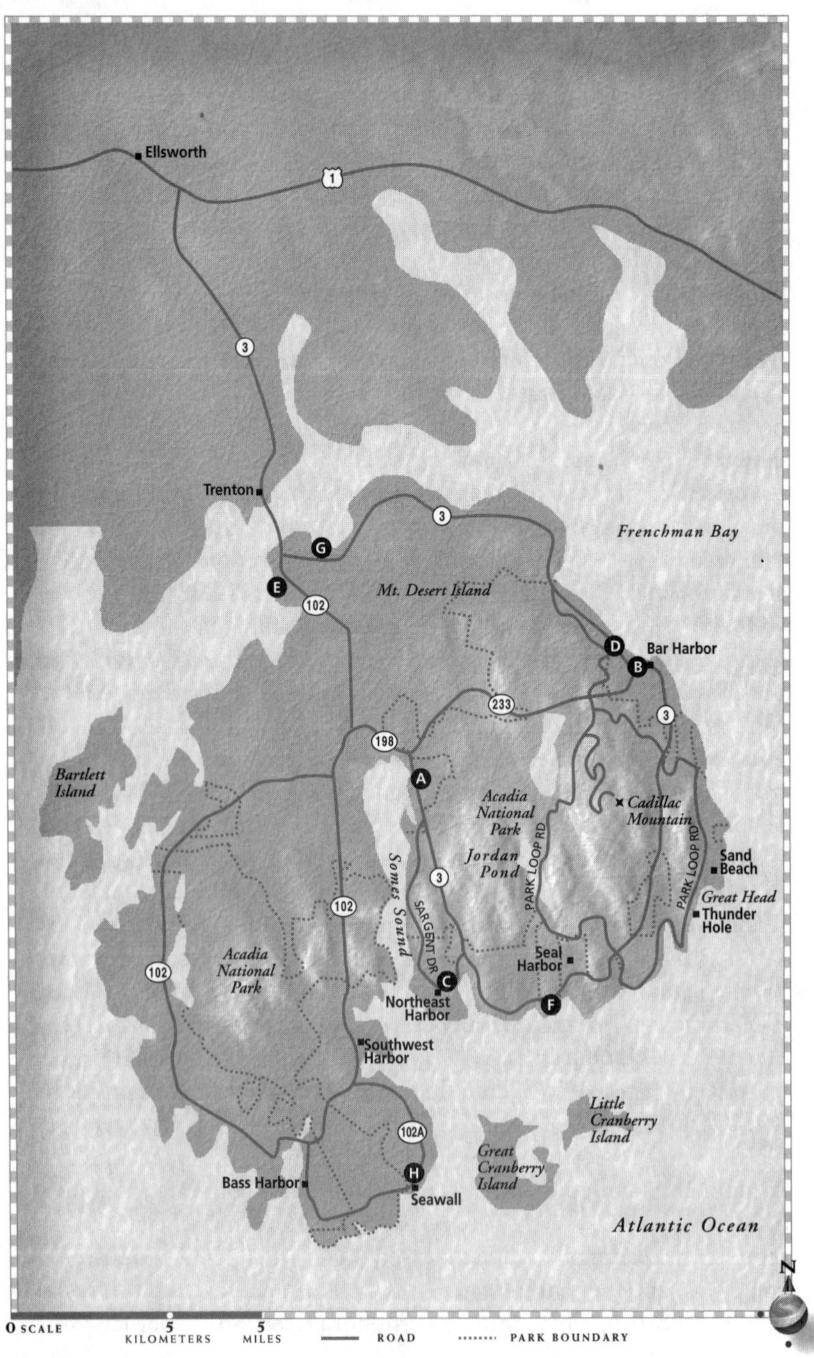

Ellsworth
1
3
Trenton
3
G
E
102
Frenchman Bay
Mt. Desert Island
D
Bar Harbor
B
233
3
198
A
Bartlett Island
Acadia National Park
Cadillac Mountain
Jordan Pond
PARK LOOP RD
PARK LOOP RD
Sand Beach
Great Head
Thunder Hole
3
Somes Sound
SARGENT DR
102
Seal Harbor
102
Acadia National Park
C
Northeast Harbor
F
Southwest Harbor
Little Cranberry Island
102A
Great Cranberry Island
H
Bass Harbor
Seawall
Atlantic Ocean
N
0 SCALE
5 KILOMETERS
5 MILES
ROAD
PARK BOUNDARY

Food

- A Abel's Lobster Pound
- B Carlo Ristorante
- B Carmen Veranda
- B Epi
- B Gaylon's Galley
- B George's
- B Jordan's Restaurant
- B Reading Room
- B Rinehart Dining Pavilion
- B Rupununi American Grill
- B Testa's
- B Thai Paradise

Lodging

- C The Asticou
- B Balance Rock Inn
- B Bar Harbor Inn
- B Holbrook House
- B Inn at Canoe Point
- C Maison Suisse Inn
- B McKay Cottage
- B Mira Monte
- B Mount Desert Island Hostel
- B Primrose Inn
- B Ridgeway Inn

Camping

- D Bar Harbor Campground
- E Barcadia Campground
- F Blackwoods Campground
- G Mount Desert Narrows Camping Resort
- H Seawall Campground

Note: Items with the same letter are located in the same town or area.

the center of town, is also lined with bed-and-breakfast inns. One of them, the **Ridgeway Inn** (207-288-9682), was originally built as a private home for J. P. Morgan's mistress around the turn of the century. Guest rooms—named for former summer cottages once owned by the well-to-do when Bar Harbor was in its heyday as a resort for the wealthy—have soothing touches such as down comforters and claw-foot tubs. The inn is open year-round. Doubles including a gourmet breakfast start at $60 in low-season, and range from $100 to $150 during the summer months.

There are countless motels and cottages along Route 3 as you approach Bar Harbor from Ellsworth. If you're not planning to visit during the month of August or on a holiday weekend, you can probably check into any of these without advance reservations. The Bar Harbor Chamber of Commerce will send you a free, useful brochure with detailed lodging listings. Write them at P.O. Box 158, Bar Harbor, ME 04609, or call (207) 288-5103 for your copy.

Northeast Harbor, only 12 miles from Bar Harbor via Route 3, can be a welcome alternative to Bar Harbor's summer throngs, and is equally convenient to Acadia. If your budget permits, the view of the harbor from **The Asticou** (207-276-3344) is first-rate and so is the service. It is best to book well in advance, particularly for August; the oceanside rooms naturally fill up first. Double rooms including breakfast start around $120 and range up to $300 ($350 for suites) including dinner and breakfast at the height of the summer season. On Main Street in the center of Northeast Harbor—but set back from the road far enough that it's nice and quiet—is the **Maison Suisse Inn** (207-276-5223, or 800-624-7668). It provides attractive guest rooms complete with four-poster beds and cozy down comforters to take the nip out of the Maine night air. The inn is open seasonally from May through October. Peak-season rates including breakfast begin at $105 for a double, $175 for a suite.

CAMPING

Blackwoods Campground, about 8 miles from Bar Harbor and 1 mile from Seal Harbor off Route 3, is the closest campground to Acadia's main loop road. Several miles from the Seal Harbor entrance to Acadia, it is operated by the National Park Service. The sites are more heavily wooded than in most private campgrounds in the area, and there's a path to the ocean. Reservations must be made through the

Destinet reservation system up to five months ahead; it's recommended that you reserve at least three weeks before your arrival. It may be possible to obtain a site on a space-available basis upon your arrival; generally, the earlier in the day you arrive, the better chance you'll have. There are bathrooms on the premises and a shower nearby. For provisions, there is a small store in Seal Harbor, but you'll find more substantial offerings at the Pine Tree Market on Main Street in Northeast Harbor about 4 miles away. Call (800) 365-2267 or write Destinet, 9450 Carroll Park Drive, San Diego, CA 92121 for reservations and current rate information. Major credit cards are accepted for reservations, and campsites cost about $16 in the height of summer. **Seawall Campground**, on Route 102A 4 miles south of Southwest Harbor, is open from late May until late September, and sites are available on a first-come, first-served basis.

Neither of the park service campgrounds have utility hookups, so you'll have to stay at one of the private campgrounds in the area if you need one. Several campgrounds are reasonably close to Bar Harbor on Route 3 between Bar Harbor and Ellsworth. **Bar Harbor Campground** (207-288-5185) is only 4 miles from the center of town and 3 miles from the main entrance to Acadia. It has modern facilities, including a heated pool, and sites range from $18 to $25. **Mount Desert Narrows Camping Resort** (207- 288-4782), 8 miles from Bar Harbor, has RV hookups and ocean sites ranging from $18 to $45). **Barcadia Campground** (207-288-3520) is on the water about 10 miles from Bar Harbor. Sites range from $17 for a non-ocean site in the off-season to $30 for an ocean site in high-season.

JUST FOR KIDS

About 12 miles west of Bar Harbor on Route 3 are 3 miles of highway with enough miniature golf courses, ice-cream parlors, paddleboats, go-cart tracks, water-slide parks—and even a small zoo—to bring any travel-weary child out of the doldrums.

SIDE TRIPS FROM BAR HARBOR

A sightseeing cruise on Frenchman Bay is an agreeable way to survey Acadia National Park and the islands of Frenchman Bay. **Whale Watcher Inc.**, next to the municipal pier in Bar Harbor, offers a variety of cruising options. Call (207) 288-3322 or (800) 508-1499 for more information. The ***Natalie Todd*** is a 129-foot, three-masted schooner that offers two-hour cruises on the bay (207-288-4585). You can also take a 1½-hour cruise on the ***Katherine***, a lobster boat equipped to carry passengers. You'll get to see how lobster traps are pulled from the ocean and view seals at play (207-288-3322). The *Katherine* departs from the same pier as Whale Watcher Inc.

Those with more time may wish to go on to Southwest and Bass Harbors, and to the western part of Acadia from Northeast Harbor. From Bass Harbor you can take a ferry to Swan's Island; another ferry operates from Northeast Harbor to the Cranberry Islands. If you are so inclined and have the opportunity to stay a day or two longer, investigate some of them on your own.

If you really want to extend your trip, Nova Scotia is just a six-hour ferry ride from Bar Harbor on the ***Bluenose***. The famous ferry departs daily for Yarmouth at 8 a.m. from mid-June through mid-September. One-way passenger fare is about $42 for adults, $38 for seniors, and $21 for children ages 5 to 12. Automobiles and mobile homes up to 20 feet long cost about $55 one-way. The ferry runs on a reduced schedule the rest of the year, and fares are lower. Call (888) 249-7245 for further information and reservations. Gambling is allowed on board once the ship reaches international waters. In Nova Scotia, the most scenic routes are along the coasts. The Cabot Trail on Cape Breton, at the easternmost end of Nova Scotia, is generally considered to be the province's most beautiful region. From Caribou, Nova Scotia, you can take the ferry to sleepy Prince Edward Island where deserted white-sand beaches meet a surprisingly warm, blue sea.

Scenic Route: Schoodic Peninsula

Schoodic Peninsula, directly across Frenchman Bay from Bar Harbor, is also part of Acadia National Park. Because of its distance from the heart of Acadia, Schoodic is much less traveled. However, it's no less scenic. Take an extra day to traverse this remote part of the park and the quiet fishing village of Winter Harbor (the harbor never freezes).

To get there from the Bar Harbor area, take Route 3 to Ellsworth and continue on U.S. 1 north to West Gouldsboro. From there, take Route 186 to Winter Harbor. The entrance to the park is at Mosquito Harbor. Shortly after the road becomes one-way there's a picnic area at **Frazier Point**. From there the road circles the peninsula, encompassing over 2,000 acres of parkland and the 440-foot **Schoodic Head** (there are hiking trails to the summit). The 7-mile-long park drive follows the shore and offers numerous vistas of the rocky coastline, **Mount Desert Island** across **Frenchman Bay**, and smaller, closer islands. ◪

SCHOODIC PENINSULA

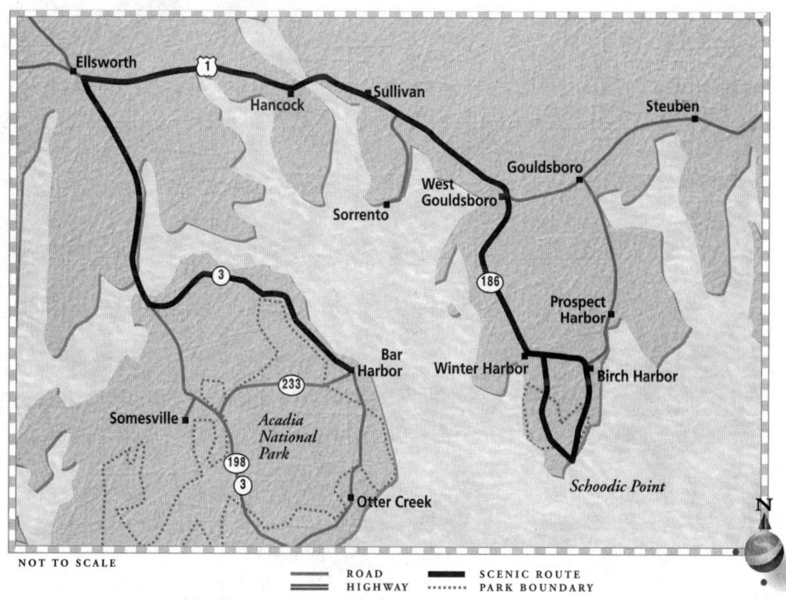

Scenic Route: Sargent Drive

The main park loop road through Acadia is the area's most scenic drive, but a short detour along Sargent Drive is certainly worth your while if you have the time. (Unfortunately for those in RVs, travel along Sargent Drive is limited to cars.) The drive begins in **Northeast Harbor** (follow the signs from the center of town) and passes some of the more exclusive residences in the area. Just after the tennis club, a turnout on the left offers a view of **Somes Sound**, the only natural fjord on the East Coast. (The spot is ideal for a picnic.) While not nearly as dramatic as Norwegian fjords (the mountains across the sound don't even top 700 feet), the scene is still a majestic one. A few short miles later Sargent Drive rejoins Routes 3 and 198.

SARGENT DRIVE

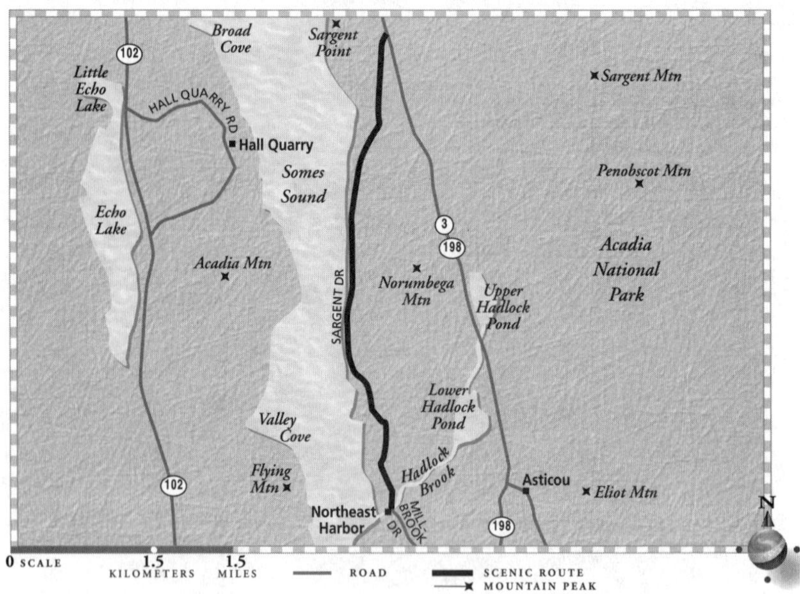

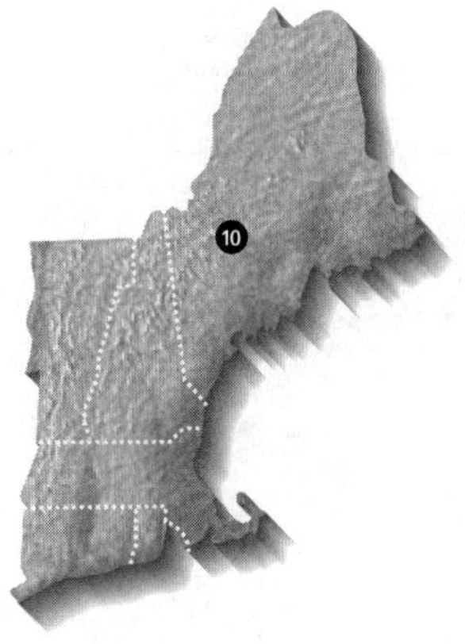

10

INLAND MAINE

For a change from Maine's coastal scenery, travel inland to the Oxford Hills region and the western part of the state that borders New Hampshire. With numerous lakes such as Kezar, Norway, Thompson, Sebago, Rangeley, and Long; a mineral- and gem-rich landscape; and numerous wooded trails where the sweet smell of pine permeates the air and waterfalls tumble down river gorges, the area is a pleasant place for hikers, rock hounds (quartz and mica are plentiful), and anglers. Villages such as Paris Hill, with its handsome Federal and Victorian homes, beckon those who appreciate classic New England architecture. The town of Bethel offers charming inns and restaurants.

Wilderness seekers will find what they are looking for in the Katahdin-Moosehead region of Maine to the north. At more than 5,000 feet, Mount Katahdin dominates the landscape—although at 40 miles in length, Moosehead Lake is impressive in its own right. Baxter State Park, which surrounds Mount Katahdin, is popular with campers and hikers, especially since it marks the northern end of the Appalachian Trail. ◪

INLAND MAINE

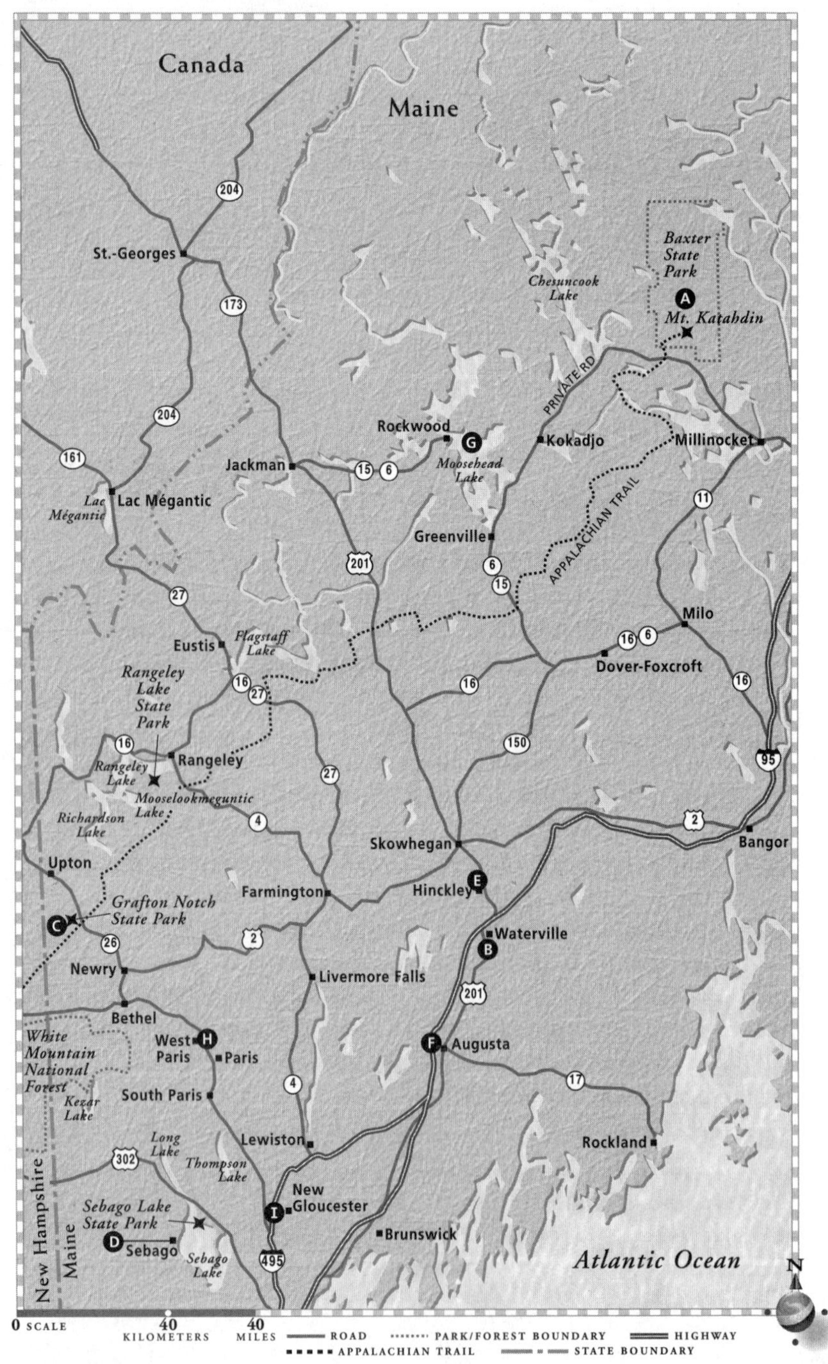

Canada
Maine
Baxter State Park
Chesuncook Lake
Mt. Katahdin
PRIVATE RD
St.-Georges
Rockwood
Kokadjo
Millinocket
Jackman
Moosehead Lake
Lac Mégantic
Lac Mégantic
Greenville
APPALACHIAN TRAIL
Milo
Eustis
Flagstaff Lake
Dover-Foxcroft
Rangeley Lake State Park
Rangeley
Rangeley Lake
Mooselookmeguntic Lake
Richardson Lake
Skowhegan
Bangor
Upton
Farmington
Hinckley
Grafton Notch State Park
Waterville
Newry
Livermore Falls
Bethel
White Mountain National Forest
West Paris
Paris
Augusta
Kezar Lake
South Paris
Lewiston
Rockland
Long Lake
Thompson Lake
New Gloucester
Sebago Lake State Park
Brunswick
Sebago
Sebago Lake
New Hampshire
Maine
Atlantic Ocean
N
0 SCALE
40 KILOMETERS
40 MILES
ROAD
PARK/FOREST BOUNDARY
HIGHWAY
APPALACHIAN TRAIL
STATE BOUNDARY

Sights

- **A Baxter State Park**
- **B Colby College Museum of Art**
- **C Grafton Notch State Park**
- **D Jones Museum of Glass and Ceramics**
- **E L. C. Bates Museum**
- **F Maine State Museum**
- **G Moosehead Lake**
- **H Perham's of West Paris**
- **I Sabbathday Lake Shaker Village**

A PERFECT DAY IN INLAND MAINE

Visit the Jones Museum of Glass and Ceramics in the morning. Follow with a picnic lunch and a swim at Sebago Lake State Park. Then travel to Newry via Route 113 north and Route 2 east through part of the White Mountain National Forest. From Newry take Route 26 northwest through scenic Grafton Notch State Park. Return to Bethel for the evening's dinner and overnight accommodations, or push on to Rangeley Lake.

SIGHTSEEING HIGHLIGHTS

★★ **Baxter State Park**—The 5,267-foot Mount Katahdin is the highlight of this 20,000-acre park in the center of northern Maine. The Appalachian Trail terminates (or begins, depending upon your perspective) at Baxter Peak, Mount Katahdin's summit. Hiking opportunities abound in this wilderness park, and many find a real sense of accomplishment in climbing Katahdin. The southern gateway to the park is via Millinocket. Pets are not allowed in the park and there are limits on vehicle size. For complete information on park regulations contact Baxter State Park Authority, 64 Balsam Drive, Millinocket, Maine 04462; (207-723-5140). (half–full day)

★★ **Moosehead Lake**—At 40 miles long and some 20 miles wide at its widest point, Moosehead is the largest lake in the Northeast. With an unspoiled beauty and abundant wildlife—moose-watching is a popular pastime here—Moosehead is a popular destination for those who enjoy lake activities without the crowds that accompany many other New England lakes. The Moosehead Trail offers snowmobilers 100 miles of groomed trails around the lake, and many hikers enjoy treks to the top of Big Squaw Mountain or Mount Kineo, both of which overlook the lake. Details: Between Greenville and Rockwood, on Routes 6 and 15. (half–full day)

★ **Colby College Museum of Art**—The museum's collection includes works by American artists such as Copley, Robert Henri, and Fairfield Porter. For a semester once every two years the museum displays its collection of French Impressionist and post-Impressionist paintings. The gallery is wheelchair accessible. Details: Colby College in Waterville; (207) 872-3696; open 10 a.m. to 4:30 p.m. Monday through Saturday, 2 to 4:30 p.m. Sunday. Admission is free. (½ hour)

★ **Grafton Notch State Park**—Route 26 runs through the notch between the 4,180-foot Old Speck and 3,812-foot Baldpate Mountains. The 3,000-plus-acre state park has numerous hiking trails—including a portion of the Appalachian Trail—and natural phenomena such as Moose Cave, and Mother Walker and Screw Auger Falls. Details: Between Newry and Upton on Route 26 at Maine's western border; (207) 824-2912; open mid-May through mid-October. A small entrance fee is charged. (1 hour–half day)

★ **Jones Museum of Glass and Ceramics**—More than seven thousand pieces of ceramics and glass, including Chinese and English porcelain, American pattern glass, and baccarat crystal are featured at this museum on the western side of Sebago Lake. Some pieces date as far back as 1200 B.C. Details: Douglas Mountain Road off Route 107 in Sebago; (207) 787-3370; open 10 a.m. to 5 p.m. Monday through Saturday, 1 to 5 p.m. Sunday May through mid-November. Admission is $5 adults, $3.75 seniors, $3 students, under 12 free. (1 hour)

★ **L.C. Bates Museum**—Artifacts at this museum range from tools used by the prehistoric people of Maine to portions of Roman frescoes. Mammoth and mastodon teeth along with native animals are part of the museum's natural history exhibits. Details: Route 201 in Hinckley; (207) 453-4894; open 10 a.m. to 4:30 p.m. Wednesday through Saturday, 1 to 4:30 p.m. Sunday May through mid-November. Admission is $2.00 adults, $1 students and children. (1 hour)

★ **Maine State Museum**—It is only natural that Augusta, the state's capital, would have a museum devoted to Maine's past. There are exhibits on the fishing, manufacturing, and logging industries that have shaped Maine's economy over the years, as well as exhibits focusing on the state's indigenous wildlife and native gemstones. The museum is wheelchair accessible. Details: In the capitol complex, State Street, Augusta; (207) 287-6740; open 9 a.m. to 5 p.m. weekdays, 10 a.m. to 4 p.m. Saturday and holidays, 1 to 4 p.m. Sunday; closed New Year's Day, Easter, Thanksgiving, and Christmas. Admission is free. (1 hour)

★ **Perham's of West Paris**—This shop is a must for rock hounds or for anyone with an interest in gems. There's a museum area where native gems and minerals are on display, as well as multiple cases filled with specimens and jewelry for sale. Perham's also provides maps for rockhounding in the area and sells equipment for gold-panning. Details: Route 26 in West Paris; (800) 371-4367; open 9 a.m. to 5 p.m. daily; closed Thanksgiving and Christmas. (½ hour)

Maine Office of Tourism

L.C. Bates Museum

★ **Sabbathday Lake Shaker Village**—The last few surviving Shakers live at this oldest Shaker community. Tours of the grounds are available during the summer months, and there's a museum as well as a gift shop with Shaker crafts. Details: 707 Shaker Road, off Route 26 in New Gloucester; (207) 926-4597; open 10 a.m. to 4:30 p.m. daily except Sunday Memorial Day through Columbus Day. (1 hour)

FITNESS AND RECREATION

The opportunities for outdoor recreation here are almost limitless. Whether you enjoy hiking, bicycling, boating, river rafting, canoeing, kayaking, swimming, downhill skiing, cross-country skiing, snowmobiling, fly fishing, ice fishing, or rock climbing, the area is bound to accommodate the activity of your choice. In the Katahdin region the **New England Outdoor Center** (207-723-5438 or 800-766-7238) specializes in white-water rafting trips and rents out snowmobiles. **Mountain Man Guide Service** (119 Knox Street in Millinocket, 207-723-8500) provides fly-fishing instruction and tours by canoe and kayak.

If you visit Maine in winter, **Sunday River** (207-824-3000) in Bethel has over 100 downhill ski trails and a 2,340-foot vertical drop. **Big Squaw Mountain** (207-695-1000) offers both alpine and cross-country skiing in the Moosehead area. With a vertical drop of 2,820 feet, **Sugarloaf** (800-THE-LOAF), in the Carrabassett Valley east of Rangeley Lake, has ski terrain to rival that of many Rocky Mountain resorts. Sugarloaf also permits snowboarding.

FOOD

With a variety of lodging and dining establishments, Bethel is a good place to base yourself while exploring the Oxford Hills and Western Lakes Region. Bethel's **L'Auberge** (207-824-2774 or 800-760-2774) has a dinner menu offering everything from veal to lobster ($15–$21). For more casual meals there's the **Sunday River Brew Company** on Route 2 outside of town on the way to the ski area. Also on Route 2, the **Good Food Store** (207-824-3734) is a perfect place to pick up picnic fixings. For French cuisine, try **Maurice's** (113 Main Street on Route 26, 207-743-7454) in nearby South Paris. Their entrées range in price from $12 to $16. Locals go to the unpretentious **Country Way Restaurant** (187 Main Street, 207-743-9783) for hearty meals and good lobster dinners at reasonable prices (dinner entrées $8–$15).

LODGING

The **Bethel Inn** (207-824-2175 or 800-654-0125) is probably the best-known inn in the area. A traditional New England inn, it's open year-round. Be sure to bring your golf clubs and tennis rackets in the summer, as the inn has good sports facilities. In the winter months the golf course becomes a haven for cross-country skiers when it is blanketed with snow. The inn also rents mountain bikes for about $30 per day. Rates, which include dinner and breakfast, start at $69 per person in the winter, and begin at $99 per person in the summer including breakfast, dinner, and golf. The inn's restaurant, which is open to the general public, offers dishes such as pan-seared duck breast topped with a raspberry walnut demi-glaze, and roasted rack of lamb with peach mint chutney. The **Sudbury Inn** (207-824-2174 or 800-395-7837) on Main Street in Bethel—just down the street from the Bethel Inn—has comfortable accommodations ($50–$150), fine dining, and a casual pub with live entertainment.

Elsewhere in the area, the **Inn at Long Lake** (207-693-6226 or 800-437-0328) has pleasant accommodations, all with private baths, color television, and air conditioning. The inn is located at the southern end of Long Lake and is just minutes from Sebago Lake. Rates range from $60 to $115. Farther north, the **Lodge at Moosehead Lake** (207-695-4400), in Greenville at the southern end of Moosehead Lake, has luxurious rooms with charming rustic touches such as totem pole bedposts and wood-carved moose headboards. Rates range from $145 to $195 and include a full breakfast.

CAMPING

There are ten campgrounds within **Baxter State Park**; reservations can be made by contacting the reservation clerk at Baxter State Park, 64 Balsam Drive, Millinocket, ME 04462. Camping costs $16 per site at **Sebago Lake State Park** (207-693-6615) off Route 302 between South Casco and Naples. Sites at **Rangeley Lake State Park** (207-864-3858) are also $16. Both parks offer swimming and fishing. If you require a full hookup or prefer the amenities provided by private campgrounds, try the **Katahdin Shadows Campground** (207-746-9349 or 800-794-KAMP) on Route 157 near Medway in the Baxter State Park area. Sites start at $16. The **Kokatosi Campground** (207-627-4642 or 800-9-CAMPIN) on Crescent Lake is centrally located for the Oxford Hills region.

INLAND MAINE

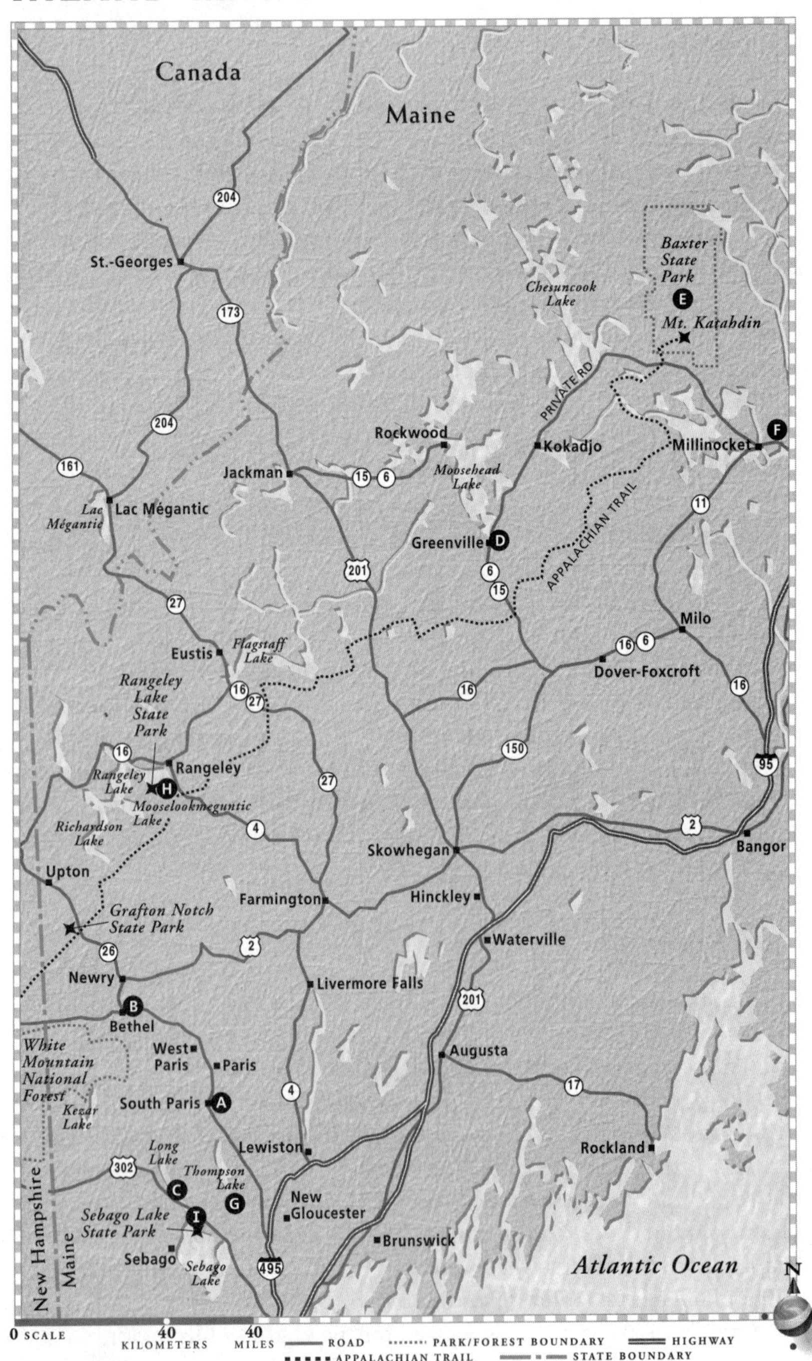

Canada
Maine
Baxter State Park
Chesuncook Lake
Mt. Katahdin
PRIVATE RD
St.-Georges
204
173
161
Rockwood
Kokadjo
Millinocket
Jackman
15
6
Moosehead Lake
Lac Mégantic
Lac Mégantic
APPALACHIAN TRAIL
Greenville
201
27
Milo
Eustis
Flagstaff Lake
16
Dover-Foxcroft
Rangeley Lake State Park
150
95
Rangeley
Rangeley Lake
Mooselookmeguntic Lake
Richardson Lake
4
2
Bangor
Skowhegan
Upton
Farmington
Hinckley
Grafton Notch State Park
Waterville
26
Newry
Livermore Falls
Bethel
White Mountain National Forest
West Paris
Paris
Augusta
17
South Paris
Kezar Lake
Lewiston
Rockland
Long Lake
302
Thompson Lake
New Gloucester
Sebago Lake State Park
Brunswick
Sebago
Sebago Lake
495
New Hampshire
Maine
Atlantic Ocean
A
B
C
D
E
F
G
H
I
N
0 SCALE
40 KILOMETERS
40 MILES
ROAD
PARK/FOREST BOUNDARY
HIGHWAY
APPALACHIAN TRAIL
STATE BOUNDARY

Food

- A Country Way Restaurant
- B Good Food Store
- B L'Auberge
- A Maurice's
- B Sunday River Brew Company

Lodging

- B Bethel Inn
- C Inn at Long Lake
- D Lodge at Moosehead Lake
- B Sudbury Inn

Camping

- E Baxter State Park
- F Katahdin Shadows Campground
- G Kokatosi Campground
- H Rangeley Lake State Park
- I Sebago Lake State Park

Note: Items with the same letter are located in the same town or area.

ARTS AND ENTERTAINMENT

Comedies and musicals are standard fare during the **Lakewood Theater**'s summer season. There are also special shows just for children. The theater is located 6 miles north of Skowhegan on Route 201. Call (207) 474-7176 for schedule and ticket information.

SIDE TRIPS IN INLAND MAINE

A trip up the **Allagash Wilderness Waterway**, from the western edge of Baxter State Park to the town of Allagash in the northernmost part of Maine, is a draw for serious backwoods campers and canoeists who prefer to be as far away from civilization as possible. The 90-plus-mile journey requires a time commitment and the ability to maneuver serious rapids. It is not for those who like their showers hot and their beds soft. (If you do go, bring plenty of insect repellent as the bugs are fierce and hungry.) Contact the Maine Bureau of Parks and Recreation at State House Station 22, Augusta, ME 04333, or call (207) 287-3821 for regulations and information.

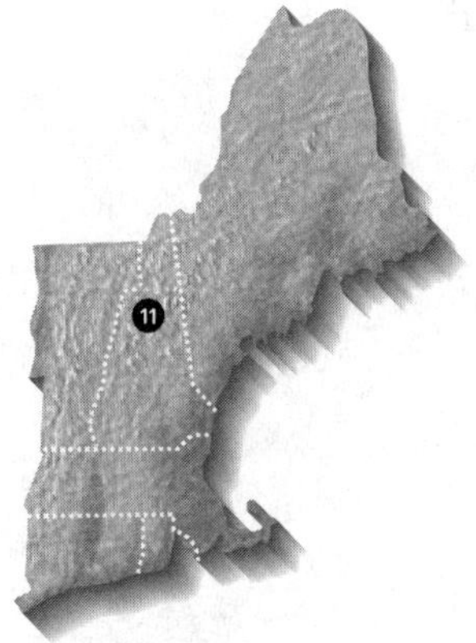

11
THE WHITE MOUNTAINS

White Mountain National Forest is a 750,000-acre expanse in central New Hampshire that encompasses much of the Presidential Range, including 6,288-foot Mt. Washington, as well as a bounty of alpine lakes, streams, cascades, and hiking trails. The Appalachian Trail traverses Mt. Washington, the highest mountain in the Northeast. One of the highest wind speeds ever recorded (231 miles per hour) was registered at the weather station atop Mt. Washington in 1934.

Because of the mountainous terrain, ski areas abound. Black Mountain is a good beginner resort. Attitash, Wildcat, Loon, and Cannon have runs for all ability levels, while Tuckerman's Ravine should be tackled by only the most expert skiers.

Mt. Cranmore in North Conway is one of the oldest ski areas in the Northeast. Although rail service is no longer available, trains used to arrive from Boston on a regular basis, dropping off skiers right in the heart of the village. The town has catered to tourists for many years, and the effects are beginning to show. In the past decade or so, factory outlets and the multitude of shoppers they bring have begun to crowd the town's charming core. Still, North Conway has its appeal, including the greatest variety of shops, restaurants, and lodging establishments in the Mt. Washington Valley. The town might be a good base for your visit to the White Mountains. ◪

THE WHITE MOUNTAINS

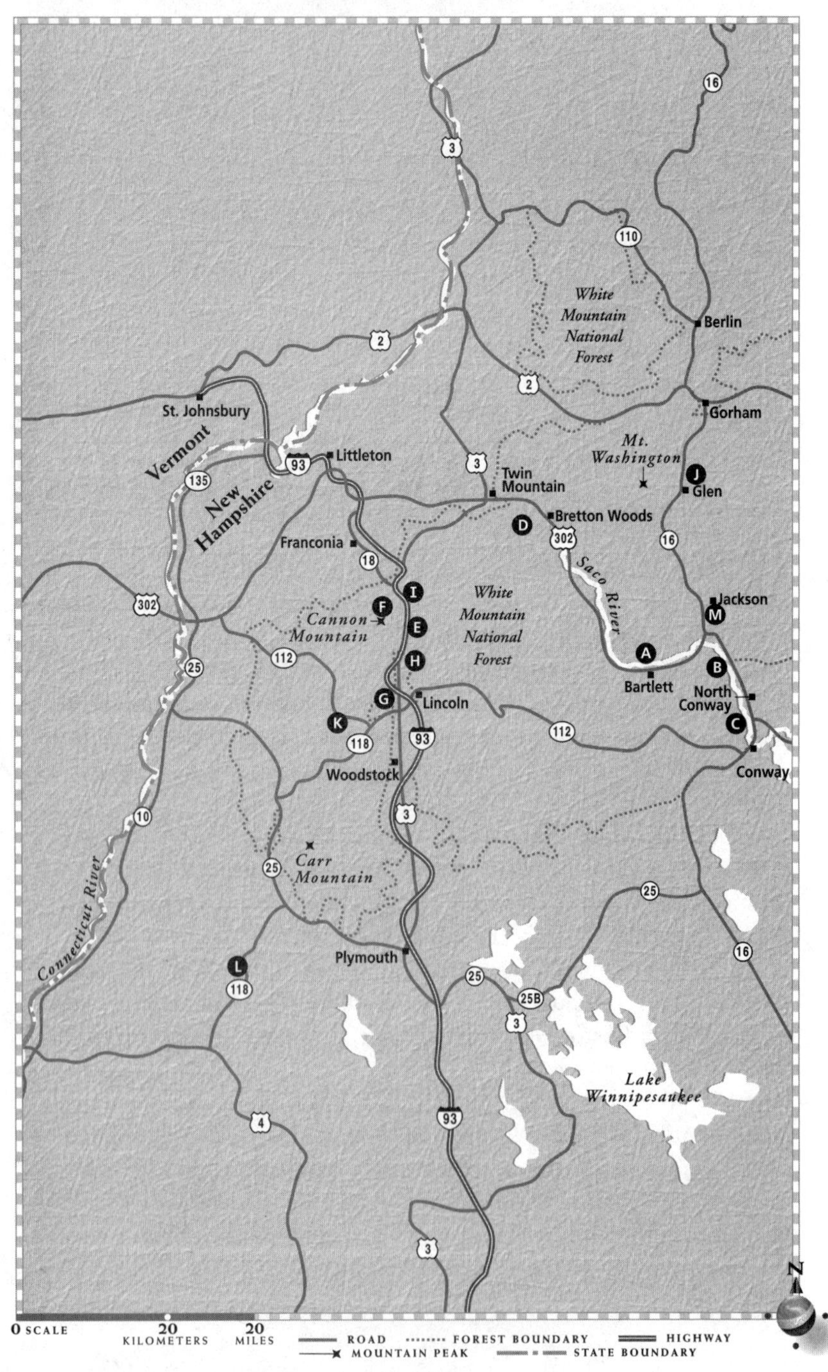

Sights

- Ⓐ Attitash Ski Area
- Ⓑ Cathedral Ledge
- Ⓒ Conway Scenic Railroad
- Ⓓ Crawford Notch State Park

Franconia Notch State Park:

- Ⓔ Basin
- Ⓕ Cannon Mountain Ski Area
- Ⓖ Fantasy Farm
- Ⓗ Flume
- Ⓕ New England Ski Museum
- Ⓕ Old Man of the Mountain
- Ⓘ Profile Lake
- Ⓖ Whale's Tail

- Ⓙ Gondola Skyride
- Ⓚ Lost River
- Ⓙ Mount Washington
- Ⓛ Ruggles Mine
- Ⓜ Storyland

Note: Items with the same letter are located in the same town or area.

A PERFECT DAY IN THE WHITE MOUNTAINS

You'll need an early start to get the most out of your day. First, drive through Crawford Notch State Park to the Cog Railway depot and take the train to the top of Mount Washington. Then drive through Franconia Notch State Park, and hike the Flume Trail. After the Flume, take the scenic Kancamagus Highway heading east, and then travel north on Route 16 to North Conway or Jackson for a well-deserved dinner and night's rest.

SIGHTSEEING HIGHLIGHTS

★★★ **Franconia Notch State Park**—This park is in the heart of the White Mountain National Forest. Franconia Notch Parkway runs from **Cannon Mountain Ski Area** (603-823-5563) at the northern entrance to the park, south to Lincoln. Cannon operates an aerial tramway mid-May through October ($8 adults, $4 children ages 6 to 12). While at Cannon, you can also visit the **New England Ski Museum** (603-823-7177 or 800-639-4181) to learn more about the regional history of the sport. Details: The museum is open noon to 5 p.m. mid-May through mid-October, and again just after Christmas for the winter ski season; closed on Wednesdays. Admission is by donation.

The turnoff to **Old Man of the Mountain** is just after Cannon Mountain and Echo Lake. This portion of cliffs overlooking **Profile Lake** was so named because, from certain angles, erosion has given the granite the appearance of an old man. Nathaniel Hawthorne wrote about the famous formation in his short story, *The Great Stone Face*. The old man's profile is depicted on many of New Hampshire's highway signs.

Other highlights of the park include the **Basin** and the **Flume**. Swirling with water, the Basin is a natural pothole formed by Ice Age glaciers and mountain cascades. There is wheelchair access. Swimming is prohibited. A well-maintained bike path runs through this section of the park, and hiking trails abound. You may wish to hike one of the trails that leave from the Basin area—they're free and likely to be less crowded than the Flume Trail.

The Flume is a narrow, moss-covered granite gorge discovered in 1808 by Jesse Guernsey, a 93-year-old woman who was hoping to find a prime fishing spot. After hiking the Flume, you can return to the visitor's center or continue on the trail to view a waterfall and natural pool. Plan to spend about 1½ hours here if you decide to hike the entire loop. Although there are buses that can take you from the visitor's center halfway to the Flume, much of the arduous walking is beyond vehicle access. There is no handicapped access. The trail is refreshingly cool on hot summer days, but on brisk autumn days you may want to bring along an extra sweater or jacket. Details: Open 9 a.m. to 5 p.m. daily (until 5:30 p.m. July 4 through Labor Day) mid-May through late October. Admission is $6 adults, $3 ages 6 to 12.

In contrast to the park's natural attractions, a small amusement park, **Fantasy Farm**, and the **Whale's Tail** (603-745-8810), a water-park, are located on U.S. 3 just below the Flume. (half–full day)

★★★ **Mount Washington**—At 6,288 feet, this is the highest peak in the Northeast. On clear days the panoramas from points along the ascent and summit are unrivaled. On top are a weather station and complete tourist facilities. Even in July the peak's climate can be quite chilly, so be sure to bring warm clothing with you. The summit can be reached by the auto road in your own vehicle at a cost of $15 for car and driver, plus $6 for each additional adult and $4 for children ages 5 to 12. The auto road is open from mid-May to late October, weather permitting. However, you should not take those bumper stickers that read "This Car Climbed Mt. Washington" lightly; the climb to the top is not easy, even for an automobile in top-notch condition. Should you prefer not to put the wear and tear on your car, vans are available to take you up the mountain. Van trips are $20 for adults, $10 for children ages 5 to 12. After spending much of your vacation behind the wheel, you may find it a welcome relief to let a tour guide do the driving. There is also cog-railway service available from the other side of Mount Washington at Bretton Woods. The round-trip by rail costs $39 for adults and takes three hours.

Of course, many hikers try their luck at climbing the mountain. Should you wish to do so, you'll need a whole day. The information center across from the entrance to the auto road can suggest trails that are right for your ability. It is fairly easy for weary hikers to get rides back down the mountain from people who have taken the auto road. Camping shelters along the trail provide sanctuary for hikers.

For a different look at Mount Washington, take the **Gondola Skyride** at Wildcat Ski Area, which faces the mountain. Details: (800) 255-6439; open 10 a.m. to 4:30 p.m. weekends Memorial Day through late June, daily July through Columbus Day. Tickets are $8 adults, $4 ages 6 to 12. (2 hours–half day)

★★ **Crawford Notch State Park**—As you travel west from Glen on Route 302 through the park, you'll pass two small waterfalls, the Silver and Flume Cascades, that slither rather than plunge down the mountainside. Both have parking areas. The better mountain view is from the Flume Cascade parking lot. The park's information center is located in a colorful train station near Twin Mountain.

As you near Twin Mountain, there is a striking view of the Mount Washington Hotel at Bretton Woods. Built in 1902, the hotel was designed to entice the privileged set, and it still holds a commanding presence over the valley. Visitors came by the trainload to visit the hotel in its heyday. Today Bretton Woods is a thriving cross-country ski mecca.

The entrance to the **Cog Railway** that climbs Mount Washington is just beyond the hotel. In the height of summer, trains run every hour on the hour until late afternoon and beginning as early as 8 a.m. Details: Call (800) 922-8825 or (603) 846-5404 for reservations and a departure schedule. The train runs from early May to mid-October. The three-hour round-trip to the summit costs $39 for adults; senior discounts and children's fares are available. The railway recommends purchasing tickets in advance. (1 hour–half day)

★ **Attitash Ski Area**—Four miles west of the junction of U.S. 302 and Route 16, this ski area in Bartlett operates an alpine slide, water park, a chairlift ride, and mountain bike trails during summer. Details: (603) 374-2368. (1–3 hours)

★ **Cathedral Ledge**—Just a few minutes from the center of North Conway, the ledge draws throngs of rock climbers and spectators alike. You'll probably find this daring sport fascinating to watch if you've never witnessed it firsthand. Climbers can be observed from below, or you can drive up the road to the top of the ledge and congratulate the climbers as they reach their goal. (½ hour)

Kancamagus Highway

★ **Conway Scenic Railroad**—The railroad runs out of North Conway's picturesque depot, which was built in 1874. Three separate excursions are available—one travels south along the Saco River to Conway (55 minutes round-trip), the second travels west to Bartlett (1¾ hours round-trip), and the third takes you all the way to the top of Crawford Notch and back (almost 5 hours round-trip). Details: Trains depart daily mid-May through October, weekends mid-April through mid-May, Thanksgiving weekend, and weekends November through Christmas. In July and August the Sunset Special leaves on Tuesday, Wednesday, Thursday, and Saturday nights at 6:15 p.m., and includes dinner ($39.95 adults, $27.95 children). Tickets for the Conway excursion are $8 adults, $5.50 ages 4 to 12; tickets for the Bartlett run are $13.50 adults, $8.50 ages 4 to 12; and the round-trip to Crawford Notch is $31.95 adults, $16.95 ages 4 to 12, $3 under age 4. First-class tickets for rides on the Gertrude Emma, a 92-year-old restored parlor car, are more expensive. Call (603) 356-5251 or (800) 232-5251 for more information. (1–5 hours)

★ **Lost River**—Moss-covered boulders and fragrant pine trees cling to the sides of this river gorge off Route 112 west of North Woodstock. Natural phenomena along the boardwalked trail have been given picturesque names such as Guillotine Rock, the Lemon Squeezer, and the Hall of Ships. For those who aren't subject to claustrophobia, there are several caves to explore. Details: (603) 745-8031; open mid-May through mid-October 9 a.m. to 5 p.m. (until 6 p.m. in July and August); the last tickets are sold one hour before closing. (1–1½ hours)

★ **Ruggles Mine**—Rock collectors may want to stop here. The mine first opened in 1803 and is known for its vast supply of mica. Visitors are allowed to take home mineral samples that they collect. Details: Near Grafton off U.S. 4 between Interstate 93 and White River Junction; (603) 523-4275; open 9 a.m. to 5 p.m. weekends only mid-May through mid-June, daily mid-June through mid-October. Admission is $12 adults, $5 ages 4 to 11. (1 hour)

★ **Storyland**—Storybook characters come to life in this amusement park that's a favorite of youngsters. Details: Route 16 in Glen; (603) 383-4293; open 9 a.m. to 6 p.m. daily Father's Day to Labor Day, 10 a.m. to 5 p.m. weekends only Labor Day through Columbus Day. Admission to all rides and performances is $16 per person, under age 4 free. (2 hours)

FITNESS AND RECREATION

Adventurous travelers may find a river trip to their liking. **Saco Bound** (Box 119, Center Conway, NH 03813; 603-447-3801) operates a variety of white-water and flat-water river trips by raft or canoe. Trips range in length from several hours to several days. Many rock climbers test their skills at Cathedral Ledge just outside North Conway (see Sightseeing Highlights). After climbing, you can cool off with a swim at neighboring **Echo Lake State Park**. There's also a mountain-stream swimming hole in nearby Jackson. Just follow the signs from Jackson toward the Eagle Mountain House. The swimming hole is about halfway up the hill on the right.

The White Mountains are home to many outstanding ski areas. **Black Mountain** (603-383-4490) in Jackson and **Mount Cranmore** (603-356-5543) in North Conway are good family mountains since they cater to all levels of ability. Mount Cranmore's skimobile tramway is a godsend to those scared of chairlifts. **Attitash** (603-374-2368 or 800-862-1600) in Bartlett, **Wildcat** (603-466-3326 or 800-255-6439) opposite the Mount Washington Auto Road, **Cannon** (603-823-5563 or 800-552-1234) in Franconia, and **Loon Mountain** (603-745-8111) in Lincoln all offer experienced skiers more of a challenge. Wildcat and Loon both have gondolas, and Cannon operates an aerial tramway. **Bretton Woods** (603-278-5000) near the cog railway to the top of Mount Washington is best known for its cross-country trails. The town of Jackson is also a major cross-country center; contact the Jackson Ski Touring Foundation at (603) 383-9355 for more information. **Tuckerman's Ravine** at Pinkham Notch is only for the most adventurous and expert skiers. There are no lifts so skiers must hike 2½ miles. Check with the White Mountain National Forest Service (603-466-2725) before tackling the ravine. Because of avalanche danger in winter, only spring skiing is allowed in the ravine.

During summer, mountain bikers can take chairlifts up to trails at Attitash, Bretton Woods, Loon, and Mount Cranmore ski areas. While many bicyclists enjoy riding through the national forest, you should check with a ranger station before embarking on backcountry trails—some trails are off-limits to mountain bikes.

Mount Cranmore's recreation center in North Conway has both indoor and outdoor tennis, an indoor swimming pool, and a climbing wall. Call (603) 356-5544 for information.

FOOD

There is fine dining on New England fare in Jackson at the **Eagle Mountain House** (603-383-9111). Moderately priced meals can be had at the **Thompson House Eatery** (603-383-9341) right in the center of town; dinner entrées range from $8.95 to $16.95, and fresh seafood specials are often available. Not too far from Jackson, the **Bernerhof Inn** (U.S. 302 west in Glen, just 2 miles from the Route 16 intersection; 603-383-4414 or 800-548-8007) serves appetizing European dishes with a Swiss flair (including Wiener schnitzel, veau Zurichoise, and salmon picatta á la Suisse), and also has accommodations for overnight guests. Dinner entrées range in price from $16.95 to $22.95, and room rates start at $90 for two.

In North Conway, just across from the railroad depot on Main Street, **Horsefeathers** (603-356-6862) offers a menu ranging from deluxe burgers to pasta and chicken entrées. The tavern atmosphere is lively, and prices are reasonable. Also in North Conway's center, **Bellini's** (Seavey Street, 1 block up from Main Street; 603-356-7000) serves Italian specialties including homemade pastas prepared in delicious combinations. Try the fettucini with prosciutto, spinach, and mushrooms in a light cream sauce. If you have room, their desserts are also scrumptious. Dinner entrées start at $10.

LODGING

A covered bridge leads to the town of Jackson, which lies between North Conway and Mount Washington. Although Jackson is home to Black Mountain downhill ski area, the town is best known as a cross-country skiers' haven. There are plenty of cozy bed and breakfasts around to care for tired winter and summer visitors alike. It is central enough to be a good base for sightseeing in the White Mountains but tends to be a little quieter and less crowded than neighboring North Conway. The **Eagle Mountain House** (800-966-5779 or 603-383-9111) in Jackson is a charming resort on a quiet country road with beautiful mountain views. The rooms in the restored hotel are comfortably elegant and start around $69 during low-season and climb up to $149 during the summer and fall-foliage seasons. Tennis, golf, and swimming are all available at the resort as well. Follow signs up Carter Notch Road from the center of Jackson.

The **Wentworth** (603-383-9700 or 800-637-0013), right in the

WHITE MOUNTAINS

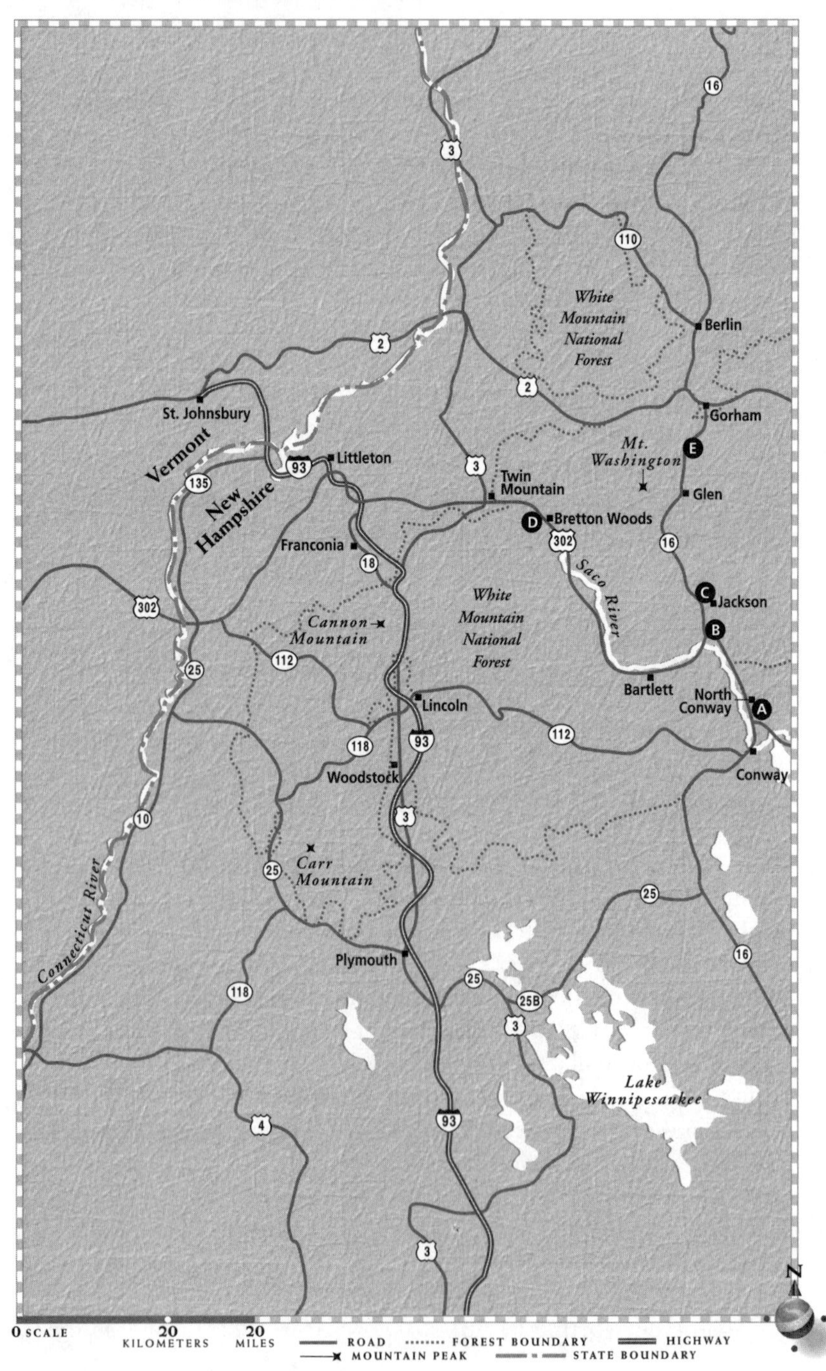

Food

- Ⓐ Bellini's
- Ⓑ Bernerhof Inn
- Ⓒ Eagle Mountain House
- Ⓐ Horsefeathers
- Ⓒ Thompson House Eatery

Lodging

- Ⓐ Cranmore Inn
- Ⓒ Eagle Mountain House
- Ⓒ Inn at Thorn Hill
- Ⓓ Mount Washington Hotel & Resort

Lodging *(continued)*

- Ⓐ Scottish Lion
- Ⓒ Wentworth
- Ⓐ White Trellis Motel

Camping

- Ⓔ Dolly Copp Campground
- Ⓑ Glen Ellis Family Campground

Note: Items with the same letter are located in the same town or area.

heart of Jackson, has been welcoming guests for over a century. Golfers will enjoy the Wentworth's golf course. Rates, which start at $150 for two, include a country breakfast and a five-course dinner in the candlelit dining room. Golf packages are also available. The **Inn at Thorn Hill** (603-383-4242 or 800-289-8990), in a home designed by renowned architect Stanford White, is another lovely lodging option in Jackson village. Rooms are tastefully decorated with Victorian furnishings, and rates starting at $75 per person include lodging, a hearty breakfast, and a gourmet evening meal.

The **Cranmore Inn** (603-356-5502 or 800-526-5502), only 1 block from the center of North Conway on Kearsarge Street, is more reasonably priced than many other inns in town yet offers the same services. A comfortable room for two costs from $48 to $86 per night (depending on the season), and includes an ample breakfast in the inn's sunny breakfast room. There are several sitting rooms and a swimming pool on the premises. Mount Cranmore ski area is only five minutes away.

Route 16 in North Conway is lined with numerous inns and

motels, but rooms can become scarce at the height of fall foliage and on big ski weekends. If you're calling ahead, try the **Scottish Lion** (603-356-6381 or 888-356-4945). The rooms are pleasant, meals have a Scottish slant, and there is a lively pub in which to unwind after a long day of sightseeing or skiing. Rooms including a full breakfast start at $59 in low-season and run up to $110 during peak times. The inn also operates a Scottish import shop next door. The **White Trellis Motel** (603-356-2492), which has pleasant mountain views, makes more of an effort than most to create an attractive atmosphere with flowering window boxes and ivy-covered trellises. Doubles start at $45. You might also want to try booking a room through the Mount Washington Valley Chamber of Commerce Lodging Bureau (603-356-3171 or 800-367-3364).

If you prefer full resort amenities and a dramatic setting to an in-town location, then the 95-year-old **Mount Washington Hotel & Resort** (603-278-1000 or 800-258-0330) in Bretton Woods more than fits the bill. Prominently situated at the base of the Presidential Range, the massive white hotel with its bright red roof and 900-foot-long veranda is hard to miss. Activities at the resort include golf, tennis, and swimming, and there's a supervised day camp available for families traveling with children. Room rates, which include a full dinner and breakfast, start at $185 for two people midweek and $225 on weekends. Call for reservations and information on special packages.

CAMPING

Dolly Copp Campground (named for an innkeeper who left her husband of 50 years by announcing at a party that "fifty years is long enough for any woman to live with one man") is a national forest campground with 176 sites near the base of Mount Washington off Route 16, 6 miles south of Gorham. Reservations can be made by calling (800) 280-CAMP. If you arrive without a reservation, sites are assigned on a first-come, first-served basis. RVs are allowed, but hot showers and electrical hookups are not available. Sites cost about $12 per night. The campground is open from mid-May to late September.

Glen Ellis Family Campground, on U.S. 302 just west of the Route 16 junction, is convenient to Jackson, North Conway, and area travel routes. If you are low on provisions, restock at the supermarket next to the entrance. The campground itself has complete sanitary and recreational facilities. Sites start at $16 per night, and some are adjacent to the Saco River. The campground operates from Memorial Day to Columbus Day, and July is the busiest month. Call (603) 383-4567 for information in-season or (603) 539-2860 for inquiries during the winter.

ARTS AND ENTERTAINMENT

The **Eastern Slope Playhouse** next door to the Eastern Slope Inn on Main Street in North Conway presents professional musical productions during the summer months. Call (603) 356-5776 for schedule and ticket information.

SHOPPING

To the dismay of locals who've seen their once quiet village become snarled with traffic, North Conway has become a center for factory outlet stores in recent years. Visiting shoppers now clog Route 16 as they look for bargains. If you enjoy outlet shopping, Calvin Klein, Anne Klein, and OshKosh B'Gosh are among the outlets you'll find here.

Scenic Route: Kancamagus Highway

The Kancamagus Highway (Route 112), which runs from Conway to the Pemigewasset River at Lincoln, is a well-known scenic route in the White Mountains (and the only federally designated scenic byway in northern New England). The 34-mile route, which is flanked by mountains up to 4,500 feet high, is a pretty drive year-round but especially during fall foliage.

Named for an Indian chief and paved since 1964, the highway is dotted with scenic overlooks, picnic areas, and multiple trailheads. Some of the more popular hikes include the half-hour **Rail 'n' River Trail**, which begins at the Passaconaway Historic Site near the Jigger Johnson Campground, the 3.5-mile hike to **Greeley Ponds** (the trail begins 9.5 miles east of Lincoln), and the 2.5-mile **Boulder Loop Trail**, which starts at the Covered Bridge Campground. Just outside Lincoln is **Loon Mountain** with downhill skiing, a gondola skyride, and mountain biking.

KANCAMAGUS HIGHWAY

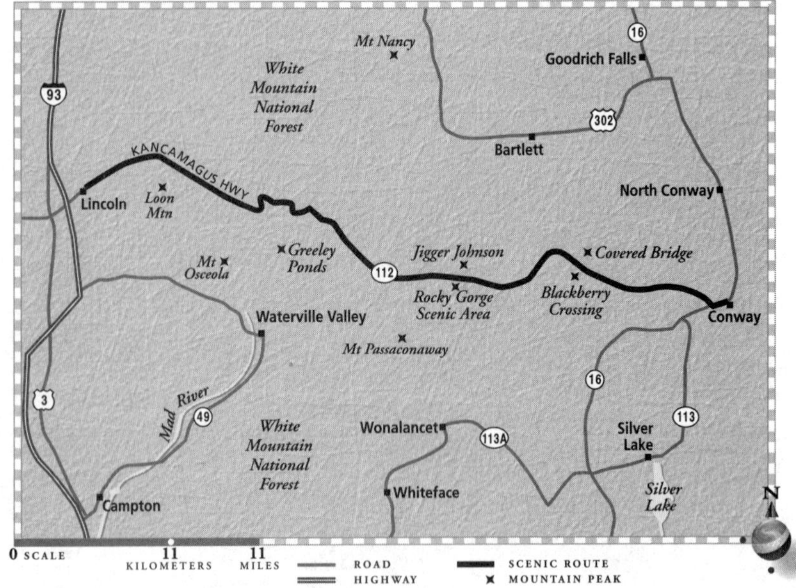

12 NEW HAMPSHIRE LAKES

Twenty-five miles in length and twelve miles in width, Winnipesaukee is New Hampshire's largest lake. Neighboring Squam Lake, second largest, is known for its beauty, resident loons, and the movie *On Golden Pond*, which was filmed on the lake and earned its stars, Henry Fonda and Katharine Hepburn, Oscars in 1981. Collectively, Winnipesaukee, Squam, and a handful much smaller tarns make up the New Hampshire lakes region.

Since the land around Squam Lake is primarily privately owned, there is limited public access there. So most visitors to the area spend their time on Winnipesaukee. The town of Weirs Beach is perhaps the most touristy spot on Winnipesaukee, complete with a honky-tonk boardwalk and a resort-style beach. Despite its commercial nature, Weirs Beach does provide beautiful views of the lake, and boat excursions leave from there often.

Other towns that border Winnipesaukee include Meredith at the north end, offering fine views down the length of the lake, and Wolfeboro on the east side, claiming to be the oldest summer resort in America. For a bird's-eye view of the lake and beyond, you can visit the Castle in the Clouds in Moultonboro. Tiny Center Sandwich, north of Winnipesaukee and east of Squam, has a number of charming nineteenth-century structures, while Tamworth, almost at the Maine border, is home to the Barnstormers summer stock theater.

NEW HAMPSHIRE LAKES

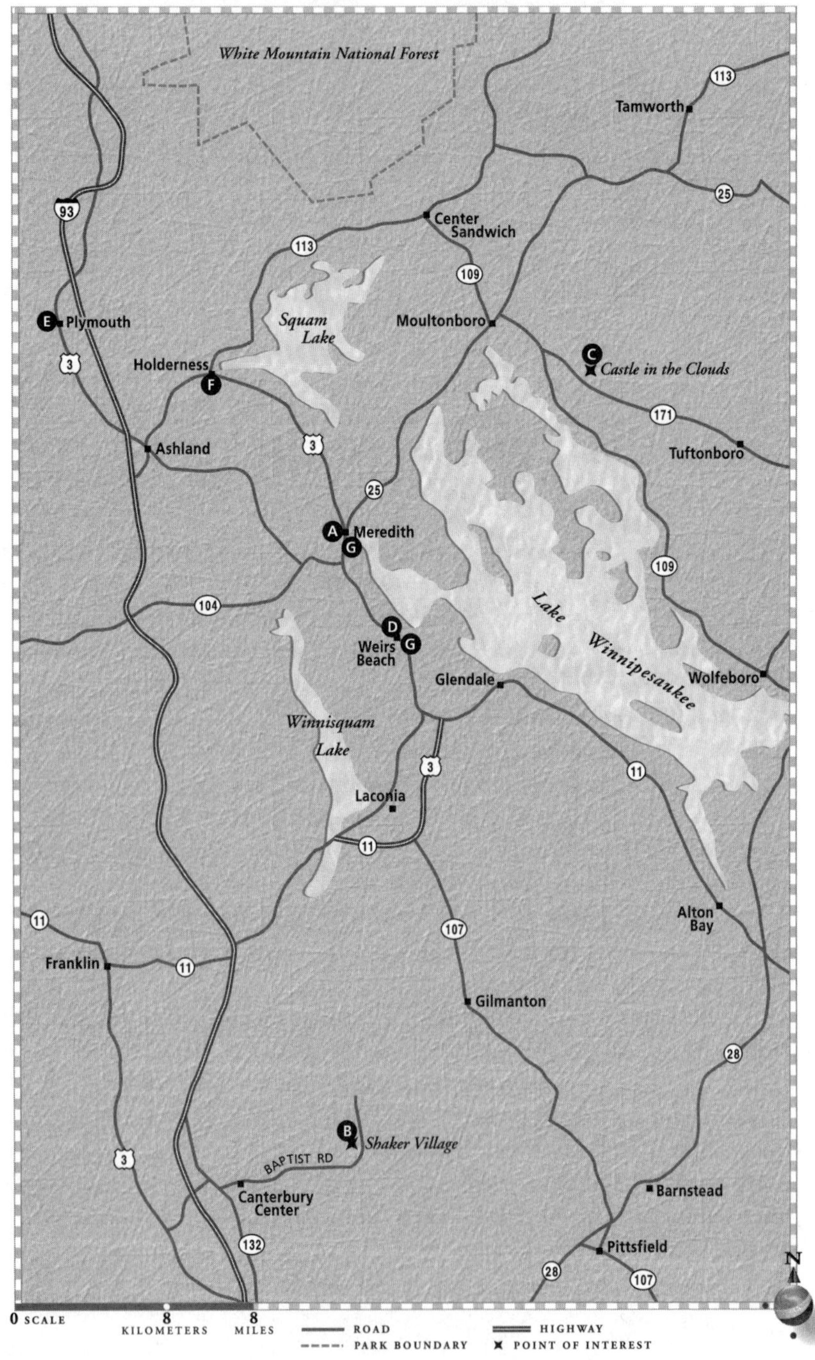

Sights

- **A** **Annalee's Gift Shop and Doll Museum**
- **B** **Canterbury Shaker Village**
- **C** **Castle Springs**
- **D** **Lake Winnipesaukee Cruises**
- **E** **Polar Caves**
- **F** **Science Center of New Hampshire**
- **F** **Squam Lake Tours**
- **G** **Winnipesaukee Railroad**

Note: Items with the same letter are located in the same town or area.

A PERFECT DAY IN THE LAKES REGION

Start your day south of Winnipesaukee in Canterbury and tour the Shaker village there. Drive to Ellacoya State Beach south of Glendale on the southwestern shore of Winnipesaukee for a picnic lunch and a swim. Then head to Weirs Beach and take a cruise on the lake. Afterward, take in a theatrical performance at the Barnstormers Theater in Tamworth.

SIGHTSEEING HIGHLIGHTS

★★ **Canterbury Shaker Village**—At this hilltop village in the pretty New Hampshire countryside, far removed from the rest of the world, you can tour 24 buildings left by the Shakers, a religious sect that had about 6,000 members nationwide at its peak in the mid-1800s. Today the Shaker population has dwindled to seven. The reason the Shakers have not flourished is not for lack of industry—they practice celibacy. Unlike other religious groups who eschew modern conveniences, the Shakers were actually quite remarkable inventors. At the village you can see the washing machine they invented in 1858 that could handle up to four loads of laundry at once, as well as the unique drying system they created. They used knitting machines to mass-produce sweaters which they then sold to the army and Ivy League schools (hence the "Shaker sweater"), and developed special tips for chair legs so that you could tilt back in your chair without the legs ever leaving the ground. The 90-minute guided tour also visits the 1792 meeting house with its "separate but equal" entrances for men and women, and the one-room schoolhouse where the Shaker (often adopted orphans) and local children were taught.

The Creamery restaurant in the village serves lunch from 11:30 a.m. to 2:30 p.m. daily, and offers Shaker dinners by candlelight on weekends. Details: 288 Shaker Road in Canterbury; (603) 783-9511; open 10 a.m. to 5 p.m. daily May through October, weekends in November, December, and April. Admission is $8.50 adults, $4 ages 6 to 15. (2 hours)

★★ **Lake Winnipesaukee Cruises**—You can cruise Winnipesaukee on the 230-foot-long *M/S Mount Washington* late May through late October. Evening Moonlight Dinner/Dance Cruises are available at the height of the summer season. Call for departure times and ticket information. Details: Cruises leave from Weirs Beach, (603) 366-2628. Day cruises are about $15 adults, $7 children (kids under 4 are free with an adult). Dinner cruises are $25 to $39 per person. (3–4 hours)

★★ **Squam Lake Tours**—Two Holderness-based companies offer guided cruises of Squam Lake that take you to see Church Island, the lake's renowned loons, and where the movie *On Golden Pond* was filmed. Details: (603) 279-4405 or (603) 968-7577 for departure schedule and ticket information. Both companies charge about $10 adults, $5 children. (2 hours)

★ **Castle Springs**—This is somewhat of a commercial operation as it is owned by the Castle Springs bottled water company. The operation consists of a hilltop stone mansion overlooking Winnipesaukee, a tram ride to the natural source of the company's spring water, and tours of the water bottling plant and Castle Springs' microbrewery. Details: Route 171 in Moultonboro; (603) 476-2512 or (800)-729-2468; open 9 a.m. to 5 p.m. weekends only early May through early June, daily early June through Labor Day; open 9 a.m. to 4 p.m. Labor Day through mid-October. Admission, which includes a tour of the 1910 mansion and a tram ride, is $10 adults, $9 seniors, $7 children over 10, free for ages 10 and under. Horseback riding on the 5,000-acre grounds costs $25 for one hour. (2 hours)

★ **Science Center of New Hampshire**—Otters, fox, deer, bears, and bald eagles are a few the animals you'll see along the trails at this 200-

acre nature center. There's also an aviary and an activities center for children. In the summer and early fall you can take a nature cruise on Squam Lake. Details: Route 113 in Holderness; (603) 968-7194; open 9:30 a.m. to 4:30 p.m. daily May through October. Admission is $6 adults, $4 children. (1–2 hours)

★ **Winnipesaukee Railroad**—Take a lakeside scenic rail trip in a restored historic railroad car. Excursions leave from Weirs Beach and Meredith. Details: (603) 279-5253. The railroad operates on weekends only Memorial Day through late June, then daily through Labor Day, and weekends only Labor Day through fall foliage. Tickets that allow you to get on and off the train as many times as you'd like are about $8.50 for adults, $6.50 for children ages 4 to 11. There are also special dinner and fall foliage excursions. (2 hours)

Annalee's Gift Shop and Doll Museum—Several hundred felt dolls created by doll maker Annalee Thorndike are on display in the museum. Annalee has been creating the posable dolls since 1934, and now must employ many other craftspeople to help her keep up with the demand for dolls. Details: Route 104 in Meredith; (603) 279-6542 or (800) 433-6557; the museum is open daily Memorial Day through October; the gift shop is open year-round. Admission is free. (½ hour)

Polar Caves—You can tour six glacial caves at this park. Details: Route 25 in Plymouth; (603) 536-1888 or (800) 273-1886; open 9 a.m. to 5 p.m. daily early May through mid-October. Admission is $9 adults, $4.50 ages 6 to 12. (1 hour)

FITNESS AND RECREATION

If you'd like to venture out on Winnipesaukee on your own power, there are a number of outdoor adventure outfitters located in Wolfeboro who can rent you the equipment needed to participate in the sport of your choice. **Winnipesaukee Kayak Company** (1 Bay Street, 603-569-9926) rents kayaks and can provide instruction. **Dive Winnipesaukee** (603-569-8080) rents sailboats, canoes, windsurfers, tubes, and Jet Skis, and also teaches scuba diving. Sport fishermen can rent fully equipped fishing boats from **Gadabout Golder Guide Service** (79 Middleton Road, 603-569-6426).

FOOD AND LODGING

Meredith, at the northwestern tip of Winnipesaukee, is a fairly central place to base yourself for the lakes region. Rooms at the **Inn at Bay Point**, which range from $150 in low-season up to $250 in high-season, have balconies with lovely views of the lake and the mountains in the distance. Rooms at the inn's sister property, the **Inn at Mill Falls** (603-279-7006 or 800-622-MILL), are not as luxurious and do not have views, but they are still comfortable. They're also less expensive, starting at $70 per night. The inn has an indoor pool, and in some rooms you can hear the 40-foot waterfall that once powered the old mill next door. Now the mill houses gift shops and **Giuseppe's** (603-279-3313), a friendly, casual spot with live musical entertainment and Italian cuisine at reasonable prices ($4.95–$15.95). Children's portions and prices are available. A short drive from the inn, at the junction of Routes 4 and 104, is the enormous **Hart's Turkey Farm** (603-279-6212), serving home-style meals and specializing in turkey. The restaurant is family oriented and a children's menu is available.

Farther south, in Glendale below Weirs Beach, the **Inn at Smith Cove** (603-293-1111) offers pleasant bed-and-breakfast accommodations overlooking a boat-filled cove on the lake. Rates start at $80 per night for a double room and breakfast for two.

On the opposite side of the lake, the **Wolfeboro Inn** (800-451-2389 or 603-569-3016) in Wolfeboro has its own beach and a supply of rowboats. The inn has just over 40 guest rooms; some are located in the original 1812 inn and some are in a newer wing with lake views. The inn's dining room serves New England cuisine while the casual Wolfe's Tavern serves pub fare and has a good beer selection. A lake cruise in the inn's own diesel-powered excursion boat is included in the room rate of $80 to $210.

The **Corner House Inn** (603-284-6219), in the quiet village of Center Sandwich just a few miles from Squam Lake, has been in continuous operation for over a century. The three guest rooms are larger than typical bed-and-breakfast rooms, hold two beds each, and have Victorian antiques, canopy beds, and handmade quilts. A full breakfast is included in the room rate of $80 for two people. The dining room, which opens to the public for lunch and dinner, serves homemade soups, sandwiches, and salads at noon, and dishes such as brandied peach duckling and lobster and scallop pie in the evening ($10.95–$19.95).

Tamworth, to the northeast of the lakes region and a little off the beaten path, is worth a visit to see a production at the Barnstormers Theater. The **Tamworth Inn** (800-NH-2-RELAX), just down the street from the theater, is the most convenient lodging to the Barnstormers. Rooms at the inn have country furnishings, and out back there's a swimming pool and an expansive lawn that leads to the Swift River. Rates for two including breakfast start at $95, and range from $120 to $145 including breakfast and dinner. Roast leg of lamb, duckling, and pork tenderloin are a few of the dinner offerings, and profiteroles are the inn's dessert specialty.

CAMPING

Ellacoya State Park (603-271-3628), on the lake in Gilford, has 38 RV campsites and a small beach. Sites, including hookups, cost $30 per night. **White Lake State Park** (603-271-3627) on Route 16 in Tamworth has 200 campsites, showers, a store, and a beach on the small lake. Sites go for $15 to $20 and canoe rentals are available. The campground is open May through October. **Clearwater Campground** (603-279-7761 or 800-848-0328) off Route 104 in Meredith has both tent and RV sites, as well as showers, laundry facilities, and a sandy beach. They also have boats for rent for use on lake Pemigewasset. If you're traveling with kids, they might enjoy camping at **Yogi Bear's Jellystone Park** (603-968-9000) on Route 132N in Ashland. In addition to all the standard amenities, the family camping resort offers miniature golf, a video arcade, canoes, rowboats, kayaks, and a snack bar.

ARTS AND ENTERTAINMENT

For almost 70 years the **Barnstormers Theater** in Tamworth has been staging professional theatrical productions during the summer. Past productions have ranged from *The Fantasticks* to *Uncle Vanya*. Tickets go for under $20. Call the box office at (603) 323-8500 for tickets and a current schedule. The **New Hampshire Music Festival** (603-524-1000) sponsors a variety of concerts throughout the summer in several locations in the lakes region. Broadway shows take center stage at the **Lakes Region Summer Theatre** (603-279-9933 or 800-643-9993) on Route 25 in Meredith. The season runs June through September.

For those who like their entertainment fast and exciting, the

NEW HAMPSHIRE LAKES

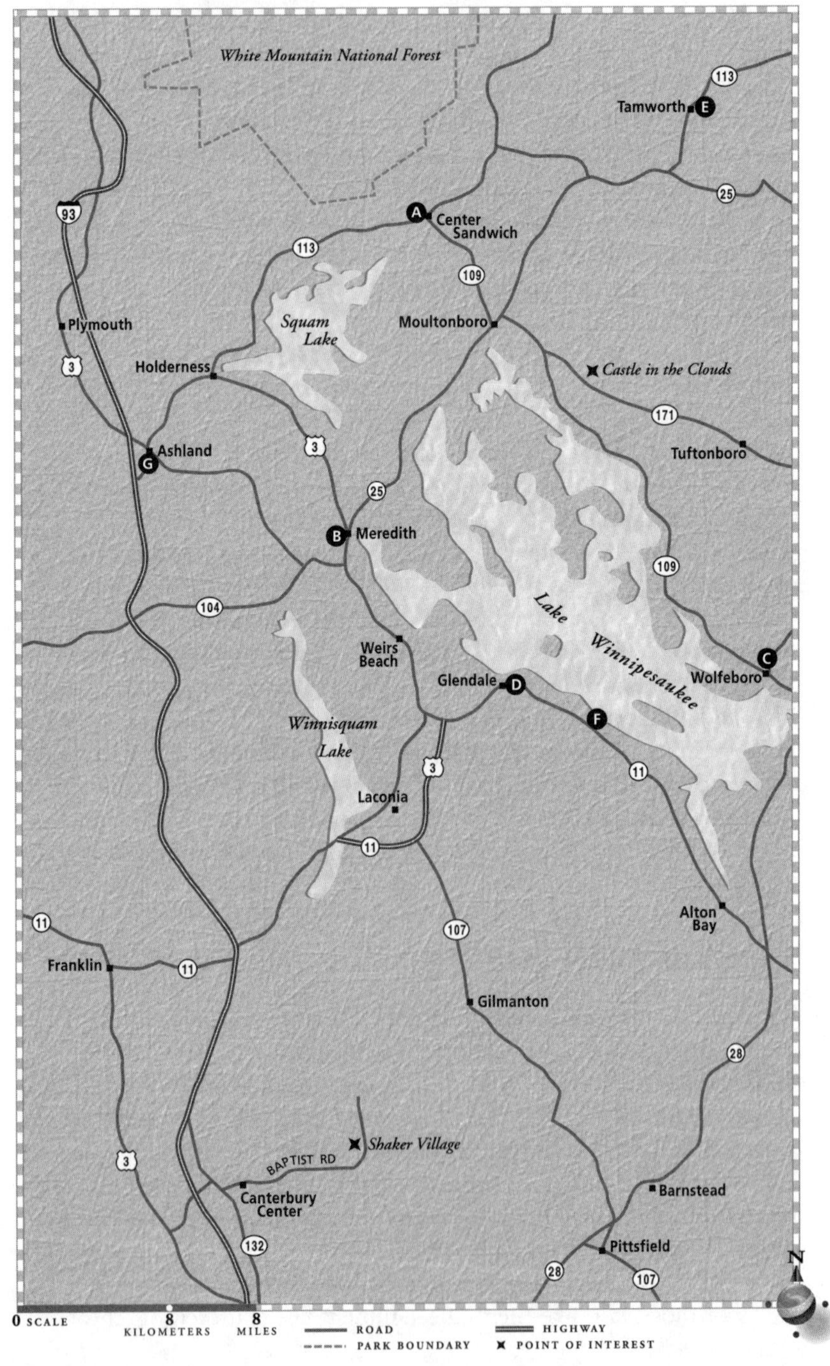

White Mountain National Forest
Tamworth
E
113
25
93
A
Center Sandwich
113
109
Squam Lake
Plymouth
Moultonboro
3
Holderness
Castle in the Clouds
171
Tuftonboro
Ashland
G
3
25
B
Meredith
109
104
Lake Winnipesaukee
Weirs Beach
C
Wolfeboro
Glendale
D
F
Winnisquam Lake
3
11
Laconia
11
Alton Bay
11
107
Franklin
11
Gilmanton
28
Shaker Village
BAPTIST RD
3
Canterbury Center
Barnstead
132
Pittsfield
28
107
N
0 SCALE
8 KILOMETERS
8 MILES
ROAD
PARK BOUNDARY
HIGHWAY
POINT OF INTEREST

Food

- Ⓐ Corner House Inn
- Ⓑ Giuseppe's
- Ⓑ Hart's Turkey Farm
- Ⓒ Wolfeboro Inn

Lodging

- Ⓐ Corner House Inn
- Ⓑ Inn at Bay Point
- Ⓑ Inn at Mill Falls

Lodging *(continued)*

- Ⓓ Inn at Smith Cove
- Ⓔ Tamworth Inn
- Ⓒ Wolfeboro Inn

Camping

- Ⓑ Clearwater Campgound
- Ⓕ Ellacoya State Park
- Ⓔ White Lake State Park
- Ⓖ Yogi Bear's Jellystone Park

Note: Items with the same letter are located in the same town or area.

Lakes Region Greyhound Park (603-267-7778 or 800-240-DOGS) on Route 106 in Belmont has live dog racing, as well as simulcast Thoroughbred, harness, and dog races from other tracks around the country. **New Hampshire International Speedway** (603-783-4931) in Loudon has a number of NASCAR and Indy League events each year as well as motorcycle racing.

SHOPPING

For outlet shopping there is the **Lakes Region Factory Stores** (800-832-3590) shopping center in Tilton. However, many of the notable stores in the area are crafts oriented. For example, there's the **Keepsake Quilting** store (603-253-4026) on Route 25B in Centre Harbor which claims to be the largest quilt shop in America. It offers shoppers the choice of some 6,000 bolts of fabric. **Basket World** (603-366-5585 or 800-528-3304) on Route 3 in Weirs Beach has handmade baskets and wicker furniture. Some of the highest quality crafts made by New Hampshire potters, jewelers, artists, weavers, and woodworkers can be found in the seven **League of New Hampshire Craftsmen** shops located around the state. Three of the stores can be found in the lakes region: There's a store on the village green in Center Sandwich

(603-284-6831), another at 64 Center Street in Wolfeboro Falls (603-569-3309), and a third on Route 3 in Meredith (603-279-7920). The **Mills Falls Market Place** adjacent to the lake in Meredith has 15 shops in and around a nineteenth-century mill. They include the **Innisfree Bookshop** (603-279-3905) with a good selection of children's books; **Oglethorpe** (603-279-9909), a fine arts and crafts gallery; and the **Catalog Outlet Store** (603-279-6006). The **Old Country Store**, which has been operating in the center of Moltonboro since 1781, is worth a stop if you've always wanted to see a typical New England country store complete with penny candy and hardware.

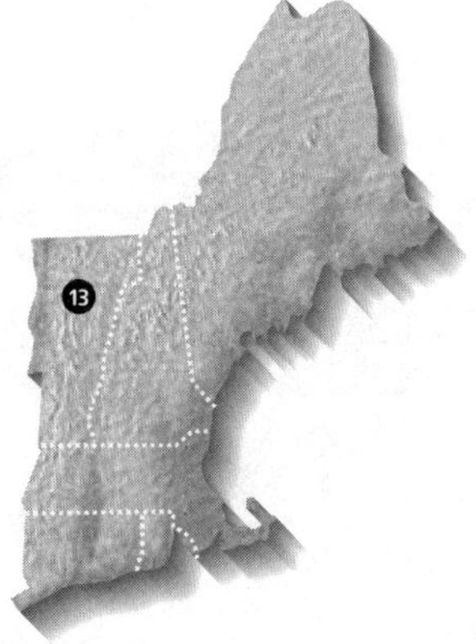

13
NORTHERN VERMONT

Almost more than any other northeastern state, Vermont embodies the spirit of New England that many travelers hope to discover when they visit this part of the United States. Picture-perfect town greens, winding river valleys, and the beautiful Green Mountains that turn gentle pastel shades at sunset all seem nearly unspoiled by modern development.

Northern Vermont also offers the appealing city of Burlington (Vermont's largest city, although small by comparison to most), located on the shores of Lake Champlain and home to the University of Vermont. Just south of Burlington is the Shelburne Museum—one of the nation's best American folk art museums.

Northern Vermont has some of the most distinctive scenery in the state, ranging from the relatively low elevation of 95 feet above sea level at Lake Champlain to the state's highest point of 4,393 feet atop Mount Mansfield. Majestic Mount Mansfield is the focal point of Stowe—Northern Vermont's premier ski resort and a charming town in its own right. ◪

NORTHERN VERMONT

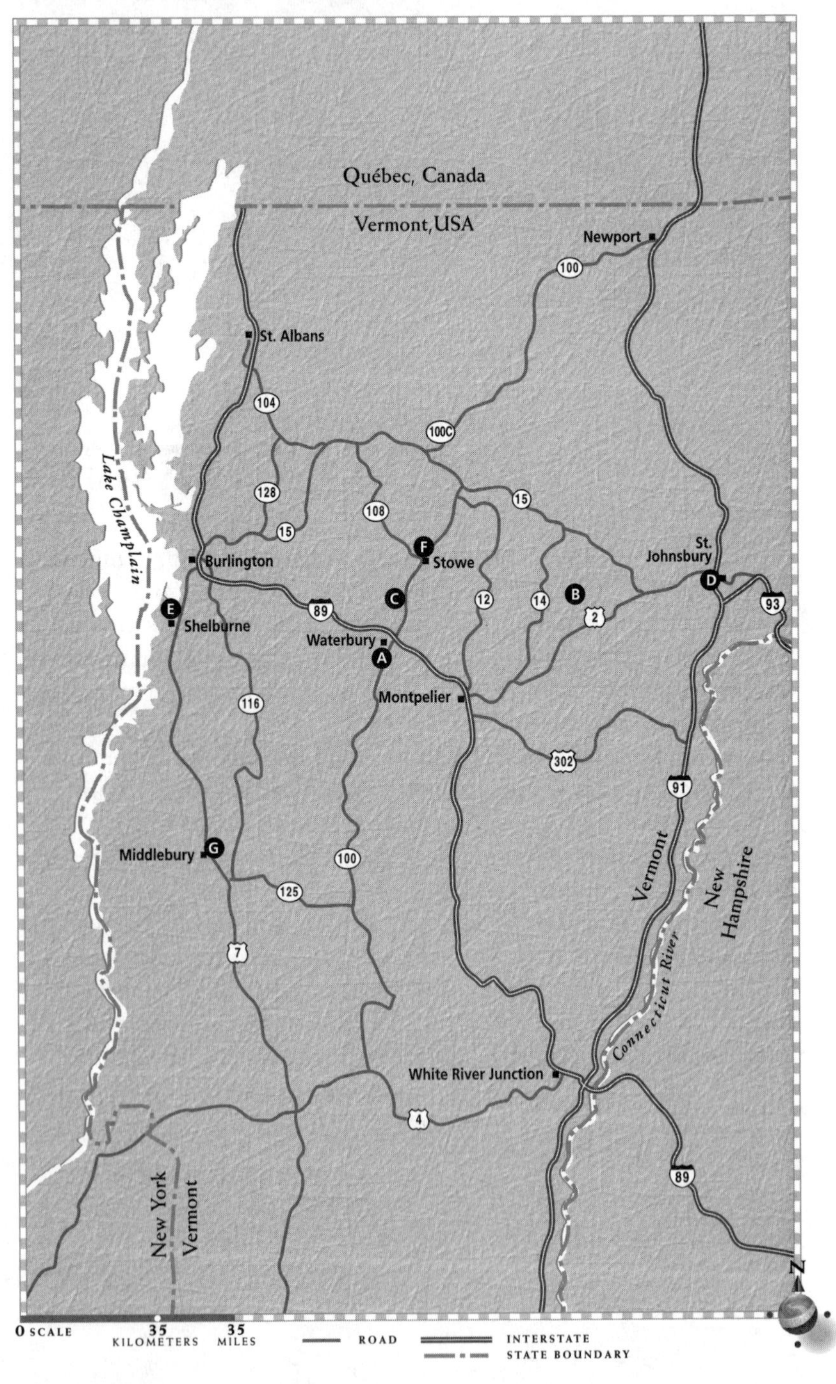

Québec, Canada
Vermont, USA
Newport
100
St. Albans
104
100C
Lake Champlain
128
108
15
15
F
Stowe
St. Johnsbury
Burlington
D
93
E
Shelburne
89
C
12
14
B
2
Waterbury
A
Montpelier
116
302
91
Middlebury
G
100
125
Vermont
New Hampshire
Connecticut River
7
White River Junction
4
89
New York
Vermont
N
0 SCALE
35 KILOMETERS
35 MILES
ROAD
INTERSTATE
STATE BOUNDARY

Sights

- Ⓐ Ben & Jerry's Ice Cream Factory
- Ⓑ Cabot Factory Tour
- Ⓒ Cold Hollow Cider Mill
- Ⓓ Maple Grove Museum and Factory
- Ⓔ Shelburne Museum
- Ⓕ Stowe Mountain Resort

Food

- Ⓕ Miguel's Stowe Away
- Ⓖ Otter Creek Bakery
- Ⓕ Whip Bar & Grill

Lodging

- Ⓕ Green Mountain Inn
- Ⓔ Inn at Shelburne Farms
- Ⓖ Middlebury Inn
- Ⓕ Topnotch Resort and Spa
- Ⓕ Trapp Family Lodge

Note: Items with the same letter are located in the same town or area.

A PERFECT DAY IN NORTHERN VERMONT

There are two quite different but very enjoyable days that might qualify for "a perfect day in Northern Vermont." One is to spend the day in nature by hiking (or skiing if you visit in winter) in the Stowe area, and perhaps sneaking off to the Ben & Jerry's factory for a tour and samples. The other is to visit the Shelburne Museum, and afterward, if there's time, take a boat ride on Lake Champlain or window shop in downtown Burlington.

SIGHTSEEING HIGHLIGHTS

★★★ **Shelburne Museum**—Generally considered to have one of the country's best collections of Early American antiques and folk art, this delightful museum covers 45 acres and has 37 period homes housing its collection of art, china, silver, scrimshaw, Native American artifacts, carousel animals, decoys, weathervanes, ship figureheads, and antique toys and dolls. Some of the unique structures include a lighthouse, a round barn, a side-wheeler boat called the SS *Ticonderoga*, and a private railroad car. Built in the late 1800s, the latter has a plush interior of mahogany paneling, velvet upholstery, and modern bath and kitchen facilities.

Not to be missed is the Hat and Fragrance House, which contains much more than its name implies. Within its walls you'll find an especially fine assemblage of antique quilts, handwoven rugs, handmade lace, embroidered samplers, and costumes. The old-time country store, apothecary shop, and doctor's and dentist's offices in the general store building are fascinating; and the Electra Havemeyer Webb Memorial Building has Degas, Manet, Rembrandt, and Monet originals. Details: Route 7, Shelburne, a few miles south of Burlington, (802) 985-3344; open 10 a.m. to 5 p.m. daily mid-May to mid-October. Admission (permits entrance on two consecutive days) is $17.50 adults, $7 ages 6 to 14. (half–full day)

After visiting the museum, you may wish to see nearby **Shelburne House and Farms** owned by Electra Havemeyer Webb's family. The estate, built in 1899, is stunningly set on Lake Champlain. Park architect Frederick Law Olmstead was consulted in the landscape design of the property. The estate now serves as an elegant inn. Details: Bay and Harbor Roads, (802) 985-8686. (1 hour)

★ **Ben & Jerry's Ice Cream Factory**—The tour of Ben & Jerry's main factory—outside of Waterbury on the road to Stowe—is fun for the whole family. Half of the nominal tour fee goes to charity, the rest goes for the delectable ice cream samples fresh off the production line. If the samples only whet your appetite for more, you can purchase cones when you're done with the tour. There's also a gift shop selling products with the company's logo. Details: Route 100, Waterbury, (802) 244-5641. (1 hour)

★ **Stowe Mountain Resort**—When the ski slopes are not covered with snow, this resort operates an alpine slide on Little Spruce, an in-line skate park at the base of Spruce Peak, and, for wonderful views from the top of Mount Mansfield, the Mountain Auto Toll Road and Gondola at Stowe. Details: (802) 253-3000. (1–3 hours)

Cabot Factory Tour—Cabot is known in Vermont and beyond for its dairy products—its cheeses in particular. The company is actually a cooperative owned by 1,800 dairy farmers. At the visitor's center on Main Street in Cabot (between Waterbury and St. Johnsbury) you can tour the factory to see how the cheese is made, then sample the product in the gift shop. Details: Main Street, Cabot, (802) 563-2231; open 9 a.m. to 5 p.m. daily June through October, closes at 4 p.m. the rest of the year; closed on Sundays during January. Admission is $1 adults, children under 12 free. (If you don't plan to make it as far east as Cabot, the company has an annex store on Route 100 in Waterbury where you won't get a factory tour but you can still sample the cheese. The annex is open daily from 9 a.m. to 6 p.m. Call (802) 244-6334 for details. (1 hour)

Cold Hollow Cider Mill—Cold Hollow does a lot of advertising, so you may find yourself stopping out of curiosity. Unfortunately, there really isn't much to see. The cider press and jelly kitchen aren't exactly exciting, but the cider samples are tasty, as are the other Vermont-made gourmet foods available for sampling and purchase. Details: On Route 100 between Waterbury and Stowe; (802) 244-8771 or (800) 3-APPLES. (1 hour)

Maple Grove Museum and Factory—If you happen to be as far east as St. Johnsbury and you're a maple syrup lover, you may want to visit this museum on U.S. 2. The museum is really just a small cottage where sugaring tools are displayed and syrup boils in a flat vat. Of more interest is the video on maple syrup making that plays continuously in the gift shop, and the tour of the factory where maple candy is made. Details: U.S. 2 in St. Johnsbury; (802) 748-5141; tours offered weekdays year-round every 12 minutes from 8 to 11:45 a.m. and from 12:30 to 4:15 p.m. Admission is $1 adults, under 12 free. (½ hour)

FITNESS AND RECREATION

Stowe is one of the premier ski areas in New England, so if you're a downhill skier and you visit in winter, don't miss the opportunity to ski here (800-253-4SKI). In warmer months hikers will find miles of trails to keep them busy in the Stowe/Mount Mansfield area. If you take Route 108 from Stowe to Jeffersonville, you'll find plenty of picnic areas as well as entrances to hiking trails alongside the road. (At one point the road becomes very steep, narrow, and curvy, making driving tricky, but only for a short stretch.)

Stowe's in-town recreational path stretches 5 miles from the Village Church to the mountain foothills. If you're an active traveler but left your equipment at home, **Action Outfitters** (802-253-7975) can rent you anything from a mountain bike to a canoe to in-line skates.

FOOD AND LODGING

Restaurants and accommodations are plentiful in Stowe, making it a good stopping place for a night or two. Perhaps the best-known hotel in Stowe is the **Trapp Family Lodge** (802-253-8511 or 800-826-7000), run by the Trapp family of *The Sound of Music* fame. With its chalet-style buildings bursting with flower boxes, and unrivaled views of Stowe below and the mountains beyond, the lodge easily lives up to its motto: "A little of Austria . . . a lot of Vermont." As one might guess, entrées such as Wiener schnitzel in the lodge's dining room have a distinctive Austrian flavor as well. During summer there are outdoor evening concerts in the Trapp Family Meadow. Doubles range in price from about $90 in low-season to $350 during peak weeks.

For those who like to indulge themselves, the **Topnotch Resort and Spa** (802-253-8585 or 800-451-8686) on the Mountain Road (Route 108) has fine accommodations and a full-service spa that includes a restorative hydromassage waterfall. Double occupancy rates are $140 to $240 per day.

The **Green Mountain Inn** (802-253-7301 or 800-786-9346), right in the heart of the village, is on the National Register of Historic Places. Built in 1833, the inn is centrally located and offers double rooms ranging in price from $90 to $310. Guests also have use of a health club. As its name suggests, the inn's **Whip Bar & Grill** specializes in grilled foods. The restaurant also has children's menu and an affordably priced Sunday brunch. For additional lodging choices in Stowe, there is an excellent reservation service (802-253-7321 or 800-24-STOWE) that can help you book a room in your price range.

If you're dining out while in town, and crave something other than New England fare, try **Miguel's Stowe Away** (802-253-7574 or 800-245-1240) for Mexican food. So popular are the restaurant's chips and salsa that they are packaged and sold in gourmet shops throughout the country. Located on Mountain Road, the restaurant has a children's menu as well as a "gringo menu" for those who can't handle spicy cuisine. Miguel's also offers overnight accommodations at reasonable rates. Doubles, which range in price from $40 to $120, include the use of the inn's hot tub and your choice of an American or Mexican breakfast. One of the nicest inns in the Burlington area can be found at the **Inn at Shelburne Farms** (802-985-8498 or 802-985-8686). Owned by the Webb family, who started the Shelburne Museum (see Sightseeing Highlights), the inn is truly worth the splurge and is open from late May through mid-October. Doubles range in price from $100 to $250. Visitors can tour the farm daily late May through mid-October beginning at 9:30 a.m.; the last tour leaves at 3:30 p.m. The farm makes its own delicious cheddar cheese that can be purchased at the farm store and visitor's center. Proceeds go to the farm's nonprofit conservation education organization.

In addition to the Inn at Shelburne Farms, there are numerous motels along U.S. 7 between Shelburne and Burlington. If you have time, travel one hour south to Middlebury, a pleasant college town bisected by Otter Creek Falls. The **Middlebury Inn** (802-388-4961 or 800-842-4666) is the town's most popular place to stay. Doubles are $90 to $180. The **Otter Creek Bakery** at 1 College Street has terrific breakfast pastries, bread sticks, and picnic fixings.

SIDE TRIPS IN NORTHERN VERMONT

For a truly out-of-the-ordinary experience take a llama trek into the mountains. **Northern Vermont Llama Company** (802-644-2257) operates half-day and full-day treks. The excursions leave from Smuggler's Notch, just over the mountain from Stowe.

Ferry rides across **Lake Champlain** to New York state are a pleasant way to see the lake and the Adirondack and Green Mountains that surround it. If you do venture out on the lake, be sure to keep an eye out for "Champ." Lake Champlain's fabled creature is said to rival the Loch Ness monster. Ferries operate from Burlington late May through late October, and the crossing takes one hour each way. Call (802) 864-9804 for departure times and fares. (If you really want to extend your trip, Montreal, Canada, is only about two hours north of Burlington.)

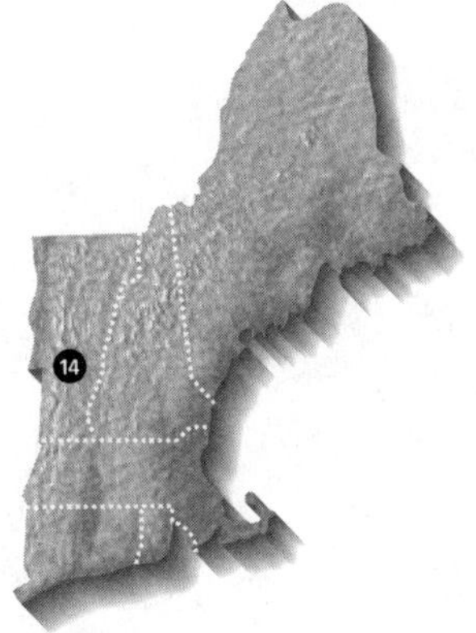

14

CENTRAL VERMONT

Central Vermont is home to the popular ski areas of Killington and Pico, rustic covered bridges, the picturesque Green Mountains, the 165-foot Quechee Gorge, the city of Rutland (home of the Vermont State Fairgrounds), and Woodstock—a quintessential New England town. Marble quarrying and processing the sweet sap of sugar maple trees have long been among the area's most valuable industries.

Charming Woodstock is a village that appears to be untouched by crime or hardship. It's a model town with elegant Federal-style homes surrounding a lovely town green. Even the grass looks perfectly groomed. Some of the bells in Woodstock's churches were made by Paul Revere. A tourist information booth on the green provides answers to visitors' questions, and the Town Crier Chalk Board in the center of the business district lists the goings-on for the day.

Billings Farm, a working farm museum, Dana House Museum, run by the Woodstock Historical Society, and the Vermont Raptor Center are all located in Woodstock. Other area attractions, including Quechee Gorge, Simon Pearce Glassworks, and Sugarbush Farm—a maple sugar farm—are all within easy driving distance of town. In short, Woodstock is an ideal place to base yourself when visiting the surrounding region.

CENTRAL VERMONT

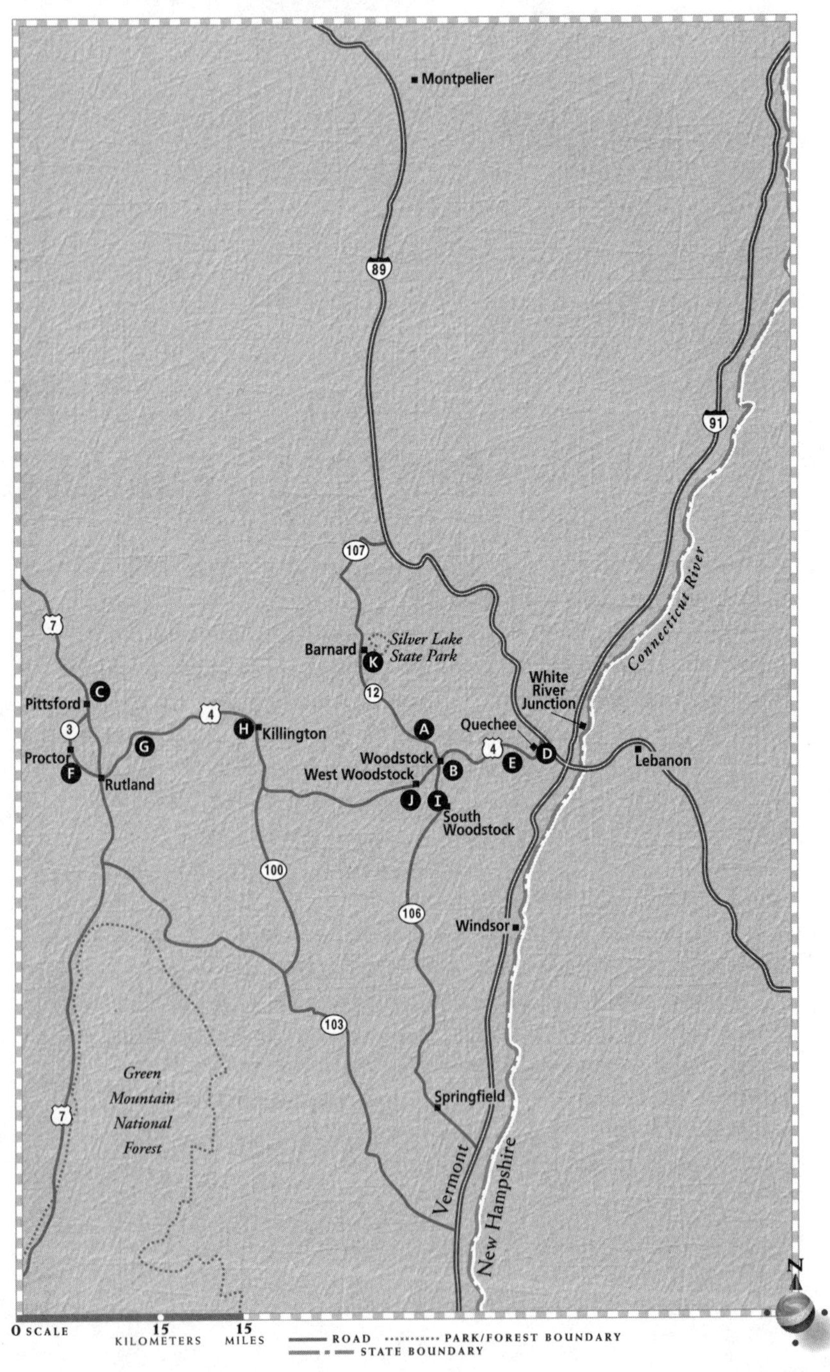

Sights

- **A** Billings Farm and Museum
- **B** Dana House Museum
- **C** New England Maple Museum
- **D** Quechee Gorge
- **D** Simon Pearce Glass
- **E** Sugarbush Farm
- **F** Vermont Marble Exhibit
- **B** Vermont Raptor Center
- **G** Wilson Castle

Food

- **B** Bentley's Restaurant
- **H** Hemingway's
- **I** Kedron Valley Inn
- **B** The Prince and the Pauper
- **G** Red Clover Inn
- **D** Simon Pearce Restaurant
- **B** Spooner's Restaurant
- **B** Woodstock Inn and Resort

Lodging

- **B** Braeside Motel
- **I** Kedron Valley Inn
- **J** Lincoln Inn at the Covered Bridge
- **K** Maple Leaf Inn
- **G** Red Clover Inn
- **B** Woodstock Inn & Resort

Camping

- **D** Quechee Recreation Area
- **K** Silver Lake Family Campground

Note: Items with the same letter are located in the same town or area.

A PERFECT DAY IN CENTRAL VERMONT

Begin your day dramatically with a hike down into Quechee Gorge followed by a visit to Simon Pearce to watch the glassblowers and eat lunch in the old mill. Visit Wilson Castle outside of Rutland in the afternoon; or, if you prefer, make agriculture the focus of your afternoon with visits to the Sugarbush Maple Farm and the Billings Farm and Museum. Hole up in a cozy country inn for your evening meal and night's accommodation.

SIGHTSEEING HIGHLIGHTS

★★ **Billings Farm and Museum**—The farm offers a look at rural Vermont life of a century ago. You can help hand-churn butter, see how cows were milked the old-fashioned way, and watch wood-carving demonstrations. Details: Off Route 12 north of Woodstock, (802) 457-2355; open 10 a.m. to 5 p.m. daily May through October, 10 a.m. to 4 p.m. weekends November and December. Admission is $6.50 adults, $5.50 students and seniors, $3 ages 5 to 12. (2 hours)

★★ **Quechee Gorge**—In Quechee, Vermont, on U.S. 4, only a few miles from the Vermont/New Hampshire state line, a bridge crosses the dramatic 165-foot-deep Quechee Gorge. Take the 1-mile hike to the bottom of the gorge, or just stretch your legs on the short (¼-mile) walk to view the waterfall that empties into the river below. Picnic tables are adjacent to the gorge. (1 hour)

★★ **Wilson Castle**—This nineteenth-century castle is set on 115 acres. Built by a Vermont doctor and his wealthy British wife, the castle is filled with an eclectic mix of European and Oriental pieces. Although the paint is peeling here and there, the hand-painted and hand-stenciled ceilings are unusual, and the colorful stained- and etched-glass windows throughout the house are quite beautiful. A Louis XV chair used by several popes, an ornate jewel case, an inlaid pool table, and a handsome curly maple fireplace in the master bedroom are a few of the other furnishings worth special note. Details: On West Proctor Road off Business U.S. 4, west of Rutland about ½ mile from the Route 3 north turnoff; (802) 773-3284; open 9 a.m. to 6 p.m. daily for guided tours mid-May through late October. Combination tickets for the castle, the Vermont Marble Exhibit, and New England Maple Museum nearby are available. (1½ hours)

★ **Dana House Museum**—Woodstock artifacts, period furnishings, antique costumes, tools, and toys make up the majority of the exhibits at this small museum operated by the Woodstock Historical Society. Details: 26 Elm Street; (803) 457-1822; open 10 a.m. to 5 p.m. Monday through Saturday and 2 to 5 p.m. Sunday May through October; open weekends in December. Admission is free. (1 hour)

★ **New England Maple Museum—**This museum offers exhibits, demonstrations, and a slide show designed to educate the public about the processing of one of Vermont's most famous products—maple syrup. Tastings are available, and you can buy the sweet confection in the gift shop. Details: On Route 7 in Pittsford a few miles north of Rutland; (802) 483-9414; open daily March through December. (½ hour)

★ **Simon Pearce Glass**—A right-hand turn at the first blinking light after Quechee Gorge bridge will take you over one of New England's rustic covered bridges and into "downtown" Quechee. There, Simon Pearce has completely renovated the old mill so you can watch glassblowers and potters at their crafts. You can also inspect the modern hydraulic power system that now fuels the ovens. The handmade glassware and pottery is sold in the gift shop along with natural fiber fabrics. There is a fine restaurant on the premises as well. Details: (802) 295-1470; the shop is open 10 a.m. to 5 p.m., and you can watch glassblowing during those same hours, except from 1 to 2 p.m. when the craftsmen take their lunch. Admission is free. (½ hour)

★ **Sugarbush Farm**—At this maple farm you can visit a maple sugarhouse to learn about processing the sweet syrup. Although spring is the sugaring season, the farm is open year-round. Sugarbush also makes cheese. Details: From Simon Pearce in Quechee, continue on River Road for several miles past lush green golf courses and farms, turn onto Hillside Road, and follow signs to Sugarbush. (802) 457-1757 or (800) 281-1757; call for hours of operation. (½ hour)

★ **Vermont Marble Exhibit**—Proctor, a small town about 8 miles from Rutland, calls itself the "marble capital of the world." At the Vermont Marble Exhibit on Main Street, visitors can see marble sculptors at work. There is also a film explaining the natural forces that create marble and the steps taken to mold this stone for artistic and functional purposes. There are examples of Vermont marble throughout Proctor and in nearby Manchester Village, where the sidewalks are made of the stone. Details: 62 Main Street, Proctor; (802) 459-2300; the exhibit is open 9 a.m. to 5:30 p.m. daily mid-May through late October, 9 a.m. to 4 p.m. Monday through Saturday in winter. Combination tickets are available to the exhibit, Wilson Castle, and the New England Maple Museum. (1 hour)

★ **Vermont Raptor Center**—Woodstock boasts this unusual museum at Vermont's Institute of Natural Science. At the outdoor museum, visitors can view more than 25 species of New England hawks, owls, and eagles, including bald eagles and the great horned owl. Details: On Church Hill Road about 1½ miles from the Woodstock town green; (802) 457-2779; open 10 a.m. to 4 p.m. daily, closed Sunday November through April. Admission is $5 adults, $2 ages 5 to 15. (1 hour)

FITNESS AND RECREATION

There are three marked jogging trails in the village of Woodstock; pick up trail maps at the Woodstock Inn. The **Woodstock Recreation Department** (802-457-1502) has two outdoor pools, and the **Woodstock Sports Center** (802-457-6656) has an indoor pool as well as fitness rooms. Bikes can be rented in Woodstock from **Woodstock Sports** (802-457-1568). **Silver Lake State Park** (802-234-9451) in nearby Barnard offers both swimming and boat rentals. For downhill skiing try **Suicide Six** (802-457-1666), only 3 miles from Woodstock. More extensive trail systems can be found less than 25 miles away at **Killington** (802-773-1500) and **Pico** (802-775-4345). Killington has more than 100 trails and a 3,081-foot vertical drop. The **Woodstock Ski Touring Center** (802-457-6674) offers 37 miles of groomed trails as well as cross-country ski rentals and lessons.

FOOD

Woodstock Inn and Resort has a fine-dining restaurant as well as the more casual Eagle Cafe. Savory herbs, light sauces, and fresh local ingredients combine to give meals at the **Kedron Valley Inn** in South Woodstock their distinguished reputation. **The Prince and the Pauper** (802-457-1818) on Elm Street in the center of Woodstock has a prix fixe menu that changes weekly, but you can expect to see dishes such as poached salmon and roast duckling.

Bentley's Restaurant (802-457-3232), also in Woodstock center, serves dishes ranging from veal to Szechuan to fresh salads, and has a good selection of microbrewed beer. On weekends there's live entertainment and a jazz brunch on Sunday. Dinner entrées average about $15. Families may want to try **Spooner's Restaurant** (802-457-4022) in the Sunset Farm Barn on U.S. 4 just east of Woodstock center. It has a children's menu, and specialties include western-style beef and traditional New England fare. Prices are moderate.

Near Rutland, the **Red Clover Inn** serves tasty cuisine in three intimate, candlelit dining rooms. The menu changes daily. Appetizers are creative, the wine list is extensive (over 130 selections), and desserts are tempting. Entrées range from $15 to $24. On Route 4 in Killington, **Hemingway's** (802-422-3886) receives consistently high ratings for its food. Reservations are recommended.

In Quechee, the **Simon Pearce Restaurant** (802-295-1470)—located in an old mill straddling the Ottauquechee River and Falls—offers tasty cuisine in a unique setting. The table settings are comprised of handblown glass and hand-thrown pottery from the Simon Pearce glassworks (see Sightseeing Highlights). The menu includes soups, salads, pastas, fresh fish, and smoked meats; and, not surprisingly for an operation that stresses hand craftsmanship, the breads are homemade.

LODGING

For those seeking the comfort of a country inn combined with resort amenities such as golf, tennis, and swimming, the **Woodstock Inn & Resort** (802-457-1100 or 800-448-7900) right on the village green has double rooms starting at $150 per night. The **Braeside Motel** (802-457-1366) on the east side of Woodstock offers doubles ranging in price from $50 to $90 and has an outdoor swimming pool.

The **Lincoln Inn at the Covered Bridge** (802-457-3312) on U.S. 4 in nearby West Woodstock is a 200-year-old farmhouse overlooking the Lincoln Covered Bridge and the Ottauquechee River. Double room rates including a full country breakfast run from $100 to $140. The **Kedron Valley Inn** (802-457-1473 or 800-836-1193) on Route 106 in South Woodstock is known for its nouvelle cuisine (see Food) and has accommodations with canopy beds and country patchwork quilts. Rooms range in price from $114 to $189 including breakfast. About 10 miles north of Woodstock, in Barnard near Silver

Lake, the five-room **Maple Leaf Inn** (802-234-5342 or 800-516-2753) welcomes guests in rooms with wood-burning fireplaces, stenciled walls, handmade quilts, sitting areas, TVs, VCRs, telephones, and private baths with whirlpool tubs. Doubles including a full breakfast range in price from $100 to $150.

About 5 miles east of Rutland and ½ mile from U.S. 4, the **Red Clover Inn** (802-775-2290 or 800-752-0571) has country-cozy rooms. Dinner at the inn's restaurant (see Food) and a full breakfast are included in the per-night rate for two ($130–$265 during fall-foliage season, ski season, and holiday weekends). As you travel toward Rutland, you'll find a number of reasonably priced motels.

CAMPING

The closest camping area to Woodstock is the state-operated **Quechee Recreation Area** (802-295-2990), near the Quechee Gorge. A trail runs from the camping area to the bottom of the gorge. Both tent and RV sites are available. Fifteen minutes north of Woodstock in Barnard is the **Silver Lake Family Campground** (802-234-9974). It has 70 campsites as well as showers and a children's playground.

15
SOUTHERN VERMONT

Winters are long in this part of New England, with temperatures averaging a chilly 20 degrees. Summers are short and fairly cool—the average temperature is only about 70 degrees. Spring zips by in a flash, but autumn is glorious here. Southern Vermont sees a great deal of travelers in fall, not only because of its clear, crisp weather but also because of the abundant maple trees that turn brilliant orange and red as winter approaches.

Southern Vermont's excellent ski resorts (Bromley, Stratton, and Mount Snow) lure winter visitors. And the region's beautiful mountain vistas and charming towns with their tidy village greens provide reason enough to visit the region in any season.

All along U.S. 7, from Rutland south to Manchester Center, are views of the Green Mountains. At Arlington, covered bridges grace both sides of the highway. Historic Manchester Village, with its marble sidewalks and grand Equinox Hotel, is also worth a visit.

Farther south, Bennington was the site of a major Revolutionary War victory for colonists in 1777. Today, when you drive past Old Bennington's graceful Greek Revival and Federal-style homes, it is hard to believe that a battle ever took place there. ◘

SOUTHERN VERMONT

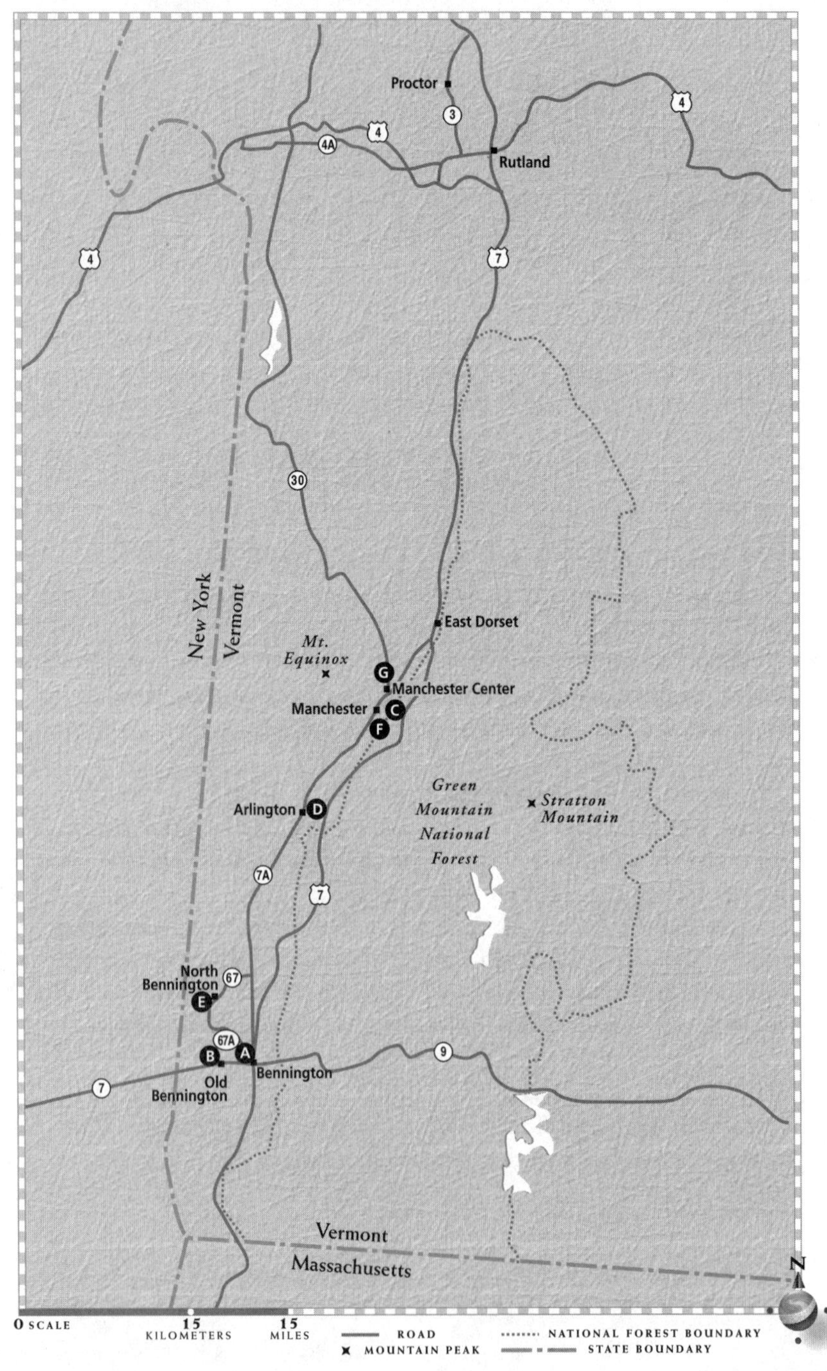

Proctor
Rutland
4
4A
3
7
30
New York
Vermont
Mt. Equinox
East Dorset
G
Manchester Center
Manchester
C
F
Arlington
D
Green Mountain National Forest
Stratton Mountain
7A
North Bennington
67
E
67A
B
A
Bennington
Old Bennington
9
Vermont
Massachusetts
N
0 SCALE
15 KILOMETERS
15 MILES
ROAD
MOUNTAIN PEAK
NATIONAL FOREST BOUNDARY
STATE BOUNDARY

Sights

- **A Bennington Museum**
- **B Bennington Monument**
- **C Hildene**
- **D Norman Rockwell Exhibition and Gift Shop**
- **B Old First Church**
- **E Park-McCullough House**
- **F Sky Line Drive**
- **C Southern Vermont Art Center**
- **G Vermont Wax Museum and Store**

Note: Items with the same letter are located in the same town or area.

A PERFECT DAY IN SOUTHERN VERMONT

In the morning, visit the Bennington Museum and Old Bennington, then head to Manchester Center for lunch and a bit of outlet shopping. After lunch, tour the Lincoln family's lovely estate, Hildene, and then end the day with a drive up Mount Equinox.

SIGHTSEEING HIGHLIGHTS

★★ **Bennington Museum**—The museum holds works by famed American folk artist Grandma Moses, who started to paint in her 70s and continued well into her 90s. The collection also includes Early American furniture, glassware, pottery, military artifacts, and household items such as pedal-operated sewing machines. Details: Approximately ½ mile from the Bennington Monument on Route 9; (802) 447-1571; open 9 a.m. to 5 p.m. daily, until 6 p.m. June through October; closed Thanksgiving and the week of Christmas through New Year's Day. Admission is $5 adults, $4.50 students and senior citizens, free for children under 12; family admission is $12. (1½ hours)

★★ **Hildene**—This stucco Georgian Revival mansion was built and owned by Robert Todd Lincoln, son of Abraham Lincoln. Hildene remained in the Lincoln family until 1975 and is now open to the public. The furnishings, including a 1,000-pipe player organ (complete with over 240 rolls of music) and a stovepipe hat worn by the president, belonged to the Lincolns. Set in the Manchester Valley, Hildene's expansive front lawn was used as a driving range by avid golfer Robert Todd Lincoln. The estate's formal English-style gardens were designed by his daughter, Jesse, after she returned from England. Many special events such as polo, symphony concerts, sleigh rides, and cross-country skiing take place on the estate's "meadowlands." Details: South of Manchester Village on Route 7A; (802) 362-1788; open for tours 9:30 a.m. to 5:30 p.m. May through October; the last tour of the day leaves at 4 p.m. Admission to the house is $7 adults, $2 ages 6 to 14, free for children under 6. (1½ hours)

★ **Bennington Monument**—This monument—completed in 1891—commemorates the Battle of Bennington and is the centerpiece of lovely Old Bennington. It warrants a visit on any clear day for the view, and it is a must at the height of fall-foliage season. You can see three states—Massachusetts, New York, and Vermont—from the observation deck. An elevator takes you to the top of the 306-foot structure. The well-groomed houses that line the road leading to and from the monument are also worth a look. Details: Open 9 a.m. to 5 p.m. daily April through October. Admission is $1 adults, 50 cents children. (½ hour)

★ **Norman Rockwell Exhibition and Gift Shop**—More a gift shop than a museum, this place has hundreds of Rockwell magazine covers on display but no original works. There is a film presentation on the artist. I prefer the Rockwell Museum in Stockbridge, Massachusetts, which has many Rockwell originals. But if you don't plan to visit Stockbridge, and you're a Rockwell fan, then this will have to suffice. Details: Route 7A in Arlington; (802) 375-6423; open 9 a.m. to 5 p.m. daily May through October, 10 a.m. to 4 p.m. the rest of the year. Admission is $1. (½ hour)

★ **Old First Church**—Adjacent to the town green in Old Bennington, this is a lovely example of early-nineteenth-century church architecture in New England. Perhaps more interesting, though, is the church's graveyard with headstones dating back to the Revolutionary War. Poet Robert Frost is buried here. (½ hour)

★ **Park-McCullough House**—This lovely 35-room Victorian mansion was once home to two Vermont governors. The house is filled with family antiques and beautiful details such as a stained-glass skylight and intricately patterned frosted-glass light fixtures. Special "Victorian Christmas" tours are run during the holidays. Details: Corner of Park and West Streets in North Bennington; (802) 442-5441; open for tours 10 a.m. to 4 p.m. mid-May through October; the last tour leaves at 3 p.m. Admission is $5 adults, $4 seniors, $3 ages 12 to 17. (1 hour)

★ **Sky Line Drive**—For better views of the Green Mountains, take the 5-mile-long Sky Line Drive to the top of Mount Equinox, the highest peak in the Taconic Range. The drive is particularly dramatic at the height of fall foliage. There are a number of picnic areas and hiking trails on the way up and an inn at the 3,835-foot summit, but despite the view, you're better off opting for accommodations down in the village. Details: Entrance to the auto road is on Route 7A south of Manchester Village; open 8 a.m. to 10 p.m. daily May 1 to November 1. A toll is charged. (1 hour)

★ **Southern Vermont Art Center**—After viewing the changing exhibits by local artists, take a walk in the sculpture garden or on the botany trail, or have lunch in the attractive garden café where the menu changes daily. Details: West Road in Manchester; follow signs from Route 7A just south of Manchester Center; (802) 362-1405; open 10 a.m. to 5 p.m. Tuesday through Saturday, noon to 5 p.m. Sunday mid-May through October; call for winter hours. Admission is $3 adults, 50 cents students, free for children under 13. (1 hour)

Vermont Wax Museum and Store—The Kennedys (JFK and Jackie), Gandhi, and Columbus are among the 85 famous figures you'll see sculpted in wax at this museum and gift shop. Details: Intersection of Routes 11 and 30 in Manchester Center; (802) 362-0609; open daily—call for hours. (1 hour)

FITNESS AND RECREATION

Hikers should visit the U.S. Forest Service office on Route 30 just east of Manchester Center for local hiking suggestions.

Downhill skiers will be pleased to know that both **Stratton** (802-297-2200 or 800-STRATTON) and **Bromley** (802-824-5522) Mountains are convenient to the Manchester area. The two mountains have a combined total of 21 lifts and 129 trails. Bromley also operates an Alpine Ride during summer months for about $5 per person. There are cross-country ski centers located at Stratton (802-297-1880) and at the **Equinox Ski Touring Center** (802-362-4700) in Manchester

Village. Ski and snowshoe rentals are available at both centers, and the Equinox also has an ice-skating rink. Twenty-two kilometers of trails crisscross **Hildene**, Robert Todd Lincoln's estate, starting in mid-December. The trails are open from 9 a.m. until dusk daily. Call (802) 362-1788 for information.

The Battenkill River, running from Manchester southwest through Arlington, is frequented by canoeists. **Battenkill Canoe Ltd.** (802-362-2800 or 800-421-5268) at 1 River Road in Arlington can set you up with the canoe trip of your choice.

Battenkill Sports Bicycle Shop (802-362-2734 or 800-340-2734) at the junction of Routes 7 and 30 in Manchester Center can fix you up with a mountain or touring bike for exploring the beautiful surrounding countryside.

FOOD AND LODGING

Reservations in southern Vermont—particularly for the Manchester area (which is the best place to stay)—are strongly advised, especially on weekends and during leaf-peeping season. At the Equinox Hotel, for example, rooms are often completely booked as much as six months in advance for peak foliage weekends. If the lodgings listed below are full during your visit, you may want to contact Manchester and the Mountains Area Lodgings (800-677-7829). They will try to locate a room for you in your price range. There is no charge for the service.

The majestic **Equinox Hotel Resort and Spa** (802-362-4700 or (800-362-4747) reigns supreme over historic Manchester Village. The historic hotel has been renovated in recent years, and now acts as a full-service resort and spa. The grand exterior appears to stretch endlessly, as do the marble sidewalks that surround the building. Carriage rides are available from the hotel's doorstep. Rooms in season cost over $150 per night for two, including breakfast. Dinner entrées in the hotel's main dining room average about $20; "lighter entrées" (really, expanded portions of appetizers) are in the $10 range. **Marsh Tavern** at the hotel has a buffet luncheon, dinner entrées from hamburgers to basil linguini ($9–$15), and evening entertainment.

The **Reluctant Panther** (802-362-2568 or 800-822-2331) on West Road right in Manchester Village has pleasant lodging and dining facilities. Room rates, which include dinner and a full breakfast, range in price from $170 to $335. The inn's restaurant features hearty soups, stews, and pies in winter, and lighter fare such as seafood and grilled dishes during summer. Dinners, such as dill-steamed striped bass with paprika cream, and quail on a marsala-shallot demi glaze, are $17 to $25.

The **1811 House** (802-362-1811 or 800-432-1811), also in the village center, was built in the 1770s but didn't become an inn until 1811. Authentically furnished with fine antiques, the house is on the National Register of Historic Places and once belonged to Mary Lincoln Isham, President Lincoln's granddaughter. Doubles range in price from $110 to $200 including a full breakfast (a two-night minimum stay is required on weekends, during fall-foliage season, and on holidays). There is a pub on the premises (open from 5 to 7:30 p.m.). The **Inn at Manchester** (802-362-1793 or 800-273-1793), just down the street on Route 7A toward Manchester Center, is open all year, has a swimming pool, and serves a complete breakfast. Rates range in price from $120 to $210. The **Seth Warner Inn** (802-362-3830), also on Route 7A, has sunny rooms with country furnishings ($80–$95 for two, including breakfast). The **Arlington Inn** (802-375-6532 or 800-443-9442) on Route 7A in nearby Arlington has been in continuous operation since 1888. Attractive guest rooms, some with fireplaces and Jacuzzis, range in price from $80 to $200 and include a full country breakfast. While you're there you might want to enjoy candlelight dining at the inn's restaurant—it's well known for its cuisine.

There are many motels in the vicinity of Manchester. Most of them are located on the outskirts of town on Routes 30, 7, and 7A. One of the nicest is the **North Shire** (802-362-2336), on Route 7A on the south side of the village. Rooms are spacious and attractively furnished and have lovely mountain views. The outdoor pool is pleasant, as are the helpful hosts, who are more than willing to provide you with sightseeing and dining suggestions. Doubles are $75 to $80 per day including a continental breakfast. Rooms cost $5 more per day during fall-foliage season.

If your lodging establishment doesn't serve food, the Manchester area has plenty of restaurants to satisfy just about any food craving. If you're in the mood for something with a little spice, **Candelero's Mexican Restaurant** (802-362-0836) on Main Street in Manchester Center should fit the bill. The guacamole is prepared tableside. Try the mole—a unique Mexican sauce made with chocolate. For breakfast, there's **Up For Breakfast** (802-362-4204), also on Main, where breakfast dishes are far from ordinary. Or you can indulge in pancakes at the **Pancake House** (802-362-3496) just south of the Route 7A/Route 30 junction. The **Park Bench** (802-362-2557), nearby on Route 7, is popular for lunch. **Christo's** (802-362-2408), next to Up for Breakfast,

SOUTHERN VERMONT

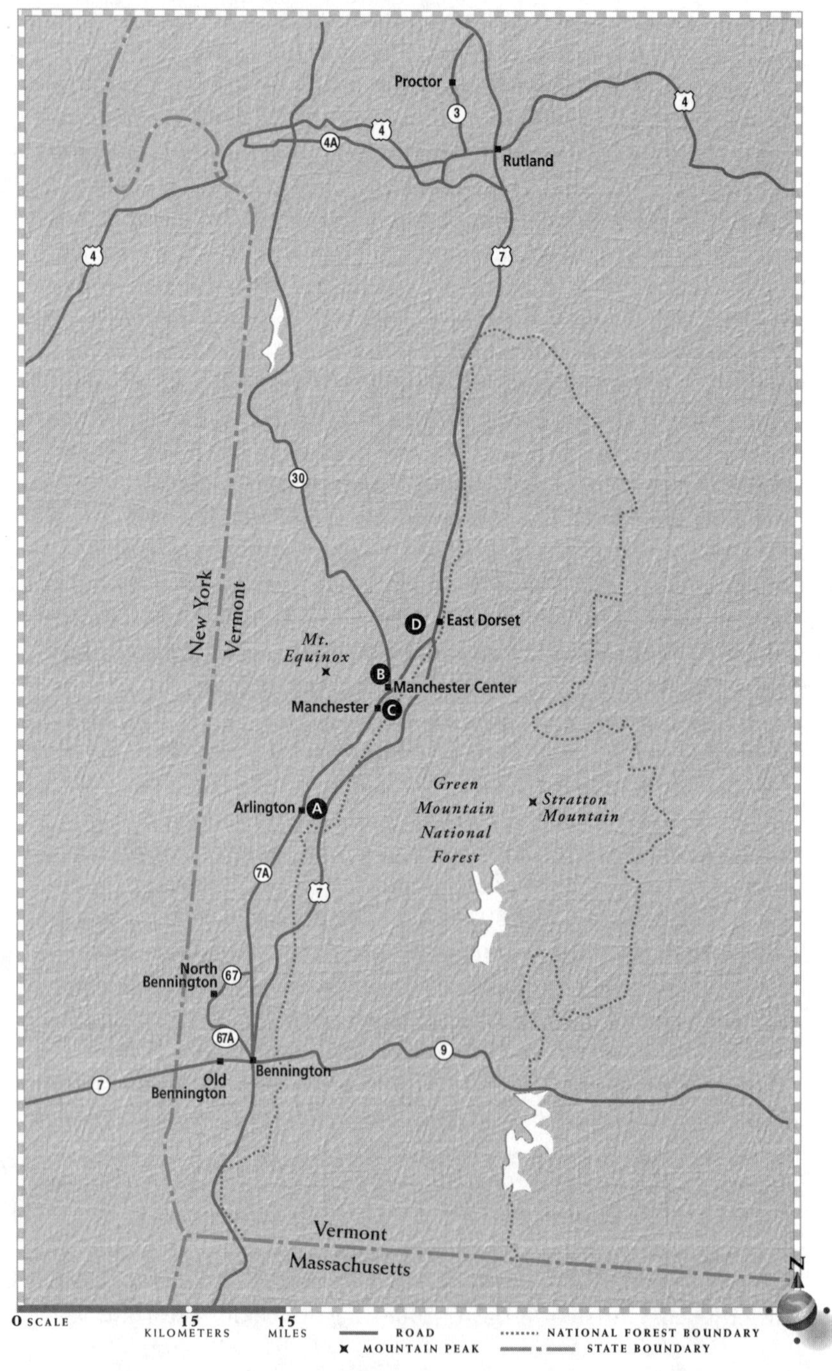

Proctor
3
4
4A
4
Rutland
4
7
30
New York
Vermont
D
East Dorset
Mt.
Equinox
B
Manchester Center
Manchester
C
Green
Mountain
National
Forest
Stratton
Mountain
Arlington
A
7A
7
North
Bennington
67
67A
9
Old
Bennington
Bennington
7
Vermont
Massachusetts
N
0 SCALE
15
KILOMETERS
15
MILES
ROAD
MOUNTAIN PEAK
NATIONAL FOREST BOUNDARY
STATE BOUNDARY

Food

- (A) Arlington Inn
- (B) Ben & Jerry's
- (B) Black Swan
- (B) Candelero's Mexican Restaurant
- (B) Christo's
- (C) Equinox Hotel Resort and Spa
- (C) Marsh Tavern
- (B) Pancake House
- (B) Park Bench
- (C) Reluctant Panther
- (B) Up For Breakfast

Lodging

- (C) 1811 House
- (A) Arlington Inn
- (C) Equinox Hotel Resort and Spa
- (C) Inn at Manchester
- (B) North Shire
- (C) Reluctant Panther
- (C) Seth Warner Inn

Camping

- (A) Camping on the Battenkill
- (D) Emerald Lake State Park

Note: Items with the same letter are located in the same town or area.

features pizza and pasta at reasonable prices ($5.75–$9.50). For dessert, Vermont's own **Ben & Jerry's** ice-cream shop just a couple of doors down is hard to resist. The **Black Swan** (802-362-3807) on Route 7 between Manchester Center and the historic village is renowned for its continental cuisine. Fresh seafood, pasta, game, and seasonal specialties range in price from $11 to $22.

If you want to ship home some of Vermont's celebrated cheddar cheese, the Grand Union supermarket in Manchester Center is one of the best places in the area to purchase it. The supermarket also sells Vermont maple syrup and prepared salads.

CAMPING

Emerald Lake State Park (802-362-1655), in East Dorset about 8 miles north of Manchester Center on U.S. 7, has camping, swimming, a nature trail, and boating on a beautiful green lake. The camping area has 105 sites, no hookups, 35 lean-tos, bathrooms, and pay showers. Canoes and rowboats can be rented for an outing on the lake. Call for reservations.

Camping on the Battenkill (802-375-6663) is a private

campground with both tent and RV sites, plus swimming and fishing on the Battenkill River. The campground, located on Route 7A in Arlington, is open from mid-April through October. Rate range from about $16 to $20 per campsite. Call for reservations.

PERFORMING ARTS

During June, July, and August, enjoy summer-stock theater at the **Dorset Playhouse** on Route 30, 5 miles north of Manchester Center. The playhouse stages a variety of productions—including plays for children and *The Nutcracker* during the holidays—throughout the year. Call (802) 867-5777 for ticket information.

SHOPPING

Manchester Center has an array of tidy shops interspersed with Ralph Lauren, Donna Karan, J. Peterman, and Liz Claiborne outlets, among others. The Northshire Bookstore at the intersection of U.S. 7 and Route 30 is one of the better bookstores in New England, and is definitely worth a visit. Orvis, the mail-order giant, has its flagship store on Route 7A in Manchester. The Equinox Valley Nursery on Route 7A is known for its colorful seasonal displays. The nursery's annual fall pumpkin patch is especially festive.

SIDE TRIPS IN SOUTHERN VERMONT

Lake George, New York, a very popular resort, is only 43 miles from Rutland. To get there, continue on U.S. 4 west from Rutland to Fort Ann. Then take Route 149 west to U.S. 9 and follow it north.

Fort Ticonderoga, about 50 miles northwest of Rutland in Ticonderoga, New York, is also a popular tourist destination. To get to the fort, continue on U.S. 4 west at Rutland to Whitehall, then take Route 22 north to Ticonderoga. The fort is open from 9 a.m. to 5 p.m. daily mid-May through mid-October, until 6 p.m. in July and August. Horse-racing fans visiting the area in August may want to take a 35-mile detour from Arlington, Vermont, to Saratoga Springs, New York. In addition to being recognized for Thoroughbred horse-racing and its natural springs, Saratoga also lays claim to many fine homes. The **National Museum of Racing and Thoroughbred Hall of Fame** is in Saratoga, as well as the unusual **Petrified Sea Gardens**.

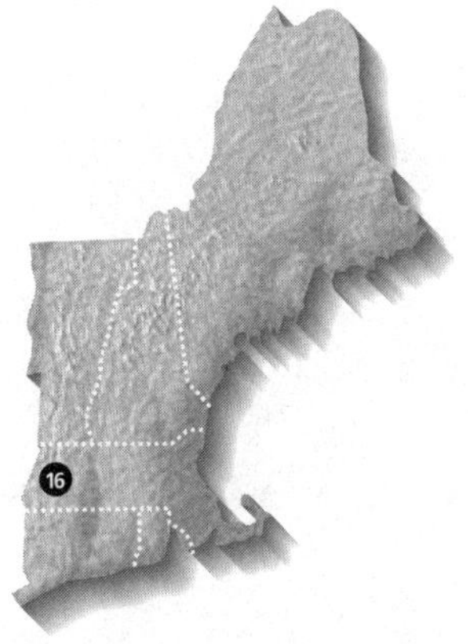

16
THE BERKSHIRES

The Berkshires offer the visitor much in the way of outdoor recreation, such as golf, skiing, and hiking, and in cultural events such as the Boston Symphony Orchestra at Tanglewood. With the picturesque villages of Stockbridge and Lenox, and the beauty of the Berkshire hills themselves, it's no wonder the area has remained a popular resort for more than 100 years. Considering the Berkshires are only three hours from both New York City and Boston, it's amazing that the area is not overrun with souvenir shops, factory outlets, and T-shirt stores designed to take advantage of the tourist dollar. Thanks to careful planning, though, most towns remain much as they were when Norman Rockwell painted here in the 1950s, and many have changed little in the last century.

Williamstown, at the northern edge of the Berkshires, is the quintessential college town. Williams College dominates almost every aspect of town life, providing the residents of the sleepy Berkshire community with a wealth of cultural activities other rural communities lack. Sheffield, at the southern end of the Berkshire region, is known for antiques. ◪

THE BERKSHIRES

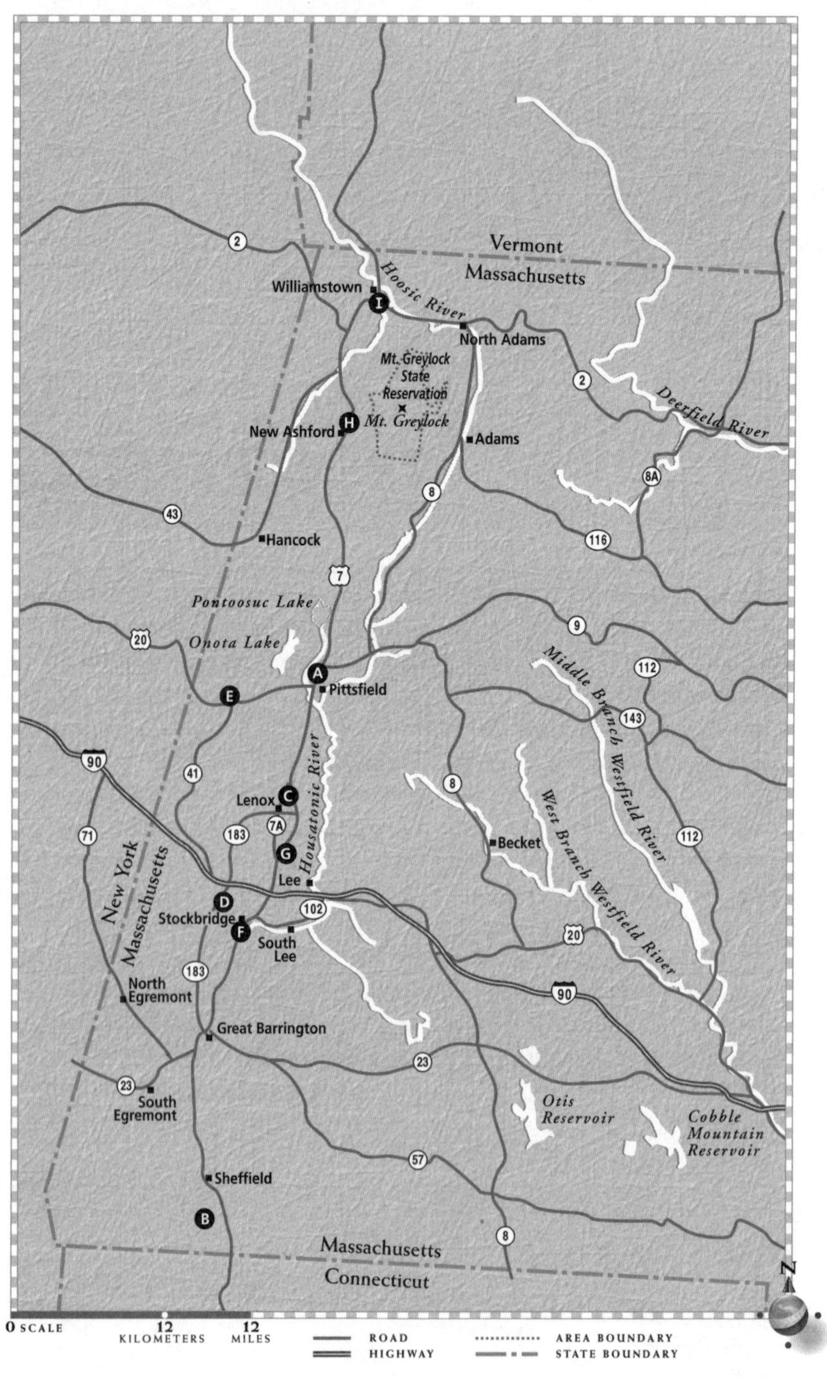

Vermont
Massachusetts
Hoosic River
Williamstown
North Adams
Mt. Greylock State Reservation
Mt. Greylock
New Ashford
Adams
Deerfield River
Hancock
Pontoosuc Lake
Onota Lake
Pittsfield
Middle Branch Westfield River
Housatonic River
Lenox
West Branch Westfield River
Becket
Lee
New York
Massachusetts
Stockbridge
South Lee
North Egremont
Great Barrington
South Egremont
Otis Reservoir
Cobble Mountain Reservoir
Sheffield
Massachusetts
Connecticut
N
0 SCALE
12 KILOMETERS
12 MILES
ROAD
HIGHWAY
AREA BOUNDARY
STATE BOUNDARY

Sights

- **A** **Arrowhead**
- **B** **Bartholomew's Cobble**
- **C** **Berkshire Botanical Garden**
- **A** **Berkshire Museum**
- **C** **Berkshire Scenic Railway Museum**
- **D** **Chesterwood**
- **E** **Hancock Shaker Village**
- **F** **Merwin House**
- **F** **Mission House Museum**
- **G** **The Mount**
- **H** **Mount Greylock**
- **F** **Naumkeag**
- **D** **Norman Rockwell Museum**
- **I** **Sterling and Francine Clark Art Institute**
- **I** **Williams College Art Museum**

Note: Items with the same letter are located in the same town or area.

A PERFECT DAY IN THE BERKSHIRES

Either spend a leisurely morning at Hancock Shaker Village, picnicking on the grounds at lunch, or enjoy the works of Impressionist masters at the Clark Art Institute. In the afternoon, visit Chesterwood, then go window-shopping in Stockbridge. Evening plans should be determined by the weather. If it is good, opt for a picnic dinner on "the lawn" at Tanglewood and stay to watch a concert. If rain threatens, dine at the Red Lion Inn and then head to Jacob's Pillow for a dance performance.

SIGHTSEEING HIGHLIGHTS

★★★ **Hancock Shaker Village**—Allow at least two hours to explore this village—one of the best examples of the everyday life of an unusual religious sect called the Shakers. There are live demonstrations of Shaker crafts such as broom making and basket weaving. The descriptive panels in each room describe different aspects of Shaker life. Don't miss the unique round barn. Two one-hour tours daily at 10:30 a.m. and 2 p.m. take you through part of the village. If you are unable to time your visit for a guided tour, you are free to tour the complex on your own. For a truly uncommon evening, visit the village for a candlelight Shaker dinner and tour. You'll tour the village and then dine on traditional Shaker dishes while seated communal style at one of the long tables in the "Believers Room." The dinner events usually begin at 5 p.m. on Saturday evenings during summer and early fall, and run about $35 per person. There are picnic tables outside the visitor center. Details: Junction of Routes 41 and 20 in Hancock; (413) 443-0188; open 9:30 a.m. to 5 p.m. daily Memorial Day weekend through the third weekend in October, 10 a.m. to 3 p.m. in April, May, and November. Admission is $10 adults, $8 students and seniors, $4.50 ages 6 to 12, $25 for families. (2 hours–half day)

★★★ **Sterling and Francine Clark Art Institute**—This museum has room after room of stunning French Impressionist paintings, including Renoirs and Monets, and works by noted American painters such as Homer, Cassatt, and Sargent. The fine collection also includes English silver and works dating back to the fifteenth century. Details: 225 South Street, Williamstown, (413) 458-9545; Open 10 a.m. to 5 p.m. Tuesday through Sunday; closed Thanksgiving, Christmas, and New Year's Day. Admission is free. (1½ hours)

★★ **Chesterwood**—This was the summer home of sculptor Daniel Chester French, who is known for the Lincoln Memorial in Washington, *The Minute Man* statue in Concord, Massachusetts, and many other works that adorn governmental buildings. Plaster castings of his works are displayed in his barn, home, and studio. Many of his works were so large he had to transport them out of his studio on railroad tracks just to see how they'd look in the sunlight. Each summer, usually beginning July Fourth weekend, contemporary sculpture from local artists is on exhibit throughout the 12-acre grounds and along the nature trail. Other annual events include an antique show in May, a flower show in July, and Christmas at Chesterwood. The museum is operated by the National Trust. Details: Off Route 183 in Stockbridge; (413) 298-3579; open 10 a.m. to 5 p.m. daily May through October. Admission is $7 adults, $3.50 ages 13 to 18, $1.50 ages 6 to 12, and includes a tour of the home; admission to the grounds only is reduced. (1½ hours)

★★ **Norman Rockwell Museum**—In 1993 the museum moved from its previous quarters in the quaint "Old Corner House" on Main Street in downtown Stockbridge to this $4.4-million facility on Route 183 just west of town. Now exhibits include the venerated artist's studio, and the museum can display up to one-third of its more than 500 Rockwell works at a time. Devoted Rockwell fans will enjoy this choice collection, and those previously indifferent to Rockwell will become converts when they witness firsthand the clarity and vitality of his oils. Details: (413) 298-4100; open 10 a.m. to 5 p.m. daily May through October; open 11 a.m. to 4 p.m. Monday through Friday and 10 a.m. to 5 p.m. weekends November through April; closed on Christmas, Thanksgiving, and New Year's Day. Admission is $9 adults, $7 students, $2 ages 6 to 18, $20 for families. The studio is closed November through April so admission is reduced during those months. (1 hour)

★★ **Williams College Art Museum**—The museum's collection ranges from ancient Greek vases to Andy Warhol pop art. A gallery is devoted to the artist brothers, Maurice and Charles Prendergast. Details: Main Street, Williamstown, (413) 597-2429; open 10 a.m. to 5 p.m. Tuesday through Saturday, 1 to 5 p.m. Sunday year-round; closed Thanksgiving, Christmas, and New Year's Day. Admission is free. (1 hour)

★ **Arrowhead**—Author Herman Melville made his home here for 13 years during the mid-1800s. See the room where Melville penned *Moby Dick* and several other novels. Details: 780 Holmes Road in Pittsfield; (413) 442-1793; open 10 a.m. to 5 p.m. daily Memorial Day through Labor Day. (1 hour)

★ **Berkshire Botanical Garden**—This 15-acre botanical garden is a nice spot for a picnic lunch between visits to Hancock Shaker Village and Chesterwood. Details: Off Route 102 just before it intersects Route 183; greenhouses open 10 a.m. to 5 p.m. daily year-round; gardens may be toured during same hours mid-May through October. Admission to the gardens is $5 adults, $4 seniors, free for children under 12. (½–1 hour)

★ **Berkshire Museum**—The museum is a combination art and natural history museum. Its collections include everything from gemstones to boa constrictors to a fine selection of landscapes by artists of the Hudson River School. Details: 39 South Street, on U.S. 7 in Pittsfield; (413) 443-7171; open 10 a.m. to 5 p.m. Tuesday through Saturday, 1 to 5 p.m. Sunday year-round; also open 10 a.m. to 5 p.m. Monday in July and August. Admission is $3 adults, $2 students and seniors, $1 ages 12 to 18. (1 hour)

☆ **The Mount**—This was the summer estate of American novelist Edith Wharton. Visitors can tour the property during summer months. *Ethan Frome*, perhaps Wharton's most famous novel, is set in Lenox. Plays based on the author's works are presented here during July and August, and tickets to matinee performances include afternoon tea. Details: Off U.S. 7 between Lenox and Stockbridge; (413) 637-1899. Admission is $4.50 adults, $4 seniors, $2.50 ages 13 to 18. (1 hour)

☆ **Mount Greylock**—In fair weather the scenic drive over Mount Greylock offers extraordinary views of the Berkshire Mountains. The entrance to the visitor's center is off U.S. 7 just south of New Ashford. (1 hour)

☆ **Naumkeag**—This stately brick and shingle home designed by Stanford White has formal gardens open to the public. Details: ½ mile from the Red Lion Inn on Prospect Hill Road, (413) 298-3239; gardens open 10 a.m. to 5 p.m. during summer; house tours 10 a.m. to 4:15 p.m. Tuesday through Sunday Memorial Day through Columbus Day. Admission to the house and gardens is $6.50 adults, $2.50 ages 6 to 12; admission to the house or garden alone is $5. (1½ hours)

Bartholomew's Cobble—This delightful 277-acre nature preserve off Route 7A south of Sheffield, adjacent to the Housatonic River, is worth a visit if you love nature. Details: (413) 229-8600. (1–2 hours)

Berkshire Scenic Railway Museum—This model train museum in a restored 1902 train station should appeal to railroad buffs. Call for ticket and schedule information if you're interested in taking the short train ride along the Housatonic River. Details: On Willow Creek Road in Lenox; (413) 637-2210; open 10 a.m. to 3 p.m. weekends and holidays June through October. Admission is free. (1 hour)

Merwin House—This Federal-style home was built circa 1825. Details: 14 West Main Street in Stockbridge; (413) 298-4703, tours leave hourly noon to 5 p.m. Tuesday, Thursday, Saturday, and Sunday June 1 through October 15. Admission is $4 adults, $2 children. (1 hour)

Mission House Museum—Diagonally across the street from Merwin House, Mission House was built in 1739 for the Reverend John

Sargeant, the first Christian missionary to the Stockbridge Indians. The house originally stood on the hill overlooking town but was moved to its present location in 1926. Details: Main Street Stockbridge; (413) 298-3239; tours offered from 11 a.m. to 4 p.m. Tuesday through Sunday Memorial Day weekend through Columbus Day. Admission for the combined house and garden tour is $6.50 for adults; garden tour only is $5. (1 hour)

FITNESS AND RECREATION

Butternut Basin (413-528-2000) in Great Barrington, **Catamount** (413-528-1262 or 800-342-1840) in South Egremont, **Jiminy Peak** (413-738-5500) in Hancock, and **Brodie Mountain** (413-443-4752) in New Ashford are all in the Berkshire region and provide skiing terrain for all levels of ability. Brodie has the greatest vertical drop, at 1,250 feet, while Catamount straddles the Massachusetts/New York border. Brodie and Butternut both have cross-country trails as well.

Hiking opportunities in the Berkshires abound—such as climbing to the top of **Mount Greylock, Mount Everett**, or traversing the Berkshire segment of the **Appalachian Trail**. Fall visitors to the area can enjoy picking their own apples at orchards such as **Windy Hill Farm** (413-298-3217) on Route 7 in Great Barrington.

FOOD AND LODGING

You can find comfortable lodging at the **Williams Inn** (413-458-9371) on the village green in Williamstown if you plan to stay for a performance at the playhouse. Doubles range from about $100 to $150. If you're not attending the theater, base your Berkshires stay in either Stockbridge or Lenox—they are better jumping-off points for area activities. The **Red Lion Inn** (413-298-5545) in Stockbridge is one of the best-known inns in the area and deservedly so; the focal point of the town, it has been treating its guests regally for over 200 years. Double rooms at the inn start at around $150 in peak-season (May through October) and $100 in low-season. Singles and two-room suites are also available. If you are unable to book a room here, at least partake of a traditional New England meal such as prime rib, stuffed lobster, or turkey in the main dining room; or people-watch while sipping cocktails on the inn's front porch. The **Lion's Den** downstairs has pub fare and entertainment in the evenings.

THE BERKSHIRES

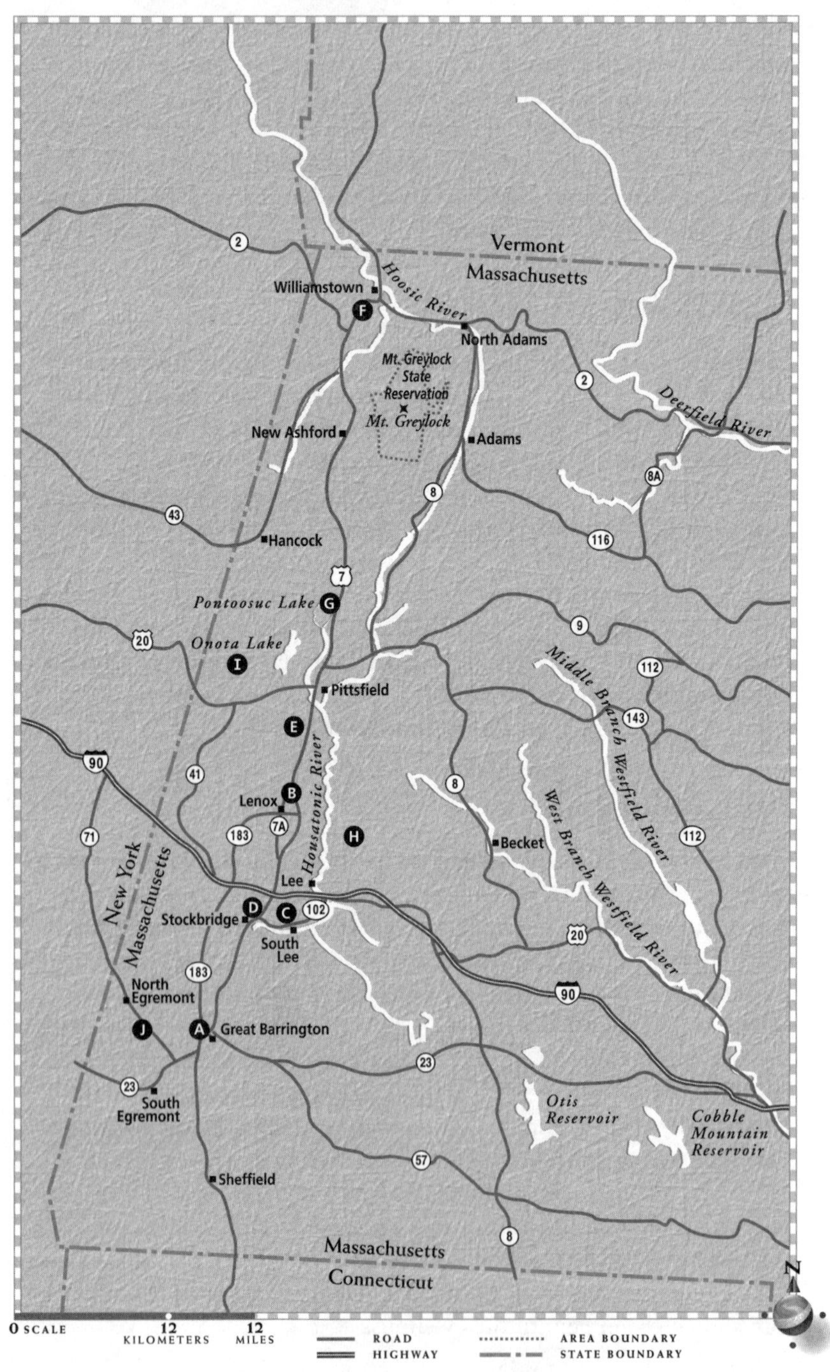

Food

- A 20 Railroad Street
- B Candlelight Inn
- C Federal House
- B Gateways Inn and Restaurant
- D Lion's Den
- D Michael's
- D Red Lion Inn

Lodging

- B Blantyre
- B Candlelight Inn
- C Federal House
- B Gables Inn
- B Gateways Inn and Restaurant

Lodging *(continued)*

- C Merrell Inn
- D Red Lion Inn
- E Susse Chalet
- B Walker House
- F Williams Inn
- A Windflower

Camping

- G Bonnie Brae Cabins and Campsites
- H October Mountain State Forest
- I Pittsfield State Forest
- J Prospect Lake Park

Note: Items with the same letter are located in the same town or area.

Lenox has its share of attractive inns right in the center of town on Walker Street. Each room in the **Walker House** (413-637-1271) is named after a famous composer and is furnished accordingly. Guests are welcome to use the inn's delightful porches or watch movies in the library. The hosts are friendly, and breakfast and afternoon tea are included in the high-season room rates of $80 to $190. The **Gables Inn** (413-637-3416) just down the street was once the home of Edith Wharton. Rooms here are also thematic; they include the Shakespeare Room, the Show Business Room, and the Presidential Room with pictures and memorabilia of past presidents. Rates, including continental breakfast at an elegantly set table, are $75 to $195 per night. There's also a pool on the premises.

Two other inns on Walker Street have restaurants and overnight accommodations. **Gateways Inn and Restaurant** (413-637-2532) has four large suites with private baths, fireplaces, and curly maple furniture for $85 to $325 in summer. Prix fixe dinners feature dishes such as breast of chicken topped with crawfish, truffle and crêpes served in a honey liqueur sauce, and medallions of monkfish stuffed with Norwegian salmon and topped with a fresh basil sauce. The menu at the **Candlelight Inn** (413-637-1555) changes seasonally but is primarily continental and American in focus. Dinner entrées range in price from $18 to $25, and lunch generally runs anywhere from $5 to $15. Try the Chocolate Chippie for dessert. Upstairs rooms range from $145 to $175 per night in season and $100 to $130 per night in the off-season.

Outside Lenox, a turreted estate has been turned into one of the area's most elegant lodging establishments. Set on 85 acres, and restored by the owners of the Red Lion Inn, **Blantyre** (413-637-3556) is truly a feast for the eyes. You'll have to have a deep pocketbook to stay at Blantyre, however, as rooms average about $250 per night (including tennis and continental breakfast).

If you want to be situated away from the tourist fray but still conveniently located for Berkshire sights, there are two pleasant inns in the quiet ex–mill town of South Lee about 1½ miles from Stockbridge. The historic **Merrell Inn** (413-243-1794 or 800-243-1794), built in 1794, has the only remaining colonial circular bar in America. Rooms are furnished with antiques, and the property borders on the Housatonic River. Double rooms, including an ample breakfast, range from $85 to $155 per night in high-season. Just across the street, the **Federal House** (413-243-1824)—known locally for its fine European cuisine—also rents rooms to overnight guests ($95–$185). Call them for dining or lodging reservations. The **Windflower** (413-528-2720 or 800-992-1993) on South Egremont Road (Route 23) in Great Barrington is a pleasant, 13-room bed and breakfast somewhat removed from Berkshire tourist traffic. All guest rooms have private baths; some have four-poster beds topped with floral comforters, fireplaces, and claw-foot tubs. Breakfasts feature homemade pastries and breads as well as a hot entrée. The inn also has an outdoor swimming pool. Rates for two range from $100 to $170.

Somewhat more affordable are the motels on U.S. 7 between Pittsfield and Lenox. The **Susse Chalet** (413-637-3560 or 800-524-2538) offers double rooms for $50 to $130 per night. More motels can also be found on U.S. 7 between Stockbridge and Great Barrington. The area abounds with country inns, but accommodations do fill up quickly on weekends. Call the **Berkshire Visitor's Bureau** (413-443-9186) for a complete list of lodging options.

For more casual and less expensive meals than those offered by the restaurants discussed above, **Michael's** (413-298-3530) on Elm Street in Stockbridge serves a variety of American dishes at moderate prices. **20 Railroad Street** (413-528-9345) in Great Barrington has tasty tavern-style food in a pleasant and comfortable milieu. Exposed brick walls add charm, and prices are reasonable.

CAMPING

Pittsfield State Forest (413-442-8992) has 31 campsites for about $10 each. However the campground does not have showers, and some facilities are unimproved. The camping season is mid-May through mid-October. The **October Mountain State Forest** (413-243-1778) in Lee does have showers and flush toilets. One of the campground's 50 sites is wheelchair accessible. The campground is open from mid-May through mid-October, and sites are about $12 per night. The October Mountain campground is more convenient for sightseeing, so reservations are strongly recommended.

Full hookups are available at **Prospect Lake Park** (413-528-4158) campground off Route 71 in North Egremont. Other amenities include showers, a camp store, lake-swimming, tennis, volleyball, and basketball. Sites start at $20 and the campground is open from mid-May through Columbus Day. **Bonnie Brae Cabins and Campsites** (413-442-3754) at Pontoosuc Lake, just off U.S. 7 several miles north of downtown Pittsfield, is another economical alternative to staying in a country inn. Open May through mid-October, Bonnie Brae has cabins that rent for $40 to $75 per night, and campsites that start at $25 per night.

PERFORMING ARTS

The **Williamstown Theatre Festival** (413-597-3400) is widely known for its high-quality summer productions. Many popular actors got their start here, and some return on occasion to hone their stage skills. Call for performance and ticket information.

A visit to **Tanglewood**, the Boston Symphony Orchestra's summer home in Lenox, is a favorite in the Berkshires. The BSO performs in the "Shed" on lovely wooded grounds, while smaller-scale concerts are given in the new concert hall. Tickets are available for seating in the Shed, but on clear nights Beethoven is best heard with a champagne picnic on the lawn. Bring your own blanket and dress warmly. Early birds can catch afternoon rehearsal performances at bargain prices. Call the box office at (413) 637-1940 for information during summer months. Contact the BSO's office in Boston (617-266-1492) for details in the off-season. Tanglewood is located off Route 183 about 2 miles south of Lenox Center.

Jacob's Pillow is also a popular summer cultural event. The dance festival features various well-known and talented traveling dance troupes. The Pillow is located in Becket on U.S. 20 about 8 miles from Lee. Call (413) 243-0745 for a performance schedule and tickets.

Other cultural events in the area include the **Berkshire Theatre Festival** (413-298-5576) in Stockbridge, the **Berkshire Ballet** (413-445-5382) and **Berkshire Public Theatre** (413-445-4634) in Pittsfield, and the **Berkshire Opera Company** (413-528-4420). Works of the Bard are presented in various Berkshire venues by **Shakespeare & Company**. Call (413) 637-3353 for ticket information.

The **Berkshire Ticket Booth** at the Chamber Office (in the Lenox Academy Building at 75 Main Street in Lenox) sells tickets to area events. The booth is open from 1 to 5 p.m. Monday through Saturday; it sells same-day discounted tickets whenever they are available.

SIDE TRIPS FROM THE BERKSHIRES

It is only a two-hour drive from the Berkshires to the **Catskill Mountains** in New York state. The Catskills are somewhat less traveled during fall than most of New England, but the scenery is no less spectacular. To get there, take U.S. 7 south to Great Barrington, then follow Route 23 west to Hudson, New York. At Hudson, cross the Rip Van Winkle Bridge to Catskill, New York.

Deerfield, about 35 miles southeast of Williamstown, Massachusetts, is one of the most perfectly preserved historic towns in New England with numerous eighteenth-century structures. While many of the buildings are privately owned by either individuals or Deerfield Academy, 12 of them are open to the public and can be toured with one admission ticket. Guided tours of the houses last 30 minutes each, so you'll need a full day if you want to visit them all. Tickets, which can be purchased at the information center on the village's main street (called the Street), are $12 for adults and $5 for ages 6 to 17. The buildings, which were built between the early 1700s and the late 1800s, are open daily from 9:30 a.m. to 4:30 p.m. except on Thanksgiving, Christmas Eve, and Christmas. Call (413) 774-5581 for information.

The **Memorial Hall Museum** on Memorial Street in the center of Deerfield has period rooms including a Victorian bedroom and a Colonial kitchen. Indian artifacts and pottery, handmade quilts, and nineteenth-century clothing are also on display. The museum is open from 10 a.m. to 4:30 p.m. Saturday and Sunday May through October. Admission is $5 for adults, $3 for students, $1 for ages 6 to 12.

If you do plan to stay in Deerfield for a day, there are picnic tables behind the information center. The **Deerfield Inn** (413-774-5587 or 800-926-3865), right across the street from the information center, is a fine lodging and dining establishment. Lunch entrées average about $10, while pheasant, veal with wild mushrooms, and venison dishes are just a sampling of the varied dinner menu which changes seasonally to take advantage of what's fresh. Dinner entrées average about $20. Overnight accommodations including afternoon tea, a full country breakfast, and perhaps a visit from one of the inn's two resident ghosts, start at $65 per person. The inn is handicapped-accessible, and two of the 23 guest rooms are specifically designed to accommodate wheelchairs—a nice plus for a historic hotel (the inn was built in 1884).

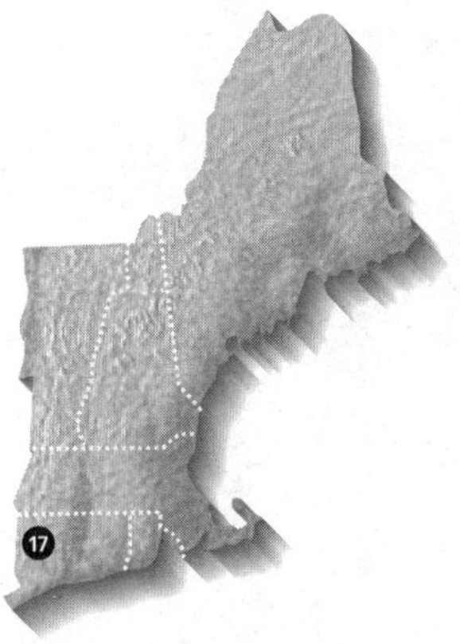

17 WESTERN CONNECTICUT

Western Connecticut, particularly the Litchfield Hills area, is the type of place where people go for a quiet weekend to escape the city and maybe to do some antiquing, fishing, lake-swimming, or light hiking. There are no big museums, outlet centers, or kitschy tourist traps here.

What draws visitors is the serene beauty of the area's rolling hills and winding Housatonic River—in West Cornwall you can cross the river on a 160-year-old covered bridge—and picture-perfect New England towns such as Lakeville, Sharon, and Salisbury. The exclusive Hotchkiss and Salisbury boarding schools, in Lakeville and Salisbury respectively, are located within a few miles of each other.

Nearby, Litchfield is a showplace for exquisite eighteenth-century estates, and the Congregational church on the town's village green is widely noted for its classic New England architecture. Litchfield, along with the neighboring town of Bantam, is also known for its antiques dealerships. ◪

WESTERN CONNECTICUT

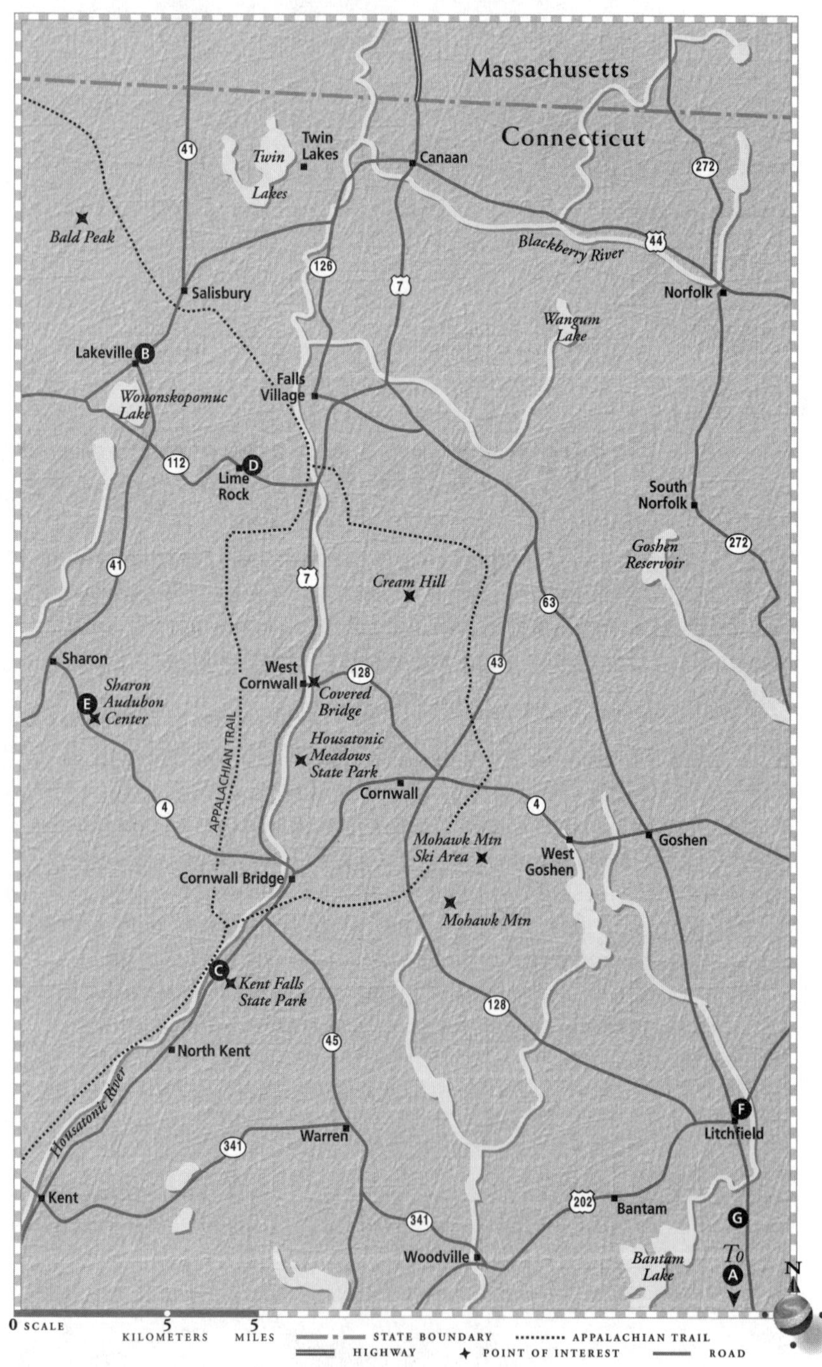
Massachusetts
Connecticut
Twin Lakes
Twin Lakes
Canaan
Bald Peak
Salisbury
Blackberry River
Norfolk
Wangum Lake
Lakeville
B
Falls Village
Wononskopomuc Lake
D
Lime Rock
South Norfolk
Goshen Reservoir
Cream Hill
Sharon
West Cornwall
Covered Bridge
Sharon Audubon Center
E
Housatonic Meadows State Park
APPALACHIAN TRAIL
Cornwall
Mohawk Mtn Ski Area
West Goshen
Goshen
Cornwall Bridge
Mohawk Mtn
C
Kent Falls State Park
North Kent
Housatonic River
F
Litchfield
Warren
Kent
Bantam
G
Woodville
Bantam Lake
To A
N
41
41
272
272
126
7
7
44
112
63
43
128
128
4
4
45
341
341
202
0 SCALE
5 KILOMETERS
5 MILES
STATE BOUNDARY
APPALACHIAN TRAIL
HIGHWAY
POINT OF INTEREST
ROAD

Sights

- Ⓐ **American Clock and Watch Museum**
- Ⓑ **Holley House Museum**
- Ⓒ **Kent Falls**
- Ⓓ **Lime Rock Park**
- Ⓔ **Sharon Audubon Center**
- Ⓕ **Topsmead**
- Ⓖ **White Flower Farm**

A PERFECT DAY IN WESTERN CONNECTICUT

Spend your morning antiquing and surveying the display gardens at White Flower Farm. Have lunch in one of the restaurants bordering Litchfield's village green, or picnic at Kent Falls. After visiting the waterfalls, explore the nature trails at the Sharon Audubon Center. Then head to the White Hart Inn in Salisbury for a good meal and comfortable overnight accommodations.

SIGHTSEEING HIGHLIGHTS

★ **American Clock and Watch Museum**—Bristol, to the east of the heart of the Litchfield Hills region, was a clock-making center for many years. The town's clock and watch museum, with over 3,000 timepieces, is in a house dating back to 1801. Be sure to time your visit so you'll be in the museum when a chorus of clocks strike the hour all at once. Details: 100 Maple Street; (860) 583-6070; open 10 a.m. to 5 p.m. daily April through November except Thanksgiving Day. Admission is $3.50 adults, $3 seniors, $1.50 children. (1 hour)

★ **Holley House Museum**—The museum complex, which includes a period home, an old-fashioned ice house, a seven-hole outhouse, a maze, and a historic garden, is designed to teach visitors what family life was like in the area during the nineteenth century. The Salisbury Cannon Museum, which depicts how cannons made in Salisbury's blast furnace were used during the American Revolution, is also part of the complex. Details: Route 44 in Lakeville; (860) 435-2878; open noon to

5 p.m. weekends mid-June through mid-October; tours leave on the hour from 1 to 4 p.m. Admission is $3 adults, $2 students and seniors, free for children under 5. (1 hour)

★ **Kent Falls**—This 200-foot waterfall is located off Route 7 about 6 miles north of Kent. There are picnic facilities, and there is a charge for parking on weekends and holidays. Details: (860) 927-3238. (¼–1 hour)

★ **Lime Rock Park**—Although it seems out of place in the pastoral landscape of western Connecticut, this auto racetrack is a popular area attraction. Details: Route 112 in Lime Rock; (800) RACE-LRP.

★ **Sharon Audubon Center**—Situated on close to 700 acres, this wildlife sanctuary has 11 miles of nature trails that wend through the woods and alongside two ponds. Recently sighted birds and notable plants in bloom are posted at the trailhead. There are picnic tables as well as an information center and gift shop. Details: Route 4 in Sharon; (860) 364-0520; the trails are open from dawn until dusk; the shop is open 9 a.m. to 5 p.m. Monday through Saturday, 1 to 5 p.m. Sunday; closed on major holidays. Admission is $3 adults, $1.50 seniors and children. (½–2 hours)

★ **Topsmead**—This Tudor-style cottage with formal gardens is open for guided tours during summer. Set on over 500 acres, the grounds are open to sledders and cross-country skiers during winter. Details: Buell Road about 1 mile east of Litchfield Center; (860) 567-5694. (1 hour)

★ **White Flower Farm**—One of the best-known and respected mail-order nurseries in the country, White Flower Farm is located just a few miles south of the center of Litchfield. Several acres of display gardens are open to the public as is a small retail store. Details: Route 63 in Litchfield; (860) 567-8789. (½ hour)

FITNESS AND RECREATION

Mohawk Mountain Ski Area (860-672-6100 or 800-895-5222), off Route 4 about 6 miles west of Goshen, has both downhill and cross-country ski trails. Rafting, canoeing, and kayaking are popular on the

Housatonic River in the warmer months. **Clarke Outdoors** (860-672-6365) in West Cornwall has boat rentals and offers guided trips, and can provide instruction to newcomers to river sports. Both **Housatonic Anglers** (860-672-4457) and **Housatonic River Outfitters** (860-672-1010) in West Cornwall are in the business of outfitting fly fishermen. Housatonic River Outfitters also rents mountain bikes. If you're in the Bantam area, try the enjoyable 1-mile hike to the stone tower atop the 1,325-foot Mount Tom; or take a swim in Bantam Lake (the beach and bathhouse are about 3 miles from Morris off Route 109).

FOOD AND LODGING

The **White Hart Inn** (860-435-0030), right in the center of Salisbury, has all the characteristics of the quintessential New England country inn—a long front porch set with wicker sofas and armchairs, cozy rooms dressed in chintz, a historic tavern, and a fine-dining room with soft lighting. The white-clapboard nineteenth-century inn has 26 guest rooms, all with private baths, air conditioning, and cable television. The rates range in price from $95 to $195 mid-April through mid-November, and are $75 to $150 during the winter months. Dinner entrées at the inn's American Grill range in price from about $17 to $26. At the seven-room **Under Mountain Inn** (860-435-0242), a home dating back to the early 1700s on Route 41 north of Salisbury, you'll be treated to genuine British hospitality—and bangers and mash—as the owner is originally from England.

The colonial **Blackberry River Inn** (860-542-5100) is listed on the National Register of Historic Places. Located on Route 44 between Canaan and Norfolk, the inn has 20 guest rooms. Some rooms come with fireplaces and Jacuzzis. Breakfast is included in the double-occupancy rate of $65 to $200. The **Litchfield Inn** (860-567-4503), on Route 202 on the edge of Litchfield, is not old but has the flavor of a traditional country inn. Guest rooms have four-poster beds and reproduction furniture, while a number of special theme rooms are decorated to honor the likes of Sherlock Holmes, Queen Victoria, and American presidents. Rates start at $95 for a double in the winter and at $100 during the rest of the year. Theme rooms are $150 in winter and $175 April through December. The inn's restaurant serves dinner entrées such as Dover sole and beef tenderloin, and dessert indulgences such as chocolate truffle cake or grasshopper mint torte.

WESTERN CONNECTICUT

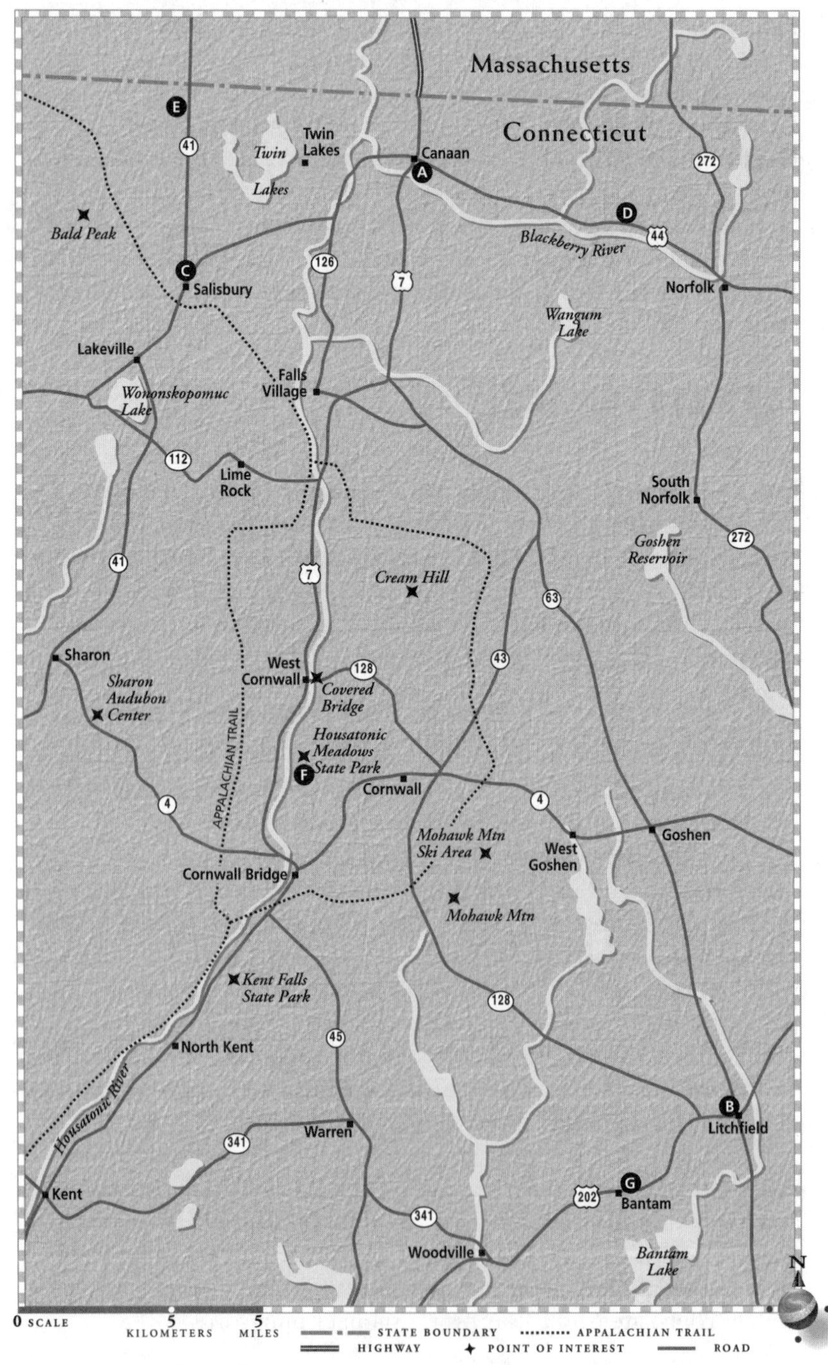

Massachusetts
Connecticut
Twin Lakes
Twin Lakes
Canaan
Bald Peak
Salisbury
Lakeville
Wononskopomuc Lake
Falls Village
Lime Rock
Blackberry River
Norfolk
Wangum Lake
South Norfolk
Goshen Reservoir
Cream Hill
Sharon
Sharon Audubon Center
West Cornwall
Covered Bridge
Housatonic Meadows State Park
Cornwall
APPALACHIAN TRAIL
Mohawk Mtn Ski Area
West Goshen
Goshen
Cornwall Bridge
Mohawk Mtn
Kent Falls State Park
North Kent
Housatonic River
Warren
Kent
Litchfield
Bantam
Woodville
Bantam Lake
0 SCALE
5 KILOMETERS
5 MILES
STATE BOUNDARY
APPALACHIAN TRAIL
HIGHWAY
POINT OF INTEREST
ROAD
N

Food

- **A** **The Cannery**
- **B** **County Seat**
- **B** **Litchfield Inn**
- **C** **Ragamont**
- **B** **Village Restaurant**
- **B** **West Street Grill**
- **C** **White Hart Inn**

Lodging

- **D** **Blackberry River Inn**
- **B** **Litchfield Inn**
- **E** **Under Mountain Inn**
- **C** **White Hart Inn**

Camping

- **F** **Housatonic Meadows State Campground**
- **G** **Looking Glass Hill Campground**

Note: Items with the same letter are located in the same town or area.

Most of the towns in this part of Connecticut are too small to have large commercial centers with lots of restaurants, but several restaurants do face Litchfield's town green. The **West Street Grill** (860-567-3885), with good bistro cuisine, is the most formal and expensive. The **County Seat** (860-567-8069) has the feel of an old-fashioned soda fountain, and selections such as hummus quesadillas are tasty and have an imaginative flair. The County Seat is also the place to stop in the morning for a breakfast bagel or pastry and a cup of coffee. The **Village Restaurant** (860-567-8307) features home-style cooking, and is the sister restaurant of **The Cannery** in Canaan (worth stopping at for a meal if you happen to be in the Canaan area around dinnertime). In Salisbury dine at the **White Hart Inn** (860-435-0030), or try the **Ragamont** (860-435-0030) on Main Street, where dinner entrées such as sauerbraten range in price from $16 to $22.

CAMPING

Housatonic Meadows State Campground—on the Housatonic River about 3 miles from the covered bridge in West Cornwall—has 95 campsites and is a popular spot for fly fishing. A hiking trail from the campground connects with the Appalachian Trail. The campground is open mid-April through Columbus Day and sites cost about $10 per night. Call (860) 672-6772 for more information.

Private campgrounds in the Litchfield area include **White Memorial Family Campground** (860-567-0089) near Bantam Lake (call for directions), **Looking Glass Hill Campground** (860-567-2050) on Route 202, and **Hemlock Hill Camp Resort** (860) 567-2267. Hemlock Hill—which offers two swimming pools and a hot tub—has the most extensive facilities of the three. Call the resort for precise directions.

ARTS AND ENTERTAINMENT

The oldest continuous chamber music festival in the country is held each summer at **Music Mountain** off Route 7 in Falls Village. Jazz and popular musical performances are also held in the concert hall. Call (860) 824-7126 for schedule and ticket information.

18 HEART OF CONNECTICUT

Connecticut's centrally located capital is truly at the state's heart. Hartford's first insurance company was founded in 1794, and today, over 300 years later, the city is still known as the insurance capital of the nation. What many people do not know is that Hartford was also a major industrial center and was at one time the country's most affluent city. Hartford was home to the country's first woolen mill, and products such as coffeemakers, typewriters, and brushes were manufactured in the city as recently as the 1950s.

When Mark Twain first came to the area 130 years ago he was moved to remark on its beauty. Today Hartford is a multiethnic city struggling to maintain its rich cultural past while trying to define what its role will be in the twenty-first century.

South of Hartford, the winding Connecticut River Valley and its sleepy towns give way to the state's Atlantic coast. Essex, located on the Connecticut River, is an attractive town whose past and present have been shaped by nautical endeavors. In 1814, during the War of 1812, the British raided Essex and burned many of the town's ships, causing great hardship to the townspeople. Today, well-kept houses are discreetly tucked away on the waterfront, while the marina is filled with pleasure craft. Other handsome river towns include Chester, with its charming galleries and antique shops; and East Haddam, with the renowned Goodspeed Opera House. ◪

HEART OF CONNECTICUT

Litchfield
Farmington
Hartford
Middletown
East Haddam
Essex
Waterbury
New Haven
Bridgeport
New London
Old Mystic
Mystic
Connecticut River
Thames River
Quinnipiac River
Housatonic River
Long Island Sound
Long Island, New York
New York
Connecticut
84
395
2
9
5
691
91
95
15
8
A
B
C
D
E
F
ROAD
HIGHWAY
STATE BOUNDARY
0 SCALE
20 KILOMETERS
20 MILES
N

Sights

- Ⓐ Antiquarian and Landmarks Society
- Ⓐ Connecticut Historical Society
- Ⓑ Connecticut River Museum
- Ⓐ Connecticut State Capitol
- Ⓒ Dinosaur State Park
- Ⓐ Elizabeth Park
- Ⓓ Gillette's Castle
- Ⓔ Hill-Stead Museum
- Ⓐ Menczer Museum of Medicine and Dentistry
- Ⓐ Noah Webster House
- Ⓐ Nook Farm
- Ⓐ Old State House
- Ⓕ Science Center of Connecticut
- Ⓔ Stanley-Whitman House
- Ⓑ Steam train and riverboat ride
- Ⓐ Wadsworth Athenaeum

Note: Items with the same letter are located in the same town or area.

A PERFECT DAY IN THE HEART OF CONNECTICUT

Catch up on literary history by visiting the homes of Harriet Beecher Stowe and Mark Twain in Hartford's Nook Farm neighborhood. From there travel down the Connecticut River to have a late picnic lunch on the grounds of Gillette's Castle, followed by a tour of the home itself. Afterward, travel to Chester and Essex for window shopping and a traditional New England dinner at the Griswold Inn; or dine at the Gelston House overlooking the river in East Haddam, and take in a show at Goodspeed Opera House. If you prefer the arts to historic homes, spend your day at the Hill-Stead Museum in Farmington and the Wadsworth Athenaeum in Hartford.

SIGHTSEEING HIGHLIGHTS

★★★ **Nook Farm**—Only a handful of houses remain from this nineteenth-century community for the literary elite of Hartford. Two are open to the public and worth seeing: the homes of Harriet Beecher Stowe and Mark Twain. The Beecher Stowe house exemplifies a conventional upper-middle-class Victorian home, whereas the more pretentious Twain house is a monument to the author's eccentricities. In both cases, many of the writers' personal effects have been preserved, among them Stowe's original paintings, Twain's bed, and the dining room chair from which the raconteur told fantastic tales to his guests and family. Tour guides recount humorous details from the authors' everyday lives. The guided tour of both homes takes approximately 1¼ hours. Details: The Twain house, (860) 493-6411, is located at 351 Farmington Street, and the Stowe house, (860) 525-9317, is next door. Stowe house open 9:30 a.m. to 5 p.m. Tuesday through Saturday, noon to 5 p.m. Sunday year-round; also open Mondays in summer. Twain house open 9:30 a.m. to 5 p.m. Monday through Saturday, noon to 5 p.m. Sunday Memorial Day through Columbus Day, and the month of December; closed Tuesdays the rest of the year. Admission to the Stowe house is $6.50 adults, $6 seniors, $2.75 ages 6 to 16. Admission to the Twain house is $7.50 adults, $7 seniors, $3.50 ages 6 to 12. (2 hours)

★★ **Gillette's Castle**—They say a man's home is his castle, and in actor William Gillette's case, that statement can be taken literally. Best known for his portrayal of Sherlock Holmes, Gillette built his castle overlooking the Connecticut River in East Haddam. The jagged stone exterior is striking, but except for several intricately carved wooden doors, the interior is fairly modest. Children will no doubt enjoy exploring the castle, and theater buffs will appreciate the Broadway memorabilia on display. The castle grounds are a Connecticut state park, so there are picnic tables available as well as a souvenir shop and refreshment stand. Skip the wooded trail unless you are in the mood to stretch your legs. Details: 67 River Road, East Haddam, (860) 526-2336; castle open 11 a.m. to 5 p.m. daily Memorial Day through Columbus Day, 10 a.m. to 5 p.m. weekends only Columbus Day through mid-December; grounds open year-round. Admission is $4 adults, $2 ages 6 to 11. (1 hour)

★★ **Hill-Stead Museum**—Hill-Stead was originally designed in 1901 as a private home for the Pope family. The house, now open to the public, is filled with choice furnishings and Impressionist paintings (Cassatt, Monet, and Manet are a few of the artists whose works you will see), and the sunken garden and surrounding grounds are lovely. Details: 35 Mountain Road in Farmington; (860) 677-4787; open 10 a.m. to 5 p.m. Tuesday through Sunday May through October, 11 a.m. to 4 p.m. Tuesday through Sunday November through April.

Admission is $6 adults, $5 seniors and students, $3 ages 6 to 12. (1 hour)

✭✭ **Wadsworth Athenaeum**—The athenaeum—the nation's oldest public art museum—is a good place to visit if you want to view a quality collection of art from a variety of periods without feeling overwhelmed. The athenaeum's collections include everything from African American art to modern works by the likes of Picasso, Dali, Calder, Miro, Arp, and Chagall. The museum's collection of Impressionist paintings is small, but it does include works by majors such as Monet and Renoir. American artists such as Homer, Whistler, Glackens, and William Merritt Chase get their due, and the museum's fine assemblage of oils by Hudson River School painters (Cole, Church, etc.) is well known in art circles. Other exhibits are devoted to Early American furniture and European decorative arts (the elaborate gilded antique platters and centerpieces from Germany are something to behold); and there's even a small wing housing ancient artifacts from Greece, Rome, and Egypt—including an Egyptian mummy. If your visit falls over the lunch hour, take time out to eat at the Museum Cafe. It serves fine meals and is a good dining choice in Hartford, especially on Sunday when not much else is open. Details: 600 Main Street in Hartford; (860) 278-2670; open 11 a.m. to 5 p.m. Tuesday through Sunday; closed major holidays. Admission is $7 adults, $5 seniors and students, $3 children over 5. Admission is free all day Thursday, and Saturday morning before noon. (2 hours–half day)

✭ **Dinosaur State Park**—Looking at Connecticut today it may be hard to believe that giant dinosaurs once roamed the area freely—but they did, and some of the country's best-preserved, fossilized dinosaur tracks can be found in Rocky Hill south of Hartford. The tracks are now protected by a geodesic dome. The park also has nature trails, and you can make a cast of a dinosaur footprint (bring your own plaster of paris). Details: West Street in Rocky Hill (take exit 23 off I-91); (860) 529-8423; open 9 a.m. to 4:30 p.m. Tuesday through Sunday; closed Mondays, Thanksgiving, Christmas, and New Year's Day. Admission is $2 adults, $1 ages 6 to 17. (1 hour)

✭ **Steam train and riverboat ride**—This excursion offers a good alternative way to see the Connecticut River and sights such as Gillette's Castle and Goodspeed's Opera House, especially if you fancy steam-powered locomotives. All trains connect with a riverboat cruise, except the last one of the day. Details: On Railroad Avenue in Essex; (860) 767-0103. Call ahead for departure times; they vary from day to day and season to season. The service operates May through October with special excursions some holiday weekends in the off-season. Tickets for the combined train and riverboat trip are $15 adults, $7.50 ages 3 to 11, free for age 2 and under; less for the train ride only. Separate tickets are not sold for the riverboat cruise. (2½ hours)

Antiquarian and Landmarks Society—The society operates a number of historic homes in Connecticut, including the Nathan Hale Homestead in Coventry and two homes in Hartford—the 1782 **Butler-McCook Homestead** (396 Main Street) and the 1854 Italianate-style **Isham-Terry House** (211 High Street). Details: The Butler-McCook Homestead is open noon to 4 p.m. Tuesday, Thursday, and Sunday mid-May through mid-October. Admission is $4 adults, $1 students. The Isham-Terry House is open by appointment only. Contact the society at (860) 247-8996 for appointments and admission information. (½ hour per home)

Connecticut Historical Society—The society's museum and library are dedicated to the education and preservation of the state's history. Details: 1 Elizabeth Street in Hartford; (860) 236-5621. The museum is open noon to 5 p.m. Tuesday through Sunday; the library is open 9 a.m. to 4:45 p.m. Tuesday through Saturday. Admission is $3 adults, free for students and children under 18. (½ hour)

Connecticut River Museum—This museum's exhibits pertain to river history. Of special interest is the replica of America's first submarine, the Turtle. It was originally constructed in 1775. Details: On the waterfront at the end of Main Street in Essex, (860) 767-8269. Open 10 a.m. to 5 p.m. Tuesday through Sunday. Admission is $4 adults, $2 ages 9 to 12, free for children under 8. (1 hour)

Connecticut State Capitol—Tour the striking, gold-domed, Gothic-style 1879 state capitol building and see the legislative process at work. Details: 210 Capitol Avenue in Hartford; (860) 240-0222. Tours offered hourly 9:15 a.m. to 1:15 p.m. weekdays year-round (there's also a 2:15 p.m. tour during July and August), and 10:15 a.m. to 2:15 p.m. Saturday April through October. Admission is free. (1 hour)

Elizabeth Park—This is the oldest municipal rose garden in the country. In addition to the roses, there are greenhouses, nature walks, and rock gardens to explore. Details: Prospect Avenue in Hartford; (860) 722-6514; gardens open dawn to dusk and greenhouses open 10 a.m. to 4 p.m. daily. Admission is free. (½ hour)

Menczer Museum of Medicine and Dentistry—This highly specialized museum will probably most appeal to those that have a particular interest in the field of medicine. Historic instruments of the trade are on display, and the building also houses a medical library. Details: 230 Scarborough Street in Hartford; (860) 236-5613; open 10 a.m. to 4 p.m. weekdays. Admission is $2 adults. (½ hour)

Noah Webster House—You can see early editions of Webster's first dictionary in the eighteenth-century farmhouse that was Webster's birthplace. Details: 227 South Main Street in West Hartford; (860) 521-5362; open 10 a.m. to 4 p.m. weekdays, 1 to 4 p.m. weekends July and August; 1 to 4 p.m. daily the rest of the year; closed Wednesday. Admission is $5 adults, $4 seniors and AAA members, $1 ages 6 to 12. (1 hour)

Old State House—This Georgian-style capitol building was designed by Charles Bullfinch (who also designed Massachusetts' state house) and constructed in 1796. About a century later, no longer big enough to adequately serve as the capitol, it was replaced by the current capitol building (see above). Details: 800 Main Street in Hartford; (860) 522-6766; open 10 a.m. to 4 p.m. weekdays, 10 a.m. to 3 p.m. Saturday. Admission is free. (½ hour)

Science Center of Connecticut—This museum has hands-on science exhibits as well as a planetarium. Details: 950 Trout Brook Drive in West Hartford (take exit 43 off I-84); (860) 231-2824; open 10 a.m. to 5 p.m. Tuesday through Saturday (Thursday until 8 p.m.), noon to 5 p.m. Sunday. Admission is $5 adults, $4 children and seniors; combination tickets including admission to a planetarium show are $2 more per person. (1–2 hours)

Stanley-Whitman House—This restored Colonial home dating to 1720 is now a National Historic Landmark and open to the public. Details: 37 High Street in Farmington; (860) 677-9222; open noon to

HEART OF CONNECTICUT

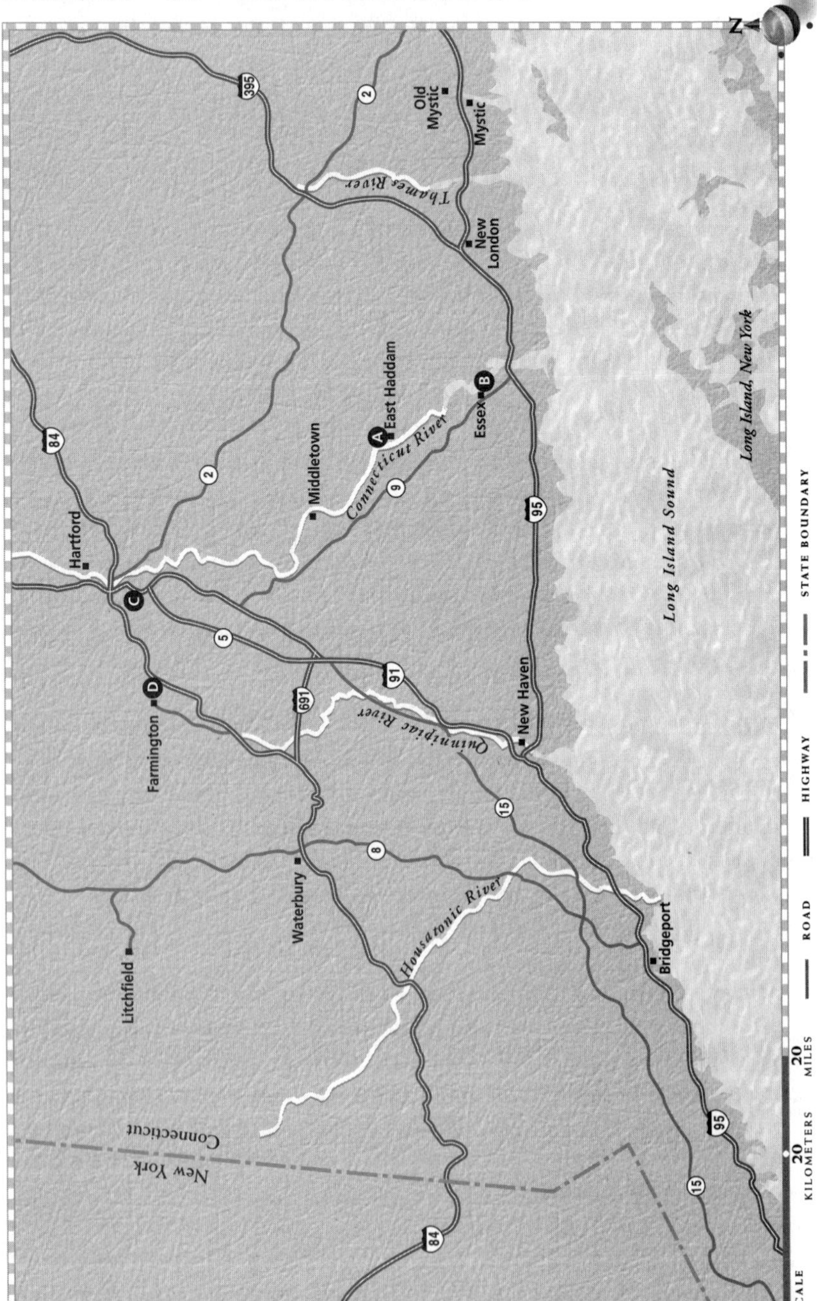

Hartford
Middletown
East Haddam
Essex
Farmington
New Haven
Waterbury
Litchfield
Bridgeport
New London
Old Mystic
Mystic
Connecticut River
Thames River
Quinnipiac River
Housatonic River
Long Island Sound
Long Island, New York
New York
Connecticut
84
395
2
9
95
5
91
691
15
8
A
B
C
D
N
0 SCALE 20 KILOMETERS 20 MILES
ROAD
HIGHWAY
STATE BOUNDARY

Food

- **A Gelston House**
- **B Griswold Inn**
- **C Ichiban**
- **C No Fish Today**
- **C Peppercorn's Grill**
- **C Pumpkinseed**
- **C The Savannah**
- **C Vito's by the Park**

Lodging

- **D Farmington Inn**
- **A Gelston House**
- **C Goodwin Hotel**

Lodging *(continued)*

- **B Griswold Inn**
- **C Holiday Inn**
- **C Mark Twain Hostel**
- **C Ramada Inn**
- **C Sheraton Hartford Hotel**

Camping

- **A Wolf's Den Family Campground**

Note: Items with the same letter are located in the same town or area.

4 p.m. Wednesday through Sunday May through October; open Sundays only November through April. Admission is $5 adults, $4 seniors, $2 ages 6 to 18. (½ hour)

FOOD AND LODGING

The **Griswold Inn** (860-767-1776) in Essex is always a popular stop in the Connecticut River Valley. The lively restaurant serves sandwiches and burgers for lunch, and traditional New England fare such as lobster, pot roast, and scrod for dinner. At midday on Sundays the inn serves an all-you-can-eat "hunt breakfast" ($12.95 per person). A collection of firearms, maritime artifacts, oils, and Currier and Ives prints graces the walls of the Griswold's several dining rooms. Lunch entrées start at $7, and dinner entrées start at $17. Servings are hearty. The inn also has 25 guest rooms ($100–$195 per night double occupancy). Reservations are strongly recommended for overnight lodging or weekend dinners.

If you're planning to see a musical at the Goodspeed Opera House in East Haddam (see page 225), the **Gelston House** (860-873-1411) next door could not be any more convenient. Its fine restaurant serves continental cuisine and overlooks the Connecticut River. Guest rooms, which also come with river views, range in price from $100 to $225 including private baths and a continental breakfast. Make reservations well in advance—there are only six rooms.

For deluxe lodgings in downtown Hartford, the century-old **Goodwin Hotel** (1 Haynes Street, 860-246-7500 or 800-922-5006) is the place to stay. The hotel's lovely Queen Anne facade is a standout among its neighbors and, inside, guest rooms have such inviting features as sleigh beds, fluffy down comforters, and Italian marble baths. Rates for doubles start at $185 mid-week and drop to as low as $89 on the weekends. The **Holiday Inn** (50 Morgan Street, 860-549-2400 or 800-465-4329) and **Sheraton Hartford Hotel** (315 Trumball Street, 860-728-5151 or 800-325-3535) are located just off I-84. Doubles start at about $120 at the Holiday Inn and around $100 at the Sheraton. The **Ramada Inn** (440 Asylum Street, 860-246-6591) is directly across the street from the capitol's expansive green lawn. Budget accommodations can be found at the **Mark Twain Hostel** (131 Tremont Street, 860-523-7255). The dormitory-style rooms cost $18 per night per person. If city lodging is not for you, the **Farmington Inn** (827 Farmington Avenue, 860-677-2821 or 800-648-9804) in Farmington is convenient to the Hill-Stead Museum, and is only 15 minutes from the city. Doubles at the inn range from $100 to $130 per night.

For dining in downtown Hartford, try **The Savannah** at the corner of Capitol and Main Street, **Peppercorn's Grill** (860-547-1714) a couple of doors away, or **Pumpkinseed**, a coffee house, nearby. **Vito's by the Park** (860-244-2217), on Gold Street across from Bushnell Park, is a pleasant Italian bistro. **No Fish Today** (860-244-2100), in a lovely old brick building on Pratt Street, specializes in seafood; and **Ichiban** (860-560-1414), in Bushnell Plaza across the street from the Wadsworth Atheneum, serves Japanese (including sushi) and Korean dishes and is one of the few downtown restaurants open on Sunday.

CAMPING

Wolf's Den Family Campground (860-873-9681) on Route 82 in East Haddam has over 200 campsites. Cabins are available for rent, but RV hookups are not.

ARTS AND ENTERTAINMENT

Goodspeed Opera House, built in 1876, is an attractive building on the banks of the Connecticut River in East Haddam, and is a regional landmark which can be toured even if you don't plan to see one of the evening performances. Broadway-bound musicals often get their trial run at Goodspeed during the season which runs from April through December. You can picnic on the river's edge prior to a show, or dine next door at the **Gelston House**. Call (860) 873-8668 for schedule and ticket information. You can tour the theater Saturday from 11 a.m. to 1:30 p.m. and Monday from 1 to 3 p.m. in summer. Admission is $2 adults, $1 children under age 12.

Being the state capital, Hartford quite naturally has an active cultural scene. Attractions include the **Hartford Ballet** (860-525-9396), the **Hartford Symphony Orchestra** (860-244-2999), and the **Connecticut Opera** (860-527-0713). The **Bushnell Memorial Hall** (166 Capitol Avenue, 860-246-6807) is home to over 300 performing arts events each year, and the **Civic Center** (860-727-8010) is the city's primary venue for major concerts and sporting events (the NHL's **Hartford Whalers** play their home games here; call 800-WHALERS). The **Charter Oak Cultural Center** (21 Charter Oak Avenue, 860-249-1207), Connecticut's first synagogue, is open for tours and hosts numerous live performances and concerts throughout the year. Pratt Street, between Trumball and Main, is the place to go in downtown Hartford for jazz music.

19 COASTAL CONNECTICUT

On Connecticut's coast, industrial ports such as Bridgeport and New London stand in stark contrast to smaller seaside towns. Among these are Lyme, where handsome homes border shady lanes, Stonington, where antique stores line narrow Main Street, and Madison, with its 2 miles of sandy beach. The importance of the sea in Connecticut's history is evident in this region, especially at Mystic Marinelife Aquarium and at Mystic Seaport Museum, a re-created nineteenth-century maritime village that recalls Mystic's origins as a center for whaling and shipbuilding.

Yet the pleasures of the Connecticut coast are not limited to the ocean. Renowned Yale University was founded in 1701 and moved to New Haven in 1716. Famous students include Bill and Hillary Rodham Clinton, as well as Presidents George Bush, Gerald Ford, and William Howard Taft. The university's Peabody Museum of Natural History has exhibits on land-based animals as well as sea creatures, while Yale's art gallery and Center for British Art are first-rate.

In coastal Connecticut, art lovers might also be interested in stopping at the Florence Griswold Museum in Old Lyme. The National Historic Landmark was once home base for the Lyme Art Colony of American Impressionist painters. ◪

COASTAL CONNECTICUT

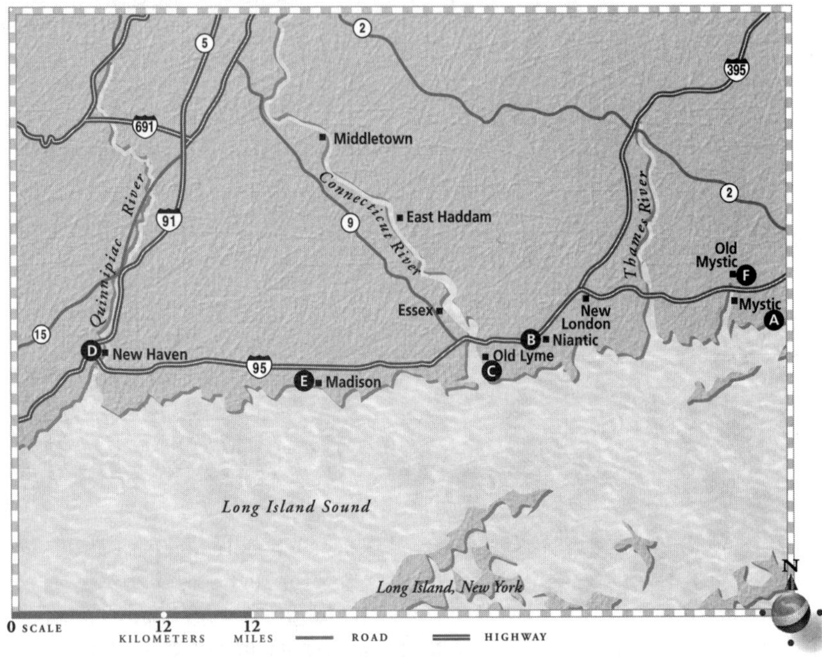

Sights

- A Captain Nathaniel B. Palmer House
- B Children's Museum of Southeastern Connecticut
- C Florence Griswold Museum
- A Old Lighthouse Museum
- D Yale University

Food

- E Inn at Cafe Lafayette

Lodging

- E Inn at Cafe Lafayette
- C Old Lyme Inn

Camping

- F Seaport Campground

Note: Items with the same letter are located in the same town or area.

A PERFECT DAY IN COASTAL CONNECTICUT

The ideal day on Connecticut's coast should be determined by your interests. If you enjoy the arts, then a visit to Yale's art museum is in order, followed by the Florence Griswold Museum in Old Lyme, perhaps squeezing in a late picnic lunch at the beach in between. If the seafaring life fascinates you, don't miss Mystic Seaport—and if you don't spend the entire day at the museum village, you might also see Mystic's Marinelife Aquarium or the Old Lighthouse Museum in Stonington in the afternoon. For those traveling with children, Mystic Seaport, the Aquarium, the New England Carousel Museum, the Denison Pequotsepos Nature Center, and the Children's Museum in Niantic all have kid appeal.

SIGHTSEEING HIGHLIGHTS

★★★ **Mystic Seaport Museum**—You'll need the better part of a day to fully explore the museum grounds. Climb aboard a whaling vessel to see the cramped quarters of deckhands and where whale blubber was processed; visit seaport shops typical of those that would have served a fishing community 100 years ago; watch boatbuilders at work; in the planetarium, learn how fishermen navigated by the stars; and in a special tribute to the America's Cup, see how sailing, once a necessary skill, has become a modern sport. A snack bar in the village serves fast-food lunches of clam cakes, burgers, or hot dogs. For more refined dining, try the Seaman's Inne next to the complex. Details: Village entrance on Route 27, less than 1 mile east of I-95; (860) 572-5315; open 9 a.m. to 5 p.m. daily in spring and fall, 9 a.m. to 8 p.m. in summer, 10 a.m. to 4 p.m. in winter; closed Christmas Day. General admission to the village is $16 adults, $8 ages 6 to 15. You'll need to buy separate tickets to take one of the steamboat cruises that leave from the village or to visit the museum's planetarium. (half–full day)

★★ **Yale University**—This prestigious member of the Ivy League is located in New Haven. Details: The visitor's information center is at 149 Elm Street; (203) 432-2300; hour-long walking tours of the campus are offered at 10:30 a.m. and 2 p.m. weekdays, 1:30 p.m. weekends. Tours are free.

Yale also has a number of museums worth a visit. The **Yale University Art Gallery** has works by Degas, Monet, Renior, van

Gogh, Picasso, and many respected American painters (Homer, Hassam, Hopper, and Eakins to name a few), as well as decorative arts. Details: 1111 Chapel Street; (203) 432-0600; open 10 a.m. to 5 p.m. Tuesday through Saturday, 2 to 5 p.m. Sunday September through July. Admission is free.

The **Yale Center for British Art**—with artwork dating back to the Elizabethan era and some 1,300 paintings, 17,000 drawings, 30,000 prints, and 22,000 rare books—has one of the most respected collections of British art in the United States. Details: 1080 Chapel Street; (203) 432-2800; open 10 a.m. to 5 p.m. Tuesday through Saturday, noon to 5 p.m. Sunday. Admission is free.

Yale's own **Peabody Museum of Natural History** is open the same hours as the Center for British Art. 170 Whitney Avenue; (203) 432-5050; open 10 a.m. to 5 p.m. Tuesday through Saturday, noon to 5 p.m. Sunday. Admission is $5 adults, $3 seniors and ages 3 to 15; free 3 to 5 p.m. weekday afternoons.

For music lovers, the university even has the **Yale Collection of Musical Instruments**. The museum has more than 800 instruments (some of sixteenth-century vintage), including a large bell collection. Details: 15 Hillhouse Avenue; (203) 432-0822; call for information as hours are limited (unfortunately for the many travelers who visit the school during summer, the museum is closed in July and August). Donations are requested. (½–1 hour per museum)

★ **Florence Griswold Museum**—At the turn of the century, Florence Griswold's residence became home to the Lyme Art Colony—a group of respected American Impressionist painters that included Childe Hassam, Will Howe Foote, Willard Metcalf, and William Chadwick. Chadwick's studio—which stands on the museum's 6-acre grounds—can be toured, as can the Griswold home, where panels painted by the former artists in residence grace the walls of the dining room. Details: 99 Lyme Street in Old Lyme; (860) 203-434-5542; open 10 a.m. to 5 p.m. Tuesday through Saturday June through November, 1 to 5 p.m. Sunday; open 1 to 5 p.m. Wednesday through Sunday the rest of the year. Admission is $4 adults, $3 students and seniors, free for children under 12. (1 hour)

★ **Mystic Marinelife Aquarium**—This is a worthwhile stop if you didn't make it to the New England Aquarium in Boston and have extra time after visiting Mystic Seaport. Exhibits include a penguin pavilion and a marine theater with daily dolphin and beluga whale demonstrations. Details: Just off I-95 at the Mystic exit; (860) 572-5955; open 9 a.m. to 7 p.m. daily July 1 through Labor Day, 9 a.m. to 5 p.m. the rest of the year; closed Thanksgiving, Christmas, New Year's Day, and the last week in January. Admission is $10.50 adults, $9.50 seniors, $7 ages 5 to 12. (1½ hours)

Captain Nathaniel B. Palmer House—This is the nineteenth-century home of the discoverer of Antarctica, Nathaniel Palmer. Details: North Water and Palmer Streets in Stonington; (860) 535-8445; open for guided tours 10 a.m. to 4 p.m. (last tour leaves at 3 p.m.) Tuesday through Sunday May through October. Admission is $4 adults, $2 ages 6 to 12. (1 hour)

Children's Museum of Southeastern Connecticut—Interactive exhibits at this kids-oriented museum include Nursery Rhyme Land, Kidsville, a scientific discovery room, a garden, and a model of the Connecticut shoreline. Details: 409 Main Street in Niantic (Route 156 between Old Lyme and New London); (860) 691-1255; open 9:30 am. to 4:30 p.m. Tuesday through Saturday, noon to 4 p.m. Sunday year-round; also open Monday noon to 4 p.m. and Friday until 8 p.m. in summer. Admission is $3 per person, free for children under 2. (1 hour)

Denison Pequotsepos Nature Center—This 125-acre establishment offers nature trails and a small natural-history museum. One trail is designed especially for blind visitors, and during the winter the trails are open for cross-country skiing. Details: Pequotsepos Road in Mystic; (860) 536-1216; open 9 a.m. to 5 p.m. Monday through Saturday, 1 to 5 p.m. Sunday May through Labor Day; closed Sunday and Monday during the off-season. Admission is $4 adults, $2 children over 5. (1 hour)

New England Carousel Museum—Take a trip back to your childhood with a visit to this museum devoted to preserving and displaying antique carousel art. Details: 193 Greenmanville Avenue (Route 27 at exit 90 off I-95); (860) 536-7862; open 10 a.m. to 5 p.m. Monday through Saturday, noon to 5 p.m. Sunday year-round; open until 6 p.m. in summer. Admission is $4 adults, $3.50 seniors, $2.50 ages 4 to 14. (1 hour)

Old Lighthouse Museum—This stone structure dating to 1823 was Connecticut's first government-operated lighthouse. Now it houses artifacts from the whaling industry and trade with Asia, as well as changing exhibits. There's a waterside picnic table in the parking lot on the point just beyond the museum. Details: 7 Water Street in Stonington; (860) 535-1440; open 10 a.m. to 5 p.m. Tuesday through Sunday May through October. Admission is $4 adults, $2 ages 6 to 12. (½ hour)

FITNESS AND RECREATION

The 2-mile long beach at **Hammonasset Beach State Park** (203-245-2785) off Route 1 in Madison is Connecticut's longest public beach, and probably the best place to go if you want to spend a day at the ocean while in the state. There are bathhouses, snack bars, bike trails, a nature center, plenty of picnic tables, and ample parking. The park is open year-round from 8 a.m. until sunset. Out-of-state vehicles are charged up to $12 on weekends during the summer. The parking fee is less on weekdays and for in-state vehicles, and there is no fee in the off-season.

FOOD AND LODGING

Mystic is a good home base for exploring Connecticut's coast because not only is it within a couple of hours from most coastal attractions, it also has a helpful tourist information center at the Mystic exit of I-95 that will help you find appropriate lodging in the area. A board lists nearby accommodations, their rates, and driving distances. The center's helpful personnel will even call ahead to secure your room. While there, be sure to peruse the menus from area restaurants and pick out the ones that best suit your tastes and budget. The tourist center is also a great source of area sightseeing information.

The **Inn at Mystic** (860-536-9604 or 800-237-2415)—on a hill overlooking the water and a marina at the junction of Route 27 and U.S. 1—has accommodations ranging from motor court rooms in shingled buildings to comfortable rooms in a traditional country inn. There are gardens, a tennis court, a restaurant, a pool, and a hot tub on the premises. Rooms in the motor court are $90 to $230 during the summer and $65 to $220 off-season. Inn rooms go for $125 to $250 per night.

If you wish to stay within walking distance of Mystic's downtown shops and restaurants, the **Whaler's Inn** (860-536-1506 or 800-243-2588) is your only lodging choice. It offers pleasant accommodations in 2-story motel-style buildings dressed up with geranium-filled flower boxes. Doubles range in price from $85 to $135 per night. Restaurants **Bravo** and the **Bagel Company** are located on the inn's ground level.

There are a number of reasonably priced restaurants and fast-food establishments in and around Olde Mystick Village, just off I-95. The **Seaman's Inne** (860-536-9649), next to Mystic Seaport, specializes in seafood and prime-rib dinners. In downtown Mystic, locals recommend the **Draw Bridge Inne** (860-536-9653), a half-block from the drawbridge on Main Street. It offers specialties for seafarers and landlubbers alike. Dinner entrées average about $15. For a simple but filling meal, try an overstuffed sandwich at **2 Sisters Deli** (860-536-1244) on Pearl Street just off Main. For breakfast, try **Bee Bee Dairy** (860-536-4577), a family-style restaurant on Main Street; and for pizza, of course, there's **Mystic Pizza,** where the Julia Roberts film of the same name was set.

In Old Lyme, diagonally across the street from the Florence Griswold Museum, the **Old Lyme Inn** (85 Lyme Street, 860-434-2600 or 800-434-5352) offers both fine dining and overnight accommodations. The inn is near busy I-95, but all is pleasant once inside the white 1850s former farmhouse with bright blue shutters. The front lawn is set for a game of croquet. Double occupancy rates, which include a continental breakfast, range in price from $100 to $160. If you want to stay at an in-town location and still be near the beach, try **The Inn at Cafe Lafayette** (800-660-8984) right on Main Street in downtown Madison. Once a nineteenth-century church, the inn now offers fine dining as well as guest rooms furnished with antiques and marble baths.

CAMPING

Seaport Campground (860-536-4044), 3 miles from the Mystic Seaport Museum, is the closest campground to Mystic's attractions. From exit 90 on I-95, take Route 27 north 1¼ miles to Route 184. Follow Route 184 east for about ½ mile and watch for the campground on your left. RV hookups and tent sites are available, and complete recreational facilities, including swimming, are on the premises. The campground is open mid-April through late October.

MYSTIC

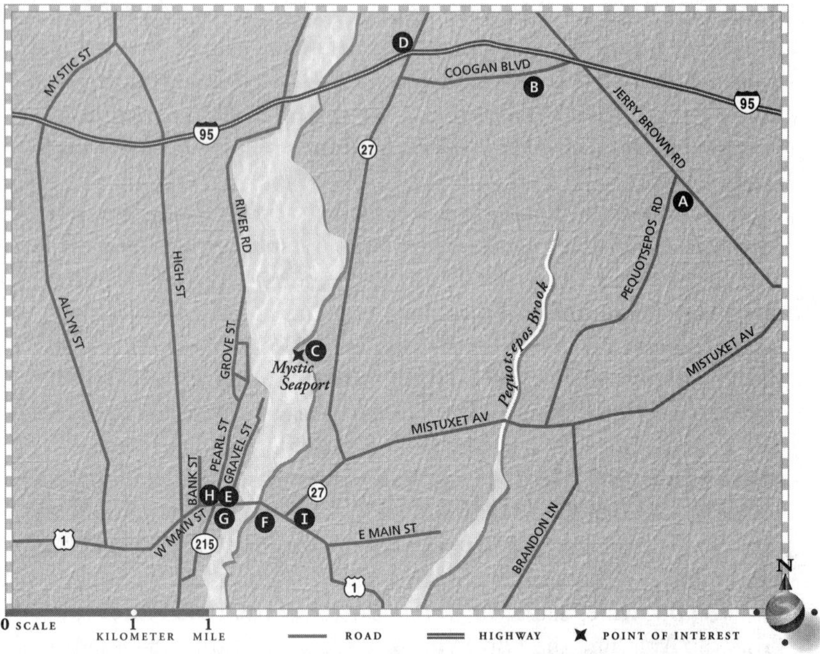

Sights

- **A** Denison Pequotsepos Nature Center
- **B** Mystic Marinelife Aquarium
- **C** Mystic Seaport Musuem
- **D** New England Carousel Museum

Food

- **E** 2 Sisters Deli
- **F** Bagel Company
- **G** Bee Bee Dairy

Food *(continued)*

- **F** Bravo
- **E** Draw Bridge Inne
- **H** Mystic Pizza
- **C** Seaman's Inne

Camping

- **I** Seaport Campground
- **F** Whaler's Inn

Note: Items with the same letter are located in the same town or area.

SIDE TRIPS FROM COASTAL CONNECTICUT

Las Vegas comes to the rural Connecticut countryside in the form of **Foxwoods Casino** in Mashantucket southeast of Norwich about a half-hour drive from Mystic. Foxwoods gets a lot of press, and even more business, because it was New England's first modern-day casino. Operated by the Pequot Indians, the casino has brought a financial boon to the once all-but-extinct tribal nation. If you're lucky a visit to the casino will be a financial boon to you as well. Be prepared, however, for a visual shock: The massive Foxwoods complex is disturbingly out-of-scale with the surrounding cornfields. Restaurants and accommodations are located within the casino complex. Even the traffic lights at each entrance appear to be programmed to make you stop—just in case you were contemplating driving by without dropping in. Call (800) FOXWOOD for details. The Mohegan Indians, no doubt seeing the success the Pequots have had, have opened their own casino and claim it is one of the country's largest. It is located in Uncasville north of New London (888-226-7711).

Those who wish to explore Long Island's exclusive **Hamptons** or sand dunes at **Montauk** can take the ferry from New London, Connecticut (several miles south of Mystic), to Orient Point on Long Island, New York. The ferry trip costs over $20 one-way for most automobiles. Unfortunately, you really do need to bring your car across to do any sightseeing. The ferry operates year-round except for Christmas Day. Sailing time is approximately 1½ hours. Call (203) 443-5281 for schedule and reservation information. To visit the Hamptons from Orient Point, take Route 25 west to Riverhead and Route 24. Follow Route 24 until it intersects with Route 27. Drive east on Route 27 to the Hamptons, then continue all the way out to the lighthouse at Montauk Point.

20 NEWPORT

Newport, Rhode Island, is a city of contrasts. Its inhabitants range from the wealthy living in turn-of-the-century mansions to military personnel stationed at the nearby naval base to the yachting crowd that invades each summer. Somehow, this city manages to satisfy all these groups in their varied pursuits—and quite competently at that.

It is also this diversity of people and attractions that makes Newport such an appealing place to visit. One can wander through a topiary garden, then visit the oldest synagogue in the United States; tour a lavish oceanfront mansion such as the Vanderbilts' Breakers, then stroll past modest colonial homes in the center of the city; shop for souvenirs in the Brick Marketplace, then admire handsome ships docked at the waterfront; dine overlooking the grass tennis courts at Newport Casino or opt for a traditional New England clambake on a sandy beach. Choices abound.

In a way, Newport was a city conceived on choices. Founded in 1639 by the Antinomians, a religious group that split off from the Massachusetts Bay Colony, the city became a refuge for others seeking religious freedom, including Sephardic Jews and Quakers.

During the American Revolution, Newport was occupied by the British. It later served as co-capital of the state. In the late 1800s, Newport was a summer playground for the very rich, while today the city of close to 30,000 residents is home to people of varied incomes and backgrounds. ◪

NEWPORT

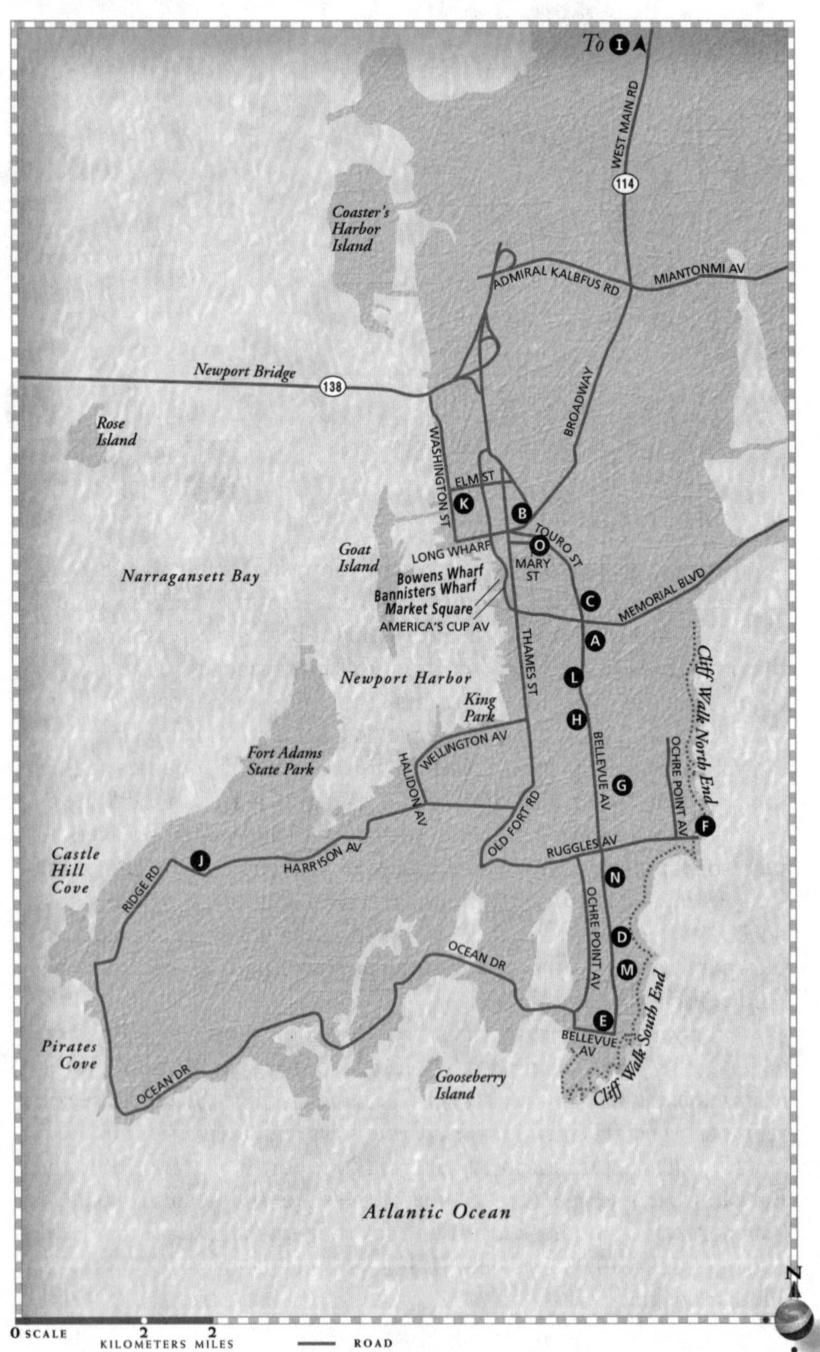

To I
WEST MAIN RD
114
Coaster's Harbor Island
ADMIRAL KALBFUS RD
MIANTONMI AV
Newport Bridge
138
BROADWAY
Rose Island
WASHINGTON ST
ELM ST
K
B
TOURO ST
O
Goat Island
LONG WHARF
MARY ST
Narragansett Bay
Bowens Wharf
Bannisters Wharf
Market Square
AMERICA'S CUP AV
C
MEMORIAL BLVD
A
THAMES ST
Cliff Walk North End
Newport Harbor
L
King Park
H
WELLINGTON AV
Fort Adams State Park
HALIDON AV
BELLEVUE AV
G
OCHRE POINT AV
F
OLD FORT RD
Castle Hill Cove
J
HARRISON AV
RUGGLES AV
RIDGE RD
N
OCHRE POINT AV
D
OCEAN DR
M
Cliff Walk South End
E
Pirates Cove
BELLEVUE AV
OCEAN DR
Gooseberry Island
Atlantic Ocean
N
0 SCALE
2
2
KILOMETERS MILES
ROAD
CLIFF WALK

Sights

- Ⓐ **International Tennis Hall of Fame**
- Ⓑ **Museum of Newport History**
- Ⓒ **Newport Art Museum**

Newport Mansions:

- Ⓓ **Beechwood**
- Ⓔ **Bellecourt Castle**
- Ⓕ **The Breakers**
- Ⓖ **Château-Sur-Mer**
- Ⓗ **The Elms**

Newport Mansions *(continued)*:

- Ⓘ **Green Animals**
- Ⓙ **Hammersmith Farms**
- Ⓚ **Hunter House**
- Ⓛ **Kingscote**
- Ⓜ **Marble House**
- Ⓝ **Rosecliff**

- Ⓞ **Touro Synagogue**

A PERFECT DAY IN NEWPORT

Begin your day with a tour of Marble House, then stroll along the Cliff Walk, a 3-mile promenade that skirts the great lawns of many of Newport's finest homes as well as the ocean some 30 feet below. Have a picnic lunch at Brenton Point State Park followed by the pièce de résistance—a tour of the sumptuous Breakers Mansion. Afterwards, head downtown for an ice-cream cone at Newport Creamery and shopping along Thames Street and the Wharf area. End the day with a seafood dinner at either the Cooke House or the livelier Black Pearl restaurant next door.

SIGHTSEEING HIGHLIGHTS

★★★ **Newport Mansions**—The Preservation Society of Newport operates six exquisite mansions (or "cottages," as they were called by their original owners), one historic home, and a topiary garden. The palatial mansions represent a lifestyle that's just about unheard of today. They were the summer homes of wealthy businessmen. The tycoons' wives, who ruled Newport society, were given up to $300,000 per season just for entertaining—and that was a century ago. You'll probably be able to appreciate only two properties in one day unless you're very energetic. Take your pick—you won't be disappointed. Details: (401) 847-1000; Marble House, the Elms, and Château-Sur-Mer are open 10 a.m. to 4 p.m. on weekends throughout the winter and are beautifully decorated for Christmas. Most of the remaining mansions are open weekends starting in April, and all are open 10 a.m. to 5 p.m. daily throughout the summer. The Breakers is open until 6 p.m. on Saturdays July through Labor Day. Since hours do vary from mansion to mansion and season to season, it is best to check with the Preservation Society for hours during your visit. Admission to most of the mansions is at least $6.50 for adults and about $3.50 for ages 6 to 11. Adult combination tickets range from $13 for any two mansions to $35.50 for all. Children's combination tickets range from $5 to $11.

The Breakers, on Ochre Point Avenue off Bellevue, is the most extravagant of all the mansions and the most popular with tourists. Designed by architect Richard Morris Hunt, who also designed the extraordinary Biltmore House in North Carolina, the Breakers was built in Italian Renaissance style for Cornelius Vanderbilt in 1895. This stately home, with 70 rooms and an abundance of gold leaf and marble throughout its interior, is almost overwhelmingly opulent. No expense was spared in its construction; it was even wired for electricity—a real rarity at the time. Children will enjoy the "Children's Cottage" on the grounds.

Château-Sur-Mer ("House by the Sea") and **Rosecliff** (on Bellevue Avenue) are also situated on the ocean. Florentine craftsmen were responsible for many of the creative touches at Château-Sur-Mer. The mansion has a stained-glass ceiling above its main hallway and a Chinese Moon Gate on its grounds. Rosecliff was designed by well-known architect Stanford White, and has the largest private ballroom in Newport. Robert Redford and Mia Farrow waltzed in this ballroom in the movie version of *The Great Gatsby*.

Marble House—appropriately named for the beautiful and rare marble throughout (more than 500,000 cubic feet of marble was used in construction)—is my personal favorite. William K. Vanderbilt had the "cottage" built for his wife's thirty-ninth birthday in 1892. (Ironically, they later divorced—but she kept the house.) The mansion cost $7 million to build, and half that again to furnish—all for a home that was used only six to eight weeks a year. A Chinese teahouse on the grounds exemplifies the wealthy's fascination with the Orient at the turn of the century.

Also on Bellevue Avenue are **The Elms** and **Kingscote**. The Elms, modeled after a French château, is known for its array of trees and shrubbery. Kingscote, built in 1839, is one of the oldest mansions open to the public. Incorporating elements of both Victorian and Gothic architecture, the estate was named after William Henry King, who acquired the property in 1864.

The **Hunter House** at 54 Washington Street is much smaller in scale than the grand "cottages," reflecting its mid-eighteenth-century time period. It was the headquarters for French naval forces during the Revolutionary War, and is now a National Historic Landmark.

The **Green Animals** topiary gardens are located on Cory's Lane off Route 114 in Portsmouth. An elephant, a giraffe, and a camel are just a few of the animal-shaped shrubs that are bound to amuse children and adults alike.

Several other stately homes, none of which are operated by the Preservation Society, are also open to the public. **Hammersmith Farms**, near Fort Adams, is often considered the most "livable" of the Newport mansions. The wedding reception for John F. and Jacqueline Kennedy was held here. Its colorful gardens were designed by Frederick Law Olmstead. Details: (401) 846-7346; open 10 a.m. to 5 p.m. weekends March and November, daily April through October; open until 7 p.m. at the height of the summer season.

Bellecourt Castle on Bellevue Avenue is owned and occupied by the Tinney family. The house is open for high tea, and guided tours are led by attendants in period costume. A gold coronation coach and art treasures from all over the world are among the items on display. Details: (401) 846-0669; open 10 a.m. to 5 p.m. daily April through October, 10 a.m. to 3 p.m. in the off-season; closed in January. Call for castle hours if you plan to visit during spring or fall. Admission is $7.50 adults, $6 seniors, $5 students, $3 children.

Beechwood, also on Bellevue Avenue, was built for the Astors. Although the home is not as lavish or well-kept as the Preservation Society mansions, the tour can be quite entertaining: Actors playing members of the Astor household greet you as a dinner guest and treat you to the family gossip of the day. Details: (401) 846-3772; open 10 a.m. to 5 p.m. mid-May through October, 10 a.m. to 4 p.m. during the off-season; closed in January. Admission "calling card" is about $8 adults, $6 children and senior citizens, $30 per family.

There are many beautifully restored colonial homes in and around Queen Anne Square 1 block from Thames Street. Explore these streets on your own or take an organized walking tour with the Newport Historical Society (82 Touro Street, 401-846-0813). Tours usually begin at 10 a.m. in the summer. (1 hour per mansion)

★ **International Tennis Hall of Fame**—The museum is adjacent to the emerald-green grass courts of the Newport Casino. The shingled casino was designed by the renowned architecture firm of McKim, Mead & White and was constructed in 1880. Professional tennis tournaments are still held here today. Tennis buffs will want to visit the museum to see its collection of trophies, costumes, and equipment, but those who don't play will probably be content to poke around the outside of the building. Details: 194 Bellevue Avenue, (401) 849-3990; open 10 a.m. to 5 p.m. daily; closed Christmas and Thanksgiving. Admission is $6 adults, $2.50 children under 16; senior-citizen discounts are available. (1 hour)

★ **Museum of Newport History**—Those who wish to delve deeper into Newport's history should visit this museum created by the Newport Historical Society. Hours: 82 Touro Street; (401) 846-0813; open hours vary—call for more information. Admission is $5 adults, $3 ages 6 to 12; family rates available. (1 hour)

★ **Newport Art Museum**—The museum is housed in the Griswold Mansion, built in 1864. American art exhibits are changes regularly. Details: 76 Bellevue Avenue; (401) 848-8200; open 10 a.m. to 4 p.m. Tuesday through Saturday, 1 to 4 p.m. Sunday September through May; open until 5 p.m. during summer. Admission is $5 adults, $4 students and seniors. (1 hour)

★ **Touro Synagogue**—Built in 1763, the oldest synagogue in the country is now a National Historic Site. Details: Touro Street, (401) 847-4794; open 10 a.m. to 5 p.m. Sunday through Thursday, 10 a.m. to 3 p.m. Friday in summer; call for winter hours. (½ hour)

FITNESS AND RECREATION

For a two-wheeled view of the island, rent bicycles from **Ten Speed Spokes** (401-847-5609) at the corner of Elm and America's Cup Avenue. At **Adventure Sports Rentals and Tours** (142 Long Wharf, 401-849-4820) you can rent everything from a mountain bike to a Waverunner to a sailboat. They also offer fishing trips, kayaking, and parasailing. Take a sailing lesson at **Sail Newport Sailing Center** (401-849-8385 in summer; 401-846-1983 in off-season) at Fort Adams State Park, or simply rent a boat if you already know how to sail.

You can take a horseback ride along the beach with **Newport Equestrian Center** (401-848-5440). If you prefer to lie on the sand rather than ride on it there are three popular public beaches in the area. **First Beach** is located in Newport at the end of the Cliff Walk and has a parking lot and bathhouse. **Second** and **Third Beaches** have better sand than First Beach, but they are located in nearby Middletown, less convenient to the center of Newport.

FOOD

The Black Pearl (401-846-5264) on Bannister's Wharf is a very popular Newport restaurant, as evidenced by the throngs of hungry diners in line to be seated. Next door at the **Cooke House** (401-849-2900), you'll find truly elegant dining upstairs for dinner, and a more casual atmosphere downstairs at the **Candy Store**. For dining in a unique setting, try **La Forge Restaurant** (401-847-0418) overlooking the grass courts at the Newport Casino. La Forge serves veal and chicken dinner entrées for about $15. Another fine restaurant is the **White Horse Tavern** (401-849-3600), the oldest operating tavern in the United States.

Numerous restaurants along Thames Street offer cheaper alternatives for eating out. **Cafe Zelda** (528 Thames, 401-849-4002) has a varied menu with everything from burgers to lobster, and prices are easy on the pocketbook. For Italian and Mediterranean specialties, try **Pronto** (464 Thames, 401-847-5251). Prices are reasonable and the mood is romantic. For dessert, visit any one of the **Newport Creamery**'s several locations for a traditional ice-cream cone. **Poor Richard's** (254 Thames Street, 401-846-8768) is the place to get breakfast.

LODGING

Stay in the heart of things at the **Inntowne** (401-846-9200 or 800-457-7803) at Thames and Mary Streets, where many of Newport's shops and restaurants are at your doorstep. Rates range from $95 to $300, depending on the season and type of accommodation. Rooms at the **Francis Malbone House** (392 Thames, 401-846-0392 or 800-846-0392) are elegantly furnished with attractive Colonial reproduction furniture. The 1760 Colonial mansion is listed on the National Register of Historic Places. A full gourmet breakfast is included in the room rate, which ranges in price from $175 to $355 in-season and from $145 to $275 off-season. The **Marriott** (401-849-1000 or 800-458-3066) on the waterfront is also convenient to Newport center. Nine of the Marriott's rooms are specially equipped for handicapped guests. Doubles run from about $170 to $240.

There are two comfortable and centrally located bed and breakfasts on quiet Clarke Street. The **Admiral Farragut** (31 Clarke, 401-848-8015 or 800-343-2863) was built in 1650. Doubles run $115 to $145 in summer and start at $60 in winter. The **Melville House** (39 Clarke Street, 401-847-0640), built in 1750, is listed on the National Register of Historic Places. Doubles are $65 to $125 in winter and $85 to $145 in summer, including breakfast and afternoon tea. One suite has a working fireplace.

For an out-of-the-ordinary night's sleep, try the **Jailhouse Inn** (13 Marlborough Street, 401-847-4638 or 800-427-9444) where bars on the windows and black-and-white-striped bedspreads are not just for show—the inn was once a jail. Doubles, including a continental breakfast, range from $95 to $225 in high-season, and from $55 to $115 in low-season.

Warm hospitality is what you'll experience at the **Marshall Slocum Guest House** (29 Kay Street, 401-841-5120 or 800-372-5120). Innkeeper Joan Wilson treats midweek guests who stay three nights or more to a complimentary lobster dinner on Wednesday evenings. Afternoon refreshments and a full breakfast (perhaps Joan's homemade hash or peach French toast) are included in the room rates: $80 for a room with a shared bath, $90 for a room with a private bath.

At the **Willows of Newport** (401-846-5486), about a five-minute walk from the Brick Marketplace, guests are served breakfast in bed by black tie–attired attendants. Hostess Pattie Murphy, a longtime resident of Newport, is happy to share her knowledge of Newport's diverse history with her guests. Many guests particularly enjoy the Willows' garden. Doubles range in price from $98 to $198.

If you prefer to be adjacent to the Cliff Walk rather than downtown, the **Cliffside Inn** (2 Seaview Avenue, 401-847-1811 or 800-845-1811) is a good choice. The lovely Victorian home is furnished with antiques, and a full breakfast and afternoon hors d'oeuvres are included in the rates ($185–$350).

For a splurge you won't soon forget, stay at the **Castle Hill Inn** (401-849-3800 or 888-466-1355) off Ocean Drive. With a room overlooking the ocean, a fireplace, and a whirlpool tub, you'll feel like a

Vanderbilt. Doubles with a private bath and water view cost more than $200 during the summer, significantly less during the winter months. The inn's restaurant is also worth a try.

Bed & Breakfast of Rhode Island (401-849-1298 or 800-828-0000) can help you locate accommodations. Their service is free of charge.

CAMPING

There are several municipal campgrounds near Newport, the closest being **Middletown Campground** (401-846-6273 or 401-846-5781) on Second Beach in neighboring Middletown. Since there are only 44 campsites, reservations are strongly recommended. Open late May through late September. Facilities include toilets, showers, and sewer hookups. On the far side of the island, **Melville Ponds Campground** (401-849-8212) off Route 114 in Portsmouth has tent sites, RV sites with hookups, and recreational facilities. The campground is open April 1 through October 31. Tent sites are $13; RV sites are $18 with water and electricity, $22 if you want a sewer hookup. If all campgrounds on the island are filled, try the one in Jamestown at **Fort Getty Recreation Area** (401-423-7211). You can fish at the campground, but you will have to cross the toll bridge to sightsee in Newport. Open during the summer months on a first-come, first-served basis. Tent sites are about $17 per night, and RV hookups are $22 per night.

SHOPPING

The Brick Marketplace on Thames Street and Bannisters and Bowen Wharves off America's Cup Avenue comprise Newport's main shopping district. Not to be missed by nautical buffs is the **Armchair Sailor Bookstore** on Lee's Wharf, which has one of the most comprehensive selections of maritime publications found anywhere.

NIGHTLIFE

Jai alai is considered to be the fastest game on two feet. See if you can keep up with the action at **Newport Jai Alai** (150 Admiral Kalbfus Road, 800-451-2500 or 401-849-5000). Rhode Island is one of the few states that allows pari-mutuel wagering on the sport. Admission is nominal to encourage betting.

NEWPORT

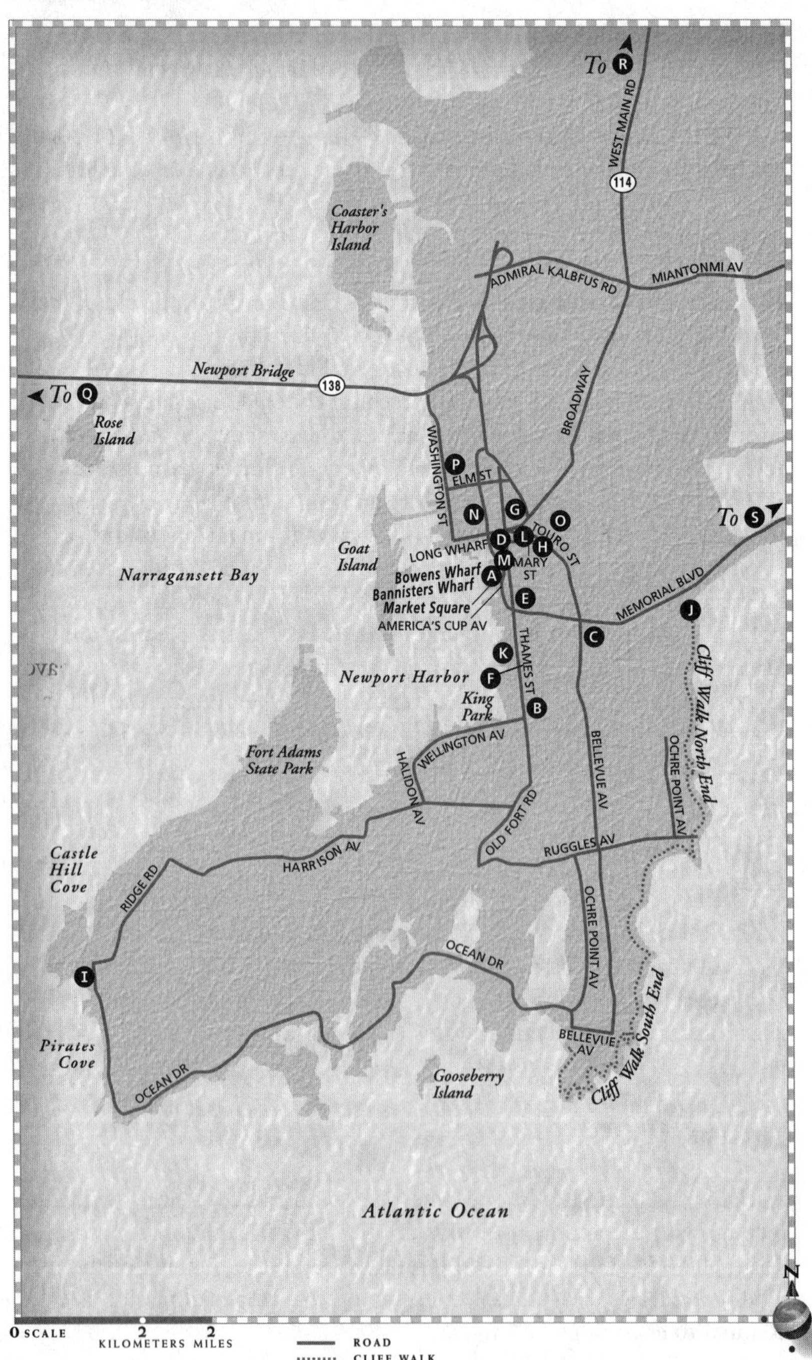

To R
WEST MAIN RD
114
Coaster's Harbor Island
ADMIRAL KALBFUS RD
MIANTONMI AV
Newport Bridge
138
To Q
Rose Island
BROADWAY
WASHINGTON ST
ELM ST
To S
Goat Island
LONG WHARF
TOURO ST
MARY ST
Narragansett Bay
Bowens Wharf
Bannisters Wharf
Market Square
AMERICA'S CUP AV
MEMORIAL BLVD
THAMES ST
Newport Harbor
King Park
Cliff Walk North End
BELLEVUE AV
OCHRE POINT AV
Fort Adams State Park
WELLINGTON AV
HALIDON AV
OLD FORT RD
Castle Hill Cove
RUGGLES AV
HARRISON AV
RIDGE RD
OCHRE POINT AV
OCEAN DR
Pirates Cove
BELLEVUE AV
Cliff Walk South End
Gooseberry Island
OCEAN DR
Atlantic Ocean
N
0 SCALE
2 KILOMETERS
2 MILES
ROAD
CLIFF WALK

Food

- Ⓐ The Black Pearl
- Ⓑ Cafe Zelda
- Ⓐ Candy Store
- Ⓐ Cooke House
- Ⓒ La Forge Restaurant
- Ⓓ Newport Creamery
- Ⓔ Poor Richard's
- Ⓕ Pronto
- Ⓖ White Horse Tavern

Lodging

- Ⓗ Admiral Farragut
- Ⓘ Castle Hill Inn
- Ⓙ Cliffside Inn

Lodging *(continued)*

- Ⓚ Francis Malbone House
- Ⓛ Inntowne
- Ⓜ Jailhouse Inn
- Ⓝ Marriott
- Ⓞ Marshall Slocum Guest House
- Ⓗ Melville House
- Ⓟ Willows of Newport

Camping

- Ⓠ Fort Getty Recreation Area
- Ⓡ Melville Ponds Campground
- Ⓢ Middletown Campground

Note: Items with the same letter are located in the same town or area.

Many of Newport's bars and restaurants offer music. Try **The Pelham** on Thames Street for jazz. **Club Thames** on America's Cup Avenue is the place to go for dancing to a contemporary beat.

SIDE TRIPS FROM NEWPORT

Need a break from sightseeing? How about a break from the world in general? If so, a trip to **Block Island** may be the answer. Only 12 miles off the coast of Rhode Island, Block Island was originally settled in 1661. The island offers visitors all of the quiet beauty, miles of beach, and dramatic cliffs of Martha's Vineyard, without the commercialism.

If you enjoy cycling past sand dunes, beach roses, lily ponds, and old stone walls; exploring wildlife refuges and lighthouses; or just lounging on the beach, Block Island will be a welcome retreat. But if you're looking for art museums, chic shops, and active nightlife, then this is not the place for you. There is only one town on the island, consisting primarily of one street lined with Victorian-era hotels and a handful of restaurants and souvenir shops.

Ferries to the island operate from Point Judith, Rhode Island, year-round, though a winter visit is not recommended. Service is more frequent during the summer, and ferries even run from Newport during the summer months. The trip from Point Judith takes a little over an hour. One-way fares are $6.60 for adults, $3.15 for children, and $10.50 and $5, respectively, for a same-day round-trip. Passenger cars cost $20.25 one way, motorcycles are $11.85, and bicycles are $1.75. Call (401) 783-4613 for reservations and a current ferry schedule. If you're lucky enough to get a legal parking spot along the street, parking is free. Otherwise it will cost you at least $5 per day.

Just about every service you'll need on the island is within a block of the ferry dock. The tourist booth in the dock parking lot can provide you with a map of the island for $1 (some bike rental places will give you an island map for free with a rental). It will guide you to the unusual gray granite lighthouse at Sandy Point, Crescent Beach, the Clayhead Nature Trail, and the wildlife refuge at Rodman's Hollow.

Across the street from the dock area you can rent a bike or moped, then shop for picnic foods at the market next door (one of the few places on the island to get provisions). While bringing your car over to the island may be cheaper than renting bikes (about $10 per day per bicycle) or mopeds (about $60 per day for two), these two-wheeled vehicles bring you closer to the island's charm.

Most of the island's accommodations are right along Old Harbor's main street. (Some have limited seasons, so be sure to call ahead if you plan to stay overnight.) The **National Hotel** (401-466-2901 or 800-225-2449), built in 1888, is the most prominent. You can't miss it as the ferry pulls into the harbor. The hotel's restaurant has pleasant outdoor dining and an excellent appetizer menu. Double rooms at the hotel go for $69 to $229, depending on the season and the view. The **Harborside Inn** (401-466-5504), with doubles including continental breakfast ranging from $69 to $199 (some rooms have shared baths), is another Victorian inn right in the town's center. The **Manisses Hotel** and the **1661 Inn** (401-466-2421 or 800-626-4773), both on the edge of town, are jointly managed. Guests staying at either can enjoy a small animal farm behind the Hotel Manisses, buffet breakfasts, and dinner. The hotel has one of the most interesting menus on the island, and dinner entrées are priced from $16. Room rates range from $50 to $335. **Finn's Seafood Restaurant** (401-466-2473) is the place to go for lobster.

Just over the Rhode Island/Massachusetts border, you'll find the **New Bedford/Fall River** area with its factory outlet stores. These stores are factory outlets in the truest sense since they are generally located on the factory premises. A guide to the outlets can be picked up at the New Bedford visitor's center.

Once a bustling whaling center, New Bedford experienced a great decline during the twentieth century. Recently, efforts have been made to restore the city to its past glory. You can see the handsome result of those efforts by rambling through the 16-block cobblestone area that comprises the historic district, originally built up in the 1760s. New Bedford's visitor's center, on Second Street in the historic district, is open from 9 a.m. to 5 p.m. Monday through Saturday, 11 a.m. to 5 p.m. Sunday.

At New Bedford's **Whaling Museum** (18 Johnny Cake Hill, 508-997-0046), exhibits range from model vessels and ships' logs to scrimshaw artwork depicting whaling expeditions. The museum offers a fascinating look at an industry and an era that have long since died out. The museum is open from 9 a.m. to 5 p.m. daily June through September. On Sundays during the winter months, the museum does not open until 1 p.m. Admission is $4.50 for adults and $3 for children.

After visiting the whaling museum, you may want to see the **Seaman's Bethel** across the street: It was the whalemen's chapel referred to in Herman Melville's *Moby Dick*. If you like period homes, the **Rotch-Jones-Duff House and Garden Museum** (508-977-1401) should be on your itinerary while you're in New Bedford. Built in what is now New Bedford's County Street Historic District, this 1834 Greek Revival home is a fine example of the "brave houses and flowery gardens" Melville described in *Moby Dick*. The museum is open from 10 a.m. to 4 p.m. Tuesday through Saturday, 1 to 4 p.m. Sunday. Admission is $3 for adults, $2 for seniors, and $1 for children 12 and over. The museum offers concerts under the stars on some summer evenings.

New Bedford's **Buttonwood Park Zoo** stands on 13 acres and is surrounded by a 90-acre park designed by Frederick Law Olmstead of Boston Public Gardens fame. The zoo is open daily from 10 a.m. to 5 p.m. Admission is $1.50 for adults and $1 for children.

If you plan to dine in New Bedford, **Freestone's Restaurant & Bar** (508-993-7477) is located in an attractive building on the corner of Williams and Second Streets. It serves sandwiches—including seafood melts—at reasonable prices; entrées are more expensive (about $12 each). **Jimmy Connor's Irish Pub** (508-997-2808), on the corner of Acushnet and Union Streets, is a good place to stop for a modestly priced burger and a draft beer. **The Last Laugh** (784 Purchase, 508-999-9812) is a bar and deli just north of the historic district. Its sandwiches are named for famous comedians such as Jackie Gleason.

The world's largest exhibit of historic fighting ships can be found in **Fall River's Battleship Cove**. Visitors can tour the USS *Joseph P. Kennedy Jr.* destroyer, a 35,000-ton battleship named *Big Mamie* that saw action in World War II, a World War II attack sub, and PT boats. The cove is open daily from 9 a.m. to 5 p.m., and admission is $8 for adults, $6 for seniors, and $4 for ages 6 to 14. The **Marine Museum** (508-674-3533) nearby has ship models, a *Titanic* exhibit, and other marine collections. The museum is open from 9 a.m. to 5 p.m. Monday through Friday, noon to 4 p.m. on weekends and holidays May through October. Call for winter hours. Admission is $3.50 for adults, $2.50 for seniors and ages 6 to 14.

Providence is Rhode Island's capital and the Ocean State's largest city. In Providence you can visit the lovely campus of **Brown University**, several historic homes, and the **Roger Williams Park Zoo** (1000 Elmwood Avenue, 401-785-3510). The zoo has some 600 specimens representing more than 160 species (including rare species such as the red panda). It also has a barn that dates back to 1891. The zoo is open from 9 a.m. to 5 p.m. daily April through October; it closes at 4 p.m. the rest of the year. Admission is $5 for adults, $2.50 for seniors and children. Providence's **Museum of Natural History** (401-785-9457) includes a planetarium at Roger Williams Park. The museum is open from 10 a.m. to 5 p.m. and admission is $2 for adults and $1 for children under 8. Planetarium shows cost $4 for adults, $3 for children 8 and over, and $1 for children under 8.

The highly respected **Rhode Island School of Design** is also located in Providence. Quite fittingly the school has the **Museum of Art at RISDE** (224 Benefit Street, 401-454-6502). Admission to the museum is $2 for adults, $1 for seniors, and 50 cents for students and children. During the school year the museum is open from 10:30 a.m. to 5 p.m. Tuesday, Wednesday, and Friday, and from noon to 8 p.m. Thursday and Sunday. In summer hours are limited to noon to 5 p.m. Wednesday through Saturday.

If you're interested in Rhode Island's history, visit the **Aldrich House** (110 Benevolent Street, 401-331-8575). The 1822 Federal-style home is open from 9 a.m. to 5 p.m. Tuesday through Friday. You can also tour **John Brown House,** (52 Power Street, 401-331-8575), an 1785 Georgian mansion with Brown family memorabilia.

21 MARTHA'S VINEYARD

Although Martha's Vineyard is only 7 miles from Cape Cod and the Massachusetts mainland, once you get there it doesn't take long to relax and leave the rest of the world behind. The island is 20 miles long by 10 miles wide at its widest point, and its population swells from around 12,000 year-round residents to almost 62,000 in summer. Even so, if you venture out of the main towns, you can almost always find a quiet spot to call your own. It's the island's gentle beauty and sense of seclusion that draw visitors year after year. Many celebrities, including Carly Simon and Walter Cronkite, call the vineyard home.

Discovered by British explorers John Bereton and Bartholomew Gosnold in 1602, Martha's Vineyard was named after Gosnold's daughter and for the abundance of grapes that once covered the island. Now the island holds three main towns, Vineyard Haven, Oak Bluffs, and Edgartown, with stretches of beach and sand dunes in between. Edgartown, the most elegant of the towns, showcases the prosperity that the whaling trade brought to nineteenth-century New England communities. Vineyard Haven is the quietest of the three towns, while Oak Bluffs, with its colorful Victorian "gingerbread" houses and active nightlife, is more flamboyant. The most dramatic scenery on the island is at Gay Head, where chalky cliffs meet the sea. ◪

MARTHA'S VINEYARD

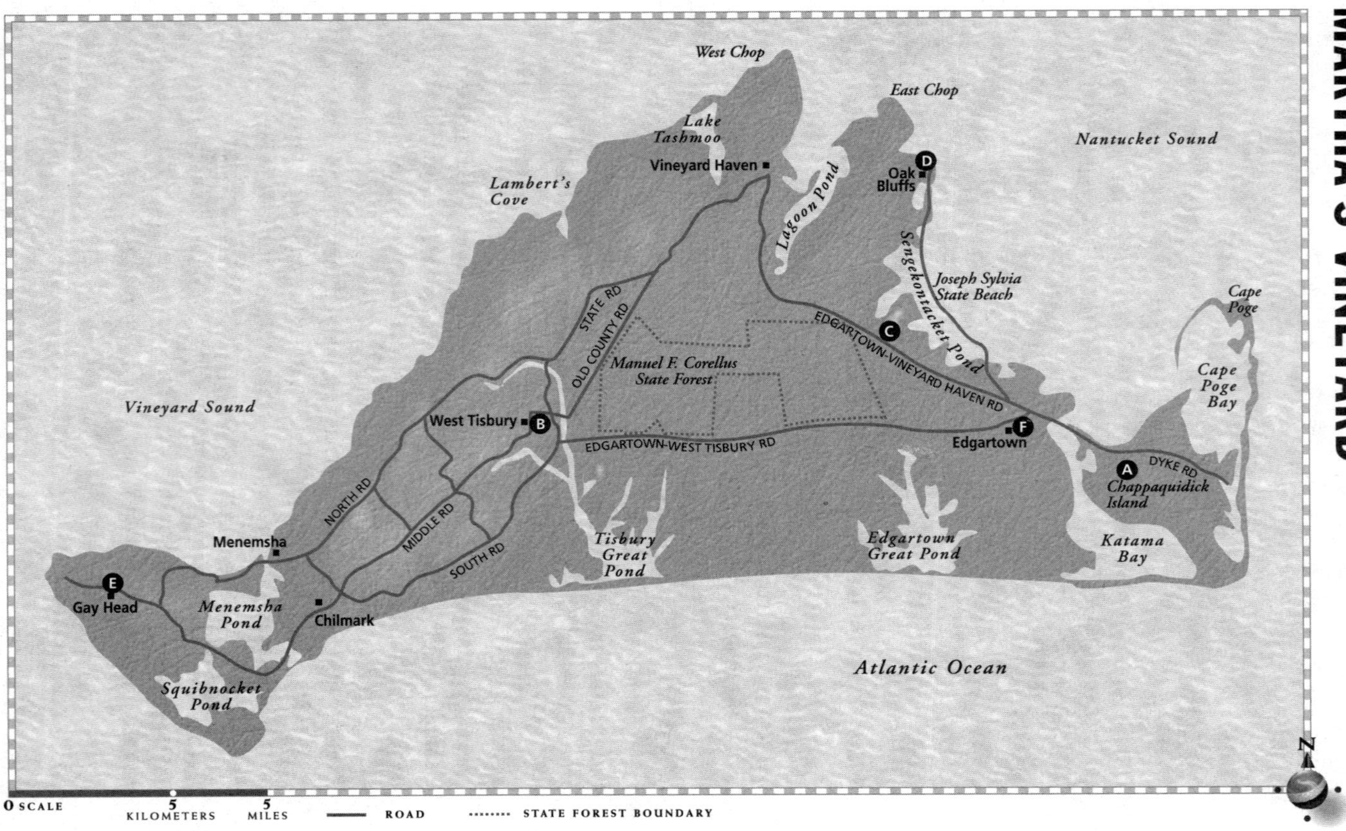

Sights

- **A Chappaquiddick Island**
- **B Chicama Vineyards**
- **C Felix Neck Sanctuary**
- **D Flying Horses Carousel**
- **E Gay Head**
- **F Vineyard Museum**

A PERFECT DAY ON MARTHA'S VINEYARD

Pack a picnic lunch, rent a moped, and set out to explore the island with Gay Head as an ultimate destination. After visiting Gay Head, look for a quiet stretch of beach and soak up the sun for a few hours. Later in the afternoon, head to Edgartown for window-shopping and a good meal.

GETTING TO MARTHA'S VINEYARD

Boats to Martha's Vineyard leave from either Woods Hole or Hyannis on Cape Cod, but if you wish to bring your car to the Vineyard you must take the **Steamship Authority** ferry from Woods Hole. **Hy-line** (508-778-2600) boats take passengers only to the Vineyard from Hyannis, and although the trip is longer and more expensive than from Woods Hole, it may be more convenient, depending upon where you are staying on the Cape. The first ferry to the Vineyard from Woods Hole usually leaves around 7 a.m., and even earlier during summer. Sailing time from Woods Hole is approximately 45 minutes, and boats arrive in either Oak Bluffs or Vineyard Haven, only a few miles apart.

Passenger fares one-way from Woods Hole to Martha's Vineyard are about $5 for adults, $2.50 for ages 5 to 12. Fares for automobiles can cost more than $40 one-way at peak times, and run as little as $20 during the winter months. Reservations for automobiles are *strongly* recommended during summer months. Although it may seem expensive to bring a car over, when you consider that moped rentals are at least $50 a day, it may be worth the fare, particularly if you decide to stay more than one day or if there are more than two people in your party. Call the Steamship Authority in Woods Hole (508-548-3788) for the ferry schedule and reservation information.

Cape Air offers flights to Martha's Vineyard from Hyannis, Boston, and New Bedford. The one-way airfare runs about $120 from Boston, $40 from New Bedford, and $35 from Hyannis, with discounts available for round-trip ticket purchases. The Boston flight, which takes just over half an hour, is the longest of the three flights. Call (508) 771-6944 or (800) 352-0714 for reservations and a flight schedule.

TRANSPORTATION ON MARTHA'S VINEYARD

Traveling by moped is one of the easiest ways to get around the island. You don't have to worry about finding a parking space when you discover that deserted stretch of beach, and you can travel much faster than on a bicycle. There are clearly marked and well-maintained bicycle paths on the island. Moped and bicycle rental places abound in Vineyard Haven, Edgartown, and particularly in Oak Bluffs. Many operations claim they have the lowest rates on the island. You may want to shop around, but my experience has been that rates tend to be fairly consistent from one place to the next and that your time is better spent sightseeing than looking for a bargain-priced moped rental. Daily rentals cost at least $50 in-season for a moped that seats two fairly comfortably. Bicycle rentals run about $15 per day.

Budget (408-693-1911) has several car rental locations on the island, should you prefer traveling on four wheels. To see the island from the seat of a Harley-Davidson or a 1964 Mustang convertible, contact **Vineyard Classic Cars** at (408) 693-5551. They rent classic automobiles (and motorcycles) by the hour, day, and week, and will come pick you up.

Numerous taxi services and sightseeing operators will greet you right at the boat and offer to take you around the island. During the summer months **Martha's Vineyard Transportation Services** operates shuttles between the major towns. Call (408) 693-1589 or 693-0058 for schedule information and bus stop locations.

SIGHTSEEING HIGHLIGHTS

★★ **Gay Head**—The jagged cliffs at Gay Head offer the most dramatic scenery on the island. Gay Head, which also has a lighthouse, is at the opposite end of the island from the towns of Oak Bluffs, Edgartown, and Vineyard Haven. (½ hour)

★ **Chappaquiddick Island**—Many visitors to Martha's Vineyard enjoy an excursion to Chappaquiddick. A ferry runs from the waterfront in Edgartown to the island from 7:30 a.m. to midnight during summer. Fares are nominal and prices are even quoted for horses and cattle in case you brought yours along. The ferry runs as needed and must be one of the shortest ferry crossings you'll ever experience. (1 hour)

★ **Vineyard Museum**—Most people don't come to Martha's Vineyard to spend their time in museums, but if inclement weather forces you indoors, this museum and library are dedicated to preserving island history through exhibits of maritime artifacts, scrimshaw, and antique clothing. Details: Cooke and School Streets; (508) 627-4441; open 10 a.m. to 5 p.m. daily July 4 through Labor Day; call for off-season hours. Admission is $5 adults, $3 ages 7 to 15. (½ hour)

Chicama Vineyards—In keeping with the island's origins, Martha's Vineyard now has this active vineyard in West Tisbury. Details: Stoney Hill Road; (508) 693-0309; open 11 a.m. to 5 p.m. Monday through Saturday, 1 to 5 p.m. Sunday in summer. (½ hour)

Felix Neck Sanctuary—This wildlife refuge is operated by the Massachusetts Audubon Society. The self-guided trails that wind through marshlands offer glimpses of birds and native wildlife in their natural habitat. Details: 1 mile off the Edgartown-Vineyard Haven road, about halfway between the two towns (turn at the sign); (408) 627-4850; open until 7 p.m. Admission is $3 adults, $2 children. (1 hour)

Flying Horses Carousel—If you're traveling with kids, a visit to this carousel at the bottom of Circuit Avenue in Oak Bluffs is a must-see. Dating back to 1876, it is the oldest working carousel in the United States. Details: (408) 693-9481; operates 10 a.m. to 10 p.m. daily mid-June through August; limited hours Easter through mid-June and September through Columbus Day. Rides are $1. (½ hour)

FITNESS AND RECREATION

The beaches on the Vineyard are lovely. Perhaps the most accessible beach to the public is **Joseph Silvia State Beach**, which runs along the road between Edgartown and Oak Bluffs. Park your vehicle on the side

MARTHA'S VINEYARD

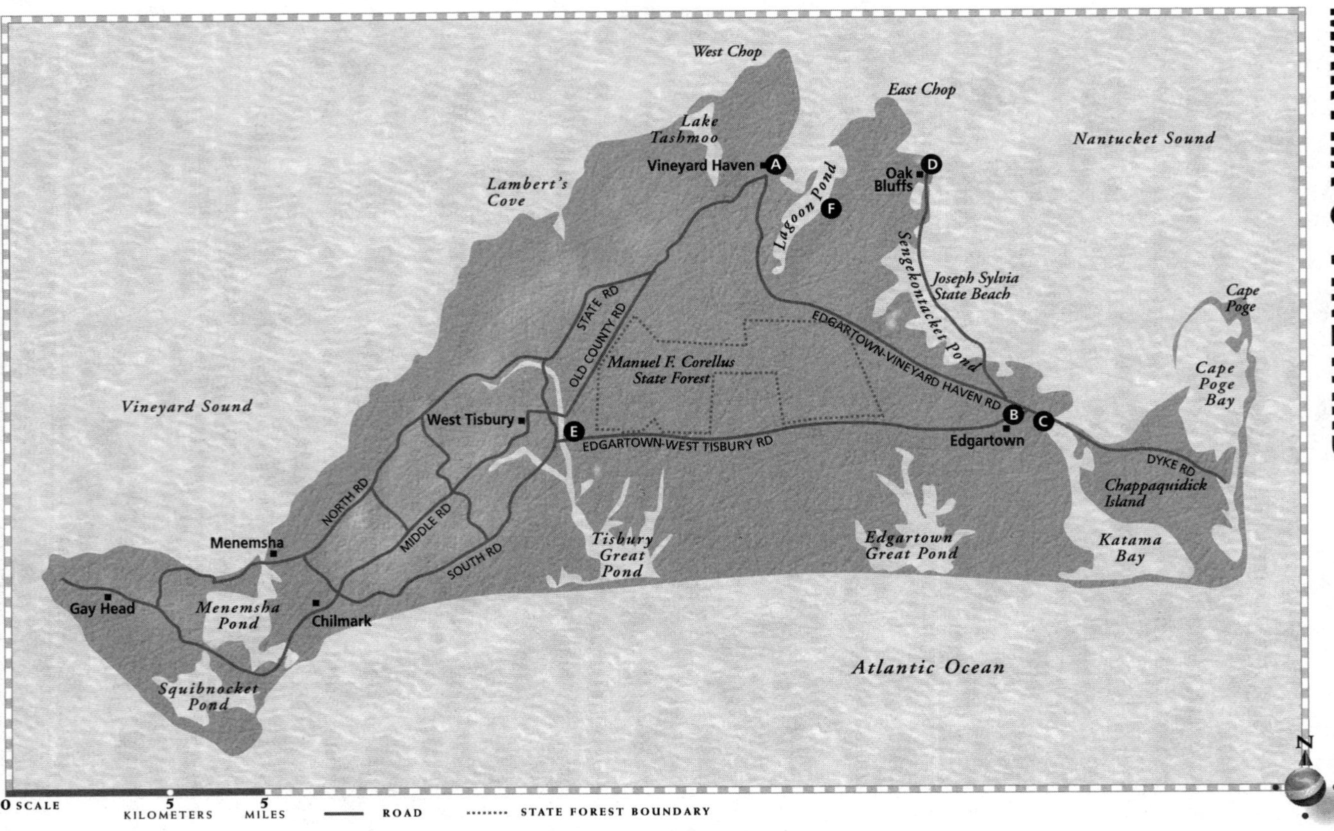

Food

- **A Black Dog Tavern**
- **B Navigator Restaurant and Boathouse Bar**
- **B O'Brien's Restaurant**
- **C The Quarterdeck**
- **D Seasons Bar 'n' Grille**
- **B Shiretown Inn & Restaurant**
- **B Wharf Restaurant**

Lodging

- **B Charlotte Inn**
- **B Daggett House**
- **B Hob Knob Inn**

Lodging *(continued)*

- **E Manter Memorial AYH Hostel**
- **D Oak Bluffs Inn**
- **B Victorian Inn**
- **D Wesley Hotel**

Camping

- **C Martha's Vineyard Family Campground**
- **F Webb's Camping Area**

Note: Items with the same letter are located in the same town or area.

of the road, hop over the dunes, and stretch out. Warning: As tempting as it may be, overnight camping is not allowed.

Bicycling is one of the most popular activities on Martha's Vineyard (see above for rental information). There are clearly marked and well-maintained bike paths all over the island.

FOOD

There are plenty of dining choices on the island, especially in summer. In Edgartown, the **Navigator Restaurant and Boathouse Bar** (508-627-4320) at the foot of Main Street and the **Wharf Restaurant** (508-627-9966) across the street both serve seafood. The Navigator, which overlooks the water, offers lunches for about $8 and dinner for about $19. In summer, the Navigator also has a light-dinner menu in the $10 range. If your appetite runs to dishes such as roast rack of lamb Dijon, veal scallopini, or prime rib, try the **Shiretown Inn &**

Restaurant (508-627-6655). Dinner entrées start around $20, and there is a pub on the premises. **O'Brien's Restaurant** (508-627-5850) on Upper Main Street features both seafood and pasta dishes in a comfortably elegant and candlelit setting. Outdoor dining in the rose garden is a pleasant option in nice weather. For the cheapest ocean-front table in town, get a burger or fried clams to go from **The Quarterdeck** near the Chappaquiddick ferry, and sit on the docks.

In Oak Bluffs meals are usually casual, and on Circuit Avenue you can get anything from steak and seafood to subs, pasta, and pizza. **Seasons Bar 'n' Grille** (124 Circuit, 508-693-7129) is pleasant and informal, and serves good pub-style food at reasonable prices.

The **Black Dog Tavern** (508-693-9223), in Vineyard Haven, is one of the most popular establishments on the island. Even President Clinton ate here when he visited. But don't let the word "tavern" mislead you—Vineyard Haven is a dry town, so no liquor is served. Prices at the Black Dog are steep, and some feel that the restaurant is beginning to ride on its reputation and that the quality of the food is not what it once was.

If you travel to Gay Head and forget to pack a picnic, there are several fast-food establishments there that offer fried-clam platters and the like.

LODGING

For sumptuous accommodations in Edgartown, the **Charlotte Inn** (508-627-4751) on South Summer Street fits the bill. It provides country-inn comfort in restored nineteenth-century homes that originally belonged to sea captains. High-season doubles start at $250 and suites cost as much as $650; low-season rates are about half that. The lovely **Victorian Inn** (508-627-4784) on South Water Street was once a whaling captain's home as well, and is now listed in the National Register of Historic Places. Prices are $125 to $265 in high-season, and start at $70 in the off-season for rooms furnished with canopy beds and antiques. A gourmet breakfast, served outside in the garden during the summer and inside in front of the fire in the winter months, is included in the room rates. The **Daggett House** (59 North Water Street, 508-627-4600 or 800-946-3400)—a country inn on the water in Edgartown—was built in 1660 and has a secret stairway. Doubles cost from $85 to $285 during the winter months, and $150 to $400 in summer. The **Hob Knob Inn** (128 Main Street,

508-627-9510 or 800-696-2723) is another handsome home originally built for a sea captain. Rooms are decorated in chintz with antiques, king beds, and down comforters. Doubles range in price from $125 to $250 in low-season and $185 to $375 in summer. Rates include a full breakfast, and in winter months an afternoon tea is also served.

The **Oak Bluffs Inn** (508-693-7171 or 800-955-6235), at the corner of Circuit Avenue and Pequot Avenue in Oak Bluffs, is painted flamboyantly in pink to exemplify the lighter side of Victorian architecture. Rates range from $115 to $160 during the summer, and start as low as $80 in the off-season. The **Wesley Hotel** (505-693-6611 or 800-638-9027), on Lake Avenue overlooking Oak Bluffs Harbor, has been restored, and is typical of many turn-of-the-century seaside hotels. High-season double rooms with shared baths are $65, doubles with private baths are $125 to $175.

Perhaps the least expensive lodging on the island can be found at the **Manter Memorial AYH Hostel** (508-693-2665) on the Edgartown-West Tisbury road 3 miles west of the airport. Dormitory-style accommodations cost $12 per night per person for AYH members and $15 for non-members. The hostel is open from April through mid-November.

CAMPING

There are two campgrounds on Martha's Vineyard: **Webb's Camping Area** (508-693-0233) on Barnes Road several miles southwest of Oak Bluffs and **Martha's Vineyard Family Campground** (508-693-3772) on the Edgartown-Vineyard Haven road a little over a mile from the ferry dock. Martha's Vineyard Family Campground is open mid-May through mid-October. Tent sites for two are $25 per night, RV sites are $28. Webb's is open mid-May through mid-September, with nightly rates starting at $26. Both campgrounds have facilities for RV and tent campers, as well as children's playgrounds and camp stores.

NIGHTLIFE

Of the three main towns, Oak Bluffs has the most active nightlife on the Vineyard. The **Atlantic Connection Nightclub** (508-693-7129) and some its neighboring bars on Circuit Avenue can be jam-packed during summer months. Many of the patrons are college students working on the island during school break.

22 NANTUCKET

Thirty miles from the Massachusetts coast, Nantucket Island is a sparkling oasis in the Atlantic. During its heyday, Nantucket was the third largest city in Massachusetts—trailing only Boston and Salem. Evidence of the island's onetime whaling prominence can be seen in the facades of graceful Federal, Greek Revival, and Georgian-style homes that border Nantucket town's cobblestone streets (made with stones once used for ships' ballast); and in the railinged roofwalks atop the many fine homes used by early residents as lookouts for incoming whaling ships. Shingled cottages in Siasconset on the other side of the island are more modest, yet no less respectable, reminders of the seafaring life. In between are miles of low-lying moors and soft sand beaches.

Nantucket is a delightful getaway. Fine galleries, boutiques, and restaurants abound in handsome Nantucket town, while historic sights such as the Old Mill, the Fire Hose Cart House, and the Old Gaol serve as reminders of the island's past. For some, finding a deserted stretch along one of Nantucket's 82 miles of glorious beach is all the retreat they need to make the two-hour boat trip from the mainland worthwhile. ◪

NANTUCKET

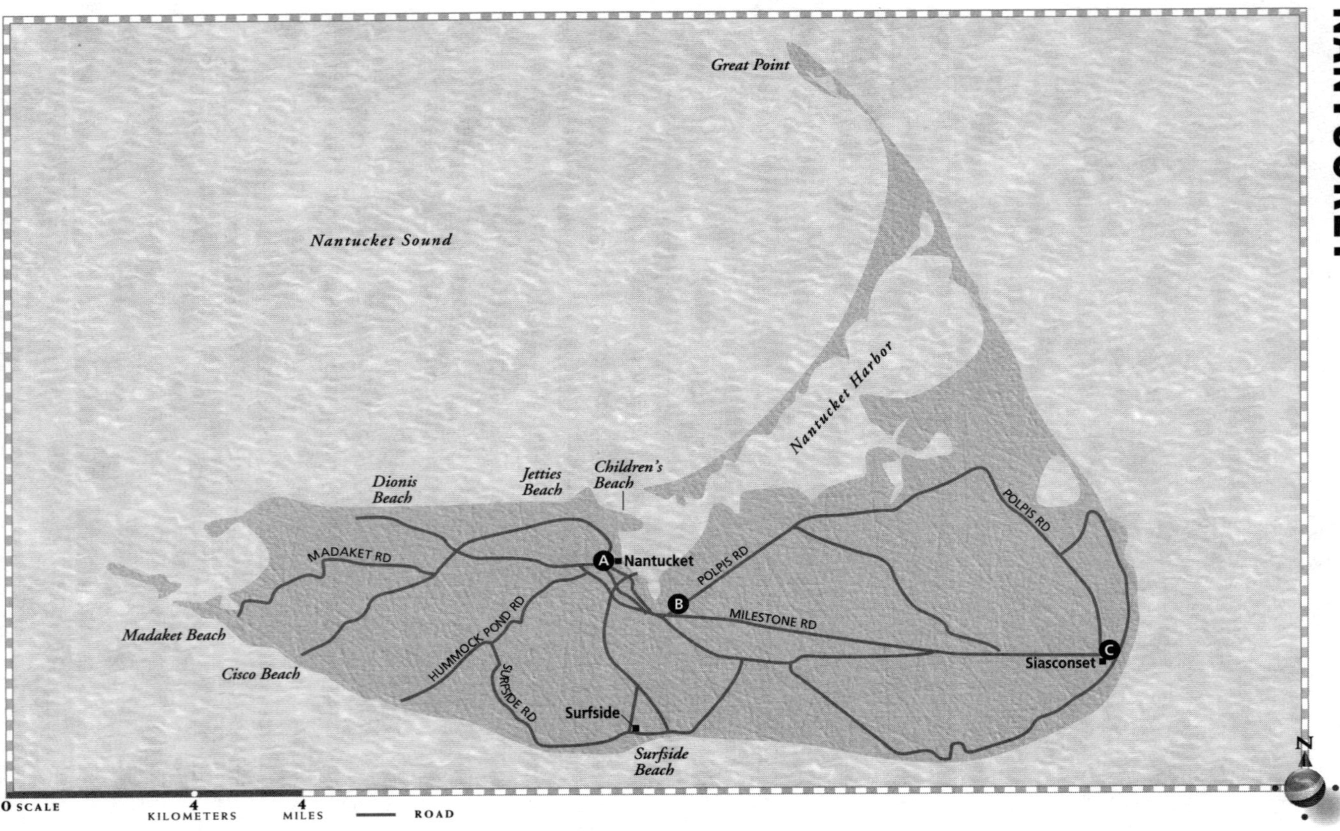
Great Point
Nantucket Sound
Nantucket Harbor
Dionis Beach
Jetties Beach
Children's Beach
Nantucket
A
B
C
MADAKET RD
POLPIS RD
POLPIS RD
MILESTONE RD
HUMMOCK POND RD
SURFSIDE RD
Siasconset
Madaket Beach
Cisco Beach
Surfside
Surfside Beach
N
0 SCALE
4 KILOMETERS
4 MILES
ROAD

Sights

Ⓐ **Maria Mitchell Science Center**

Ⓐ **Nantucket Atheneum**

Ⓐ **Nantucket Historical Association**

Ⓑ **Nantucket Life-Saving Museum**

Ⓒ **Siasconset**

Note: Items with the same letter are located in the same town or area.

A PERFECT DAY ON NANTUCKET

After breakfast at the Downyflake, browse through Nantucket's shops in the morning, and perhaps visit one or two Nantucket Historical Association sites. Lunch at the Rose & Crown, and then bicycle to Siasconset where you can wander down inviting residential lanes, relax on the beach, or travel out to the lighthouse. If you're in the mood for an elegant dinner, dine at the Chanticleer; if not, try the less formal Sconset Café. If the weather is especially nice, you might opt for a picnic dinner on the beach instead.

GETTING TO NANTUCKET

To get to Nantucket, **Steamship Authority** (508-771-4000 in Hyannis or 508-228-0262 in Nantucket) boats leave from South Street in Hyannis, while **Hy-Line** (508-778-2600 in Hyannis or 508-228-3949 in Nantucket) boats leave from Ocean Street, which intersects with South Street. Because of their proximity to one another, and because fares from Nantucket (about $11 for adults and $5.50 for children ages 5 and over) are about the same on both lines, it is possible to take the Hy-Line out to the island and return by the Steamship Authority, or vice versa, giving you more departure times to choose from. Sailing time from Hyannis on traditional ferries takes a little over two hours to Nantucket. Hy-Line also has a high-speed catamaran service which makes the trip in just over an hour, but tickets, as one might expect, are costlier at $29 one way ($52 round-trip) for adults, and $23 one way ($39 round-trip) for children ages 1 to 12. Cars can travel on Steamship Authority ferries only, at a rate of $100 one way in the height of summer. Since Nantucket is so small, it really makes more sense to leave your car on the mainland and travel by alternative means once on the island. However, if you are planning an extended stay, the cost of rental vehicles on the island may exceed the cost of bringing your own automobile.

Hy-Line also operates an inter-island ferry from Oak Bluffs on Martha's Vineyard to Nantucket from early June to mid-September. The ferry takes passengers only. It departs Oak Bluffs three times a day and costs $11 for adults and $5.50 for children ages 5 and older. Bike rentals are $4.50.

If you're short on time or are prone to seasickness, there is another way to get to Nantucket from the mainland. Flights, which take only 20 minutes from Cape Cod and cost about $65 round-trip for adults, can be an appealing option for some. **Nantucket Airlines** (508-228-6234 or 800-635-8787) and **Island Airlines** (508-228-7575 or 800-248-7779) have frequent flights between Hyannis and Nantucket, while **Cape Air** (508-771-6944 or 800-352-0714) offers service between Nantucket and Boston, New Bedford, and Hyannis.

GETTING AROUND THE ISLAND

Nantucket is small and flat enough so that you can get around rather easily by bicycle. Rentals cost about $15 per day; you should have no trouble locating the rental shops as you come off the boat. Moped rentals are much more expensive—at least $50 per day for a two-person vehicle. However, if you can afford it, renting a moped may make sense because they allow you to cover much more ground in a short period of time. Most bike rental establishments also offer mopeds.

If you haven't brought your automobile over on the ferry and decide once you're on the island that you'd prefer to rent a car rather than travel by bicycle or moped, there are a number of car rental agencies on Nantucket. **Windmill Auto Rental** (508-228-1227 or 800-228-1227) rents everything from convertibles to jeeps, **Don Allen Auto Service** (508-228-5666 or 800-258-4870) rents Fords, **Affordable Rentals** (508-228-3501) has cars as well as mopeds, and **Budget** (888-228-5666) has a branch on the island.

Barrett's Tours (20 Federal Street, 508-228-0174 or 800-773-0174) operates a shuttle service to Siasconset, Jetties, Surfside, and Madaket Beaches in the summer, and offers guided tours.

SIGHTSEEING HIGHLIGHTS

★★ **Nantucket Historical Association**—The association operates a number of period homes, museums, and monuments, representing four centuries of Nantucket history. The sights are located throughout the town of Nantucket. Pick up the "Historic Nantucket" brochure—which maps out the route—from the tourist office on the corner of Chestnut Street, just 1 block from Main Street.

The tour begins at the **Thomas Macy Warehouse** on Straight Wharf, then continues to the **Whaling Museum** on Broad Street near Steamboat Wharf. Just next door is the **Peter Fougler Museum and Research Center** building where genealogical charts and ships' logs are on display. The period homes include **The Oldest House**, built in 1686 and considered to be the oldest house still standing on the island; the **Hadwen House**, a stately Greek Revival built in 1845 at the height of the whaling era; and **Thomas Macy-Christian House**. You can also visit the **Old Gaol**, built in 1805; the **Old Mill**, built in 1746 and still operational today; the **Quaker Meeting House**, dating to 1838; the **Fair Street Museum** next door, containing Nantucket

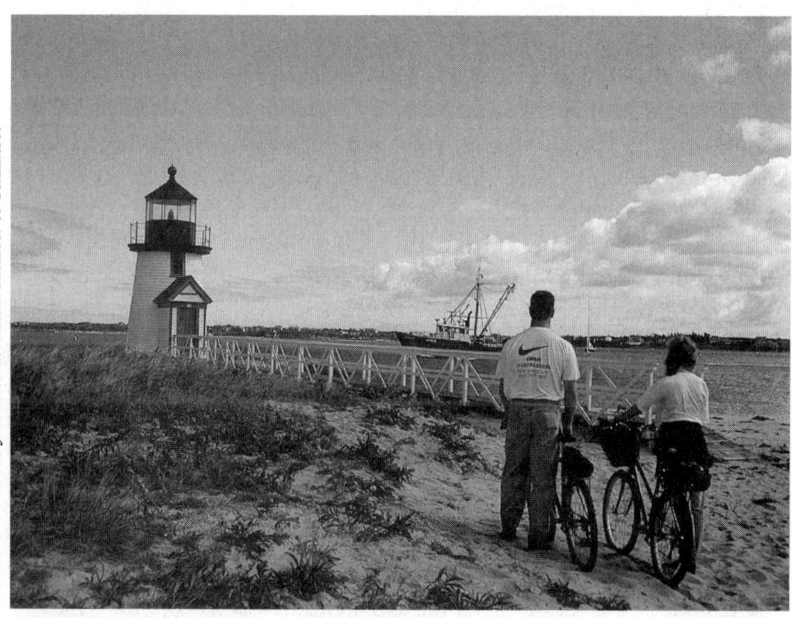

On the beach in Nantucket

decorative-arts exhibits; and the **Fire Hose Cart House**, which contains nineteenth-century firefighting equipment and was built in 1866. Details: (508) 228-1894; buildings close at 5 p.m. Admission charges to the various buildings range from $2 to $5, or you can buy a visitor's pass that will admit you to all of them: $10 adults, $5 children ages 5 to 14. (half–full day)

★★ **Siasconset**—In Siasconset (called Sconset by locals) there are no official sights to see, but the town's often-deserted beach, quiet seaside lanes, and charming weathered cottages are enough to warrant the 7½-mile trip from Nantucket center. One of my favorite walks is along the footpath that runs between some of Siasconset's most beautiful homes and the sand dunes that protect the houses from the sea. To reach the footpath, proceed straight from the market in the town's center to the row of houses overlooking the beach. When you come to the end of the row, at a house named Casa Marina, turn right (just to the left of the house) on what looks like a driveway. Where the driveway veers back to the main road, continue straight ahead onto the lawn. This is the beginning of the footpath, which will lead you across people's lawns (this is legal, but be considerate). The path runs from the village out to Sankaty Head Lighthouse. (1–2 hours)

★ **Maria Mitchell Science Center**—Dedicated to the nation's first prominent woman astronomer, the center operates a science library, a small natural science museum, an aquarium, and an observatory. It also maintains the astronomer's birthplace, which was built in 1790 and boasts the only public roofwalk on the island. Details: 7 Milk Street. Open 10 a.m. to 4 p.m. Tuesday through Saturday in summer. Admission is $3 adults, $1 children under 14; a combination ticket to the birthplace, the natural history museum (called the Hinchman House), and the aquarium is $5 adults, $2 children.

For information on the center, stop in at the library at 2 Vestal Street (508-228-9198). It houses Mitchell's papers as well as books on astronomy. The library is open year-round and operates on the same hours as the rest of the center during the summer, and from 2 to 5 p.m. Wednesday through Friday, 9 a.m. to noon on weekends during the off-season. (½ hour per site)

Nantucket Atheneum—If libraries are of interest to you, than the Nantucket Atheneum on India Street in the heart of downtown

Nantucket may be worth a visit. The handsome Greek Revival–style building was constructed in 1847, and has recently been restored. Scrimshaw and ship models, as well as over 40,000 volumes, are among the library's collections. Maria Mitchell (see above) was the Atheneum's first librarian. Details: India Street, (508) 228-1110. (½ hour)

Nantucket Life-Saving Museum—This museum claims to be the only one of its kind in the world. Exhibits include lifeboats, historic photographs, and artifacts from the *Andrea Doria*—the Italian liner which met its untimely end off the coast of Nantucket in July of 1956. Details: Polpis Road outside of town, (508) 228-1885; open 10 a.m. to 4:30 p.m. Tuesday through Saturday mid-June through mid-September. (½ hour)

FITNESS AND RECREATION

Those with time to beachcomb may want to visit **Children's Beach**, **Jetties Beach**, and **South Beach**, all within walking distance from downtown Nantucket. **Dionis Beach**, 3 miles south of town, offers calm waters for swimming. Adventurous swimmers will enjoy the surf at **Madaket**, **Surfside**, and **Siasconset**. Serious surfers find **Cisco Beach** to their liking.

There are bike paths to Siasconset, Madaket, and Surfside Beaches, and another that runs along Cliff Road. The bike path across the island's central moors is for mountain bikes only.

FOOD

Sconset Café (508-257-4008), in Siasconset Center, serves both lunch and dinner. With entrées such as Indonesian grilled shrimp and shrimp stuffed artichokes, the café offers an interesting twist to its seafood dishes that one doesn't come across in many New England restaurants. Lunch entrées range in price from $7 to $13, dinner entrées begin at $17.50. The café is only open during the summer, as is the market around the corner where you can pick up fresh sandwiches, pasta, and potato salad to take with you to the beach.

Chanticleer Inn (508-257-6231), also in Siasconset, specializes in French gourmet fare and is considered by many to be the best restaurant on the island. Festive flowers and a brightly painted carousel horse greet diners in the restaurant's garden courtyard, making outdoor

NANTUCKET

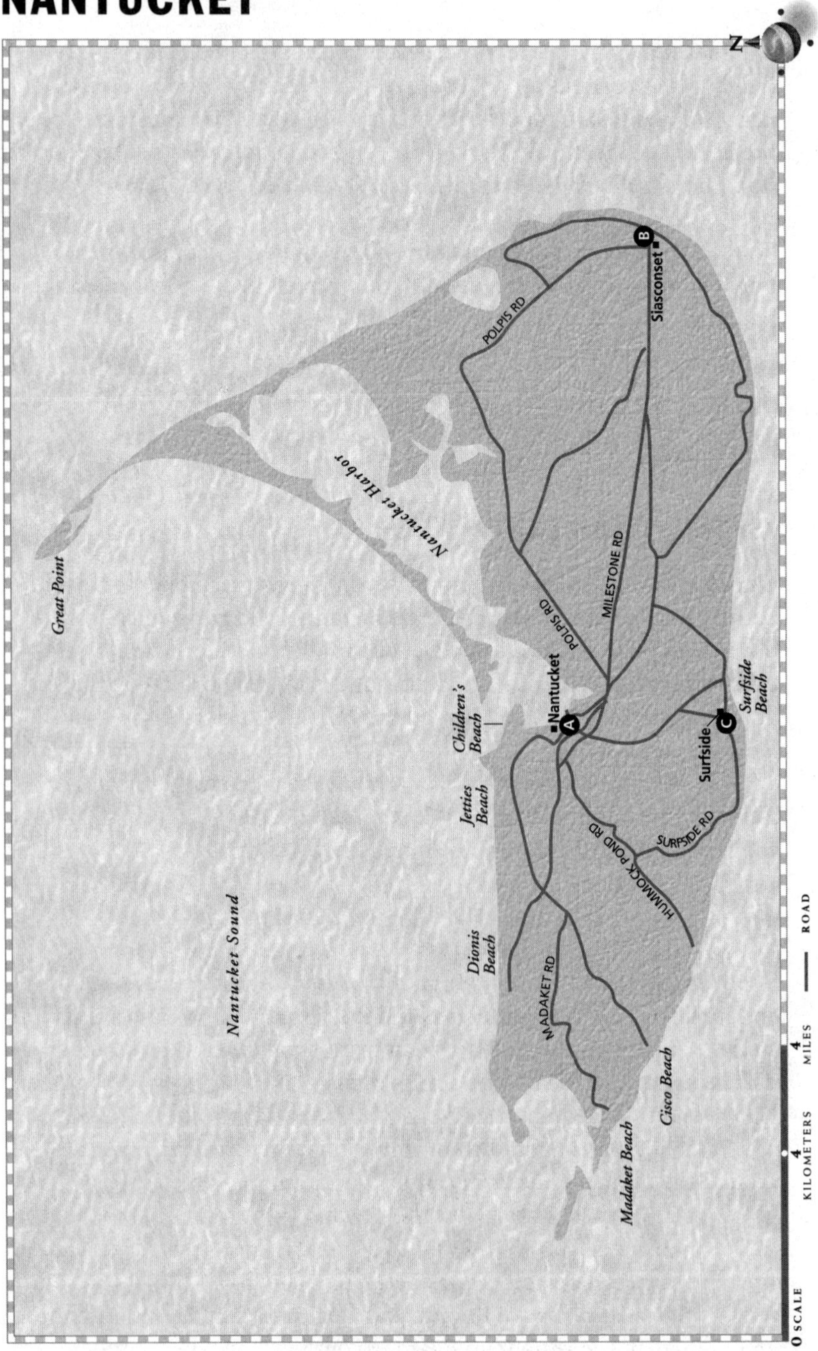

N

Great Point
Nantucket Harbor
POLPIS RD
Siasconset
B
MILESTONE RD
POLPIS RD
Nantucket
A
Children's Beach
Jetties Beach
Surfside Beach
Surfside
C
SURFSIDE RD
HUMMOCK POND RD
Dionis Beach
MADAKET RD
Nantucket Sound
Cisco Beach
Madaket Beach

0 SCALE 4 KILOMETERS 4 MILES
ROAD

Food

- Ⓐ Arno's
- Ⓐ Atlantic Cafe
- Ⓑ Chanticleer Inn
- Ⓐ Downyflake
- Ⓐ Henry's Sandwiches
- Ⓐ Rose & Crown
- Ⓑ Sconset Café

Lodging

- Ⓐ 18 Gardner Street
- Ⓐ Brass Lantern Inn
- Ⓐ Centre Street Inn

Lodging *(continued)*

- Ⓐ Jared Coffin House
- Ⓐ Nesbitt Inn
- Ⓐ Periwinkle Guesthouse
- Ⓐ Sherburne Inn
- Ⓑ Summer House Inn
- Ⓑ Wade Cottages

Camping

- Ⓒ Star of the Sea AYH Hostel

Note: Items with the same letter are located in the same town or area.

dining a must in good weather. However, the atmosphere, cuisine, and service will cost you: Lunch entrées start in the mid-teens and it's hard to sit down to dinner for less than $40 per person.

In downtown Nantucket on South Water Street, the **Atlantic Cafe** (508-228-0570) and, several doors down, the **Rose & Crown** (508-228-2595), both offer satisfying meals in a pub atmosphere ($6.95–$19.95). For casual fare, there are numerous fast-food joints on the road leading to the Steamship Authority boat dock. One of them, **Henry's Sandwiches** (508-228-0123) on Steamboat Wharf, makes great subs. For a hearty, down-home traditional breakfast, try the **Downyflake** (508-228-4533) on South Water Street. They have terrific homemade doughnuts. **Arno's** (508-228-7001), at 41 Main Street, has a good selection of omelettes and breakfast entrées. They also have a children's menu.

LODGING

Your lodging choices in Siasconset are limited to **Wade Cottages** (508-257-6308), which has a three-night minimum, and the **Summer**

House Inn (508-257-4577), which has a restaurant. Both overlook the ocean and offer pleasant accommodations. Wade Cottages opens in late May and operates through September. The midweek rate for a room with a private bath is $505 for three nights in the height of summer, and drops to $310 from late September through Columbus Day. Lodging at the Summer House includes private sitting rooms and marble Jacuzzis. Rates start at $325 in high-season, and are less off-peak. The inn closes for the season at the end of September.

The **Jared Coffin House** (29 Broad Street, 508-228-2400 or 800-248-2405) in downtown Nantucket, one of the better-known inns on the island, is open all year. Guest rooms are spread out among six dwellings, the oldest dating to the 1700s. The inn also operates a respectable restaurant, Jared's, with courtyard dining in the summertime, and a cozy bar. Dining prices are moderate, while doubles go for $150 to $200 in high-season and start at $85 in the winter. Rates include breakfast. The **Nesbitt Inn** (21 Broad Street, 508-228-0156), just down the block at in a large, friendly Victorian, is reasonably priced at $65 to $132 per night for double occupancy.

The town of Nantucket has a seemingly endless list of bed and breakfasts, yet remarkably they fill up quickly during the height of summer. Nantucket Accommodations (508-228-9559) is a reservation service that can help you find a room. Try the **Sherburne Inn** (508-228-4425) where rooms are decorated with four-poster and canopy beds. Originally built as a silk factory in 1835, the Sherburne is rumored to have a ghost. Doubles range in price from $125 to $175 in high-season, and start at less than $100 per night in the off-season. Lodgers will not be disappointed with the quality and comfort of **18 Gardner Street** (508-228-1155 or 800-435-1450) where double rooms rent for $110 to $300 per night.

There is also a string of guest houses on North Water Street. Two of them are the **Brass Lantern Inn** (508-228-4064 or 800-377-6609) and the **Periwinkle Guesthouse** (508-228-9267 or 800-588-0078). Summer room rates run from $125 to $185 at the Brass Lantern and from $110 to $195 at the Periwinkle. On nearby Centre Street, the **Centre Street Inn** is decorated with English pine antiques, white wicker furniture, and Laura Ashley and Ralph Lauren fabrics. Cranberry sour cream coffee cake is a specialty at breakfast, which is included in the room rate of $90 to $175 in high-season (rates are reduced in the off-season). Accommodations at the inn range from a single room with a shared bath to a suite with its own sitting room and fireplace.

CAMPING

There are no campgrounds on Nantucket, but **Star of the Sea AYH Hostel** (508-228-0433) in Surfside does give budget travelers a lodging option. Dormitory-style beds rent for $12 per night for members, and $15 per night for non-members. The oceanside hostel is 3½ miles from the ferry. It is open April 1 through the end of October. Reservations are essential.

ARTS AND ENTERTAINMENT

Places like the **Rose & Crown** (see above) and **The Brotherhood** (23 Broad Street) offer live entertainment. Bluegrass, jazz, acoustic, and folk music performances are standard fare for the **Cross Rip Coffeehouse** (2 Centre Street, 508-228-7617). Performances are held in the basement of the Methodist church. The **Actor's Theatre of Nantucket** (508-228-6325) performs popular plays, concerts, and children's matinees throughout the summer (mid-June through September). The **Nantucket Musical Arts Society** (508-228-1287) presents Tuesday evening concerts during July and August, and the **Theatre Workshop of Nantucket** (508-228-4305) is a community theater open year-round. Free outdoor concerts sponsored by the Nantucket Parks and Recreation Department are held at Children's Beach in July and August. Cinema lovers should enjoy the five-day-long **Nantucket Film Festival** which takes place each June. Contact the organizers at ACKFEST@aol.com or (212) 642-6339 for additional information about festival events.

SHOPPING

Shopping is a popular pastime on Nantucket, particularly when the always changeable New England weather makes beachcombing out of the question. In addition to the expected fudge and souvenir shops, there are high-quality galleries, antique stores, and specialty boutiques to tempt the serious shopper. Visit **Claire Murray's** (115 Water Street, 508-228-1913) for wonderful hand-hooked rugs; **Handblock** (42 Main Street, 508-228-4500) for colorful linens, pottery, and clothing; **Erica Wilson** (25 Main Street, 508-228-9881) for needlepoint creations; and **Majolica** (1 Old North Wharf, 508-228-4443) for Italian ceramics. The **Golden Basket** (44 Main Street, 508-228-4344) and **Diana Kim**

England Goldsmiths (56 Main Street, 508-228-3766) make Nantucket lightship basket charms in gold; and **The Lightship Shop** (Miacomet Avenue, 508-228-4164), 1½ miles from downtown on the way to Surfside, makes the traditional, tightly woven baskets topped with scrimshaw.

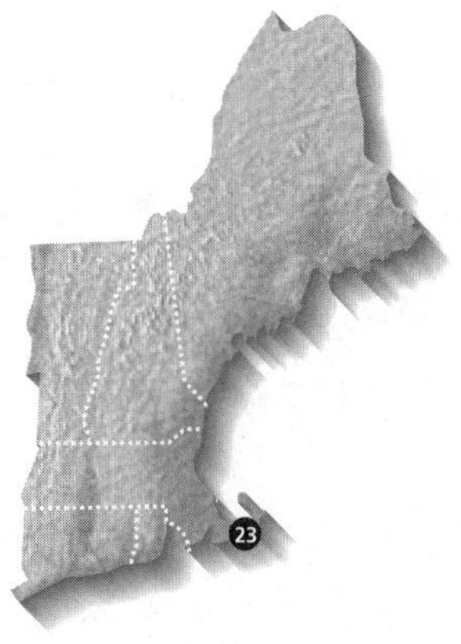

23 CAPE COD

Cape Cod juts out into the Atlantic Ocean from the Massachusetts mainland like an arm flexing its biceps. At the base of the arm is the town of Sandwich—a quintessential Cape Cod village, with neatly shingled houses, gentle tidal marshes, and many sights to occupy the out-of-town visitor. In 1997 the town of Sandwich celebrated its 360th birthday.

If you follow scenic Route 6A from Sandwich down the arm of the Cape, you'll pass through other quaint towns such as Barnstable and Yarmouth. Some of the Cape's most beautiful homes are at the peninsula's elbow in the lovely town of Chatham. Chatham also has a lighthouse on Shore Road off Route 28. The pristine beaches of the Cape Cod National Seashore border the Atlantic as you travel back up the forearm.

Provincetown, forming Cape Cod's hand, feels as if it should be remote. Yet somehow, the latest trends in food, fashion, and art still manage to find their way out to the town at the tip. Once, Provincetown was the Pilgrims' first stopover in the new land. Today, the art, tourist, and gay communities all vie for space along Provincetown's harbor, making the town a busy place during the summer months. ◪

CAPE COD

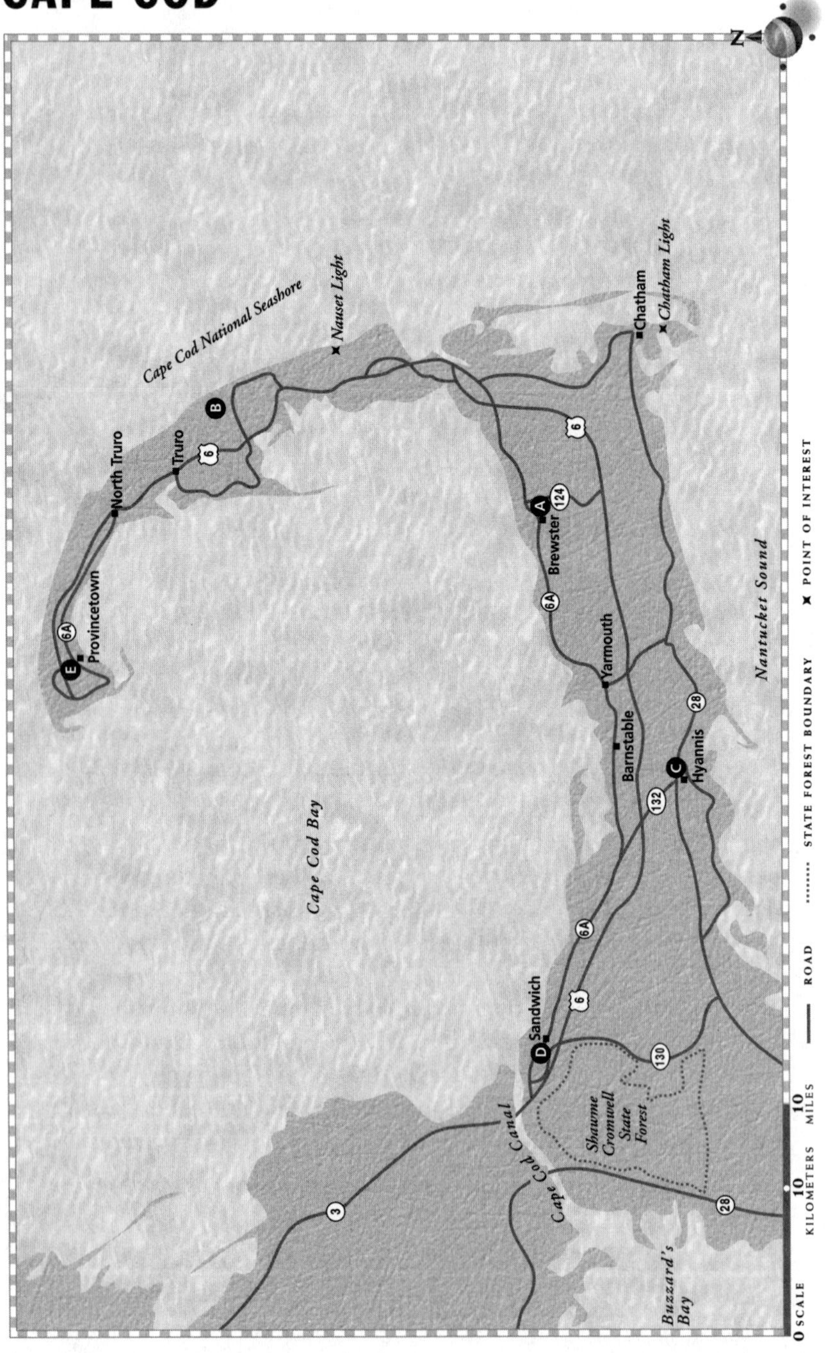

Provincetown
6A
E
North Truro
Truro
6
B
Cape Cod National Seashore
Nauset Light
Chatham
Chatham Light
Brewster
A
124
6
6A
Yarmouth
Barnstable
Hyannis
C
28
132
Cape Cod Bay
Nantucket Sound
6A
6
Sandwich
D
130
Shawme Cromwell State Forest
Cape Cod Canal
3
28
Buzzard's Bay
0 SCALE
10 KILOMETERS
10 MILES
ROAD
STATE FOREST BOUNDARY
POINT OF INTEREST
N

Sights

- **A** **Cape Cod Museum of Natural History**
- **B** **Cape Cod National Seashore**
- **C** **Cape Cod Potato Chip Factory**
- **D** **Green Briar Nature Center and Jam Kitchen**
- **D** **Heritage Plantation**
- **D** **Historic Homes of Sandwich**
- **A** **New England Fire and History Museum**
- **E** **Pilgrim Monument and Provincetown Museum**
- **E** **Provincetown Art Association and Museum**
- **E** **Provincetown Heritage Museum**
- **D** **Sandwich Glass Museum**
- **D** **Thornton Burgess Museum**
- **D** **Yesteryears Doll Museum**

Note: Items with the same letter are located in the same town or area.

A PERFECT DAY ON CAPE COD

In good weather, pack a picnic lunch and head to the Cape Cod National Seashore; spend part of the day hiking and the rest of the day stretched out on a beach towel. If Mother Nature is not cooperating, spend the day in the Sandwich area between Heritage Plantation and the Sandwich Glass Museum. Dine at the Sagamore or Daniel Webster Inn, saving room for an ice-cream cone at O'Brien's for dessert.

SIGHTSEEING HIGHLIGHTS

★★★ **Cape Cod National Seashore**—The national seashore stretches from the eastern half of the Cape's elbow all the way out to its fingertips at Provincetown, offering the visitor miles of nature trails, beaches, and wind-sculpted sand dunes peppered with beach grass. You won't be able to cover all 27,000 acres of the seashore in an afternoon, but a ranger at the Salt Pond Visitor's Center (off U.S. 6 in Eastham) can send you off in the direction of Nauset Lighthouse, a good hiking trail, or a remote beach. There's a marsh trail right behind the visitor's center, as well as a nature trail especially designed for the blind. You can park at Nauset

Beach for $5 per day, and there is a bathhouse facility available in season. From the nearby Coast Guard station you can see the place where Henry Beston's "Outermost House" once stood before it was washed away with the extreme tides created by the blizzard of 1978. The seashore is open to the public year-round. (full day)

★★ **Heritage Plantation**—The prettiest time to visit the plantation is in early June when the rhododendrons are in full bloom, but the beautifully landscaped 76-acre grounds are handsome in any season. American folk art, Currier & Ives lithographs, antique firearms, and early automobiles are among the plantation's other attractions. The antique cars, housed in a replica of the Shaker Round Barn at Hancock, include a vibrant green and yellow Duesenberg designed for Gary Cooper. The art museum houses a carousel to entertain the children while you view the Currier & Ives collection. Buses run at regular intervals between the museums. Details: Grove and Pine Streets in Sandwich, ½ mile from Sandwich Center, (508) 888-3300; open 10 a.m. to 5 p.m. daily mid-May through late October. Picnicking on the grounds is not allowed. Admission is $8 adults, $7 seniors, $4 ages 6 to 18, free for children 5 and under. (2 hours)

★★ **Sandwich Glass Museum**—The museum houses a fine collection of glassware made in the 1800s by the Boston & Sandwich Glass Company and the Cape Cod Glass Works. Exhibits include an explanation of glass manufacturing procedures and a chronology of the Sandwich operation. Details: Across from Town Hall Square in Sandwich Center, (508) 888-0251; open 9:30 a.m. to 4:30 p.m. daily April through October, 9:30 a.m. to 4 p.m. Wednesday through Sunday the rest of the year; closed in January. Admission is $3.50 adults, 50 cents for children over 5. (1 hour)

★ **Provincetown Art Association and Museum**—Changing exhibits include works by respected American artists such as Milton Avery, as well as promising newcomers. Details: 460 Commercial Street; (508) 487-1750; open noon to 5 p.m. and 8 to 10 p.m. in summer; call for off-season hours. Admission is $3 adults, $1 children, students, and seniors. (½ hour)

★ **Provincetown Heritage Museum**—Artifacts pertaining to the sea make up the majority of the museum's exhibits; the focal point is the

64-foot-long half-scale model of the *Rose Dorothea*, a turn-of-the-century fishing vessel. It is the largest indoor boat model in the world. Details: At the corner of Commercial and Center Streets; (508) 487-7098; open 10 a.m. to 6 p.m. in summer. Admission is $3 adults, free for children under 12. (½ hour)

★ **Pilgrim Monument and Provincetown Museum**—You will have no trouble locating the monument because, at 255 feet, it is the tallest all-granite structure in the United States. It affords marvelous views of the Cape and South Shore on clear days. Museum exhibits spotlight outer Cape Cod history. Unfortunately, handicapped access is limited as there is no elevator to the top of the monument. Visitors must use ramps and stairs to climb to the top. Details: off Route 6 at the tip of Cape Cod, (508) 487-1310; open 9 a.m. to 5 p.m. daily, until 7 p.m. in summer. Admission is $5 adults, $3 ages 4 to 12. (1 hour)

Cape Cod Museum of Natural History—The museum features exhibits highlighting the flora and fauna of Cape Cod. Details: Route 6A in Brewster; (508) 775-7253; open 9:30 a.m. to 4:30 p.m. Monday through Saturday, 12:30 to 4:30 p.m. Sunday May through mid-October; closed Monday the rest of the year. Admission is $4 adults, $2 ages 6 to 12. (½ hour)

Cape Cod Potato Chip Factory—If you're a potato-chip lover, you may want to tour this factory in Hyannis. The tour is self-guided, free, and you even get a complimentary bag of chips at the end of the tour. Details: Breeds Hill Road in Independence Park off Route 132 opposite the Cape Cod Mall; (508) 775-7253; open for tours 10 a.m. to 4 p.m. Monday through Friday. (½ hour)

Green Briar Nature Center and Jam Kitchen—If you're traveling with small fans of Peter Rabbit and the famous briar patch, then you may want to visit Green Briar Nature Center and Jam Kitchen. You can watch homemade jams bubbling away in the kitchen, visit "Peter Rabbit," then take the nature trail around the "old briar patch" that served as an inspiration for Thornton Burgess's marvelous children's tales. Details: Discovery Hill Road off Route 6A east of Sandwich, between Sandwich Center and Quaker Meeting House Road, (508) 888-6870; open 10 a.m. to 4 p.m. Monday through Saturday, 1 to 4 p.m. Sunday; there is storytelling at the museum in July and August. (½ hour)

Historic Homes of Sandwich—There are a number of historic homes in Sandwich, all within a 3-block radius of Town Hall Square. There's a water-operated stone mill, **Dexter's Grist Mill**; and **Hoxie House**, the oldest house on Cape Cod. Hoxie House was originally built in the 1600s and restored in 1960. Details: 130 Water Street; open 10 a.m. to 5 p.m. Monday through Saturday, 1 to 5 p.m. Sunday June through September. Admission for each site is $1.50 adults, 75 cents for children; combination tickets to both sites are $2.50 adults, $1 children. (1 hour)

New England Fire and History Museum—This small Brewster museum has antique fire-fighting equipment, a replica of Ben Franklin's firehouse, and a diorama of Chicago's great fire. Details: Route 6A, Brewster, (508) 896-5711; open 10 a.m. to 4 p.m. Monday through Friday, noon to 4 p.m. weekends mid-May through mid-October; open by appointment the rest of the year. Admission is $4.75 adults, $4.25 seniors, $2.50 ages 5 to 12. (½ hour)

Thornton Burgess Museum—This was the home of the children's books author, and some first editions of his books and his original artwork are on display here. Details: 4 Water Street, just up from the mill in Sandwich, (508) 888-6870; open 10 a.m. to 4 p.m. Monday through Saturday, 1 to 4 p.m. Sunday April through December; open Tuesday through Sunday January through March. Admission is by donation. (½ hour)

Yesteryears Doll Museum—This museum has a fascinating collection of rare and antique dolls as well as dollhouses. Details: Pilgrim's First Parish Meetinghouse on Main Street, Sandwich, (508) 888-1711; Open 10 a.m. to 4 p.m. Monday through Saturday mid-May through October. Admission is $3 adults, $2.50 seniors, $2 children. (½ hour)

FITNESS AND RECREATION

The **Cape Cod Rail Trail** is a bike path that runs up the center of the Cape along an old railway line. **Rail Trail Bike Shop** (508-896-8200) adjacent to the trail in Brewster rents bicycles, and they even have baby seats and tagalong trailers for those traveling with children that are too young to ride on their own.

FOOD

If you're staying in the Sandwich area, the dining room at the **Dan'l Webster Inn** has a fine reputation. It serves such favorites as filet mignon and baked scrod in lobster sauce. If dinner entrées averaging about $20 are too steep for your budget, a little west of Sandwich Center on 6A is the **Sagamore Inn** (508-888-9707), a favorite with locals. Pressed-tin ceilings amplify the sound of diners, and crowded tables create an atmosphere that is always animated. The fare includes fresh seafood, New England–style dinners, and Italian specialties at moderate prices. **The Beehive** (508-833-1184), a sunny yellow, tavern-style eatery on Route 6A east of Sandwich Center, serves seafood and tasty sandwiches at very reasonable prices. **O'Brien's** on 6A in East Sandwich is the place to go for homemade ice cream—there's always a tempting array of flavors to choose from, and the scoops are generous. If your lodging does not provide breakfast, try the casual **Marshland Restaurant** (508-888-9824) on Route 6A near Sandwich Center. Portions are large, but the prices are not. If you like microbreweries, **Cape Cod Brew House** (720 Main Street, 508-775-4110) in Hyannis brews its own beer. The brewhouse also offers a varied menu (everything from burgers to shrimp cerveza—shrimp sautéed in draught beer) and has reasonable prices ($5–$12).

In Provincetown, for a different sort of dining experience, try **Old Reliable Fish House** (229 Commercial Street, 508-487-9742). It has a mixed menu of Portuguese and Yankee specialties. The restaurant is on the water with outdoor seating in season. Dinner prices range from $8 to $12 for regular entrées, and start at $14 for lobsters. **Ciro & Sals** (508-487-0049) on Kiley Court is known statewide for sumptuous northern Italian creations. Prices are $9 to $20, and reservations are strongly recommended. **Vorelli's** (226 Commercial Street, 508-487-2778) serves Italian as well as seafood, and has a nice atmosphere. Dinner entrées range from $14 to $18. The restaurant also has a raw bar. Also on Commercial Street, **The Mew's** (508-487-1500)—which was once a stable—and **Pepe's** (508-487-0670) are popular places for seafood, while **Cafe Blase** (508-487-9465) serves good sandwiches at moderate prices and has a pleasant sidewalk café in the summertime. There is no shortage of sub shops and pizza joints in town, and ice cream lovers are bound to be tempted by Provincetown's many ice-cream parlors.

CAPE COD

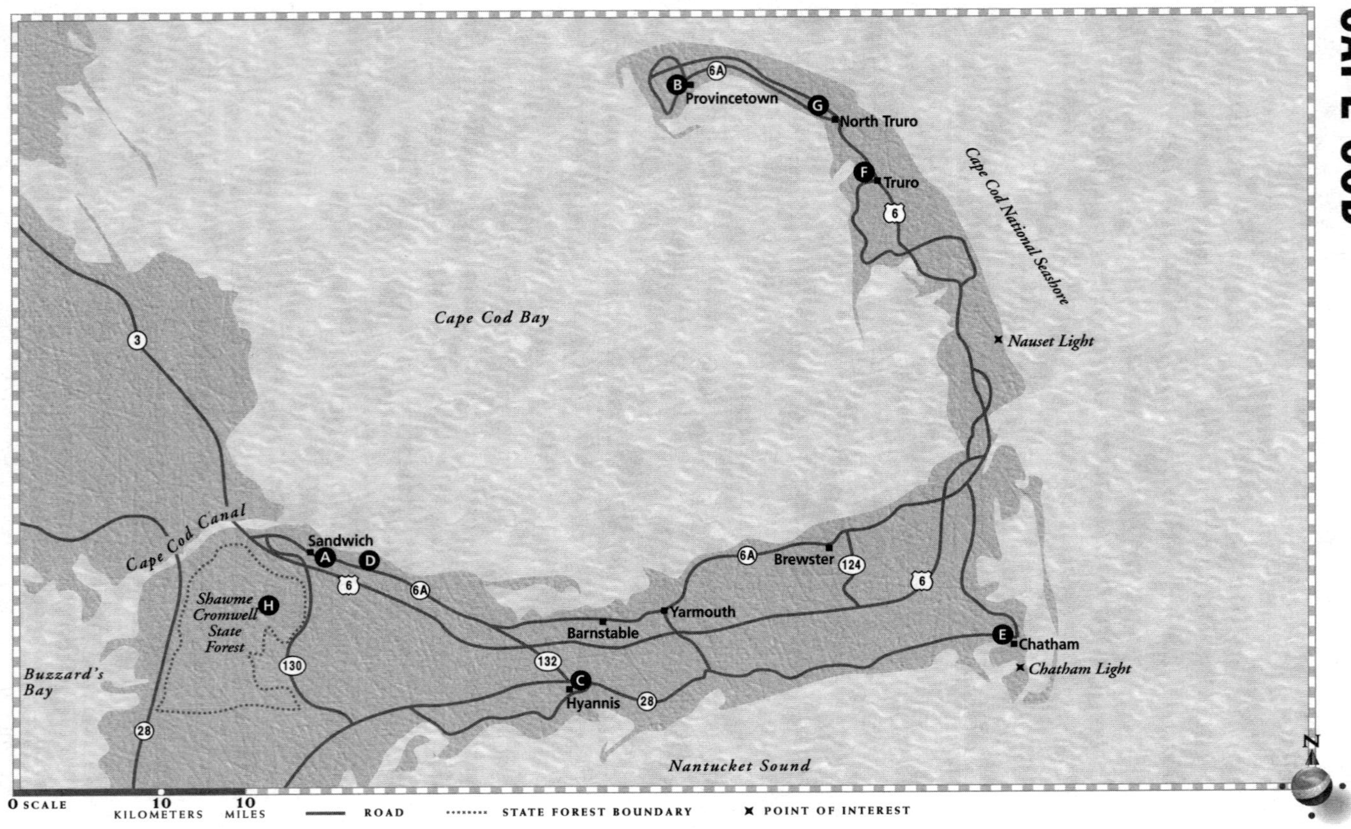

Provincetown
North Truro
Truro
Cape Cod National Seashore
Nauset Light
Cape Cod Bay
Cape Cod Canal
Sandwich
Shawme Cromwell State Forest
Buzzard's Bay
Barnstable
Yarmouth
Brewster
Chatham
Chatham Light
Hyannis
Nantucket Sound
6A
6
124
3
28
130
132
N
0 SCALE
10 KILOMETERS
10 MILES
ROAD
STATE FOREST BOUNDARY
POINT OF INTEREST

Food

- **A** The Beehive
- **B** Cafe Blase
- **C** Cape Cod Brew House
- **B** Ciro & Sals
- **A** Dan'l Webster Inn
- **A** Marshland Restaurant
- **B** The Mew's
- **D** O'Brien's
- **B** Old Reliable Fish House
- **B** Pepe's
- **A** Sagamore Inn
- **B** Vorelli's

Lodging

- **B** Anchor Inn
- **A** Captain Ezra Nye Guesthouse
- **E** Chatham Bars Inn
- **E** Chatham Wayside Inn
- **E** Cranberry Inn
- **A** Dan'l Webster Inn

Lodging *(continued)*

- **A** Earl of Sandwich Motor Manor
- **A** Isaiah Jones Homestead
- **F** Little America Hostel
- **B** Outermost Hostel
- **B** Somerset Guesthouse
- **D** Spring Garden Motel
- **E** Wequassett Inn
- **B** White Wind Inn
- **D** Wingscorton Farm Inn

Camping

- **B** Coastal Acres Camping Court
- **B** Dune's Edge Campground
- **G** Horton's Camping Resort
- **G** North of Highland Camping Area
- **G** North Truro Camping Area
- **A** Peter's Pond Park
- **H** Shawme Crowell State Forest

Note: Items with the same letter are located in the same town or area.

LODGING

Sandwich makes a wonderful place to base yourself when exploring the inner Cape. Accommodations may be plentiful in nearby Hyannis, but Sandwich is more convenient to sights, almost as conveniently located to beaches, and has a lot more charm than Hyannis. On Sandwich's Main Street, the **Dan'l Webster Inn** (508-888-3622 or 800-444-3566) will bathe you in four-star comfort you won't have to sell your soul for. Double rooms run from $100 to $200 per night depending on the season, and children under 12 stay free in the same room with their parents. The inn also offers packages that include breakfast and dinner starting at $80 per person. Reservations are strongly recommended.

Sandwich also has choice bed and breakfasts in the town center. Across from the Dan'l Webster, friendly hosts greet you at the **Captain Ezra Nye Guesthouse** (800-388-2278 or 508-888-6142), built in 1829. Rates are $85 to $105 per night including breakfast—quite reasonable for the area. The **Isaiah Jones Homestead** (508-888-9115 or 800-526-1625), also on Main Street, is elegantly furnished with four-poster beds and other Victorian pieces. Modern conveniences are not overlooked—one room has its own Jacuzzi. Doubles range from $75 to $135 in low-season and $95 to $155 in high-season.

You'll find a wide assortment of motor inns and cottages along scenic 6A in Sandwich. On the upper end is the mock Tudor-style **Earl of Sandwich Motor Manor** (508-888-1415 or 800-442-3275), with doubles ranging from $45 to $89. The attractive cedar-shingled **Spring Garden Motel** (508-888-0710 or 800-303-1751), with flowering window boxes, a swimming pool, and cozy rooms is in East Sandwich on the edge of a tidal marsh. Continental breakfast is included in the room rate of $67 to $85. If you would like to wake up to a rooster crowing and other sounds of a working farm, **Wingscorton Farm Inn** (508-888-0534), across the road from the Spring Garden Motel, offers fine accommodations ($125 to $175 per night including a full breakfast).

The lovely town of Chatham is another pleasant spot to base yourself on the Cape for overnight accommodations. The **Chatham Wayside Inn** (512 Main Street, 508-945-5550 or 800-391-5734) and the **Cranberry Inn** (359 Main Street, 508-945-9232 or 800-332-4667) are both located downtown. The Wayside has a dining room and a heated swimming pool. Four-poster beds and fireplaces highlight the rooms at the Cranberry Inn. A continental breakfast, which often includes freshly baked cranberry muffins, is included in the room rate.

The **Chatham Bars Inn** (508-945-0096 or 800-527-4884) and the **Wequassett Inn** (508-432-5400 or 800-225-7125) are Chatham's two upscale waterfront resorts. Both offer on-property tennis, fine dining, and swimming (the Chatham Bars Inn has its own private beach), and there's a golf course nearby. Doubles at the Chatham Bars Inn start at around $100 per night.

In Provincetown, the **Anchor Inn** (175 Commercial Street, 508-487-0432) has a wonderful porch for people-watching and an attractive garden in front. Rooms rent for about $110 to $145 in the summer, $65 to $95 in the off-season. Also open year-round is the **White Wind Inn** (508-487-1526) just across the street. Some of the rooms have balconies and fireplaces, and pets are allowed. Doubles go for $115 to $195 in the summer, and $75 to $125 in the off-season. The **Somerset Guesthouse** (508-487-0383 or 800-575-1850) on the corner of Commercial and Pearl Streets has reasonable rates. Rooms with shared baths range from $65 to $85 in the summer; doubles with private baths go for $85 to $115 in the summer and $70 to $80 in the winter.

Route 6A in nearby Truro has a string of cottages and motels on the beach. Accommodations there vary in quality, but are an option if you want to stay on the beach, or if you are traveling with a family and find in-town bed and breakfasts too expensive for your whole crew. If you have trouble finding lodging in the area, try calling Provincetown's Chamber of Commerce (508-487-3424) for assistance. Budget travelers should be aware that the **Little America Hostel** (508-349-3889) in Truro and the **Outermost Hostel** (508-487-4378) in Provincetown have accommodations for about $12 per person per night.

CAMPING

Shawme Crowell State Forest (508-888-0351) on Route 130 in Sandwich has 280 sites and is open mid-April through Columbus Day, although camping in contained vehicles is permitted during the winter months. Restrooms with showers are available, and campsites are much less expensive than at most other campgrounds on the Cape. **Peter's Pond Park** (508-477-1775) in Sandwich has both tent and trailer sites. Located on a freshwater pond, the 500-site campground is open mid-April through mid-October, and is handicapped accessible. Sites start at $17 per night.

At the other end of the Cape, **Coastal Acres Camping Court** (508-487-1700) on the West Vine Street Extension is the closest campground to downtown Provincetown. They do have a three-night minimum stay requirement for reservations, but you could call on the day of your arrival and see if they have space available. Sites for two people cost $20 for a tent and $27 for RV hookups. The campground is open April through October. **Dune's Edge Campground** (508-487-9815) off U.S. 6 is just a little farther from town but still convenient, and borders on sand dunes of the national seashore. Sites start at $21 per night, and the campground is open May through September. In North Truro there are three campgrounds you might try if Coastal Acres and Dunes Edge are full. They are **Horton's Camping Resort** (starting at $16 per site; 508-487-1220 or 800-252-7705); **North of Highland Camping Area** ($18 per site; 508-487-1191), which is open seasonally; and **North Truro Camping Area** ($7.50 per person, $15 per-site minimum; 508-487-1847), which is open all year.

SIDE TRIPS FROM CAPE COD

If you have time to spend in the area, the **Cape Cod National Seashore** has enough beautiful coastline to occupy nature enthusiasts and beach bums alike for many days. There is always a new dune to investigate.

Whale-watching is also an interesting pastime in this part of the world. The ***Portuguese Princess*** shuttles eager marine mammal watchers daily from Provincetown, April through November, to view the whales in their natural habitat. Call (508) 487-2651 or (800) 442-3188 for reservations. Tickets start at about $17.50 per person. **Provincetown Whale Watch** (508-487-3322 or 800-992-9333) also operates cruises out of Provincetown. The company offers discounts for passengers on their early morning expeditions. If you don't plan to travel as far out as Provincetown, **Hyannis Whale Watcher Cruises** depart from Barnstable's Harbor. Finbacks and humpbacks are among the types of whales you may spot, and the company will issue a rain check in "the remote event there are no sightings" on your trip. Tickets are $23 for adults, $19 for seniors, and $15 for ages 4 to 12. Call (508) 362-6088 or (800) 287-0374 for cruise information and reservations.

Scenic Route: Route 6A Cape Cod

Route 6A runs from Sagamore, where the Cape is joined to the mainland by the Sagamore Bridge, to Orleans, where it merges with Route 6—the Cape's busy central highway. The route is a peaceful thoroughfare that lazily winds through some of the Cape's prettiest and most historic villages. The quintessentially Cape Cod houses that you'll see along the way—shaded by leafy trees and bordered by well-maintained lawns and colorful gardens; freshly painted with contrasting shutters, or quaint with weathered shingles—are as essential to the route's appeal as the terrain itself.

The first required stop along 6A is **Sandwich Center**, just a short detour off the main route. The town, which was incorporated over 350 years ago and is the oldest town on Cape Cod, has a lovely church, several historic homes open to the public, and a number of museums worth a visit. Once you're back on 6A, the route's charm begins to become apparent. Handsome residential stretches are interspersed with soggy cranberry bogs, gentle marshlands, and tasteful commercial establishments (antique shops,

ROUTE 6A CAPE COD

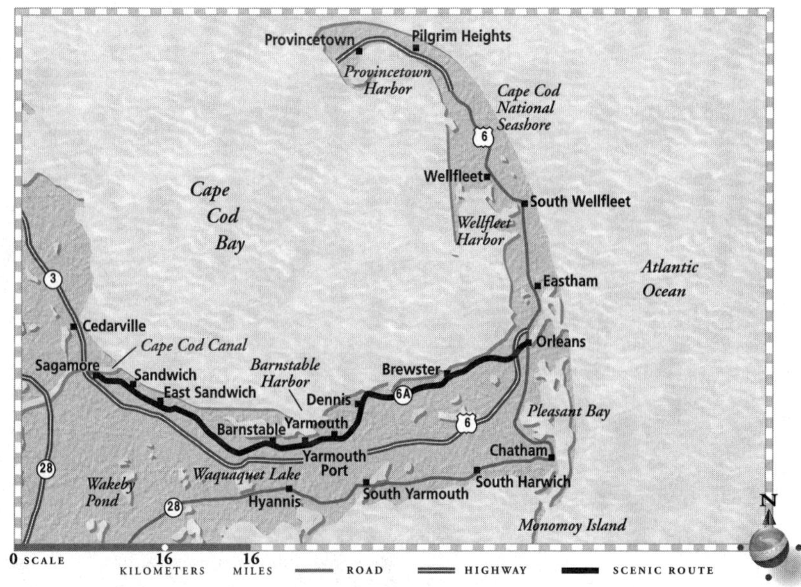

galleries, bookshops). Local children plunge into the chilly waters from the small bridge that crosses over **Scorton Creek** in East Sandwich, and canoeists gently ply the creek's current as they look for wildlife hidden in the marshes.

Further along 6A you'll pass through **Barnstable**, where the library dates to 1644; **Yarmouth Port**, where you can stop for a refreshment at **Hallet's Drugstore's** old-fashioned soda fountain; and **Brewster**, which once had more sea captains in residence than any other town in the United States and is now home to several small museums as well as a water-powered grist mill operating since the 1660s.

Route 6A ends in Orleans. From there you can follow Route 6 to **Provincetown** (be sure to stop at the beaches of the national seashore along the way) or head south to **Chatham** along Route 28. ◪

24
PLYMOUTH AND THE SOUTH SHORE

The name South Shore refers to the towns that stretch along the Massachusetts shore from Boston south to Cape Cod. These towns include Quincy, where two U.S. presidents were born, and pretty coastal villages such as Duxbury, Cohasset, and Hingham.

Settlements here date to the early 1600s—Quincy to 1624, Cohasset to 1614 with the arrival of Captain John Smith, Hingham to 1635, and Duxbury to 1627, when Pilgrims such as John Alden and Miles Standish, in search of more farmland, moved into the area. Plymouth, some 35 miles south of Boston, is the most celebrated of the South Shore towns. And rightly so. It was in Plymouth that the Pilgrims settled in 1620, beginning the first real colonization of North America.

Today the Pilgrims' legacy can be explored at multiple sights in and around Plymouth, such as Plimoth Plantation, the *Mayflower II*, Pilgrim Hall, and Plymouth Rock. In the nineteenth century, Plymouth was home to the world's largest rope factory—a site that is now a complex of shops and eateries known as Cordage Park Marketplace.

For those preferring natural attractions, the South Shore boasts a number of wildlife sanctuaries, World's End Reservation in Hingham, and Atlantic beaches—Duxbury is a favorite among local beachcombers. The South Shore's seaside climate also provides the perfect environment for growing cranberries, and cranberry bogs abound, particularly around Plymouth. ◪

PLYMOUTH AND THE SOUTH SHORE

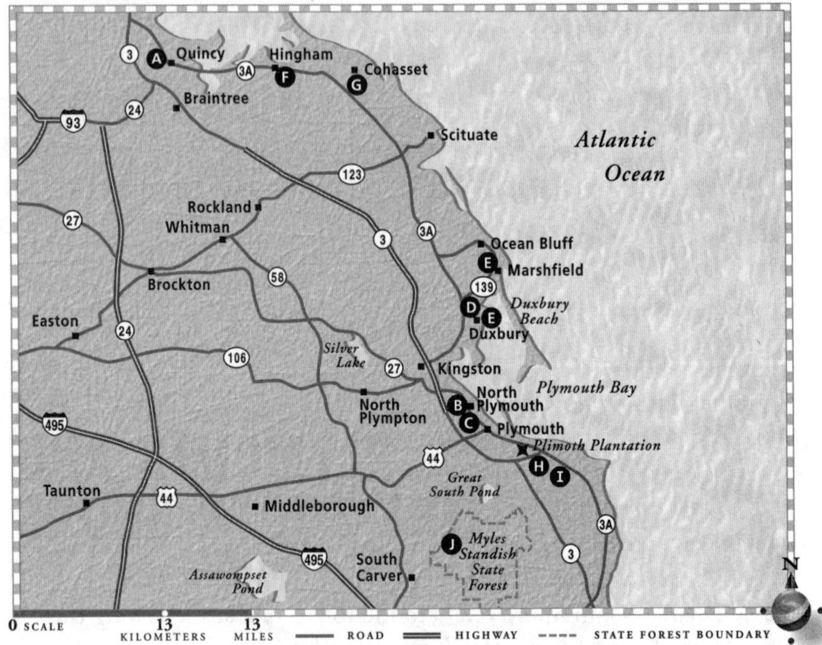

Sights

- **A** Adams National Historic Site
- **B** Children's Museum of Plymouth
- **C** Cordage Park Marketplace
- **D** John Alden House
- **E** Massachusetts Audubon Society
- **D** Old Burying Ground
- **F** World's End Reservation

Food

- **G** Kimball's by the Sea
- **B** Sam Diego's

Lodging

- **H** Foxglove Cottage
- **H** Pilgrim Sands Motel

Camping

- **I** Indianhead Campground
- **J** Myles Standish State Forest

Note: Items with the same letter are located in the same town or area.

A PERFECT DAY ON THE SOUTH SHORE

Begin your day at Plimoth Plantation, where the Pilgrim life of 1627 has been re-created. For lunch, feast on a fried-clam platter from Wood's (get it take-out so you can picnic on the harbor). In the afternoon, take Route 3A north through Duxbury, Marshfield, Cohasset, and Hingham—possibly detouring from the main road to look at some of the South Shore's elegant homes. Next, visit the Adams home in Quincy before heading to Boston or back to Plymouth for your evening meal and overnight accommodations.

SIGHTSEEING HIGHLIGHTS

★★★ **Plimoth Plantation and the *Mayflower II***—Both the plantation and the ship are run by the same nonprofit organization. The plantation is a living museum exemplifying everyday seventeenth-century Pilgrim life and that of nineteenth-century Native Americans in the neighboring Wampanaog settlement. In the Pilgrim village of thatched cottages, costumed guides play the parts of the original settlers tending to their farm animals, gardens, and everyday chores. They claim to know nothing of modern times but are happy to explain how and why things were done in 1627. Several miles away, the *Mayflower II* is docked in Plymouth Harbor adjacent to Plymouth Rock. Since historians weren't (and still aren't today) really sure what happened to the original *Mayflower*, this replica was built in England in the 1950s. On board, costumed guides relate the events of the fateful 1620 voyage, and you can see the cramped conditions under which the Pilgrims traveled. Details: Plantation Route 3A and Warren Avenue, (508) 746-1622; both sights open 9 a.m. to 5 p.m. daily April through November; *Mayflower II* is open until 7 p.m. late June through Labor Day. Admission to the plantation is $15 adults, $9 ages 6 to 17. Admission to the ship is $5.75 adults, $3.50 ages 6 to 17. Combination tickets are $18.50 adults, $16.50 seniors and students, $11 ages 6 to 17. (half day)

★ **Adams National Historic Site**—The site is actually comprised of houses at several different locations. The houses were the homes and birthplaces of U.S. presidents John Adams and John Quincy Adams, writers Henry and Brooks Adams, and envoy Charles Adams. The tour of the home at 135 Adams Street in Quincy is the most worthwhile of the three. Tour guides provide in-depth historical information to go along with the family artifacts on display. The library is especially interesting. If you wish to see the birthplaces as well, the tour guides can provide directions. Details: 135 Adams Street; the birthplaces are at 133–141 Franklin Street in Quincy; (617) 773-1177; open 9 a.m. to 5 p.m. daily mid-April through mid-November. Admission is $2 adults, free for children under 16. (1 hour per home)

✯ **Cordage Park Marketplace**—The marketplace, now filled with factory outlet stores and boutiques, is of interest because it stands on the site of a nineteenth-century rope manufacturing plant. The Plymouth mill was the world's largest and employed an army of workers. The prints and photographs on display throughout the marketplace will give you some sense of the factory's magnitude. Details: On Route 3A about 1 mile north of downtown Plymouth. (1 hour)

✯ **Cranberry World**—Outside the museum building is a small cranberry bog where you can see how this one of only three native American fruits is grown. Inside there are exhibits that show how the tangy fruit is harvested and demonstrate how it has been used over the years. The museum is operated by Ocean Spray, and samples of cranberry refreshments are free. Details: 225 Water Street, Plymouth, (508) 747-1000; open 9:30 a.m. to 5 p.m. daily May through November. Admission is free. (½ hour)

✯ **Pilgrim Hall Museum**—The museum—which is on the National Register of Historic Places—houses personal belongings of the Pilgrims, including Governor William Bradford's Bible and Myles Standish's sword. Details: 75 Court Street on Route 3A in the center of Plymouth; (508) 746-1620; open 9:30 a.m. to 4:30 p.m. daily February through December; closed Christmas. Admission is $5 adults, $4 seniors, $2 ages 6 to 15. (1 hour)

✯ **Pilgrim Path**—In addition to leading you to the *Mayflower II*, Plymouth Rock, and the Pilgrim Hall, this trail will take you to other historic buildings throughout Plymouth. You'd have to spend a lot of time in Plymouth to see them all, but here's a sampling of what's available:

Sparrow House was built in 1640 and is the oldest house in Plymouth. Now the museum houses rotating exhibits and a craft gallery. Details: 42 Summer Street; (508) 747-1240; open 10 a.m. to

5 p.m. daily except Wednesday late May through late December. Admission is $1.50.

The **Court House and Museum** on Town Square operated as a municipal building longer than any other courthouse in America. It's open daily in the summer, and admission is free. **Howland House** is currently the only house in Plymouth that an original Pilgrim actually lived in. Tours are given by costumed guides. Details: 33 Sandwich Street; (508) 746-9590; open 9 a.m. to 5 p.m. daily (tours are offered 10 a.m. to 4:30 p.m.) late May through mid-October. Admission is $3.50 adults, $2.50 students and seniors, 75 cents ages 6 to 12.

Spooner House, built in 1749, was the home of Bourne Spooner, founder of the Plymouth Cordage Company. The house remained in the Spooner family until 1954. Many of the original furnishings are on display. Details: Open late May through mid-October. Admission is $2.50 for adults, 50 cents for children.

The lovely **Antiquarian House** was frequented by Daniel Webster and has a number of unusual octagonal rooms. Details: 126 Water Street; open late May through mid-October. Admission is charged. The **Mayflower Society Museum**—with eighteenth-century furnishings—is in a beautiful home dating to 1745. It is the headquarters of the General Society of *Mayflower* Descendants. Details: 4 Winslow Street; open 1:30 to 3:30 p.m. Monday through Friday. Admission is $3 adults, 50 cents for children.

For a map and complete listing of sights along the Pilgrim Path, contact the Plymouth Area Chamber of Commerce at 91 Samoset Street, Plymouth, MA 02360. (¼–1 hour per site)

★ **Plymouth National Wax Museum**—Overlooking Plymouth Rock and Harbor from atop Coles Hill, the museum uses wax figures to re-create events in Pilgrim history. Details: 16 Carver Street; (508) 746-6468; open 9 a.m. to 5 p.m. daily March through November. Admission is $5 adults, $2 children. (1 hour)

★ **Plymouth Rock**—There is nothing extraordinary about this enshrined rock other than the fact that it symbolizes the Pilgrims' first settlement and thus is a cornerstone of American colonization. Visiting Plymouth Rock is probably comparable to kissing the Blarney Stone—all Americans should make a pilgrimage once in a lifetime, whether the rock is engrossing or not. Details: Water Street on Plymouth's waterfront. (¼ hour)

Children's Museum of Plymouth—This museum has kid-oriented interactive exhibits and games. Details: 46–48 Main Street; (508) 747-1234; open 10 a.m. to 5 p.m. daily (until 7 p.m. in summer). Admission is $3.50; free for children under 2. (1 hour)

John Alden House—This is the home of the famous *Mayflower* couple, John and Priscilla Alden. Details: 105 Alden Street in Duxbury; (781) 934-9092; open Tuesday through Sunday late June through early September. Admission is $2.50 adults, $1 children under 12. (½ hour)

Massachusetts Audubon Society—The society operates three wildlife refuges on the South Shore that are open to the public. The regional office is located at the North River sanctuary at 2000 Main Street in Marshfield, where there's a library and gift shop, as well as a river trail through a red maple swamp and a second trail through woodlands. The Daniel Webster sanctuary on Winslow Cemetery Road in Marshfield is home to nesting tree swallows, bobolinks, kestrels, and bluebirds. The North Hill Marsh sanctuary on Mayflower Street in Duxbury offers walking trails through marshland. Details: Admission is $3 for adults, $2 for seniors and ages 3 to 12. Trails are open from dawn to dusk year-round. Call (781) 837-9400 for gift shop hours. (1 hour per sanctuary)

Old Burying Ground—On Chestnut Street in Duxbury, this is the cemetery where Myles Standish and other passengers from the *Mayflower* are buried. (½ hour)

World's End Reservation—This 250-acre shoreline park in Hingham was designed by Frederick Law Olmstead, whose work you may have seen in the Boston Public Gardens as well as at other locations on your New England trip. (½ hour)

FOOD

In Plymouth, **McGrath's Restaurant** (508-746-9751) overlooking the harbor in downtown is a popular spot for seafood. Prices are moderate. Restaurants are plentiful along Water Street at the waterfront. There are also informal eat-in or take-out seafood shacks out on the piers. Try **Wood's** (508-746-0261) on Town Pier where a fried-clam plate will easily satisfy two hungry appetites. **Sam Diego's** (51 Main Street, 508-747-0048), in a building that was a fire station in the early 1900s, serves up Mexican food, a fun atmosphere, and refreshing margaritas. The John Carver Inn's informal **Hearth 'n' Kettle Restaurant** (see Lodging) is family friendly. It offers a children's menu and has toys to keep kids occupied during meals. Farther up the coast, **Kimball's by the Sea** (124 Elm Street, 781-383-6650) overlooks the water in Cohasset and is known for its seafood.

LODGING

In Plymouth, the **Pilgrim Sands Motel** (Route 3A, 508-747-0900 or 800-729-7263) is a popular lodging choice because of its oceanfront location and proximity to Plimoth Plantation. Doubles start at $50 in low-season, and run from $93 to $123 in summer. The **Sheraton Plymouth at Village Landing** (180 Water Street, 800-325-3535) is adjacent to the Village Landing Marketplace, not far from Plymouth Rock. Double rooms start at around $100 per night, and it is best to make reservations several weeks ahead during the summer. The **Governor Bradford Motor Inn** (800-332-1620 or 508-746-6200) is right on Plymouth's waterfront. Motel-style rooms have refrigerators and coffeemakers, and range in price from $58 to $105 for double occupancy in the off-season and from $79 to $119 in high-season. The **John Carver Inn** (508-746-7100 or 800-274-1620) in Plymouth's town center is run by the same people who operate the fine Dan'l Webster Inn in Sandwich. Doubles range in price from $65 to $105 in high-season, and children under age 18 can stay for free if they are in the same room with their parents. If you prefer bed-and-breakfast accommodations, try **Foxglove Cottage** (101 Sandwich Road, 508-747-6576 or 800-479-4746). The pink clapboard home is convenient to Plimoth Plantation, and is just a few miles from downtown Plymouth. The three guest rooms have private baths and fireplaces, and rates including breakfast start at $80 per night.

CAMPING

Indianhead Campground (508-888-3688), south of Plymouth off Route 3A, is one of the closest camping areas to Plymouth's attractions. The campground has complete hookups and recreational facilities including miniature golf, aquabikes, canoes, and rowboats. Sites start at

PLYMOUTH

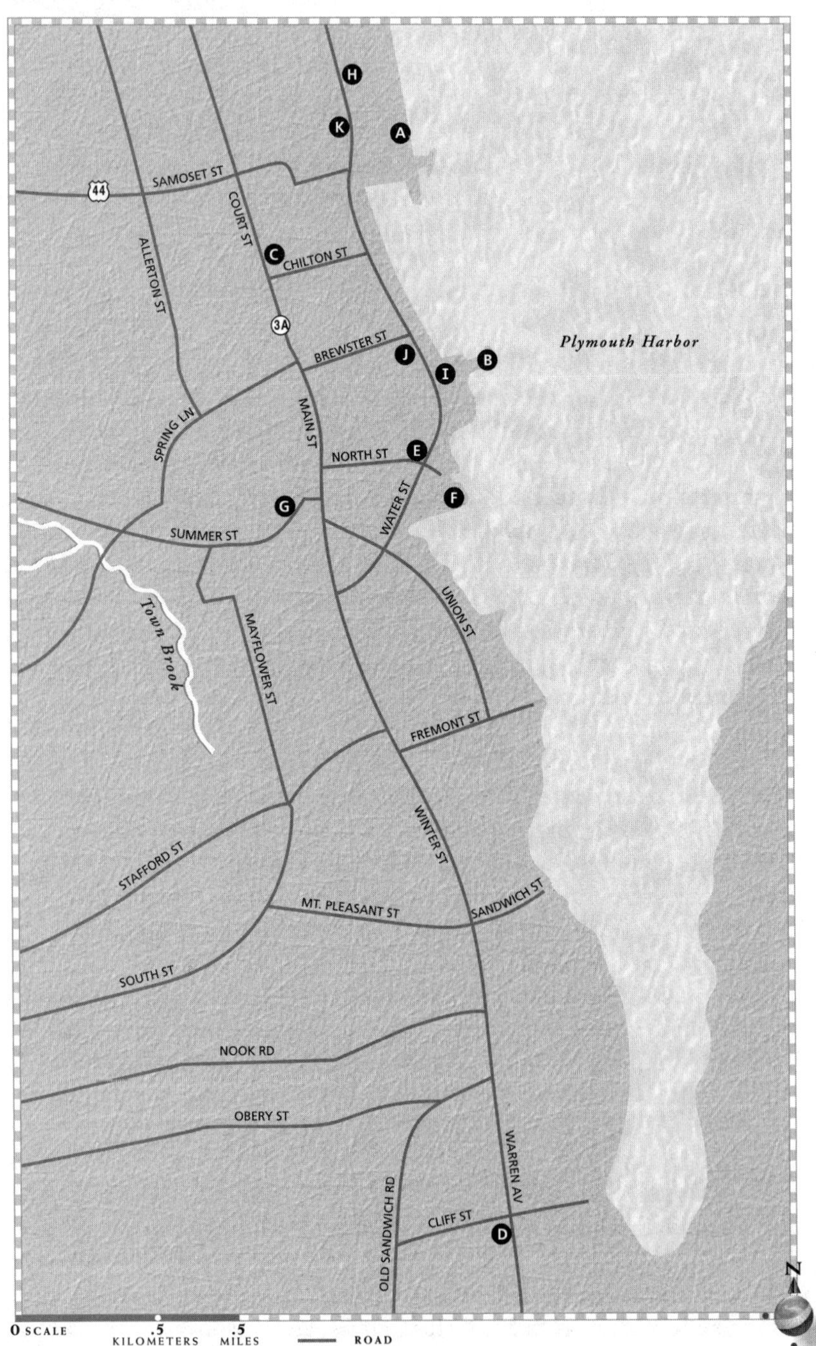

Plymouth Harbor
SAMOSET ST
44
COURT ST
ALLERTON ST
CHILTON ST
3A
BREWSTER ST
SPRING LN
MAIN ST
NORTH ST
WATER ST
SUMMER ST
Town Brook
UNION ST
MAYFLOWER ST
FREMONT ST
WINTER ST
STAFFORD ST
MT. PLEASANT ST
SANDWICH ST
SOUTH ST
NOOK RD
OBERY ST
WARREN AV
OLD SANDWICH RD
CLIFF ST
H
K
A
C
J
I
B
E
F
G
D
N
0 SCALE
.5 KILOMETERS
.5 MILES
ROAD

Sights

- A Cranberry World
- B *Mayflower II*
- C Pilgrim Hall Museum
- D Plimoth Plantation
- E Plymouth National Wax Museum
- F Plymouth Rock

Food

- G Hearth 'n' Kettle
- H McGrath's Restaurant
- I Wood's

Lodging

- J Governor Bradford Motor Inn
- G John Carver Inn
- K Sheraton Plymouth at Village Landing

Note: Items with the same letter are located in the same town or area.

$20 per night for two. **Myles Standish State Forest** (508-866-2526), about 10 miles from Plymouth off Route 58 in South Carver, has 475 campsites plus swimming, hiking, boating, and fishing. Sites are about $12 per night.

BEACHES

Plymouth has a public beach with a bathhouse, parking lot (for up to 200 cars), and lifeguards. The 5-mile-long **Duxbury Beach** is probably the most popular beach for swimming on the South Shore. It also has lifeguards and facilities, and its parking lot holds up to 1,400 cars. Both beaches charge a parking fee.

25
NEW ENGLAND FESTIVALS

Each New England state has its share of folk festivals ranging from arts and crafts fairs to lobsterfests. These regional events are a fun way to soak up local culture, and I've listed some of the area's best and most colorful below.

CONNECTICUT

May

Lobsterfest, Mystic Seaport Museum, **Mystic**

June

Yale–Harvard Regatta on the Thames River, **New London**
Taste of Hartford, **Hartford**
Farmington Antiques Weekend, **Farmington**
Sea Music Festival, Mystic Seaport, **Mystic**

July

Riverfest, **Hartford**

August

Native American Festival, Haddam Meadows State Park, **Haddam**
Mark Twain Days, **Hartford**

October

Chowderfest, Mystic Seaport Museum, **Mystic**

December

First Night, Hartford
Victorian Christmas, Gillette Castle State Park, **East Haddam**
Christmas at Mystic Seaport, **Mystic**

For a complete list of Connecticut events, write Tourist Events, Department of Economic Development, 865 Brook Street, Rocky Hill, CT 06067.

MAINE

January

New Year's Eve Celebration, **Portland**

February

Cross-Country Ski Festival, **Bethel**
Winter Carnival, **Lincoln**

June

Lobster Race, **Bar Harbor**
Old Port Festival, Old Port, **Portland**
Down East Jazz Festival, **Rockport**

July

Seafood Festival, **Bar Harbor**
Schooner Days, Rockland Harbor, **Rockland**
Annual Dulcimer Festival, **Bar Harbor**
House and Garden Day, **Camden**
Antique Auto Days, **Boothbay Railway Village**
Arts and Crafts Show, **Camden**
Chickadee Quilters Show, **Bridgton**

August

Lobster Festival, **Rockland**
Maine Arts Festival, **Portland**
Annual Blueberry Festival, **Rangeley**

September

Annual Fiddlers Show, **Kennebunk**
Half-marathon, **Bar Harbor**
Fryeburg Fair, **Fryeburg**

October

Fall Festival, **Camden**
Chowder Festival, **Bar Harbor**
Annual Harvest Festival, **York**

December

Christmas Prelude, **Kennebunkport**
Christmas by the Sea, **Camden**
Harbor Lights Festival, **Boothbay**

For the most current events calendar, contact the Maine Publicity Bureau at 97 Winthrop Street, Hallowell, ME 04347 (207-289-2423).

MASSACHUSETTS

January

First Night New Year's Eve Celebration, **Boston**

March

St. Patrick's Day Parade, **South Boston**

April

Boston Marathon, **Boston**
Daffodil Festival, **Nantucket**
Reenactment of Paul Revere's Ride, **Boston**
Reenactment of the Battle of Lexington and Concord, **Lexington**

May

Lilac Sunday, Arnold Arboretum, **Jamaica Plain**
Art Newbury Street, **Boston**
Wool Days, **Sturbridge Village**
Boston Kite Festival, Franklin Park, **Boston**
Sheep Shearing Days, **Hancock Shaker Village**
Chesterwood Antique Car Show, **Stockbridge**

June

Dairy Festival, **Boston**
Cape Cod Chowderfest, **Hyannis**
Salem Maritime Festival, **Salem**
Nantucket Film Festival, **Nantucket**

July

Boston Pops Concert and Fourth of July Fireworks Display, The Esplanade, **Boston**
Bastille Day, Marlborough Street, **Boston**
Chowderfest, **Boston**
Tisbury Street Fair, **Martha's Vineyard**
Edgartown Regatta, **Martha's Vineyard**
Marblehead Race Week, **Marblehead**
USS *Constitution* Turnaround, **Boston**
Harborfest, **Boston**
Lowell Folk Festival, **Lowell**
Barnstable County Fair, **Barnstable**

August

Annual Antiques Show, Hancock **Shaker Village**
Mayflower Lobster Festival, **Plymouth**
Marshfield Fair, **Marshfield**
Annual Sandcastle and Sculpture Day, Jetties Beach, **Nantucket**

September

Cambridge River Festival, **Cambridge**
Eastern States Exposition, **West Springfield**
Bourne Scallop Festival, **Buzzard's Bay**
Essex Clamfest, **Essex**
Cranberry Festival, **Harwich**
Waterfront Festival, **Newburyport**
Cape Ann Road Race, **Gloucester**

October

Head of the Charles Regatta, Charles River, **Cambridge**
Mt. Greylock Ramble, **Adams**
Topsfield Fair, **Topsfield**

November

Hammond Castle Museum Medieval Feast, **Gloucester**
Plimouth Plantation Thanksgiving Day, **Plymouth**
Old Sturbridge Village Thanksgiving Day, **Sturbridge**

December

Old Deerfield Christmas Sampler, **Deerfield**
Christmas Stroll, **Nantucket**
Chowderfest, Vineyard Haven, **Martha's Vineyard**
Christmas at Hancock Shaker Village, **Hancock**
Main Street at Christmas, **Stockbridge**
Christmas on Cape Ann

For more information on Bay State festivals, contact the Commonwealth of Massachusetts Office of Travel and Tourism, 100 Cambridge Street, 13th Floor, Boston, MA 02202.

NEW HAMPSHIRE

February

Dartmouth Winter Carnival, **Hanover**
Chocolate Festival, Mt. Cranmore, **North Conway**

April

Old Man of the Mountain Race, Attitash, **Bartlett**

June

Mt. Washington Road Race, **Mt. Washington**
Annual Fiddler's Contest, **Lincoln**
Jazz Festival, **Portsmouth**

July

Mid-summer Arts and Crafts Fair, Loon Mountain, **Lincoln**

September

World Mud Bowl Championships, Hog Coliseum, **North Conway**
Highland Games, Loon Mountain, **Lincoln**

October

Fall Foliage Festival, Loon Mountain, **Lincoln**

December

Candlelight Stroll, Strawberry Banke, **Portsmouth**

For more detailed information on New Hampshire festivals, contact the State of New Hampshire, Office of Vacation Travel, P.O. Box 856-RC, Concord, NH 03301 (603-271-2666).

RHODE ISLAND

January

Polar Bears Dip, New Year's Day, Newport Beach, **Newport**

May

Thayer Street Art Festival, **Providence**
Pasta Cookoff, **Block Island**

June

Outdoor Art Festival, **Newport**
Taste of Block Island Seafood Festival, **Block Island**
Great Chowder Cook-off, Newport Yachting Center, **Newport**
Secret Garden Tour, **Newport**
Kidfest, **Newport**

July

Black Ships Festival, **Newport**
Newport Music Festival, Newport Mansions, **Newport**
Newport Tennis Week, **Newport**
Newport Regatta, **Newport**

August

Triathlon, Block Island
JVC Jazz Festival at Newport, **Fort Adams**
Great Gatsby Ball, Rosecliff, **Newport**

September

Newport International Boat Show, **Newport**

November

Block Island's Annual Shopping Stroll, **Block Island**

December

Christmas in Newport, **Newport**

For a free descriptive brochure of Newport County's numerous cultural events, call or write the Newport Tourism and Convention Authority, P.O. Box 782, Newport, RI 02840 (401-849-8048).

VERMONT

May

Spring Farm Festival, Billings Farm Museum, **Woodstock**
Covered Bridges Half Marathon, **Woodstock to Quechee**

June

Hot Air Balloon Festival, **Quechee**
Cow Appreciation Day, Billing Farm Museum, **Woodstock**
Antique Classic Car Show, Hildene, **Manchester**
Flower Festival, **Stowe**

July

Killington Music Festival, **Killington**

August

Fools-A-Float, **Burlington**
Scottish Festival, **Quechee**
Bennington Battle Day Weekend, **Bennington**

September

Vermont State Fair, **Rutland**
Shelburne Harvest Festival, **Shelburne**
Stratton Arts Festival, **Stratton Mountain**

October

Art in the Park Fall Foliage Festival, **Rutland**
Vermont Sheep and Wool Festival, **Killington**
Apples and Crafts Fair, **Woodstock**

December

Wassail Festival, **Woodstock**

For additional information about ongoing activities and events in the state, contact the Vermont Chamber of Commerce, Box 37, Montpelier, VT 05601 (802-223-3443).

APPENDIX

METRIC CONVERSION CHART

1 U.S. gallon = approximately 4 liters
1 liter = about 1 quart
1 Canadian gallon = approximately 4.5 liters

1 pound = approximately $^1/_2$ kilogram
1 kilogram = about 2 pounds

1 foot = approximately $^1/_3$ meter
1 meter = about 1 yard
1 yard = a little less than a meter
1 mile = approximately 1.6 kilometers
1 kilometer = about $^2/_3$ mile

90°F = about 30°C
20°C = approximately 70°F

Planning Map: New England

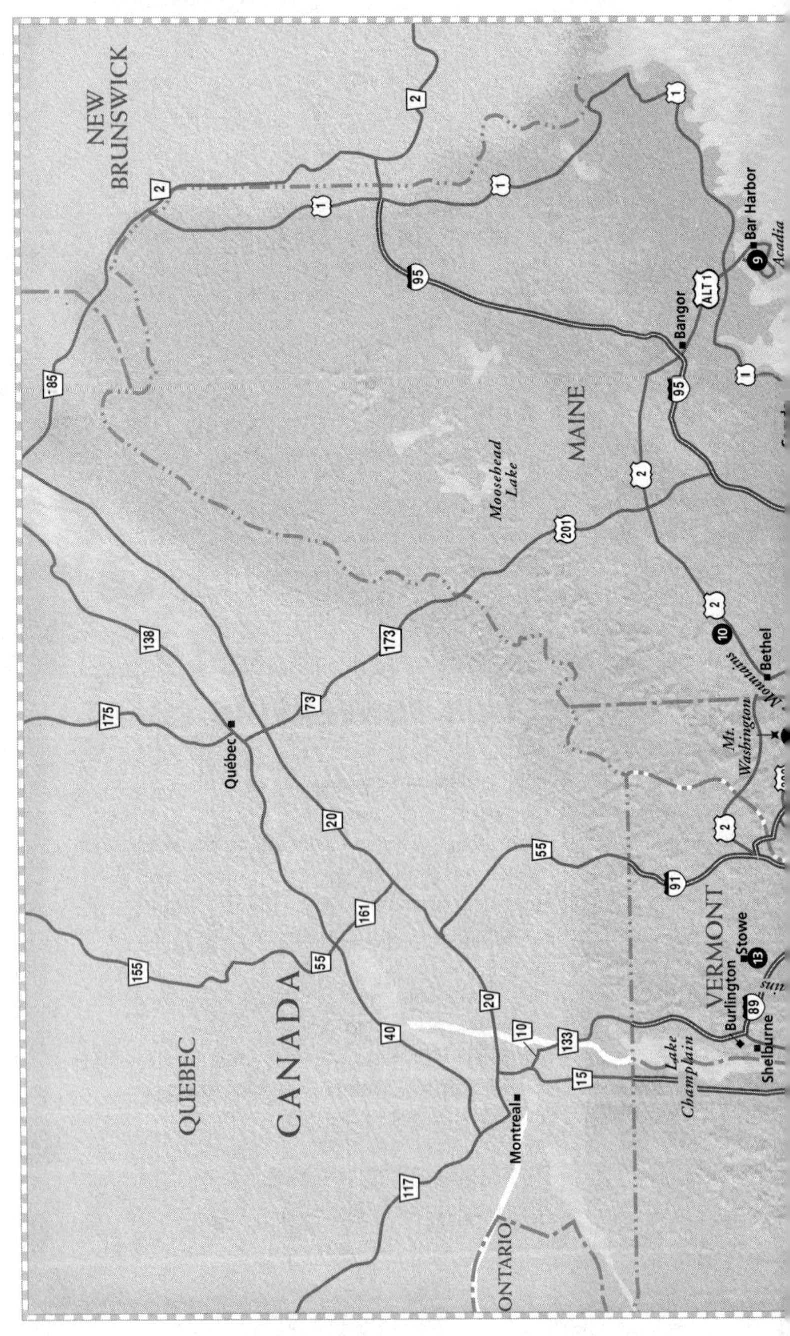

You have permission to photocopy this map.

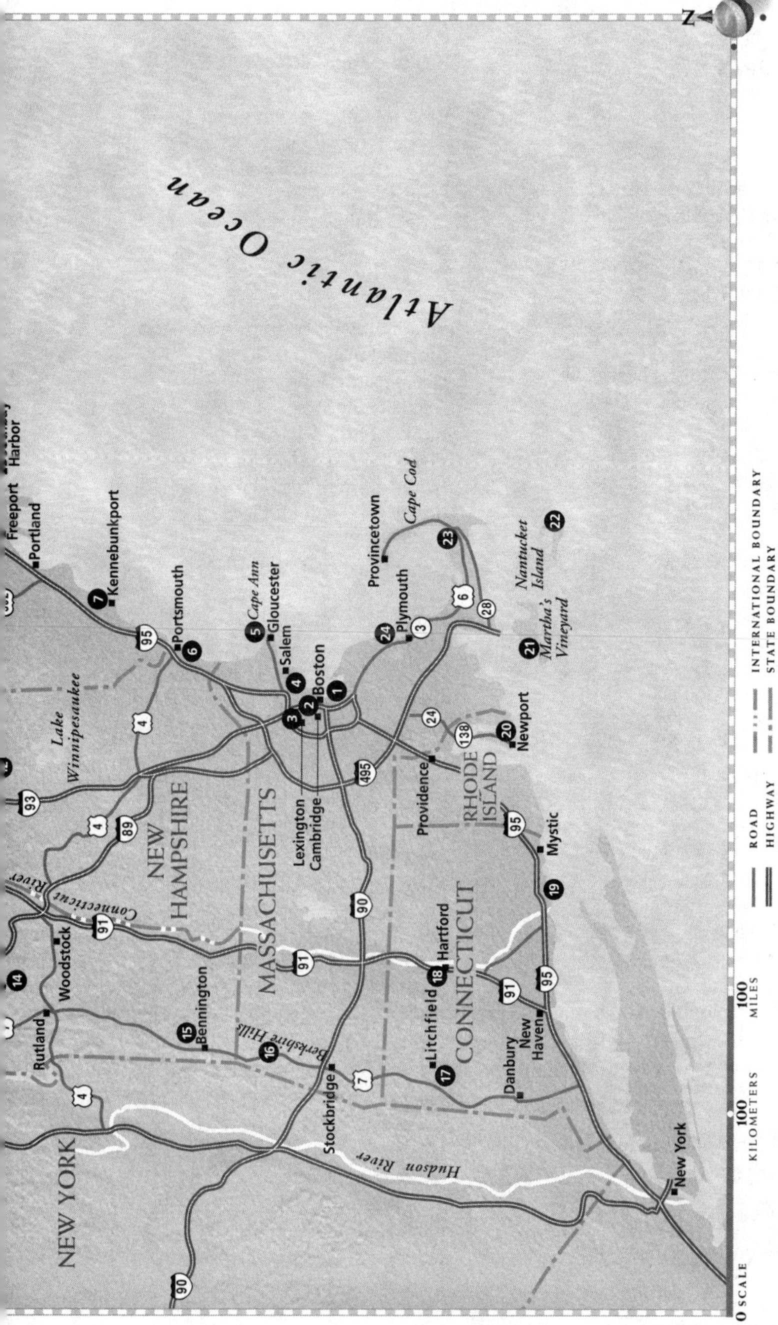

N
Atlantic Ocean
NEW YORK
NEW HAMPSHIRE
MASSACHUSETTS
CONNECTICUT
RHODE ISLAND
Freeport
Portland
Harbor
Kennebunkport
Portsmouth
Cape Ann
Gloucester
Salem
Boston
Lexington
Cambridge
Provincetown
Cape Cod
Plymouth
Martha's Vineyard
Nantucket Island
Newport
Providence
Mystic
Hartford
Litchfield
Danbury
New Haven
New York
Stockbridge
Berkshire Hills
Bennington
Woodstock
Rutland
Lake Winnipesaukee
Connecticut River
Hudson River
1 2 3 4 5 6 7 14 15 16 17 18 19 20 21 22 23 24
95 93 91 90 89 495 4 6 7 3 24 28 138
ROAD
HIGHWAY
INTERNATIONAL BOUNDARY
STATE BOUNDARY
0 SCALE
100 KILOMETERS
100 MILES

INDEX

Abbe Museum, 122
Acadia, 119–132
Acadia National Park, 121–122
Adams National Historic Site, 289–290
Albacore Park, 91
Allagash Wilderness Waterway, 141
America's Stonehenge, 96
American Clock and Watch Museum, 209
American Repertory Theatre, 60
Annalee's Gift Shop and Doll Museum, 161
Antiquarian and Landmarks Society, 220
Antiquarian House, 291
Arnold Arboretum, 35
Arrowhead, 197
Attitash Ski Area, 148

Back Bay, 49
Barnstormers Theater, 163
Basin, 146
Batholomew's Cobble, 198
Baxter State Park, 135
beaches, 73, 86, 105, 122, 232, 243, 255, 257, 267, 295
Beauport, 82
Ben and Jerry's Ice Cream Factory, 170
Bennington Monument, 186
Bennington Museum, 185
Berkshire Ballet, 204
Berkshire Museum, 197
Berkshire Opera Company, 204
Berkshire Public Theatre, 204
Berkshire Scenic Railway Museum, 198
Berkshire Theatre Festival, 204
Berksire Botanical Garden, 197
The Berkshires, 193–205
biking, 38, 102, 113, 123, 188, 242, 257
Billings Farm and Museum, 178
Black Heritage Trail, 35
Block Island, 247–248
Boothbay Land Trust Preserves, 112
Boothbay Railway Village, 109–110
Boston, 25–52
Boston Athenaeum, 35
Boston Ballet, 47
Boston Beer Company, 35
Boston Bruins, 48
Boston Celtics, 48
Boston Children's Museum, 34–35
Boston Museum of Fine Arts, 29
Boston Museum of Science, 32
Boston Pops, 46
Boston Public Gardens, 32–33
Boston Public Library, 37
Boston Red Sox, 48
Boston Symphony Orchestra, 46
Boston Tea Party Ship and Museum, 35
Brattle Theatre, 60
Brick Store Museum, 101
Bunker Hill Monument, 32
Bunker Hill Pavilion, 32
Busch Reisinger Museum, 56
Bushnell Memorial Hall, 225
Butler-McCook Homestead, 220

Cabot Factory Tour, 170–171
Cadillac Mountain, 122
Cambridge, 53–61
Camden Hills State Park, 110
Cannon Mountain Ski Area, 145
Canterbury Shaker Village, 159–160
Cape Ann, 79–88
Cape Ann Historical Museum, 82
Cape Cod, 273–286
Cape Cod Melody Tent, 284
Cape Cod Museum of Natural History, 277
Cape Cod National Seashore, 275–276, 284
Cape Cod Potato Chip Factory, 27
Captain Nathaniel B. Palmer House, 231
Castle Springs, 160
Castle Tucker, 110–111
Cathedral Ledge, 148
Catskill Mountains, 204
Central Vermont, 175–182
Chappaquiddick Island, 255
Charter Oak Cultural Center, 225
Chesterwood, 196
Chicama Vineyards, 255
Children's Museum, 91–92
Children's Museum of Maine, 100
Children's Museum of Plymouth, 292
Children's Museum of Southeastern Connecticut, 231

Christian Science Center, 37
Civic Center, 225
Court House and Museum, 291
Coastal Connecticut, 227–236
Coastal New Hampshire, 89–96
The Coffin House, 82
Cog Railway, 147–148
Colby College Museum of Art, 136
Cold Hollow Cider Mill, 171
Computer Museum, 33
Concord Museum, 63
Connecticut Historical Society, 220
Connecticut Opera, 225
Connecticut River Museum, 220
Connecticut State Capitol, 220
Conway Scenic Railroad, 149
Cop's Hill Burial Ground, 31
Cordage Park Marketplace, 290
Court House and Museum, 291
Cranberry World, 290
Crawford Notch State Park, 147–148

Dana House Museum, 179
DeCordova Museum and Sculpture Park, 67–68
Deerfield, 204–205
Denison Pequotsepos Nature Center, 231
Dexter's Grist Mill, 278
Dinosaur State Park, 219
Dole-Little House, 82
Dorset Playhouse, 192
Downtown Crossing, 49

Eastern Slope Playhouse, 155
Elizabeth Park, 220
Emerson's House, 63

Fair Street Museum, 265–266
Faneuil Hall Marketplace, 31, 49–50
Fantasy Farm, 146
Farnsworth Art Museum, 110
Felix Neck Sanctuary, 255
Fenway Park, 48
festivals, 297–304
Fire Hose Cart House, 266
Florence Griswold Museum, 230
Flume, 146
Flying Horses Carousel, 255
Fogg Art Museum, 56
Fort Ticonderoga, 192
Foxwoods Casino, 235
Franconia Notch State Park, 146
Freedom Trail, 30–32

Gate House, 122
Gay Head, 254
Gelston House, 225
Gibson House Museum, 37
Gillette's Castle, 218
Gondola Skyride, 147
Goodspeed Opera House, 225
Governor John Langdon House, 92
Grafton Notch State Park, 136
Granary Burying Ground, 30
Great Head, 122
Great Meadows Wildlife Refuge, 64
Green Animals, 241
Green Briar Nature Center and Jam Kitchen, 277

Hadwen House, 265
Hammonasset Beach State Park, 232
Hammond Castle Museum, 81
Hamptons, 235
Hancock Shaker Village, 195–196
Hartford Ballet, 225
Hartford Symphony Orchestra, 225
Harvard University, 55
Haymarket, 50
Heart of Connecticut, 215–225
Heritage Plantation, 276
Hildene, 185–186
Hill-Stead Museum, 218–219
historic homes of Sandwich, 278
history, 7, 13–14
Holley House Museum, 209–210
House of Blues, 60
House of Seven Gables, 71–72
Howland House, 291
Hoxie House, 278

Inland Maine, 133–142
Institute of Contemporary Art, 37
International Tennis Hall of Fame, 242
Isabella Stewart Gardner Museum, 33
Isham-Terry House, 220
Isle of Shoals, 94
Isleboro, 118

Jacob's Pillow, 204
John Alden House, 292
John F. Kennedy Library and Museum, 33–34
John Hancock Observatory, 34
Jones Museum of Glass and Ceramics, 136
Jordan Pond, 122

Kancamagus Highway, 156
Kent Falls, 210
King's Chapel, 30

Lake Champlain, 173
Lake George, 192
Lake Winnipesaukee Cruises, 160
Lakes Region Greyhound Park, 165
Lakes Region Summer Theatre, 161
Lakewood Theater, 141
L.C. Bates Museum, 136
Lee Mansion, 78
Lexington and Concord, 61–68
Lime Rock Park, 210
L.L. Bean, 100–101
Longfellow Natural Historic Site, 56
Lost River, 149
Lowell National Historical Park, 68

Maine Coast Railroad, 112
Maine Maritime Museum, 101
Maine State Museum, 137
Maple Grove Museum and Factory, 171
Marblehead, 77–78
Maria Mitchell Science Center, 266
Marine Resources Aquarium, 112
Martha's Vineyard, 251–260
Massachusetts Audubon Society, 292
Massachusetts Bay Brewing Company, 37
Mayflower Society Museum, 291
Menczer Museum of Medicine and Dentistry, 221
Merwin House, 198
Mid-Coast Maine, 107–118
Mission House Museum, 198–199
MIT Museum, 56–57
Moffat-Ladd House and Gardens, 92–93
Monhegan, 117–118
Montauk, 235
Montpelier, 111
Moosehead Lake, 135–136
The Mount, 198
Mount Auburn Cemetery, 57
Mount Desert Oceanarium, 122–123
Mount Greylock, 198
Mount Washington, 147
Museum of Cultural and Natural History, 56
Museum of Newport History, 242
Museum of the National Center of Afro-American Artists, 37–38
Museum of Our National Heritage, 64
Music Mountain, 214
Musical Wonder House, 112
Myopia Hunt Club, 86–87
Mystic Marinelife Aquarium, 230–231
Mystic Seaport Museum, 229

Nantucket, 261–272
Nantucket Atheneum, 266–267
Nantucket Film Festival, 271
Nantucket Historical Association, 265–266
Nantucket Life-Saving Museum, 267
National Museum of Racing and Thoroughbred Hall of Fame, 192
Naumkeag, 198
New Bedford/Fall River, Massachusetts, 249
New England Aquarium, 34
New England Carousel Museum, 231
New England Fire and History Museum, 278
New England Maple Museum, 179
New England Quilt Museum, 68
New England Ski Museum, 145–146
New Hampshire International Speedway, 165
New Hampshire Lakes, 157–166
New Hampshire Music Festival, 163
Newport, Rhode Island, 237–250
Newport Mansions, (The Breakers, Chateau-Sur-Mer, Rosecliff, Marble House, The Elms, Kingscote, Hunter House, Hammersmith, Bellecourt Castle, Beeachwood), 239–241
Newport Art Museum, 242
Nichols House Museum, 38
Nickels-Sortwell House, 111
Noah Webster House, 221
Nook Farm, 217–218

Norman Rockwell Exhibition and Gift Shop, 186
Norman Rockwell Museum, 196–197
North Bridge, 63
North Shore Music Theatre, 86
Northern Vermont, 167–173
Northern Vermont Llama Company, 173

Ogunquit Playhouse, 105
Old Burying Ground, 292
Old City Hall, Boston, 30
Old Corner Bookstore, 30
Old First Church, 186
Old Gaol, 265
Old Lighthouse Museum, 232
Old Man of the Mountain, 146
Old Manse, 64
Old Mill, 265
Old North Church, 31
Old Port Exchange District, 101
Old South Meeting House, 30
Old State House, Connecticut, 221
Old State House, Massachusetts, 30–31
Old Sturbridge Village, 51
The Oldest House, 265
Olson House, 112
Orchard House, 64
Owl's Head Transportation Museum, 111

Park Street Church, 30
Park-McCulloug Park, 186–187
Paul Revere House, 31
Peabody Essex Museum, 71
Peabody Museum of Natural History, 230
Penobscot Marine Museum, 110
Perham's of West Paris, 137
Peter Fougler Museum and Research Center, 165
Petrified Sea Gardens, 192
Pierce/Hicborn House, 31
Pilgrim Hall Museum, 290
Pilgrim Monument and Provincetown Museum, 277
Pilgrim Path, 290
Pioneer Village, 72
Plimoth Plantation and the *Mayflower II*, 289
Plum Island and Parker River National Wildlife Refuge, 81
Plymouth and the South Shore, 287–295
Plymouth National Wax Museum, 291
Plymouth Rock, 291
Polar Caves, 161
Pontine Movement Theater, 94
Portland Ballet, 105
Portland Museum of Art, 100
Portland Players, 105
Portland Stage Company, 105
Portland Symphony Orchestra, 105
Portsmouth Music Hall, 94
Profile Lake, 146
Providence, 250
Provincetown Art Association and Museum, 276
Provincetown Heritage Museum, 276–277
Prudential Building, skywalk, 34

Quaker Meeting House, 265
Quechee Gorge, 178
Quincy Market, 31

recommended reading, 23–24
Ropes Mansion, 77
Route 6A Cape Cod, scenic route, 285–286
Ruggles Mine, 149
Ryles Jazz Club, 60

Sabbathday Lake Shaker Village, 138
Sackler, 56
Salem, 69–78
Salem Maritime National Historic Site, 72
Salem Trolley, 77
Salem Wax Museum of Witches and Seafarers, 72
Salem Witch Museum, 72
Sand Beach, 122
Sandwich Glass Museum, 276
Sargent Drive, 132
Schoodic Peninsula, 131
Science Center of Connecticut, 221
Science Center of New Hampshire, 160–161
Seacoast Repertory Theatre, 94
Seashore Trolley Museum, 101

Semitic Museum, 56
Sharon Audubon Center, 210
Shelburne House and Farms, 170
Shelburne Museum, 169–170
Shore Village Museum, 111
Siasconset, 266
Simon Pearce Glass, 179
skiing, 113, 138, 148, 150, 156, 170, 171–172, 180, 187–188, 199, 210–211
Sky Line Drive, 187
Sleepy Hollow Cemetery, 64–65
Society for the Preservation of New England Antiquities (SPNEA), 82
Southern Maine, 97–106
Southern Vermont, 183–192
Southern Vermont Art Center, 187
Sparrow House, 290–291
Spencer-Pierce-Little Farm, 82
Spooner House, 291
Squam Lake Tours, 160
Stanley-Whitman House, 221–223
State House, new, Boston, 30
Steam train and riverboat ride, 219–220
Sterling and Francine Clark Art Institute, 196
Storyland, 149
Stowe Mountain Resort, 170, 171–172
Strawbery Banke Museum, 91
Sugarbush Farm, 179

Tanglewood, 203–204
Thomas Macy-Christian House, 265
Thomas Macy Warehouse, 265
Thoreau Lyceum, 65
Thornton Burgess Museum, 278
Thunder Hole, 122
Topsfield Fair, 87
Topsmead, 210
Touro Synagogue, 242

USS Constitution Museum, 31–32

Vermont Marble Exhibit, 179–180
Vermont Raptor Center, 180
Vermont Wax Museum and Store, 187
Victoria Mansion, 101
Vineyard Museum, 255

Wadsworth Arthenaeum, 219
Wadsworth-Longfellow House, 101
Walden Pond, 65
The Wayside, 65
weather, 19–20
Wenham Museum, 82–83
Wentworth-Gardner House, 93
Western Connecticut, 207–214
whale watching, 50, 78, 87, 129–130, 284
Whale's Tail, 146
Whaling Museum, 265
Whistler House Museum of Art, 68
White Flower Farm, 210
White Mountains, 143–156
Widener Library, 55
Wild Garden, 121–122
Wildlife Sanctuaries, 102
Williams College Art Museum, 197
Williamstown Theatre Festival, 203
Wilson Castle, 178
Winnipesaukee Railroad, 161
Witch House, 73
Witches Dungeon, 72–73
World's End Reservation, 292

Yale Center for British Art, 230
Yale Collection of Musical Instruments, 230
Yale University, 229–230
Yale University Art Gallery, 229–230
Yesteryears Doll Museum, 278
York Institute, 102

Map Index

Acadia: Sights/Acadia National Park Sights, 120; Food/Lodging/Camping, 126

The Berkshires: Sights, 194; Food/Lodging/Camping, 200
Boston: Food/Lodging, 44

Cambridge: Sights/Harvard University, 54; Food/Lodging, 58
Cape Ann: Sights/Society of the Preservation of New England Antiquities Sites, 80; Food/Lodging/Camping, 84
Cape Cod: Sights, 274; Food/Lodging/Camping, 280

Central Vermont: Sights/Food/Camping, 176
Coastal Connecticut: Sights/Food/Lodging/Camping, 228

Downtown Boston: Sights, 26

Greater Boston: Sights, 36

Heart of Connecticut: Sights, 216; Food and Lodging/Lodging/Camping, 222

Inland Maine: Sights, 134; Food/Lodging/Camping, 140

Lexington and Concord: Sights, 62; Food/Lodging, 66

Marblehead: Food/Lodging, 76
Martha's Vineyard: Sights, 252; Food/Lodging/Camping, 256
Mid-Coast Maine: Sights, 108; Food/Lodging/Camping, 114
Mystic: Sights/Food/Camping, 234

Nantucket: Sights, 262; Food/Lodging/Camping, 268
New Hampshire Lakes: Sights, 158; Food/Lodging/Camping, 164
Newport: Sights/Newport Mansions, 239; Food/Lodging/Camping, 246
Northern Vermont: Sights/Food/Lodging, 168

Route 6A Cape Cod, scenic route, 285

planning map, 10–11
Plymouth: Sights/Food/Lodging, 295
Plymouth and the South Shore: Sights/Food/Lodging/Camping, 288
Portsmouth: Sights, 90; Food/Lodging/Camping, 95

Salem: Sights, 70; Food/Lodging/Camping, 74
Sargent Drive, scenic route, 132
Schoodic Peninsula, scenic route, 131
Southern Coastal Maine: Sights/Food/Lodging/Camping, 98
Southern Vermont: Sights, 184; Food/Camping, 190
suggested itineraries, 3–8

Western Connecticut: Sights, 208; Food/Lodging/Camping, 212
White Mountains: Sights/Franconia Notch State Park, 144; Food/Lodging/Camping, 152

You'll Feel like a Local When You Travel with Guides from John Muir Publications

CiTY-SMaRT™ GUIDEBOOKS

Pick one for your favorite city: *Albuquerque, Anchorage, Austin, Calgary, Cincinnati, Cleveland, Denver, Indianapolis, Kansas City, Memphis, Milwaukee, Minneapolis/St. Paul, Nashville, Portland, Richmond, San Antonio, St. Louis, Tampa/St. Petersburg*

Guides for kids 6 to 10 years old about what to do, where to go, and how to have fun in: *Atlanta, Austin, Boston, Chicago, Cleveland, Denver, Indianapolis, Kansas City, Miami, Milwaukee, Minneapolis/St. Paul, Nashville, Portland, San Francisco, Seattle, Washington D.C.*

TRAVEL✦SMART®

Trip planners with select recommendations to: *Alaska, American Southwest, Carolinas, Colorado, Deep South, Eastern Canada, Florida Gulf Coast, Hawaii, Kentucky/Tennessee, Michigan, Minnesota/Wisconsin, Montana/Wyoming/Idaho, New England, New York State, Northern California, Ohio, Pacific Northwest, South Florida and the Keys, Southern California, Texas, Western Canada*

Rick Steves' GUIDES

See *Europe Through the Back Door* and take along country guides to: *France, Belgium & the Netherlands; Germany, Austria & Switzerland; Great Britain & Ireland; Italy; Russia & the Baltics; Scandinavia; Spain & Portugal;* or the *Best of Europe*

ADVENTURES IN NATURE

Plan your next adventure in: *Alaska, Belize, Guatemala, Honduras*

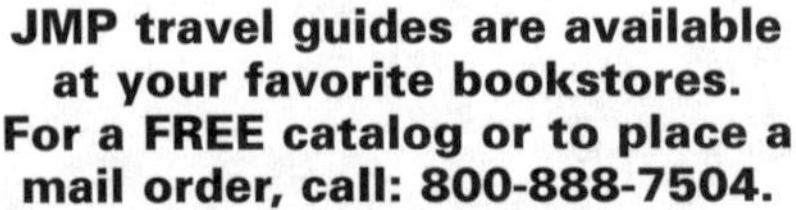

John Muir Publications • P.O. Box 613 • Santa Fe, NM 87504

Cater to Your Interests on Your Next Vacation

The 100 Best Small Art Towns in America
2nd edition
Where to Discover Creative People, Fresh Air, and Affordable Living
U.S. $15.95, Canada $22.50

The Big Book of Adventure Travel
2nd edition
Profiles more than 400 great escapes to all corners of the world
U.S. $17.95, Canada $25.50

Cross-Country Ski Vacations
A Guide to the Best Resorts, Lodges, and Groomed Trails in North America
U.S. $15.95, Canada $22.50

Gene Kilgore's Ranch Vacations, 4th edition
The Complete Guide to Guest Resorts, Fly-Fishing, and Cross-Country Skiing Ranches
U.S. $22.95, Canada $32.50

Indian America, 4th edition
A traveler's companion to more than 300 Indian tribes in the United States
U.S. $18.95, Canada $26.75

Saddle Up!
A Guide to Planning the Perfect Horseback Vacation
U.S. $14.95, Canada $20.95

Watch It Made in the U.S.A., 2nd edition
A Visitor's Guide to the Companies That Make Your Favorite Products
U.S. $17.95, Canada $25.50

The World Awaits
A Comprehensive Guide to Extended Backpack Travel
U.S. $16.95, Canada $23.95

JMP travel guides are available at your favorite bookstores. For a FREE catalog or to place a mail order, call: 800-888-7504.

John Muir Publications • P.O. Box 613 • Santa Fe, NM 87504

ABOUT THE AUTHOR

Anne E. Wright is a veteran travel writer who has written guidebooks to California and the Southwest. She has contributed to a variety of other books and publications, including *National Geographic Traveler*.

Wright was born in Cambridge, Massachusetts, and attended Tufts University, graduating with a bachelor's degree in English and classical studies. She has traveled all over New England; her favorite places are Boston—for its culture and vitality—and Nantucket—for its isolation and peacefulness.

Wright now lives in New Mexico with her husband, daughter, and two Labrador retrievers—but makes sure to get back to New England regularly.